Challenges of the Developing World

NINTH EDITION

Howard Handelman
Emeritus Professor, University of Wisconsin-Milwaukee

Rex Brynen
Professor, McGill University

ROWMAN & LITTLEFIELD
Lanham • Boulder • New York • London

Executive Editor: Traci Crowell
Assistant Editor: Mary Malley
Senior Marketing Manager: Amy Whitaker
Interior Designer: Rosanne Schloss
Credits and acknowledgments for material borrowed from other sources, and reproduced
with permission, appear on the appropriate page within the text.

Published by Rowman & Littlefield
An imprint of The Rowman & Littlefield Publishing Group, Inc.
4501 Forbes Boulevard, Suite 200, Lanham, Maryland 20706
www.rowman.com

6 Tinworth Street, London SE11 5AL, United Kingdom

British Library Cataloguing in Publication Information Available

Library of Congress Cataloging-in-Publication Data Available

ISBN: 978-1-5381-1666-1 (pbk : alk. paper)—ISBN: 978-1-5381-1667-8 (ebook)

♾™ The paper used in this publication meets the minimum requirements of American
National Standard for Information Sciences—Permanence of Paper for Printed Library
Materials, ANSI/NISO Z39.48-1992.

Printed in the United States of America

In Memory of Howard Handelman (1943–2018)

Brief Contents

Contents

Tables

Preface

THE DEVELOPING WORLD TODAY CONSISTS of more than 150 countries and around 6.2 billion of the world's 7.4 billion people. These low- and middle-income countries also make up around half of all global economic activity.

In the West, however, the popular image of much of the developing world often tends to one of two extremes, viewing these areas as either exotic tourist destinations, or as lands of unremitting poverty, deprivation, repression, and violence. Certainly most of Africa, Asia, the Middle East, and the Americas do indeed suffer from social and economic underdevelopment—one of the key characteristics, after all, that leads us to categorize them as "developing." Life expectancy in Sierra Leone or Côte d'Ivoire is only in the low fifties; less than a quarter of Cambodians or Nigerians have access to safely managed water supplies; per capita income in the United States is more than seventy times higher than it is in Burundi. Parts of the Middle East and sub-Saharan Africa suffer from political violence, even civil war. Millions of refugees and other migrants have fled conflict, repression, or lack of opportunity to find better lives for themselves and their families.

Yet, the picture is much more complex—and, in many cases, more positive—than this stereotype would suggest. The world's largest democracy is not in the West, but India. If China is not already the world's largest economy (and it depends on how you calculate it), it soon will be. Major progress has been made in many countries in improving economic and social conditions. Indeed, the last several decades have seen, across most of the developing world, one of the most rapid transformations in living conditions in human history. All of this is underpinned by a diverse array of political processes and policies, reflecting differences in history, society, and culture.

Challenges of the Developing World examines and analyzes the politics of developing countries in Africa, Asia, Latin America, the Caribbean, and the Middle East. In doing so, it does not embark on detailed examination of a few particular political systems. Instead, it focuses on key issues, common challenges, and important dynamics. It is our intent to provide the reader with a better understanding of the political and other processes at play, and thereby equip them with analytical tools and insights that will be of lasting value.

NEW TO THIS EDITION

This latest edition of the text contains a number of changes intended to address important emerging issues in the developing world.

- *The Sustainable Development Goals and social and economic progress in the developing world.* Because media coverage tends to focus on the "bad news" stories—war, famine, disaster—we are careful to underscore the remarkable progress many developing countries have experienced in recent decades. We also note the growing importance of environmental issues, including the shared global challenge of climate change.
- *Democracy, democratization, and the risks of democratic "backsliding."* We have updated our discussion to highlight the key challenges facing democracy in the developing world today. Particular attention is devoted to the Middle East, where the 2011 Arab Spring has today produced one new democracy but also return to dictatorship and devastating civil wars.
- *Corruption.* This has emerged as a key challenge to economic development and political legitimacy alike, and so in the ninth edition we devote an entire chapter to its causes and consequences, as well as anti-corruption measures. Our discussion emphasizes the extent to which corruption is often simultaneously rooted in both economics and politics, with political leaders using access to state resources to reward loyalists and consolidate their power.
- *Religion and politics.* The rise of religious fundamentalisms (especially in parts of the Middle East and broader Muslim world, but in other areas and religions too) deserves careful attention. We also explore the challenges of ethnic politics and cultural pluralism in Africa, Asia, and the Middle East.
- *Gender and development.* We continue to focus attention to the status of women in the politics of developing countries. In this edition, we also address the situation of sexual (LGBT+) minorities.

No text is capable of fully examining the individual political and socio-economic systems of so many highly diverse countries. Instead, as noted earlier, we will look for common issues, problems, and potential solutions. We start in chapter 1 by exploring the nature of underdevelopment and then consider the leading theories attempting to explain underdevelopment and development. Chapter 2 turns attention to the imperatives of economic development, highlighting the various policy choices facing developing countries (and the politics underpinning them). Chapter 3 discusses what has been one of the most important political changes in world politics during the late twentieth and early twenty-first centuries—the wave of democratic transitions that has swept over the developing nations of Africa, Asia, Latin America, and the Middle East (as well as southern Europe and the former Soviet bloc) in the past four decades. But, this edition also analyzes the risk of a "democratic recession," and the persistence of both authoritarian politics and "hybrid regimes" that combine electoral mechanisms with illiberal and undemocratic politics. Chapter 4 combines both economic and political issues as it explores the problem of corruption. Chapters 5–6 examine the impact of religion and ethnic pluralism on politics in developing countries, exploring both coexistence and conflict. In chapter 7, our attention turns to gender, and the important role it plays in shaping social, economic, and political opportunities. Chapter 8 discusses rural land concentration and poverty and their political consequences. It outlines the explosive urban growth across the developing world and analyzes both the problems and opportunities presented by this huge demographic change. It describes the many challenges the urban poor face regarding housing, employment, and crime and also their political activities. Next, chapter 9 on revolutionary change considers the definition of revolutions, how revolutions start, whether they succeed, and how they govern. We also examine the current and future prospects for revolution in the developing world. Chapter 10 on the military in politics shows that despite the declining frequency of military coups, military institutions still play a significant role in the politics of many developing countries—and underscores the point with an analysis of the role that the military played in shaping the various "Arab Spring" uprisings.

SUPPLEMENTS

Rowman & Littlefield is pleased to offer several resources to qualified adopters of *Challenges of the Developing World* and their students that will make teaching and learning from this book even more effective and enjoyable.

- **Test Bank**. For each chapter in the text, test questions are provided in multiple choice, true-false questions, and essay formats. The test bank is available to adopters for download on the text's catalog page at http://textbooks.rowman.com/handelman9e.
- **Testing Software**. This customizable test bank is available as either a Word file or in Respondus 4.0. Respondus 4.0 is a powerful tool for creating and managing exams that can be printed to paper or published directly to the most popular learning management systems. For more information, see http://www.respondus.com.
- **Companion Website**. Accompanying the text is an open-access Companion Website designed to engage students with the material and reinforce what they have learned in the classroom. For each chapter, flash cards and self-quizzes help students master the content and apply that knowledge to real-life situations. Students can access the Companion Website from their computer or mobile device; it can be found at http://textbooks.rowman.com/handelman9e.
- **eBook**. The full-color eBook allows students to access this textbook anytime and anywhere they want. The eBook for *Challenges of the Developing World* includes everything that is in the print edition in vibrant color and features direct links to the Companion Website where students can access flash cards and self-quizzes to help test their understanding of the major concepts and terminology in each chapter. The eBook can be purchased at https://rowman.com/ISBN/9781538116678 or at any other eBook retailer.

ACKNOWLEDGMENTS

Because of the broad geographic and conceptual scope of any book on politics in the developing world, we are particularly indebted to others for their kind help and advice. We would like to thank the many people at Rowman & Littlefield who have worked with us. We particularly appreciate Traci Crowell and Mary Malley for their guidance and support on this edition. We also appreciated and benefited from the comments of the many reviewers of the book—Michael Cairo, Brian Kessel, Sunil K. Sahu, and Angela Wolfe. We owe a particular debt to our respective spouses, Dr. Kristin Ruggiero and Alex Brynen, for their insights and other assistance. The quality of this book benefited enormously from their many insights, suggestions, and corrections. The usual caveat, of course, applies: Any remaining errors of fact or interpretation are our own responsibility.

Howard Handelman
Professor Emeritus, Department of Political Science
University of Wisconsin–Milwaukee

On a final note, Howard sadly passed away after we had finalized revisions for the 9th edition and as this book was going to press. Having used earlier editions of his text to teach many thousands of my own students over the years, I already knew how important he felt it was that political science should be made accessible rather than dense and jargon-laden, and how he always sought to break down stereotypes and build greater understanding of the developing world. Working with him on this edition, my admiration grew only more. He will be sadly missed.

Rex Brynen
Professor, Department of Political Science
McGill University

About the Authors

HOWARD HANDELMAN was professor emeritus at the University of Wisconsin–Milwaukee at the time of his death in 2018. He had served as director of the Center for Latin American and Caribbean Studies, chair of the Department of Political Science, and chair of the Department of Spanish and Portuguese. His books include *Struggles in the Andes: Peasant Political Mobilization in Peru*; *Mexican Politics: The Dynamics of Change*; *Democracy and Its Limits: Lessons from Asia, Latin America, and the Middle East*; *Politics in a Changing World*; and *Paying the Costs of Austerity in Latin America*.

REX BRYNEN is professor of political science at McGill University, where he specializes in Middle East politics, peacebuilding, and humanitarian operations. He is author or coauthor of *Beyond the Arab Spring: Authoritarianism and Democratization in the Arab World*; *A Very Political Economy: Peacebuilding and Foreign Aid in the West Bank and Gaza*; and *Sanctuary and Survival: The PLO in Lebanon*, and editor or coeditor of eight other books on political liberalization, refugees, the Arab-Israeli conflict, and regional security. In addition, he has served as a member of the policy staff of the Canadian Department of Foreign Affairs and as a consultant on development issues to the World Bank and United Nations agencies.

1

Understanding Underdevelopment

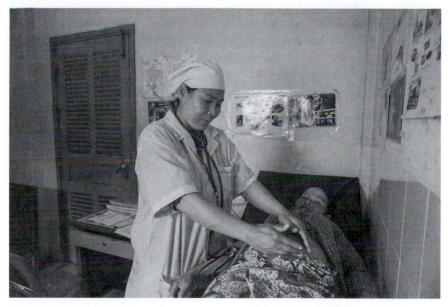

A nurse checks the health of a pregnant woman at a village health center in rural Cambodia. Because of such programs, the maternal mortality rate in Cambodia has fallen more than threefold since 2005, and the infant mortality rate has dropped by more than half. Worldwide, development initiatives by governments and aid agencies have reduced child deaths by 6 million per year since 1990. *Source*: Brian Atkinson/Alamy Stock Photo.

MEDIA COVERAGE OF THE LESS DEVELOPED COUNTRIES of Africa, Asia, the Middle East, the Caribbean, and Latin America tends to concentrate on what might be termed the "bad news"—civil wars in Syria and Yemen; terrorism in Afghanistan and Somalia; ethnic and religious conflict in Iraq and Myanmar (Burma); political repression in China, Egypt, and Venezuela; and famine in South Sudan. Indeed, the problems currently plaguing many parts of the developing world appear daunting, and some of these problems exist in industrialized democracies as well, though in a milder form. In recent times, for example, both Northern Ireland and the Basque region of Spain have experienced ethnic violence and terrorism. Parts of Washington, DC, have higher infant mortality rates than Lebanon, Sri Lanka, and Thailand. Nevertheless, it is the scope and persistence of the developing world's political, economic, and social challenges that ultimately draw our attention.

At the same time, it is important to keep in mind the remarkable progress that many areas have made.[1] Average life expectancy in the developing world today is well over seventy years, a dramatic improvement from under fifty years when the colonial era ended in the 1960s.* Since 1990, the number of people living in extreme poverty has fallen by more than half, from 1.9 billion people in 1990 to 836 million by 2015. Child (under five years) mortality dropped from 90 deaths per 1,000 live births to 42—resulting in 6 million fewer child deaths per year. A higher proportion of children attend school than at any point in human history. The UNDP (United Nations Development Programme) has estimated that the level of poverty in the developing world fell faster in the last half of the twentieth century than it had in the previous five hundred years combined. While media reports can make violence and terrorism seem commonplace, and despite an upsurge in violence (largely in the Middle East) during the past decade, the risk of war-related death was much higher through much of the twentieth century—and, indeed, most centuries before that—than it is today.

Understanding processes of development and underdevelopment is a complex task complicated by theoretical debates between scholars and a profusion of changing terminology. Even the names given to the politically and economically less developed nations vary, with each having its own assumptions: the acronym **LDC**, for example, was once used to refer to "*less* developed countries," but is now increasingly used to refer to the "*least* developed countries"—that is, only the poorest among them. There are currently forty-seven LDCs recognized by the UN, ranging from Afghanistan to Zimbabwe. The World Bank refers to low-income

---

* Average life expectancy in the developing world is now at the same level as it was in the (much richer) United States in the 1970s. Indeed, the citizens of some developing countries (Singapore, South Korea, Chile, Costa Rica) now live longer than Americans. However, life expectancies are very much lower in the poorest developing countries.

(thirty-one countries), lower-middle (fifty-three), upper-middle (fifty-six), and high–income (seventy-eight) countries, with the first three of these generally corresponding with what is usually thought of as the developing world. Developing countries were once commonly referred to as the "**third world**," and at times analysts will refer to them as the global "**South**" (in contrast to the industrialized "North"—although not all developing countries are in the southern hemisphere). In order to avoid repetitious usage, we interchangeably use the terms "**less developed countries**," "**developing world**," and "**developing countries**."*

DEVELOPING WORLD COMMONALITIES: THE NATURE OF UNDERDEVELOPMENT

The study of comparative politics is about understanding patterns of similarity and difference across political systems, and the causal relationships that shape these. What sorts of policies do countries adopt to promote economic and social development, and what effects do these have? What common elements can be seen in the social needs and political challenges of growing urban areas? Why do some countries experience ethnic conflict and military coups? What factors contribute to successful democratic transition? These are the sorts of issues this textbook addresses.

Developing countries vary widely in terms of history, culture, size, and economy. However, they also generally share a number of common characteristics. All of them, by definition, suffer from at least some aspects of political, economic, or social underdevelopment. Although some of East Asia's **newly industrializing countries** (NICs)—for example, South Korea and Singapore—are no longer economically underdeveloped, they still share a vulnerability to global economic forces and continue to suffer from aspects of political underdevelopment. On the other hand, Costa Rica and Uruguay are relatively well developed politically and socially but manifest a number of economic underdevelopment problems. In short, while some developing countries are underdeveloped in all major aspects of modernization, others are far more advanced in some aspects of development than in others.

While the basic disciplinary approach of this text is political science, it also draws on approaches from anthropology, economics, and sociology in exploring the dynamics and issues that characterize development. Before addressing any of this, however, it is useful to first unpack a little more the characteristics of the "developing world."

---

* This is not to say that the "developed" countries have themselves finished developing, or that there is a single model or outcome of development.

The Historical Origins of the Developing World

Many important characteristics of the contemporary developing world were shaped by the experience of **colonialism** during the fifteenth through early twentieth centuries. During this period, most of the world's territory and population came under the control of European powers, seeking access to raw materials, new markets, and geostrategic advantage over their rivals.

In the Americas, "discovery" by Columbus and other European explorers in the late fifteenth century was rapidly followed by colonial conquest—and then, in many areas, substantial European settlement, too. This resulted in the destruction of more than 90 percent of the indigenous population through warfare, exploitation, and most especially the arrival of Old World diseases in the New World. In addition, an estimated 12 million Africans were brutally enslaved and transported to the Americas, mainly to work on agricultural plantations. With the precolonial societies in the Americas destroyed or marginalized, new societies—marked by the class and racial inequalities born of the colonial experience—took their place. Most of the Americas gained independence from European colonialism earlier than other parts of the world, starting with the United States in the late eighteenth century, followed by Latin America in the early nineteenth century.

Unlike the Americas, where conquest preceded large-scale trade, European trade with Asia stretched back to antiquity. However, the Age of Discovery from the fifteenth century onward spurred the growth of maritime commerce and increased the economic importance of the area to Europe. First the Portuguese, and then the Dutch, British, and French, built trade relationships, established military outposts to protect these trading routes, and eventually seized control of territory from local rulers. Even the United States became a colonial power, acquiring the Philippines from Spain in 1898 following the Spanish-American War.

Unlike the Americas, however, local populations in Asia tended to be larger or more robust, and colonial settlement was much more limited. Thus, Western powers imposed their will and economic interests, reshaping local societies in the process—but did not destroy them in the way characteristic of colonialism in the Americas.

In sub-Saharan Africa, some coastal areas had come under European control quite early, to protect maritime trade routes to Asia. The area also suffered the ravages of the slave trade. However, with the interior of the continent difficult to access and fewer raw materials and markets immediately evident, it was not until the late nineteenth and early twentieth centuries that a European "scramble for Africa" took place. In the four decades before the First World War, the proportion of the continent under European colonial control grew rapidly, from around 10 percent in 1870 to around 90 percent by 1914.

The Middle East was one of the last areas to come under European rule, in large part because of much of it was still under the control of the

Ottoman Empire. As Ottoman power declined, however, European powers stepped in—most dramatically with the defeat of Ottoman forces by the allies during the First World War.

Decolonization in Africa and Asia took place much later than it had in the Americas. European powers had been weakened by the Second World War, and the two new superpowers, the United States and the Soviet Union, saw colonialism as an anachronism. In the 1950s and 1960s, almost four dozen new states gained their independence. In most countries this transition was hastened by growing anticolonial protest and nationalist mobilization by the local population. In some cases—such as in Vietnam and Algeria against the French, Angola and Mozambique against the Portuguese, or South Yemen against the British—it even involved substantial armed violence against the foreign occupier.

Why does any of this history matter for the study of contemporary politics? Scholars continue to debate the legacies of colonial rule, although none doubt that it could sometimes be very brutal: the infamous exploitation of the Congo by King Leopold II of Belgium, for example, is believed to have directly or indirectly caused millions of African deaths. It was during the colonial period that territories were divided, borders were drawn, and economies and their associated infrastructures were established to serve European needs—all with effects that would last well beyond the colonial era. During and immediately after colonial rule in Africa and Asia, foreign companies or European settlers often controlled most of the lucrative economic assets. In Kenya, Mozambique, and Vietnam, for example, white settlers owned the large agricultural plantations that produced export crops such as bananas, sugar, and rice. Elsewhere, large foreign corporations owned the mines and oil fields that produced considerable wealth in the Middle East, Africa, and Asia. These foreign firms produced almost all South Africa's diamonds, Iraq's oil, Guinea's bauxite (aluminum), Zambia's copper, and Malaysia's tin.

European rule also imposed legal systems and political administrations. In doing so it sometimes aggravated social cleavages through the use of divide-and-rule tactics by the colonial power. Ethnic, religious, and tribal tensions in Sudan, South Sudan, Uganda, and Rwanda have all been attributed, in part, to prior colonial policy. Colonial powers had only a limited interest in developing local capacities, meaning that many countries emerged from this period as weak states with untested political structures and contested political identities. Just as the American Revolution fundamentally shaped the future character of the United States, processes of decolonization elsewhere also had important implications for postcolonial politics. This was especially true in cases where a powerful local nationalist movement emerged, or where liberation took place as a consequence of violent uprising.

The colonial era occurred during a period when European power and technology was rapidly developing as a consequence of political change, scientific advances, and then the Industrial Revolution. Today, however, some parts of the developing world—notably in East Asia—are developing rapidly. China's economy, for example, is expected to surpass that of the United States in total size (although not level of development or individual income) within the next decade or so, if it has not done so already.

Economic Underdevelopment

Perhaps the most salient characteristic of many developing countries is poverty. At the national level, this is manifested by some combination of low per capita income, unequal income distribution, poor infrastructure (including communications and transportation), and limited use of modern technology. At the grassroots level, economic underdevelopment connotes widespread scarcity, substantial unemployment, substandard housing, poor health conditions, lower literacy and educational levels, and inadequate nutrition.

While most developing countries are much poorer than those in Western Europe and North America, there is also considerable variation among them and between world regions. Table 1.1 compares the per capita gross national income (GNI), human development, life expectancy, and educational level of the developing world's major regions with those of the United States.* **Purchasing power parity** (PPP) means that income has been adjusted to reflect differences in local prices (e.g., the lower price of foodstuffs in some countries) so as to give a comparable measure of actual purchasing power. As the first data column indicates, per capita income in the United States is more than three times higher than in the Arab States and almost sixteen times higher than sub-Saharan Africa.† Of late, however, many developing nations have been slowly narrowing that gap by growing at a faster economic rate than the United States and other developed countries.

The second data column in table 1.1 shows the **Human Development Index (HDI)** score for these regions. The HDI is a composite statistic of life expectancy, education, and per capita income indicators. The highest possible HDI score a country or region may achieve is 1.000 and the lowest is 0.000 (though, in real life, no country or region falls at either

---

* Gross domestic product (GDP), gross national product (GNP), and gross national income (GNI) are all measures of the size of an economy. GDP is the value of all goods and services produced within the country in a year, while GNP and GNI adjust this total to account for incomes earned by foreign residents and nonresidents. For most countries the differences are relatively minor.

† "Arab states" or "Arab world" refer to countries with primarily Arabic-speaking populations located in the Middle East and North Africa. "Sub-Saharan Africa" consists of those African nations that are located south of the Sahara Desert (i.e., south of the Arab countries of North Africa).

Table 1.1   Income and Human Development

Region	GNI per Capita (PPP)	Human Development Index (HDI)	Life Expectancy at Birth (years)	Average Years of School
United States	53,245	.920	79.2	13.2
Sub-Saharan Africa	3,383	.523	58.9	5.4
East Asia	12,125	.720	74.2	7.7
South Asia	5,799	.621	68.7	6.2
Arab States	14,958	.687	70.8	6.8
Latin America and the Caribbean	14,028	.751	75.2	8.3

Source: United Nations Development Programme (UNDP), *Human Development Report, 2016.*

of these extremes). Most development specialists consider the HDI to be a much better measure than per capita GNI of a nation's quality of life. For example, as the table shows, the Arab states have the highest per capita income of any developing region listed in the first data column. But their comparatively high GNI per capita ($14,958) is inflated by the huge oil and gas income that the governments of some countries in the region (such as Saudi Arabia and Qatar) earn and is not an accurate reflection of how well the average person lives. We can see this in the HDI scores, where the Arab states fall well behind East Asia and Latin America and the Caribbean.

The next two data columns demonstrate that life expectancy and educational levels in the Arab States, South Asia, and, especially, sub-Saharan Africa are also substantially lower than in the United States (and other developed nations), with East Asia and Latin America and the Caribbean falling in between.

Table 1.2 moves from the economic performance of developing world regions to an examination of individual countries in each of those areas: Mozambique and South Africa (both in sub-Saharan Africa); Morocco (North Africa); India, Pakistan, and China (South and East Asia); Chile, Mexico, and Brazil (Latin America). The table also includes Germany, to allow a comparison with a highly developed country. The first data column in the table, GNI (gross national income) indicates each country's per capita income adjusted for PPP. The data again illustrate the tremendous gap in living standards between the most developed and the less developed countries, as well as the considerable variation within the developing world.

While **per capita income**—that is, the total size of the economy divided by the population—is a useful indicator of a country's level of economic

Table 1.2   Income and Income Inequality

Country	GNI per Capita (PPP)	Gini Index	Income Ratio*
Germany	49,530	.270	4.3
Mozambique	1,190	.456	9.9
South Africa	12,860	.625	17.9
Morocco	7,700	.408	7.2
India	6,490	.352	5.6
Pakistan	5,580	.307	5.3
China	15,500	.465	12.2
Chile	23,270	.505	15.7
Mexico	17,740	.482	12.8
Brazil	14,810	.497	—

Source: United Nations Development Programme (UNDP), *Human Development Report*; CIA, *The World Factbook*; The World Bank, *World Development Indicators*.
* Ratio of the average income of the richest 20 percent of the population to the poorest 20 percent.

development, it does not give us a complete picture of living conditions because it fails to take into account how equitably that income is distributed. For example, two nations may have the same per capita incomes, say $20,000 annually; however, in country A, 40 percent of the population is poor, with annual incomes lower than $7,000, while the wealthiest 25 percent of the populace has an average income of $75,000. Whereas in country B, with the same average income, earnings are far more evenly distributed, with almost everyone making between $15,000 and $25,000 annually. Thus, while the countries have the same average incomes, country A has far more unequal income distribution and many more people living in poverty.*

Data columns 2 and 3 in the table measure how equally or unequally income is distributed in each country. The **Gini Index** (column 3) is a mathematical measure of the level of equality in each of the countries. A Gini score of 0.000 would indicate that a country has perfect equality—that is, families in the country have the exact same income; there are no richer people and no poorer people. A Gini score of 1.000 would indicate that one family (or person) makes all the country's national income and the rest of the population earns nothing. Of course, in reality, neither of these extremes exists and no country has an index score of 1.000 or 0.000, or any score close to those. The country with the highest Gini Index in the world—where income is most unequal—is the tiny African country of Lesotho (Gini

---

*If we hypothetically say that anyone earning less than $10,000 annually falls below the poverty line, then well over 40 percent of country A's population are poor, while few, if any, people in country B live in poverty.

Index = 0.632) and the country with the greatest income equality is Finland (Gini Index = 0.215).

In the table, Germany has a Gini Index of 0.270, indicating low inequality, a score fairly representative of Western Europe's industrialized states. South Africa's index of 0.625 reflects the fact that it is the second most unequal country in the world. Chile, like many Latin American countries, also exhibits considerable inequality (0.505). Income distribution in Pakistan (0.307) is more equitable, despite the very considerable poverty in that country.

Column 3 offers another way of measuring a country's level of equality or inequality of income distribution. It gives the ratio of the average income of people in the richest quintile (richest 20 percent) of the population to the incomes of people in the poorest quintile (poorest 20 percent) of the country. The table shows that South Africans from among the richest quintile of the country's population on average earn 17.9 times as much as their fellow countrymen in the poorest quintile. In Chile, the country in the table with the second highest Gini Index, people in the richest quintile earn 15.7 times those in the poorest quintile. Among the most equal nations in the table, Germans in the richest quintile earn "only" a bit over four times as much as their poorest compatriots and Pakistanis in the richest quintile earn "only" 5.3 times as much as the poorest one-fifth.

Looking at countries worldwide, we can discover a number of regional patterns, which correspond to the picture presented in table 1.2. The former communist countries of Central and Eastern Europe (including Ukraine, Belarus, Moldova, Romania, Hungary, and Albania)—not shown in table 1.2—generally have the greatest income *equality*, reflecting their past communist governments' (roughly 1945–89) confiscation of most of the property belonging to urban businessmen and rural landowners.

Western Europe's highly economically developed, capitalist countries as a group tend to have the second highest level of income equality, as illustrated by Germany in the table. This partially reflects the substantial influence of left political parties and labor unions in the twentieth century. This is particularly true of the Scandinavian and Nordic countries (Finland, Sweden, Norway, Denmark, and Iceland), whose long tradition of democratic socialism has produced some of the most equal income levels in the world. The United States, lacking a strong leftist political party or union tradition, has the most *unequal* income distribution of any economically developed nation in the world. Its richest quintile earns 18.5 times as much as those in the bottom 20 percent of the income scale (with a Gini Index of 0.450).

In general, developing countries tend to have more unequal income distribution than highly developed nations, but there is considerable variation within the developing world. Latin America—as table 1.2 suggests—has the most unequal income distribution of any world region, due largely to the pattern established during Spanish (and Portuguese) colonial rule prior to the nineteenth century. Following their conquest of the Americas, the Spanish concentrated land ownership in the hands of the colonizers, leaving the original indigenous population with small plots of land or landless. Even after independence and after many Latin American countries began to industrialize in the late nineteenth or early twentieth centuries, income (and wealth) in the region remained highly unequal. In countries with large indigenous populations (Indian or Mestizo)—such as Bolivia, Guatemala, Ecuador, and Peru—or large black and biracial populations—including Haiti and Brazil—opportunities for the lower class to experience upward mobility were further reduced due to racial discrimination.

As the data in table 1.2 suggest, Asia has the lowest rate of inequality of any part of the developing world. With some notable exceptions (Sri Lanka, Thailand, China, and Malaysia), Asian nations have Gini Indices below .400, which indicate much greater income *equality* than Latin American or many African countries (most notable, South Africa, as shown in the table). Indeed, it is rather surprising to see that income is more equally distributed in India—with its caste system and extensive poverty—than in the United States.*

To a large extent this can be attributed to extensive **agrarian** (land) **reforms** carried out in the region, which redistributed some (or, occasionally, all) the large agricultural estates to either state farms (in the case of communist land reforms) or directly to peasants (small farmers). The communist governments of Vietnam, Laos, and Cambodia confiscated all the large, private farms that had existed under the old order and either turned them into state farms, cooperatives (which the peasant co-op members officially control, but the government actually runs), or individual plots. In reaction to Asia's communist revolutions, the governments of South Korea and Taiwan initiated extensive land redistribution to the rural poor in order to prevent peasant radicalization. In addition, these governments have bolstered crop prices in order to reduce the substantial income gap that almost all developing nations have between their (more affluent) urban areas and the poorer rural regions (see chapter 8 for a more extensive analysis of the urban-rural income gap, agrarian reform, and government agricultural price policies in the developing world). Today, after their industrialization and extensive economic development, the two countries have some of the most equal income distributions in the world.

---

* As indicated in table 1.2 and previously in the text. This means that the poor in India get a larger share of the economic "pie" (the total national income) than do the American poor. Income is also more equally distributed in Indonesia, Pakistan, and Bangladesh than in the United States. But, since the total "pie" is much larger in the United States than in these countries, the poor in the United States still have a much higher standard of living than their Asian counterparts.

China stands out as a great exception. Table 1.2 shows that, despite its communist revolution, the nation currently has a relatively high degree of income inequality. After the victory of the communist Red Army in 1949, Mao Zedong's government introduced a number of reforms to reduce the great disparity between rural and urban incomes that had long existed. However, these policies (including agrarian reform) were inefficient and often highly repressive. Beginning in the 1970s, the government introduced free-market (capitalist) economic policies so that today, while the communists still control the government, the economy is substantially based on private enterprise. These reforms have made the Chinese economy very productive and have made China a world-leading economic power but have also produced considerable economic inequality within the country.

Of all the regions in the developing world, sub-Saharan Africa has the most varied levels of economic equality and inequality. At one extreme, South Africa has perhaps the world's most unequal distribution of income (table 1.2). From the colonial era through to 1994, the country's white minority (accounting for less than 20 percent of the population) held absolute political and economic control, while keeping the black majority in poverty. While the black majority has held political power for over twenty years, the country still suffers from tremendous economic inequality. In the remainder of the continent income distribution varies considerably depending on such factors as the extent to which land was concentrated in European hands during the colonial period, the level of ethnic disparities between different tribal groups, and the degree of government-initiated economic redistribution since independence.

Today income is very unequally distributed in the Central African Republic, Botswana, and Zimbabwe (all with Gini Indices exceeding 0.500) and relatively equally distributed in Mauritania, Tanzania, Burkina Faso, and Uganda (all with indices under 0.400). The predominantly Arab countries of North Africa, including Egypt, Morocco (see table 1.2), Tunisia, and Algeria tend to have moderate to low levels of inequality, due both to state welfare policies and Islamic principles of social responsibility.

Social Underdevelopment

Poverty in developing countries is associated with poor social conditions such as high infant mortality and low literacy rates, which in turn reduces opportunities for human development in other areas. If these countries are to further develop economically, politically, and socially, they must extend and improve their educational systems and, thereby, raise the rate of literacy. An educated workforce contributes to higher labor productivity. Moreover, improved education also expands mass political participation and contributes to greater government accountability to the governed.

Thus, not surprisingly, political scientists have found that countries with higher literacy rates are more likely to attain and maintain democratic governments.[2]

Greater **gender equality** has also been shown to contribute greatly to social development. Female education has very positive effects on infant mortality rates, for example, while improving women's access to the labor market can provide a substantial boost to economic development. The relationship between gender and development will be more fully explored in chapter 7.

Table 1.3 presents data on several important indicators of social development. The first data column lists each country's HDI and how that score ranks in comparison with other countries anywhere in the world. The highly developed countries of Norway, Australia, Switzerland, and Germany—not shown in the table—have the world's highest HDI (from 0.949 to 0.926). The lowest HDI in the world are in the sub-Saharan African countries of Central African Republic, Niger, and Chad (with indices of 0.352 to 0.396)—also not in the table. In table 1.3, listing only developing countries, Cuba (ranked 68th in the world) and Iran (69th) have the highest HDI while Zambia (139th), Pakistan (147th), and Nigeria (152nd) have the lowest indices.

In general, countries with greater average incomes throughout the world, not surprisingly, tend to have higher HDI, but that is not always true. The next column shows each country's world ranking on average income minus its rankings on HDI. Thus, if country A had the 40th highest per capita income in the world, but had the 20th highest HDI score, it would have a positive (GNI-HDI) score of +20. On the other hand, if country B's per capita income ranked 30th in the world (higher than country A), but its HDI score was only 34th in the world, it would have a

Table 1.3 Human Development and Literacy

Country	HDI (rank)	Per Capita GNI Rank Minus HDI Rank	Adult Literacy Rate (%, age 15+)
Morocco	.647 (123)	−4	72
Nigeria	.527 (152)	−23	60
Zambia	.579 (139)	+7	85
Iran	.774 (69)	NA	87
Thailand	.740 (87)	−11	94
Pakistan	.550 (147)	−10	56
India	.624 (131)	−4	72
Bolivia	.674 (118)	+6	95
Cuba	.775 (68)	+48	99
Brazil	.754 (79)	−1	93

Source: UNDP, *Human Development Report*; CIA, *The World Factbook*; World Bank.

negative (GNI-HDI) score of −4. In this column of the table, any country with a positive score has "overachieved" (i.e., its HDI rank is higher than we might have predicted based on its GNI rank) and, conversely, any country with a negative score has "underachieved." The primary reason why a country overachieves is that its government has allocated a greater percentage of its spending toward improving health, sanitation, and education, while underachieving governments have spent a lower percentage of their revenue on improving these services. Greater social and gender equality also contributes to improved performance.

Cuba (+48) is the greatest overachiever in the table, while Zambia (+7), though a desperately poor country, still had an HDI higher than its GNI would predict.* Some of the greatest overachievers among developing countries not shown in the table are Madagascar (+25), Sri Lanka (+21), Jamaica (+16), and Chile (+16). At the other end of the table, Nigeria (−23) is the greatest underachiever. But even greater underachievers not shown in the table include Equatorial Guinea (−79), Kuwait (−48), Gabon (−46), Iraq (−30), and Saudi Arabia (−26). Virtually all of the world's greatest underachievers are petroleum producers that have largely failed to fully translate their oil wealth into a greater quality of life for their citizens. Iraq has also been seriously hurt by its prolonged civil war, while Equatorial Guinea has suffered from perhaps the world's most corrupt and rapacious government (see chapter 4).

The last column again shows how widely social conditions vary among less developed countries, with Pakistan and Nigeria having an adult literacy rate of only 56 and 60 percent, respectively, while Bolivia, Brazil, Cuba, and Thailand are over 90 percent literate. In recent decades many developing nations have raised their literacy rates dramatically. Of the 112 developing nations with literacy rates reported by UNICEF, three-quarters are over 70 percent literate (including two-fifths of all developing countries over 90 percent literate), while only 12 percent of all developing countries are less than half literate.†

Finally, table 1.4 presents additional measures of the quality of people's lives: life expectancy (male and female), the percentage of the population living in poverty, and the percentage of people who have completed primary school. The first two data columns reveal how much lower life expectancy is in most sub-Saharan African nations (as illustrated by Nigeria and Zambia) and, to a somewhat lesser extent, in South Asia (India and

---

* Again, Zambia's +7 score does not mean that it has a good HDI rank—it most certainly does not—only that its HDI rank is not as bad as might have been expected by its even lower GNI rank.

† That is to say that of the 112 developing nations measured, 46 of them have literacy rates of over 90 percent, 38 are 70–89 percent literate, 15 have literacy rates of 50–69 percent and only 13 were less than half literate.

Table 1.4   Quality of Life/Social Indicators

Country	Life Expectancy		Population Living in Poverty (%)	Children Who Complete Primary School (%)
	Male	Female		
Morocco	73.8	80.1	15.6	NA
Nigeria	52.4	54.5	50.9	68
Zambia	50.8	54.1	54.4	74
Iran	69.8	73.1	NA	NA
Thailand	71.5	78.0	1.0	94
Pakistan	65.0	69.0	45.6	68
India	67.3	69.9	55.3	61
Bolivia	66.4	72.1	20.6	92
Cuba	76.4	81.1	NA	97
Brazil	73.2	80.9	2.4	96

Source: CIA, *The World Factbook*; The World Bank, *Databank*; UNDP, HDI; UNICEF.

Pakistan). While malnutrition, deadly diseases such as malaria, and, in some cases, civil violence account for much of that, a number of African countries experienced sharp declines in life expectancy in the 1990s and early 2000s because of the HIV/AIDS pandemic, especially in Southern Africa (including Zambia). Pakistan and India are still plagued by a high rate of infant mortality.

The next column presents the percentage of the population living in poverty, as measured in UNICEF's multivariate measure of key factors such as nutrition, child mortality, years of schooling, and access to potable water, electricity, and toilets. Here again, countries representing South Asia and sub-Saharan Africa have by far the highest rates of poverty—about half or more of the population in India, Zambia, Nigeria, and Pakistan, whereas less than 10 percent of the population of Thailand, Brazil, and Cuba fall below the poverty line.*

The last column presents the percentage of children who have completed primary school. Here again there have been substantial improvements through most of the developing world, so that even in very poor countries—such as India, Pakistan, and Nigeria—61–68 percent of children have completed primary school. Some of the most dramatic gains in the developing world have been in education and literacy.

---

* The UNICEF measure of poverty sets the poverty line far below what it would be in developed countries, such as the United States or Italy. That is, a significant portion of the Thai or Brazilian population falling above these poverty lines would be considered to be poverty-stricken in developed countries. Cuba did not release sufficient statistics to ascertain the percentage of its population in poverty, but HDI and other Cuban statistics suggest that only a small percentage of its population would fit the UNICEF measure of poverty.

A Palestinian child takes notes in a UN school for refugees in Gaza. Education is an important key to social development around the world. Conflict, however, can make that difficult: more than half of the 65 million refugees and other forcibly displaced persons around the world are children. *Source*: Shareef Sarhan/UNRWA

Political Underdevelopment

When Western political scientists first began to study less developed countries systematically, they soon recognized that evaluating political systems in cultural and socioeconomic settings very different from their own was challenging. While many modernization theorists believed that governments in the developing world should model themselves after Western industrialized democracies, they were also mindful of important differences between the regions that limited that possibility. For example, recognizing that most Western European countries did not fully democratize until they were well along the path to industrial development, scholars were often reluctant to criticize authoritarian governments in countries still at the early stages of economic development. A number of African social scientists added to the debate by arguing that their continent had extensive village- and tribal-based democracy that adequately substituted for competitive elections at the national level. Others feared that, in the ethnically divided countries of Africa and Asia, multiparty systems would inevitably develop along ethnic lines, further contributing to national disintegration.

Conscious of such challenges, many political scientists proposed political standards that they felt were free of ideological and cultural biases.

Political development, they suggested, involves the creation of specialized and differentiated government institutions that effectively carry out necessary functions, such as collecting tax revenues, defending national borders, maintaining political stability, stimulating economic development, improving the quality of human life, and communicating with the citizenry. In addition, they argued, developed governments are responsive to a broad segment of society and respect the population's fundamental freedoms and civil rights. Presumably, any government satisfying these standards would enjoy a reasonable level of legitimacy (i.e., its own citizens would endorse its right to govern), which encourages individuals and groups to pursue their political objectives peacefully through established political institutions rather than through violent or other illegal channels. But, too many developing countries, Paul Collier notes, suffer from "bad governance"—a combination of corruption, catering to special interests, and mismanagement.[3]

But while analysts agreed that governments should be responsive, representative, and non-repressive, many of them also believed that a political system could be considered developed even if it was not democratic, at least as that term is defined in the West. Definitions of full **democracy** generally encompass the following basic components: fair and competitive elections in which opposition parties have a realistic chance of winning; universal or nearly universal adult suffrage; widespread opportunities for political participation; free and open mass media; and government respect for human rights, including minority rights.[4] Many political scientists initially felt that it was unrealistic to expect that level of democracy to quickly flourish in developing countries. Others, concerned about the high levels of violence and instability in those political systems, claimed that the developing countries' first priority had to be political stability—even if that might initially require military rule or other forms of authoritarian government.[5]

More recently, however, troubled by extensive government repression in the developing world and the obvious failures of most authoritarian regimes, political scientists have begun to insist that democracy and some degree of socioeconomic equality must be understood as integral parts of political development.[6] Beyond its obvious ethical attractions, democracy also has pragmatic appeal. For example, governments whose citizens hold them accountable through competitive elections are more likely to be more efficient and honest (although the disappointing records of democratic governments in countries such as Kenya and the Philippines demonstrate that there are no guarantees). Similarly, free and independent forms of mass media also help keep governments accountable. The disintegration of the Soviet bloc and the fall of many dictatorships throughout the developing world suggest that authoritarian regimes may be stable in the short run but are fragile in the long term. In fact, democracies—especially those with higher levels of economic and social development—are generally less susceptible to revolutionary turmoil or other forms of mass violence.

Only a limited number of developing countries—for example, the Bahamas, Uruguay, and Costa Rica—have fully met the standards of political development and democracy just listed. Others such as Argentina, India, South Korea, and Taiwan currently satisfy most criteria. Even a cursory review of developing countries, however, reveals that most governments still fall short. At one extreme—in nations such as Somalia and Yemen—rebel groups or warlords have divided control over their country, or rebels have so undermined the national governments that political scientists label them "failed states." Elsewhere in the developing world, many governments respond disproportionately to the demands of an affluent minority. Self-perpetuating and self-serving elites have ruled many Middle Eastern and North African countries, while some sub-Saharan African governments serve the interests of dominant ethnic groups. Political corruption, bureaucratic inefficiency, and police repression are all endemic to many parts of the developing world.

In the immediate aftermath of decolonization, many countries in the developing world suffered from political instability, repression, and even civil conflict. Class-based revolutionary movements erupted in various Asian and Latin American states, and a number of African countries have been torn apart by ethnic civil wars (with some countries still suffering from such conflicts). The last decades of the twentieth century saw democracy advance in many areas of the developing world, most notably in Latin America and East Asia. That so-called "third wave" democratization now appears to have stalled, however. Chapter 3 offers a fuller account of these trends, and the factors underpinning them.

Some Relationships between the Components of Development

It is logical to assume that political, economic, and social underdevelopment are interrelated. More economically advanced countries can better educate their populations and provide them with superior health care. An educated citizenry, in turn, contributes to further economic growth and participates in politics more responsibly. Responsive and legitimate governments, constrained by competitive elections, are more likely to educate their citizens and to make informed economic decisions. Indeed, these connections are supported by empirical evidence. Wealthier countries tend to have greater life expectancies, higher literacy rates, and more stable and democratic governments.

However, these correlations are not absolute. For example, a country's literacy and infant mortality rates depend not only on its economic resources but also on government policies in the areas of education, public health, and welfare. Thus, elitist government policies in some countries have contributed to worsen social conditions (as measured by their HDI) in comparison to other nations with comparable or fewer economic resources. "Underachievers" include many petroleum-rich states such as Saudi Arabia and Kuwait. On the other hand, governments in Cuba and Chile—with strong commitments to social welfare programs—have generated higher life expectancy rates and educational levels than their economic resources alone would lead us to predict ("overachievers").

Both economic and social development tend to correlate with political development. Wealthier, more educated developing countries such as Barbados, Botswana, Costa Rica, and Taiwan tend to have more politically stable, responsive, and democratic governments than poorer nations such as Mozambique, Haiti, and Cambodia. Indeed, developing countries are much less likely to become democracies or to maintain democracy unless they have reached a minimal threshold of socioeconomic development.[7] However, as countries undergo the process of becoming more economically developed, there is not necessarily a smooth progression toward greater political stability or democracy. On the contrary, Samuel Huntington observed that while the most affluent countries in the world (e.g., Switzerland and Canada) are politically stable and the poorest countries (such as Afghanistan and Burundi) are generally politically unstable, countries that are in the mid-stages of economic development often become more unstable as their economies develop.[8] Thus, for example, some of Latin America's most economically advanced countries (including Argentina and Chile) experienced internal conflicts and political unrest in the 1960s and 1970s, resulting in the collapse of their democratic governments and the emergence of highly repressive military dictatorships. In 2001–2, nearly two decades after the restoration of democratic government, Argentina experienced economic crisis, urban rioting, and political instability that produced five presidents in a span of less than a month. Huntington explained this political instability in mid-level developing nations by suggesting that as countries modernize, the spread of urbanization, education, and mass media consumption produces an increasingly politically aware and mobilized society whose citizens make greater demands on the government. All too often, however, political institutions, particularly political parties, are not strengthened quickly enough to channel and respond to this rising tide of demands, or the government may lack the economic resources to address all these demands. As a result, he maintained, the system becomes overloaded and unstable.

Guillermo O'Donnell posited another theory explaining the rise of extremely repressive dictatorships in South America's more economically advanced nations during the 1960s and 1970s. He suggested that as those countries moved toward a higher stage of industrial growth, they required extensive new investment that they could secure only by attracting foreign capital. Such foreign investment, in turn, would materialize only if the government-controlled labor unions and kept down workers' wage demands. In order to achieve those goals, business leaders and technocrats turned to repressive military rule through what he called "bureaucratic-authoritarian states."[9]

Similarly, some scholars have argued that an authoritarian government might be helpful in the early to middle stages of industrialization in order to control labor unions and workers' wages, thereby increasing company profits and attracting new external investment. They point out that the Asian countries that enjoyed the most spectacular economic growth from the 1970s to the mid-1990s—Indonesia, Malaysia, Thailand, Singapore, Taiwan, and South Korea—were all governed by authoritarian regimes during their economic takeoffs. Although these theories have since been challenged, they indicate that the relationships between political, economic, and social development are complex. While, at least in the long run, the three generally go hand in hand, they need not progress at the same rate. Moreover, for some periods of time, they may even move in different directions.

THE CAUSES OF UNDERDEVELOPMENT

Our initial discussion suggested that there is some debate concerning the very definitions of political and socioeconomic underdevelopment. Social scientists disagree even more intensely over the underlying causes of underdevelopment and the most promising pathways to change. How, for example, do we account for constant military intervention in politics in Pakistan, political turmoil in Venezuela, and government repression in Syria? Do these problems originate from internal factors such as authoritarian cultural values, weak political parties, or misguided economic planning? Or, did foreign domination—stretching from the colonial era to today's age of **multinational corporations** (MNCs) and the International Monetary Fund (IMF)—cause many of these difficulties?

Questions about the cause of underdevelopment and pathways to development elicit very different responses from scholarly analysts. Sometimes these evaluations reflect their personal background, country of origin, or ideology. Thus, for example, theories that attribute the developing world's political unrest or economic backwardness to traditional cultural values generally have emanated from the United States or from other developed nations. On the other hand, approaches such as dependency theory and world systems theory, which view Western exploitation as the root cause of underdevelopment have been particularly popular among Latin American and African analysts. Similarly, liberal, conservative, and Marxist analysts are each drawn to different explanations.

For years, two competing paradigms shaped scholarly analyses of politics and economic change in developing countries. The first, **modernization theory**, emerged in the early 1960s as American political science's leading interpretation of underdevelopment. The second, **dependency theory**, originated in Latin America in the 1970s and offered a more radical perspective on development, one particularly popular among scholars in developing nations.

Modernization Theory: Culture, Development, and Change

During the 1950s and 1960s, as the demise of European colonialism produced a host of newly independent nations in Africa, Asia, and the Middle East, Western social scientists began to study politics and economics in the developing world more intensively. That interest produced a complex conceptual model of underdevelopment and development known as modernization theory. Its proponents included some of the most prominent figures in the study of comparative politics. For a decade or more, modernization theory reigned supreme in the study of political and economic development. Though later challenged, it has continued to influence our understanding of developing nations. While there have been variations and disagreement among modernization theorists, they generally share a number of underlying assumptions and perspectives.

Despite the tremendous array of problems facing the developing world, modernization theorists were initially optimistic about prospects for development. After all, Western industrialized democracies had also started out as underdeveloped countries. Most developing nations, they argued, could—and should—follow a path of political and economic modernization similar to the one first traveled by the advanced Western countries.

To accomplish this, modernization theorists insisted, developing nations had to acquire new cultural values and create modern political and economic institutions. Drawing on the theories of such eminent sociologists as Max Weber and Talcott Parsons, these analysts distinguished between "traditional" and "modern" values, and emphasized the important effects of **political culture**, that is, culturally rooted attitudes to authority, legitimacy, and community. They saw many traditional political and economic values as somewhat irrational or at least unscientific. For example, the Indian caste system assigned people their rank in society at birth, a rank that was difficult to change. Conversely, modern men and women, they maintained, tend to do the following: judge others by universalistic standards (appraise people based on their ability rather than caste, class, or ethnic origins); believe in the possibility and desirability of change; value science and technology; think about issues outside the sphere of the family, neighborhood, or village; and believe that average citizens can—and should—try to influence the political system. At its worst, the theory exhibited elements of ethnocentrism and condescension, implying the inferiority of other cultures. Thus, in the 1980s one of the founders of Latin American studies in the United States argued:

> There is something in the quality of Latin American . . . culture which has made it difficult . . . to be truly modern . . . which has made this part of the Western world so prone to excesses of scoundrels, so politically irrational in seeking economic growth, and so ready to reach for gimmicks.[10]

But how can a traditional society make the transition to modernity? How does a culture "modernize" its values? Modernization theorists identified education, urbanization, and the spread of mass media as central agents of change. As peasants move to cities, the theory argued, as more children attend schools that teach modern values, and as more citizens access the mass media, cultural modernization will progress. Another critical component, it was suggested, was the diffusion of modern ideas from highly industrialized nations to the developing world through the expansion of global communication, transportation, aid, and trade.

Gabriel Almond and G. Bingham Powell, depicting modernization as a rather inexorable force, contended that "the forces of technological change and cultural diffusion are driving political systems in certain directions, which seem discernible and susceptible to analysis in terms of increasing levels of development."[11] Others envisioned modernization as a process of getting developing nations to think and act "more like us" (i.e., the West). "As time goes on," Marion Levy predicted, "they and we will increasingly resemble one another. [The] more highly modernized societies become, the more they resemble one another."[12] Today, as the forces of modernization have spread McDonald's burgers and fries, computer technology, Hollywood movies, rock music, and democratic values around the world, at least some of this prophecy may seem accurate.

At the same time, modernization theory claimed, developing nations trying to modernize need to create more specialized and complex political and economic institutions to complement those cultural changes. For example, whereas a tribal culture might have a council of elders responsible for legislative, executive, and judicial activities, a modern society needs separate, specialized institutions for each of these tasks. Modernizing societies also need trained bureaucracies, which base professional advancement on merit rather than personal connections and make decisions according to uniform and consistent standards. Political parties have to channel citizens' demands and aspirations effectively to government policymakers. Eventually, it was argued, as these cultural and institutional changes progress, a modernizing society can lay the foundation for a more stable, effective, and responsive political system. During the decades after the Second World War, which featured the Cold War against Soviet communism, modernization theory became far more than an academic perspective. Its assumptions dominated US foreign policy toward the developing world, including foreign-aid programs, the Peace Corps, and the tactics used during the Vietnam War.

In time, however, many of early modernization theory's assumptions had to be modified. To begin with, it had been too optimistic and too simplistic in its initial view of change. Its proponents generally expected developing countries to achieve economic growth, greater equality, democracy, political stability, and greater national autonomy simultaneously and smoothly. As Huntington noted, the theory erroneously assumed that "all good things go together."[13] In fact, economic growth proved to be no guarantee of democracy, stability, equality, or autonomy. As we have noted, in nations such as Brazil, China, Mexico, South Korea, and Taiwan, industrialization and economic development originated and advanced for many years under the direction of authoritarian governments.

Analysts were particularly disturbed to find that the very process of social and economic modernization often ushered in political instability and violence. For example, in some of Latin America's most economically developed nations (Argentina, Chile, and Uruguay), industrial growth and greater income inequality unleashed bitter class conflict, causing the collapse of democratic institutions and the rise of repressive military dictatorships.[14] Elsewhere, in much of Africa, Asia, and the Middle East, the hopes once inspired by decolonization gave way to ethnic conflict, military coups d'état, and political repression.

Thus, the process of development often turned out to be more difficult and unpredictable than originally imagined. Modernization theory's initial optimism gave way to a revised perspective. Developing nations, this new perspective argued, would have to make hard choices between seemingly irreconcilable development goals. Concerned about growing political turmoil in many developing nations, political scientists like Samuel Huntington insisted that political stability was crucial—even if maintaining it sometimes necessitated authoritarian rule for a time. Strong institutions, he suggested, were necessary to manage and contain the new demands spurred by social change. At the same time, many economists and political scientists argued that the early stages of economic growth required wealth to be concentrated so that incipient capitalists could acquire sufficient capital for major investments.

More recently, the experiences of several countries in East Asia and Latin America have produced yet another new perspective. While certainly less naively optimistic than the earliest modernization theories, current analysis is also less pessimistic than the revisionists were. The reconciliation approach, offered by contemporary modernization theorists, maintains that, with the right policies, developing nations can simultaneously achieve goals previously thought to be incompatible.[15] Taiwan and South Korea, for example, have shown that it is possible to achieve rapid economic development together with equitable income distribution. Barbados and Costa Rica have managed to achieve democracy and stability simultaneously. Consequently, current research tries to analyze factors such as state policy, historical traditions, and cultural values that may hinder or contribute to successful development.

One of the major criticisms of modernization theory, at least as originally formulated, was that it offered an ethnocentric and simplistic view of culture. Explicitly or implicitly it suggested that the Western industrialized world was the source and model of modern ("good") values and attitudes.

More recent work on political culture is far more nuanced. It recognizes that while cultural values change over time, this change is shaped by earlier values as well as historical experience. For example, in East Asian countries, such as Japan and South Korea, traditional Confucian and Shinto beliefs may help explain why modern citizens of those countries tend to be less individualistic, more concerned with the good of the community or nation, and more family oriented than Westerners. Similarly, differing historical experiences have led to subtle but important differences between Americans and Europeans regarding role of the state—differences that help to sustain differing views on issues such as gun control, public health care, and the appropriate bounds of free speech. Scholars also agree that differences between "traditional" and "modern" cultural values are far from clear-cut. Thus, even though the United States is a highly modern society, some Americans have retained traditional values such as judging others by the color of their skin or gender. In the Middle East, reaction against social change has led some to embrace Islamic fundamentalist views that emphasize the early traditions of Islam. Yet these fundamentalist groups can also have very "modern" attitudes to political mobilization, the use of technology, the media, and political organization.

Indeed, perhaps the most striking aspect of recent work on political culture is its attention to context, complexity, and change—an aspect that will further be explored in our discussion of democracy in chapter 3. Modern opinion survey research shows that major differences in attitudes can exist within a given society based on social class, age, gender, education, and ethnicity. Mass media, economic and social change, and political experience can also cause some basic political orientations to change remarkably quickly.

Dependency Theory: The Core and the Periphery

During the 1960s and 1970s, social scientists in Latin America and the United States raised more fundamental objections to modernization theory, insisting that the revisionist modifications that we have just mentioned had failed to correct the theory's fundamental flaws. Under the banner of dependency theory, they challenged the modernizationists' most fundamental assumptions. A closely related approach was called "world systems theory."[16] Like modernization theorists, dependency scholars differ among themselves, but agree on the theory's fundamental premises.

To begin with, *dependentistas* (as dependency theorists are known) rejected the contention that developing countries can reproduce the same path to development as Western nations had, if only because the earliest industrialized nations changed the landscape for those that followed them. When Britain became the world's first industrialized nation, it faced no significant competition from other economic powers. During the colonial era, colonial powers imposed their economic interests on much of the rest world, structuring the economies of colonized countries to meet Western needs. Today, newly industrialized countries must compete against well-established industrial giants such as the United States, Japan, and Germany. In addition, Brazil's Theotonio Dos Santos argued, developing countries need to borrow capital and purchase advanced technology from highly developed countries, thereby making them dependent on economic forces beyond their borders and beyond their control.

As we have seen, modernization theory views Western influence over the developing world as beneficial, in that it spreads modern values, technology, and institutions. In contrast, dependency theorists maintain that Western colonialism and economic imperialism are precisely what first turned Africa, Asia, and Latin America into providers of cheap food and raw materials for the developed countries. Moreover, they charge, long after the developing countries had achieved political independence, wealthier nations have continued to use their economic power to sustain dependent relationships that disadvantage the developing world. Until recently, the production and export of manufactured goods and technology—the most profitable economic activities—along with major control over world finance remained primarily in the control of core nations, the *dependentistas*' label for the industrialized West. Conversely, in the past, developing countries, located in the periphery, were generally relegated to the production and export of agricultural goods and raw materials and had to trade for industrial imports on unfavorable terms. This did not mean that the core developed nations controlled every aspect of economic and political development (or underdevelopment) in the developing world, but rather dependency is

> a historical condition which shapes a certain structure of the world economy such that it favors some countries to the detriment of others and limits the development possibilities of the subordinate economies . . . a situation in which the economy of a certain group of countries is conditioned by the development and expansion of another economy, to which their own is subjected.[17]

Finally, *dependentistas* contend that economic dependence also had brought about the developing countries' political dependence on the core. Within the periphery, the argument went, political, military, and economic elites, backed by the might of the United States and other core nations, maintained a political system that benefited the powerful few at the expense of the many. Dependency theorists have noted, for example, how frequently France used to intervene militarily in its former African colonies to maintain corrupt and unrepresentative governments with which it was allied. Similarly, for many years, the United States supported friendly, but repressive, regimes such as Egypt's under the long rule of Hosni Mubarak.

As one might expect, many scholars in the developing world embraced dependency theory enthusiastically because it maintained that underdevelopment was not the developing world's "fault," but rather the result of foreign domination and exploitation. Moreover, for a time, dependency theory also challenged or displaced modernization theory in the United States and Europe as the major scholarly paradigm. As Omar Sánchez has observed, this "marks one of those rare instances in which ideas produced in the developing world come to influence the thinking of scholars in the developed world."[18]

However, just as early modernization theory had been overly optimistic about the developing countries' prospects for simultaneous economic and political development, early dependency theory turned out to be excessively pessimistic about their chances for development. Analysts such as Andre Gunder Frank had warned that less developed nations—largely confined to production of crops, minerals, and other commodities—were ruled by unrepresentative elites and were doomed to face continued backwardness. Some *dependentistas* favored nationalization, state investment, and trade protectionism as an appropriate response. Given the role of local elites in maintaining dependency, some believed that radical revolutions were the only solution.

Yet, despite the bleak prognosis of early dependency theorists, it was clear as early as the mid-1960s that nations such as Brazil and Mexico were undergoing substantial industrialization. Some two decades later, China emerged as the world's leading exporters of manufactured goods. Similarly, South Korea, Taiwan, India, Malaysia, and several other Asian nations began to enjoy rapid economic modernization and growth.

In a more sophisticated version of dependency theory, Brazil's Fernando Henrique Cardoso rejected the contention that all developing countries were condemned to underdevelopment and precluded from significant industrialization.[19] Drawing heavily from the experiences of his own country, he noted that through the active intervention of the state and the linkage of domestic firms to MNCs, some developing countries had industrialized and experienced considerable economic growth. He referred to this process as **associated-dependent development.**

Cardoso radically altered dependency theory by arguing that countries such as Argentina, Brazil, Colombia, and Mexico could modernize and expand their economies while still remaining dependent on foreign banks and MNCs for loans, investment, and technology. Brazilian industrialization, he noted, had been stimulated largely by a sharp rise in foreign, corporate investment. Still, Cardoso and his colleagues considered associated-dependent development tainted in several important ways. MNCs were making critical economic decisions affecting developing countries, but were outside the developing nations' control. Furthermore, foreign corporations tended to invest in capital-intensive (highly mechanized) production that needed fewer workers than more traditional, labor-intensive firms did, and, these new industries tended to manufacture products for more affluent middle- and upper-class consumers. Hence, unlike most Western firms, they had little incentive to raise wage levels in order to enhance working-class purchasing power. Rather than reduce poverty, *dependentistas* maintained, associated-dependent development had widened the income gap. At the same time, Peter Evans and others argued, the MNCs' alliances with Latin American economic, political, and military elites helped uphold the power of repressive regimes such as Brazil's (former) military government.

Modernization and Dependency Theories Compared

The dependency approach offered useful corrections to modernization theory. Furthermore, it highlighted important influences over developing world societies that the earlier theory had often neglected—the legacies of colonial era, and the importance of international trade, finance, and investment. In fact, many political scientists now argue that a principal characteristic defining developing nations is their dependence on the core. Consequently, these scholars still consider relatively wealthy nations such as Saudi Arabia as well as stable democracies such as Costa Rica to be part of the developing world because their economic and political systems have not advanced in other important aspects of development.

Regardless of how they view dependency theory, contemporary analysts of underdevelopment now recognize that political and economic modernization requires more than adopting new values or changing domestic political structures as modernization theory had postulated. Dependency theory shifted the focus of research from exclusively internal factors to international economic and political relationships. *Dependentistas* also helped redefine the concept of economic development. Whereas early mainstream research on economic development heavily stressed the goal of economic growth, dependency theorists also emphasized the importance of more equitable economic distribution and greater social justice. When rapid economic growth increases the concentration of wealth and income in the hands of a minority, as it frequently does, it offers limited benefits to the poor, or may even worsen their situation. Influenced by dependency theory and other leftist critiques, establishment pillars such as the World Bank reoriented their focus toward growth coupled with redistribution.

Despite its contributions, however, dependency theory suffered from serious failings. Just as early modernization theorists overemphasized the internal causes of underdevelopment, *dependentistas* erroneously attributed virtually all of the developing world's problems to external economic factors—including international trade, foreign investment, and credit—as well as political alliances linking the core nations with the developing countries' economic, political, and military elites. Furthermore, many authors portrayed developing nations as helpless pawns with no way out of their poverty. As Stephan Haggard charged, "Countries are called 'dependent' by virtue of their characteristics and remain so regardless of their action."[20] To be sure, what is striking about much of that literature is its economic determinism and neglect of domestic social or political factors. Its proponents frequently have dismissed governments in the developing world as agents of the local economic elite who colluded with Western- or Japanese-based MNCs. Consequently, there is a disturbing similarity between many of their case studies. The details of Mexican, Nigerian, or Peruvian politics and economic underdevelopment may differ in these works, but too often *dependentistas* offer identical explanations for each country's problems.

Cardoso refined dependency theory by insisting that the types of constraints imposed by core economies on the periphery varied from one developing nation to another. El Salvador may be extremely dependent—economically and politically—on the United States, while Argentina—a larger country, further from North America—has been better equipped to guide its own course. Furthermore, the effects of external influences emanating from the core are mediated by conditions within each developing country. In other words, he argued, in varying degrees, developing nations have options within the limits imposed by their dependency. For example, a country's class structure and the influence of particular classes on government policy shape the type of associated-dependent development it experiences. As he and Enzo Faletto wrote, "We conceive the relationship between external and internal forces . . . as not [being] based on mere external forms of exploitation . . . but [as] rooted in coincidences of interests between local dominant classes and international ones."[21] In other words, decisions made by governments and business leaders in the developing world do matter, and some developing countries have enjoyed notable, if still flawed, economic growth. Combining Cardoso's ideas with elements of modernization theory, Guillermo O'Donnell offered a powerful explanation for the rise of authoritarian military governments in the most developed nations of South America.[22]

However, East Asia's "economic miracle" of rapid and sustained economic growth during the past several decades—most notably in China, South Korea, Taiwan, Hong Kong, and Singapore—has confounded dependency theory. These countries have linked themselves very closely to the industrialized world through trade, credit, investments, and technology transfers. Contrary to what even the more sophisticated dependency scholars had predicted, however, they achieved spectacular economic growth coupled with comparatively equitable income distribution. Countries such as South Korea and Taiwan now have standards of living comparable to a number of Western European countries, along with relatively high-income equality. Qatar and Singapore have higher per capita incomes than Norway and the United States, while Taiwan has about the same per capita income as Germany and Australia. Moreover, in a further blow to dependency theory, first China and then India (the world's most populated nations) have become two rapidly growing economies by opening their doors to foreign trade and investment. Even Fernando Henrique Cardoso—dependency theory's most renowned exponent during his career as an academic scholar—later embraced foreign investment, trade, and technology in his second career as Brazil's finance minister and then two-term president.

Contemporary Perspectives

Today, few analysts accept either modernization or dependency theory in their entirety. In their original formulations, both approaches suffered from overgeneralizations that failed to recognize sufficiently the cultural, political, and economic differences among developing countries. The growing influence of **institutionalist approaches** to comparative politics has

Table 1.5   Under-Five Mortality Rates (per 1,000 Live Births)

Region	1990	2015
Sub-Saharan Africa	179	86
Oceania	74	51
Southern Asia	126	50
Caucasus and Central Asia	73	33
Southeastern Asia	71	27
Northern Africa	73	24
Western Asia	65	23
Latin American and the Caribbean	54	17
Eastern Asia	53	11
Developed Regions	15	6
Developing Regions	100	47

Source: United Nations, *Millennium Development Goals Report* (2015).

been one response to this. Institutionalists stress how political choices are constrained by context, structure, and historical legacies. The development of political and other institutions, they suggest, creates a degree of "path dependency"—making some future political and economic development directions more likely, and others less so. Institutionalism also often highlights the impact of critical junctures, when political decisions (like the writing of a national constitution) influence political development for many years to come.

Many recent theories and approaches, such as bureaucratic-authoritarianism (which attempted to explain the rise of military dictatorships in some of the developing world's more economically developed nations) or work on comparative democratization, have avoided overarching global explanations of development and underdevelopment, focusing instead on more specific issues. Research on interest groups, social mobilization, and contentious politics has focused on how groups organize to pursue common interests, whether within existing political structures or through more disruptive techniques. There is also growing recognition that civil conflict can cause a **conflict trap,** whereby political violence hampers development, and the resulting underdevelopment contributes to the likelihood to future violence. This has spurred greater research into the dynamics of civil war, and appropriate ways of promoting peacebuilding and post-conflict reconciliation and reconstruction.

Most contemporary analysts thus reject the very idea of a single theory of development. For one thing, the developing world is too diverse and the processes of political and socioeconomic development too complex to be explained by a single theory of change. This does not mean, however, that the insights offered by dependency and modernization theories have not been useful. Our current understanding of development draws on the strengths of both approaches, while recognizing their limitations.

HOW MUCH PROGRESS HAS BEEN MADE?

Since 1980 developing countries have suffered a number of serious economic setbacks. However, despite economic decline in Africa and Latin America during the 1980s and early 1990s, in East Asia in the late 1990s, and in many developing countries from 2008 to 2011, the developing world has enjoyed considerable social and economic development.

In 2000, all member states of the United Nations and over twenty international organizations pledged to help achieve eight **Millennium Development Goals** (MDG) by 2015: eradicating extreme poverty and hunger; achieving universal primary education; promoting gender equality and empowering women; reducing child mortality; improving maternal health; combatting HIV/AIDS, malaria, and other major diseases; ensuring environmental sustainability; and building a global partnership for development. As noted earlier in this chapter, significant gains were made during this period. Progress, however, was uneven across regions and countries. Extreme poverty (measured by the proportion of the population living on $1.25 per day) fell by 66 percent in Southern Asia, and 84 percent in Southeastern Asia, but by only 28 percent in sub-Saharan Africa. Improvements in child and maternal mortality were more evenly distributed, but the rates in sub-Saharan Africa are still much higher than those in the rest of the developing world. Table 1.5 shows under-five mortality rates around the world, indicating both the social progress that has been made and the areas where the need for improvement is greatest.

In 2015, members states of the United Nations agreed to new set of seventeen **Sustainable Development Goals** (SDGs) to be achieved by the year 2030. As the name suggests, these included increased attention to environmental concerns, including global warming, land and maritime pollution, urban development, and clean water. They also include reduced inequality and effective and accountable institutions.[23]

Official development assistance (ODA, or "foreign aid") has played an important role in such improvements, increasing from $81 billion per year in 2000 to $135 billion in 2014. However, more important still has been economic development, spurred by trade, investment, and effective government economic policies. Developing countries today attract approximately $646 billion per year in **foreign direct investment** (FDI)—that is, outside investment by private companies—accounting for almost 40 percent of the global total. They also account for a $7.9 trillion share of the world's $18.3 trillion in annual trade. The political economy of developing countries will be more fully explored in chapter 2, with particular attention to the different types of policy countries have adopted, the search for growth with equity, and the challenges of sustainable development.

Good governance is an important part of this too, with transparency, accountability, and the rule of law contributing to a positive business climate. Social development builds human capital, and a healthier, more educated, and more productive labor force—thus strengthening growth and attracting further investment.

Nonetheless, despite these impressive gains, many people in the developing world still face very difficult lives. Even with significant declines in child mortality, over 16,000 children under age five die in the developing world every day. About one-third of the adults in South and West Asia and in sub-Saharan Africa remain illiterate. Millions of people have been lifted out of extreme poverty, but many have not. The UN's Food and Agriculture Organization estimates that some 815 million people—about one in nine of the world's population—suffer from inadequate nourishment. More than half of these live in areas suffering violent conflict.[24]

Despite the general reduction in worldwide political violence since the twentieth century, conflict remains a major component of underdevelopment in some areas. Some 65 million people have been forcibly displaced by war or persecution, half of them children. Developing countries with limited resources host the vast majority of the world's refugees too. In Syria alone, half a million people may have died due to civil war. In Afghanistan, South Sudan, Yemen and elsewhere, war has inflicted a terrible toll, destroying lives and the economy. Despite efforts by the United Nations and others, these conflicts are often difficult to resolve, involving a complex and deadly interplay of domestic tensions, regional rivalries, and international geopolitics.

Corruption is another major obstacle to development, and is explored in detail in chapter 4. It is an impediment to economic growth, and an economic burden on citizens. It distorts policy and undermines the rule of law. It also causes citizens to become highly cynical about their political system, and corrodes faith in political and bureaucratic institutions. It is especially difficult to root out in authoritarian governments, where it may be deeply entrenched as part of the governing system.

Indeed, political development in the developing countries has been much more uneven than economic development. As noted in chapter 3, after decades of growing democracy around the world, indicators of political freedom are now stagnant or declining. Countries such as Venezuela, Philippines, and Turkey have slipped from democracy to hybrid regimes that combine elections with increasingly authoritarian rule. While the "Arab Spring" protests of 2011 held out the promise of greater democracy in the Middle East, only in Tunisia did such a system emerge. Elsewhere, uprisings resulted in failed transitions and renewed dictatorship (as in Egypt) or collapse into civil war (in Libya, Syria, and Yemen).

> **Practice and Review Online at**
> http://textbooks.rowman.com/handelman9e

KEY TERMS

agrarian reform
associated-dependent development
colonialism
conflict trap
democracy
dependency theory
developing countries/world
foreign direct investment (FDI)
gender equality
Gini Index
Human Development Index (HDI)
institutionalist approaches
LDCs (less or least developed
   countries)
less developed countries

Millennium Development Goals
   (MDGs)
modernization theory
multinational corporations (MNCs)
newly industrializing countries
   (NICs)
official development assistance (ODA)
per capita income
political culture
purchasing power parity (PPP)
South (global)
Sustainable Development Goals
   (SDGs)
third world

DISCUSSION QUESTIONS

1. What are the best indicators of economic and political development?
2. How does economic development affect political development, and vice versa?
3. What are the strengths and weaknesses of modernization and dependency theory respectively for the study of the contemporary developing world?

NOTES

1. United Nations, *Millenium Development Goals Report 2015*, http://mdgs.un. org/unsd/mdg/Resources/Static/Products/Progress2015/English2015.pdf.

2. Axel Hadenius, *Democracy and Development* (London: Cambridge University Press, 1992).

3. Paul Collier, *The Bottom Billion* (New York, NY: Oxford University Press, 2007), 64–75.

4. Hadenius, *Democracy and Development*; Robert A. Dahl, *Democracy and Its Critics* (New Haven, CT: Yale University Press, 1989).

5. Samuel P. Huntington, *Political Order in Changing Societies* (New Haven, CT: Yale University Press, 1968).

6. Guillermo O'Donnell and Philippe Schmitter, *Transitions from Authoritarian Rule: Tentative Conclusions about Uncertain Democracies* (Baltimore, CO: Johns Hopkins University Press, 1986); Dahl, *Democracy and Its Critics*.

7. Mitchell A. Seligson, "Democratization in Latin America: The Current Cycle," in *Authoritarians and Democrats: Regime Transition in Latin America*, eds. James M. Malloy and Mitchell A. Seligson (Pittsburgh, PA: University of Pittsburgh Press, 1987).

8. Samuel P. Huntington, *The Third Wave: Democratization in the Late Twentieth Century* (Norman, OK: University of Oklahoma Press, 1991).

9. Guillermo O'Donnell, *Modernization and Bureaucratic-Authoritarianism: Studies in South American Politics* (Berkeley, CA: University of California Press, 1973).

10. Kalman H. Silvert, quoted in J. Samuel Valenzuela and Arturo Valenzuela, "Modernization and Dependency: Alternative Perspectives in the Study of Latin American Underdevelopment," *Comparative Politics* 10, no. 4 (July 1978): 542.

11. Gabriel A. Almond and G. Bingham Powell, *Comparative Politics: A Developmental Approach* (Boston, MA: Little, Brown, 1966), 301.

12. Marion Levy Jr., "Social Patterns (Structures) and Problems of Modernization," in *Readings on Social Change*, eds. Wilbert Moore and Robert Cooke (Upper Saddle River, NJ: Prentice Hall, 1967), 207.

13. Samuel P. Huntington, "The Goals of Development," in *Understanding Political Development*, eds. Myron Weiner and S. Huntington (Boston, MA: Little, Brown, 1987).

14. See Juan Linz and Alfred Stepan, eds., *The Breakdown of Democratic Regimes: Latin America* (Baltimore, MD: Johns Hopkins University Press, 1978).

15. Huntington, "The Goals of Development."

16. Immanuel Wallerstein, *World-Systems Analysis: An Introduction* (Durham, NC: Duke University Press, 2004).

17. Theodoro Dos Santos, "The Structure of Dependence," in *Readings in U.S. Imperialism*, eds. K. T. Fann and Donald C. Hodges (Boston, MA: Porter Sargent, 1971), 226.

18. Omar Sánchez, "The Rise and Fall of the Dependency Movement: Does It Inform Underdevelopment Today?" *EIAL* (Estudios Interdisciplinarios de América Latina y el Caribe) 14, no. 2 (July–December 2003).

19. Fernando Henrique Cardoso and Enzo Faletto, *Dependency and Development in Latin America* (Berkeley, CA: University of California Press, 1979); Peter Evans, *Dependent Development* (Princeton, NJ: Princeton University Press, 1979).

20. Stephan Haggard, *Pathways from the Periphery: The Politics of Growth in Newly Industrializing Countries* (Ithaca, NY: Cornell University Press, 1990), 21–2.

21. Cardoso and Faletto, *Dependency and Development*, 26.

22. O'Donnell, *Modernization and Bureaucratic-Authoritarianism*.

23. United Nations, *Sustainable Development Goals Knowledge Platform*, https://sustainabledevelopment.un.org.

24. Food and Agriculture Organization, *The State of Food Security and Nutrition in the World 2017*, http://www.fao.org/state-of-food-security-nutrition/en.

2

The Political Economy of the Developing World

Ships loading and unloading in Durban, South Africa—the busiest port in sub-Saharan Africa. In real terms, African exports have more than doubled over the past twenty years. *Source*: Roland Knauer/Alamy Stock Photo.

ALL GOVERNMENTS, EXCEPT PERHAPS THE MOST CORRUPT and incompetent, wish to promote economic development. Economic growth, coupled with reasonably equitable income distribution, offers the promise of improved living standards and, presumably, increased popular support for the ruling regime, at least in the long run.* It also provides added tax revenues, which enhance government capacity. And, economic development can augment a nation's military strength, diplomatic influence, and international prestige. However, the obvious benefits of growth should not obscure the many difficult questions that economic development policy entails. What government policies best promote economic growth and how can the conflicting goals of economic development be reconciled? How should countries share the inevitable sacrifices required for generating early economic development? How can a nation achieve economic development without doing irreparable harm to the environment?

During the 1980s, the optimism of early modernization theorists looked ill-founded in light of sharp economic declines in Africa and Latin America. Even today, despite some obvious progress, the war on poverty remains a daunting challenge in much of South Asia and sub-Saharan Africa. At the same time, however, East Asia's spectacular growth since the 1960s and India's takeoff since the mid-1990s appear to belie dependency theory's pessimism about the limits of economic development in the periphery.

In recent decades, a substantial amount of the scholarship on developing countries has focused on its **political economy**—that is to say, the interrelated dynamics of economics, politics, and policy. This chapter focuses on several important issues: What should be the role of the state in stimulating and regulating economic growth and industrialization? What are the major strategies for development, and how might developing economies interact with the rest of the world? How should countries deal with the deep economic inequalities that normally persist, or even increase, during the early modernization process? How are these issues of economic policy linked to the processes and imperatives of domestic politics? Later, in chapter 8, we will focus on particular social, economic, and political challenges associated with rural and urban poverty.

THE ROLE OF THE STATE

The question of the state's proper economic role has been at the center of political and economic debates for hundreds of years, first in Western industrial economies, and more recently in the developing world. During the

---

* In the short term, economic growth may be politically destabilizing. However, if growth is coupled with equitable income distribution, the chances of unrest diminish.

sixteenth and seventeenth centuries, major European powers were guided by the philosophy of mercantilism, which emphasized a close relationship between state power and trade. Trade opportunities were pursued with the support of state power, including colonial conquest of new markets and sources of raw materials. At the same time, tariffs and other barriers limited imports, especially of manufactured goods.

This perspective, however, drew the fire of the eighteenth-century Scottish economist Adam Smith, who favored a very limited state that gave market forces a free hand. In the following century, Karl Marx, reacting to the exploitative nature of early capitalism, proposed giving the state a dominant economic role, at least initially, through ownership of the means of production and centralized planning. Finally, the twentieth-century economist Sir John Maynard Keynes, responding to the Great Depression, advocated a substantial degree of government economic intervention to stimulate growth, but rejected Marxist prescriptions for state ownership and centralized planning.

In recent times, the collapse of the Soviet bloc's centrally controlled economy and the implementation of free-market (capitalist) reforms in communist countries, such as China and Vietnam, have discredited the advocates of state-controlled economies. At the same time, however, no government embraces full **laissez-faire** (i.e., allowing market forces completely free rein, with no government intervention). All countries, for example, no matter how capitalist, have laws regulating banking, domestic commerce, and international trade. Most have introduced some environmental regulations and work-safety rules. In the real world, then, governments must decide where to position themselves between the extreme poles of an unregulated economy and a **command economy** (an economy that is under centralized—state—control).

For a number of reasons, this choice is particularly contentious in the developing world. The fragile nature of less developed economies, their high level of poverty, their frequently poor distribution of wealth and income, their dependence on international market forces, and their relatively unchecked damage to the environment, all have encouraged many governments to assume an active economic role. Moreover, many developing nations lack a strong entrepreneurial class and sufficient private capital for investment. As a consequence, their governments have often built the steel mills, railroads, electrical generation plants, and telecommunications infrastructure the private sector could not or would not provide. More recently, governments have been asked to protect the environment against the ravages of economic growth. Not surprisingly, then, state economic intervention traditionally has been more pronounced in the developing world than in the West. Since the 1980s, however, the spread of **neoliberal** economic policies—characterized by free trade, free markets, and relatively unrestrained capitalism—has sharply reduced government economic intervention in both the developing and the developed worlds.*

This chapter discusses a number of alternate models prescribing the role of the state in developing economies, ranging from command economies, such as North Korea's, to very limited state intervention, as in Hong Kong and Singapore. In considering these alternatives, the reader should keep in mind that these are ideal types. Few countries fit any of these models perfectly. Cuba's Marxist government, for example, permits private farming and some other small businesses. Also, many nations have introduced some mix of these approaches. While the options discussed next are not exhaustive, they cover the models most widely used in the developing countries today.

The Command Economy

Marxism began as a critique of capitalism in the Western world during the early stages of industrial development. Inherently, argued Karl Marx, capitalism produced an inequitable distribution of wealth and income with those who control the means of production (industrialists, landlords) exploiting those who worked for them (the working class, peasants). One of Marxism's appeals to its supporters was its promise of great equality and social justice. Because economic inequality often intensifies in the early stages of development, the ideology had special appeal for activists in the developing countries.

Marxist advocates further assert that only a revolutionary, communist political-economic system can free the developing countries from the yoke of dependency. That is to say, because dependency theorists believe that capitalist trade and investment in developing countries creates an exploitative relationship between core (industrial) nations and the periphery, they argued that radical change was needed.

Finally, another of communism's appeals was its establishment of a centralized state control of the economy. A command economy, first established in the Soviet Union, has two central features. First, the state largely owns and manages the means of production. This includes factories, banks, major trade and commercial institutions, retail establishments, and, frequently, farms. While all communist nations have allowed some private economic activity, the private sector has been quite limited (aside from nations such as China and Vietnam, which have largely abandoned Marxist economics in recent years). Second, in a command economy, state planners, rather than market forces, shape basic decisions governing production.

---

*In the short term, economic growth may be politically destabilizing. However, if growth is coupled with equitable income distribution, the chances of unrest diminish.

By dictating the movement of people and resources from one sector of the economy to another, communist countries such as the Soviet Union and China were able to jump-start their industrial development. During the 1920s and 1930s, "Entire industries were created [in the Soviet Union], along with millions of jobs that drew peasants away from the countryside and into higher-paying jobs and higher living standards."[1] Western estimates of Soviet economic performance during its early industrialization phase indicate that between 1928 and 1955, GNP grew at a robust average annual rate of about 5 percent. After its revolution, China also moved quickly from a backward, agrarian economy to a far more industrialized society. According to a leading authority, between 1952 and 1975, that country's economy grew at an average annual rate of 8.2 percent, while industrial output surged ahead at 11.5 percent annually.[2]

Such economic reorientation came at a severe cost. In the Soviet Union, between 2 and 4 million Ukrainian and other peasants may have died during the famine of 1932–34. In China, the "Great Leap Forward" is believed to have cost tens of millions of lives, through famine and repression. Some analysts also believe that growth rates were exaggerated.

Still, all agree that compared to Mexico, Pakistan, and most developing countries, China's growth during that period, like the Soviet Union's decades earlier, was very impressive. Small wonder that many developing countries were once attracted to communist development models.

Command economies have frequently made great strides toward reducing income inequalities. Indeed, it is in this area that some communist developing countries clearly outperformed their capitalist counterparts. In Cuba, for example, the revolution brought a substantial transfer of income from the richest 20 percent of the population to the poorest 40 percent. The poor also benefited from land reform, subsidized rents, and free health care, though some of those gains were undermined in the 1990s, following the loss of Soviet economic assistance. Greater educational opportunities for all and an extensive adult literacy program further advanced social equality. Nor was Cuba unique in this respect. Cross-national statistical comparisons indicate that communist countries as a whole had more equal income distribution than did capitalist nations at similar levels of development.

Eventually, however, the weaknesses of command economies overshadow their accomplishments.* Lacking measures of consumer demand, state planners have little basis for deciding what to produce and how much. Furthermore, centrally controlled economies typically reward producers for meeting their output quotas, with little concern for product quality. Even

---

* All command economies are also controlled by politically repressive governments. But this chapter analyzes only the economic record of command economies and not their politics.

in the best of circumstances, to be at all efficient, a centralized command economy would need a highly skilled and honest bureaucracy equipped with sophisticated and accurate consumer surveys. Unfortunately, bureaucracies in the developing world rarely have these qualities. In addition, command economies handed inordinate power to state planners. And as Lord Acton once warned, "Power tends to corrupt, and absolute power tends to corrupt absolutely."

Thus, for example, Chinese private-business entrepreneurs know that the price of doing business is bribing government officials (cadres) or their adult children. Elsewhere as well, command economies have featured a large privileged class of state and party bureaucrats (**apparatchiks**), who enjoy perquisites unavailable to the rest of the population. Furthermore, while the Soviet Union and China enjoyed rapid growth in the early decades of their revolutions, both economies eventually lost momentum as they became more complex and therefore harder to control centrally. Finally, command economies are more adept at building heavy industries such as steel mills or public works projects—projects more common in the early stages of industrialization—than they are at developing sophisticated high-tech production techniques or at producing quality consumer goods. The Soviet Union, for example, turned out impressive military hardware and powerful space rockets, but was unable to produce a decent automobile or washing machine.

By the late 1970s in China and the 1980s in the Soviet Union, as both economies deteriorated, their leaders (Deng Xiaoping and Mikhail Gorbachev, respectively) recognized the need for economic decentralization and reduced state economic control. China's subsequent transition to market socialism (a mix of free-market and socialist economics) produced the world's second-largest economy. However, in the Soviet Union and its major successor state, Russia, reforms resulted in an economic collapse that lasted for nearly a decade. The fall of Soviet bloc Communism and China's remarkable economic transformation have inspired market-oriented reforms in other command economies. Vietnam, for example, has transferred state farmland to the peasantry, attracted billions of dollars in foreign investment, and transferred a substantial portion of its industrial production from the state to the private sector. Elsewhere in Asia and Africa, governments such as Myanmar and Republic of the Congo (Brazzaville) have privatized much of the state sector (i.e., sold government-owned enterprises to private owners) and reduced government economic controls. The end of Soviet aid has undercut some of Cuba's gains in health care, nutrition, and education. Stripped of its primary benefactor, it too has been forced to accept limited free-market innovations.

In the former communist nations of Eastern and Central Europe, the demise of their command economies initially failed to improve living standards and usually lowered them sharply. Only in China and Vietnam did the transition toward free-market economics rapidly raise standards of living. In Eastern and Central Europe, especially Russia, it took a decade or more for living standards to equal or surpass their levels in the communist era. The European Union played a key role in this transformation, offering both support for economic transition and access to the large European market.

Latin American Statism

Even in capitalist developing countries, the state has often played a major economic role, trying to be an engine of economic growth. In the period between the two world wars, a number of Latin American nations first pursued **state-led industrialization**. This process accelerated during the Great Depression of the 1920s and 1930s, when countries in the region had difficulty finding markets for their food and raw material exports and, consequently, had insufficient foreign exchange for industrial imports. Argentina, Brazil, and Mexico were among the early leaders in the push toward industrialization.

Unlike communist countries, Latin American nations left most economic activity in the hands of the private sector and did not centralize control of the economy. But their governments often owned strategically important enterprises and invested in industries that failed to attract sufficient private capital. Consequently, prior to the recent privatization of state enterprises, many of the region's railroads, airlines, petroleum companies, mines, steel mills, electric power plants, and telephone companies were state owned (though many of them originally had been built by foreign corporations that were subsequently nationalized).

In a number of ways, state ownership in the region contradicted common stereotypes. First, many government takeovers were supported by the business community. To begin with, the most important nationalizations (transfers of private firms to state ownership)—including the seizures of the petroleum industries in Mexico and Venezuela, mining operations in Chile and Peru, and railroads in Argentina—only affected companies that had been owned by foreign corporations rather than local capitalists. Second, after taking control of the petroleum industry, railroads, and utilities, the state often provided the country's private-sector industries with subsidized and inexpensive transportation, power, and other needed resources. In fact, until the 1980s, conservative governments in the region were as likely to expand government ownership as were left-leaning or populist regimes. For example, during the 1960s and 1970s, Brazil's right-wing, military regime substantially increased the size of the state sector. Such nationalizations typically were broadly popular and bolstered the government's legitimacy as a defender of national interests.

In addition to owning a number of essential enterprises, the state also played a pivotal role in fomenting private-sector industrial growth. In Latin America's largest economies, the government-initiated **import-substitution industrialization** (ISI) programs in the early to mid-twentieth century. ISI (discussed more extensively later in this chapter) sought to replace imported consumer goods with domestically manufactured products. Import-substituting firms were normally privately owned, but depended heavily on government support. This included protective tariffs and quotas on competing imports, favorable exchange rates, subsidized energy and transport costs, and low-interest loans.

In countries such as Argentina, Brazil, Chile, and Mexico, these government-supported development policies were initially quite successful. From 1945 to 1970, rates of investment in Latin America were higher than in the Western industrial nations, and from 1960 to 1980, the region's manufacturing output grew faster as well.[3] Virtually every Latin American country began manufacturing basic consumer goods such as textiles, clothing, packaged food, and furniture. Larger nations such as Argentina, Brazil, and Mexico established automotive plants, steel mills, and other heavy industries. In time, industrialization altered the region's demographic and class structures. Massive rural migration to the cities transformed Latin America into the developing world's most urbanized region (see chapter 8). For decades, ISI also created blue-collar jobs and expanded the size of the middle class.

But hidden beneath these accomplishments, this strategy also promoted economic inefficiencies and income inequality. While it may have been necessary for the government to nurture industrialization in the early stages of economic development, Latin American countries maintained protectionist measures and subsidies too broadly and too long. Rather than serving as a finely calibrated tool for getting industrialization off the ground, ISI became a politically motivated juggernaut. With industrialists, the middle class, and organized labor all united behind these policies, elected officials were unwilling to wean established industries from government support and protection long after they should have become self-sufficient. Inefficient domestic industries received excessive protection; trade and fiscal policies designed to promote industrialization often harmed agricultural exports; and the income gaps widened between the urban and rural populations, between the urban middle and lower classes, and between skilled and unskilled urban workers.

Mexico illustrates both the initial accomplishments and the subsequent weaknesses of statism in the region. From the mid-1930s to 1970, the national government supplied 35–40 percent of the country's total capital investment. At the same time, the state petroleum, electric power, and railroad companies provided private industry with subsidized energy and transportation by selling those items at a loss. Government trade and labor policies protected Mexican companies from foreign competition and held down domestic wages as a means of stimulating domestic investment. As a consequence, between 1935 and 1970, industrial output grew at an average yearly rate of nearly 10 percent and GNP rose 6 percent annually, making Mexico one of the world's fastest-growing economies at that time. During the 1970s and early 1980s, however, the state's role in the economy spiraled out of control. By 1985, the government operated nearly 1,200 state enterprises (**parastatals**), involved in everything from petroleum extraction to food sales. At the same time, however, even during this era of strong economic growth, Mexico's "economic miracle" left the rural population and the urban poor behind, creating a highly unequal distribution of income and leaving substantial pockets of poverty.

Overall, Latin America's development model introduced two important areas of inefficiency, both of which typify state-led industrial growth elsewhere in the developing world. First, a large number of state-owned enterprises were overstaffed and poorly run. Contrary to the common stereotype, state enterprises are not inherently inefficient. In advanced economies such as France and Norway, governments have operated some enterprises quite productively. But few governments in the less developed world have the skilled and disciplined personnel needed to perform at that level. Furthermore, given the high rate of unemployment in almost all the developing countries, their governments are under great political pressure to hire more employees, whether the state enterprises need them or not. Consequently, parastatals are typically substantially overstaffed, with many employees who do little or nothing. Indeed, they became part of a broader system of political patronage, with economic efficiency sacrificed in the interests of maintaining support for the ruling regime.

At the same time, labor unions and middle-class groups also have lobbied state enterprises to sell consumer goods and services at highly discounted prices. For example, in the past, Argentineans rode the state railroads for a nominal fee and received highly subsidized electricity in their homes. Elsewhere in the region, governments have subsidized or controlled prices for items such as gasoline, urban bus fares, and food. Ultimately, the combination of money-losing parastatals, consumer subsidies, and subsidies to private-sector producers helped bankrupt many Latin American governments. By 1982, virtually every government in the region was deeply in debt and suffering from severe fiscal problems.

A second important weakness of Latin America's development model was the way in which ISI policies were used to support the local private sector. To be sure, governments throughout the world have effectively used protectionist measures to help infant industries get started during the early stages of development. Typically, in the ISI model, the state creates a wall of high import tariffs and quotas to protect emerging local manufacturers from foreign competition. But over time, the government needs to scale back the level of protection or else domestic firms will have little incentive to become more efficient and internationally competitive. But Latin American protectionism, rather than serving as a temporary stimulus, became embedded in the economy.

From the early 1980s to the mid-1990s, the region's severe debt crisis and economic depression compelled almost all Latin American nations to reverse their statist economic policies. For example, the Mexican government closed or privatized more than 80 percent of the country's 1,155 state enterprises, including the national airline, telephone companies, and banks. In Chile, the transition to a slimmed-down state began during the dictatorship of General Augusto Pinochet (1973–90). But when democracy was restored, the new governing coalition (including the once-radical Socialist party) continued many of Pinochet's economic policies that they had once denounced.

While these reductions in public-sector activity were necessary, they also carried a great human cost. Throughout Latin America in the 1980s and early 1990s, millions of public- and private-sector workers lost their jobs, as the new owners of privatized parastatals fired excess workers as the region endured its most serious economic recession since the 1930s. Many other state-owned, money-losing plants simply shut down. In Mexico, the government's economic restructuring program eliminated an estimated four hundred thousand jobs. For example, more than half the workers formerly employed in state steel mills were laid off when their companies were privatized. Argentina, Chile, Peru, and Venezuela had similar experiences. At the same time, reduced protectionism in much of the region opened the door to a surge of imported consumer goods, further slashing sales and jobs in local firms that were unable to compete. Finally, the reduction or elimination of government consumer subsidies sharply increased the cost of basic necessities including bread, milk, and rice.

In Mexico and Argentina, just as in Chile, populist and left-wing parties that had once been the leading advocates of government economic intervention reluctantly conceded that the state sector had grown too unwieldy and needed to be cut back. Excessive government spending, coupled with the middle and upper classes' failure to pay their fair share of taxes, had resulted in massive fiscal deficits and runaway inflation. Only by substantially cutting budgetary deficits since the 1980s have Latin America's governments been able to control inflation, which had reached rates over 1,000 percent annually in Argentina, Brazil, Nicaragua, and Peru. The debt crisis and the related economic recession contributed to a sharp decline in Latin American living standards from the early 1980s to the early 1990s (the lost decade). In Peru and Venezuela, for example, real incomes (wages that are adjusted for inflation and purchasing power) fell by nearly 40 percent.[4]

Since the 1990s, inflation has been brought under control. At the same time, the region's economy has grown at a healthier rate—more rapidly than North America's or Europe's, but not as fast as Africa's or Asia's. However, while most analysts agree that Latin America's level of state economic interventionism and protectionism had been excessive, reforms designed to scale down government often have not improved living standards, at least initially.

East Asia's Developmental State

In contrast to Latin America's economies, many Asian nations have grown at a phenomenal rate since the 1970s. South Korea, Taiwan, Hong Kong, Singapore, and China once received the most attention. But recently, India has made tremendous strides. Their impact on world trade has been enormous. China is now the world's leading exporter of manufactured goods. But several Southeast Asian economies—such as Thailand, Malaysia, and Indonesia—have also grown dramatically. From the mid-1960s until the region's financial crisis in 1997–98, Taiwan, South Korea, Singapore, Hong Kong, Thailand, Malaysia, Indonesia, and China all grew at annual rates ranging from 4 to 10 percent, and China and South Korea sometimes exceeded those rates.[5] In fact, from 1960 to the late 1990s, these economies grew almost three times as fast as Latin America's and five times as fast as sub-Saharan Africa's. While a number of East and Southeast Asian economies had serious setbacks during the late 1990s crisis, they quickly resumed rapid development. Moreover, the benefits of East and Southeast Asia's rapid growth have been distributed relatively equitably, with a far narrower gap between the rich and poor than in Latin America or Africa.

With the exception of communist China and Vietnam (which have mixed socialist and free-market economies and thus lie outside the "East Asian model"), most East and Southeast Asian countries have tied their growth to the free market. More than in other regions, the private sector has controlled most of the economy, with a relatively small state sector. Predictably, this has led conservative economists to hail the East Asian economic miracle as a triumph of unfettered capitalism, a testimony to keeping government out of the economy.

But many East Asian specialists insist that, on the contrary, governments in that region were key players in stimulating economic growth.[6] Examining the causes of Japan's spectacular postwar economic resurgence, Chalmers Johnson first formulated the notion of the **developmental state**.[7] We can best understand the meaning of this term by comparing the role of government in East Asia's high-growth capitalist nations to its function in Western nations during their initial industrial expansions some 150 years earlier. At that time, Western nations created regulatory states in which "government refrained from interfering in the marketplace, except to insure certain limited goals" (e.g., banking regulation). In contrast, the East Asian developmental states "intervene actively in the economy in order to guide or promote particular substantive goals" (e.g., full employment, export competitiveness, or energy self-sufficiency).[8]

Japan's powerful Ministry of International Trade and Industry (MITI), Johnson noted, directed the country's postwar industrial resurgence. Subsequently, South Korea, Taiwan, Singapore, Indonesia, and other industrializing nations in East and Southeast Asia adopted many features of Japan's state-guided, capitalist development model. Typically, each country had a powerful government ministry or agency "charged with the task of planning, guiding, and coordinating industrial policies."[9] They included South Korea's Economic Planning Board, Taiwan's Council for Economic Planning and Development, and Singapore's Economic Development Board, all modeled after MITI. Under the developmental state, their government economic intervention was far more extensive and direct than in the West, targeting entire economic sectors (such as agriculture or industry), whole industries (such as computers, software, and automobiles), and particular companies (such as South Korea's Hyundai).

All developmental states did not pursue identical policies. For example, the bonds between government and big business have been tighter in South Korea than in Taiwan, while state enterprises have been more important in Taiwan. In Singapore, government control over labor has been more comprehensive than in the other two countries. But in all of them, the state played an important role, guiding the private sector toward targeted economic activities and stimulating growth in areas that the government wished to expand. Sometimes, government planners even pressured particular industries or companies to specialize in certain products and abandon others.

For example, when the South Korean and Taiwanese governments wished to develop the electronics and computer industries, they intervened aggressively, rather than leaving it to the marketplace. They established relevant research institutes; granted firms in the targeted industries' preferential access to credit; temporarily required companies that had been importing those targeted products to switch to domestic manufacturers; and offered trade protection to new industries for limited periods of time. South Korea temporarily banned all imports of computers when it promoted that industry, and Taiwan did the same for textiles.[10]

While the East Asian development model's tremendous success has earned it widespread admiration, some observers have remained skeptical about its applicability elsewhere. One concern is the model's apparent political requirements. Most developmental states have been authoritarian—or what Johnson calls "soft authoritarian"—during their major industrialization push. Authoritarian rule allowed governments to repress or control labor unions and to direct management. Taiwan, South Korea, and

Indonesia all industrialized under authoritarian governments, though they have subsequently democratized. The governments of Malaysia and Singapore continue to repress democratic expression in varying degrees. Hence, there is some doubt about how the developmental state would perform under the democratic pressures now spreading across the developing world. Still, India's very impressive economic growth since 1991 addresses some of those doubts. It has adopted some elements of the East Asian development model while maintaining its democratic government.

Another important question is the transferability of East Asian political and economic institutions and policies to other parts of the developing world. The developmental state seems to require qualities that are in short supply in other developing areas: a highly skilled government bureaucracy and close cooperation between business, labor, and agriculture. In Indonesia, for example, a team of government economists known as "the Berkeley Boys" (most of them holding doctoral degrees in economics from the University of California at Berkeley) oversaw the country's economic development. India's government bureaucracy is not highly regarded, but macroeconomic planning in this country has been in the hands of some of the world's best economists (many of them having doctoral degrees from Oxford University).

South Korea's highly trained state technocrats worked closely with the country's all-powerful business conglomerates (chaebols), such as Hyundai and Samsung. Similar cooperation between sophisticated government planners and big business, together with a relatively docile working class, contributed to economic surges elsewhere in East and Southeast Asia. Outside of Asia, however, only Chile's "Chicago Boys" (economists trained at the University of Chicago) brought a comparable set of skills and enjoyed similar support from government and the business community.

While it is very possible that the model will eventually spread, few African, Latin American, or Middle Eastern nations currently offer promising conditions for its use. Furthermore, current trade liberalization under **World Trade Organization** (WTO) and support for market reforms by international financial institutions like the **International Monetary Fund** and **World Bank** means that future industrial development will probably involve less state intervention than in the initial East Asian model.*

---

* The World Trade Organization is an intergovernmental organization of over 160 states that establishes trading rules in an effort to promote freer and fairer global trade. It also has a mechanism for resolving trade disputes. The International Monetary Fund is a United Nations-affiliated international organization that assists countries in dealing with budget deficits, trade deficits, and monetary policy through technical advice and loans. The World Bank, also affiliated with the United Nations, supports economic and social development in the developing world through loans, grants, and technical advice.

The Neoliberal Model

Quite unlike the preceding models, neoliberal economics assigns government a very limited economic role. The state, it argues, should provide certain fundamental "public goods" such as national defense, police protection, a judicial system, and an educational system. It may also supply a physical infrastructure, including sewers and harbors, when it is not feasible for private capital to do so. And, perhaps it should allocate some resources to meet the most basic needs of the very poor. But neoliberal economists believe that most of the governments in the developing world have injured their economies by moving far beyond that limited role. These critics attribute Africa's and Latin America's earlier economic development problems to excessive state intervention, while they credit East and Southeast Asia's success to their governments' allegedly limited role.

Neoliberals argue that free-market forces should determine production decisions and set prices without government interference. Consequently, they condemn state policies designed to stimulate industrial growth: protective tariffs and import quotas that restrict free trade and thereby drive up prices to the consumer; artificial currency exchange rates that distort the prices of exports and imports; state subsidies to producers and consumers; and government controls on prices and interest rates. All of these policies, they argue, distort the choices made by producers, consumers, and governments. Only when these artificial constraints are removed, they maintain, will the economy "get prices right" (by letting free-market forces determine them).

For several decades, the neoliberals have generally won the debate against advocates of extensive state intervention.* Although only Hong Kong and Singapore come close to the pure neoliberal model, a large number of developing countries have moved in that direction by liberalizing their economies, deregulating the private sector, privatizing state enterprises, removing trade barriers, and freeing prices. They have also reduced subsidies for industry and for consumers, often out of budgetary necessity. In part, these changes resulted from pressures on the developing countries coming from international financial institutions—such as the World Bank and the IMF—and by the United States. In some cases such policy changes have come slowly, with regimes reluctant to alienate supporters by shifting economic gears too quickly. In other cases, they have come as part of a package of measures (known as a **structural adjustment programs** or SAPs) designed to address budget deficits and promote business-friendly reform.

------

* Since the turn of the century, leftist governments have been elected in much of Latin America (including Bolivia, Brazil, Chile, and Venezuela). But, while they have introduced many anti-poverty programs, many have moderated their previous positions and have accepted some of their predecessors' neoliberal reforms.

While analysts continue to disagree on the broader economic effects of neoliberalism, the evidence seems to indicate that reducing government intervention has often stimulated economic growth, particularly in economies that had earlier imposed extensive state intervention. For example, when India and Chile substantially reduced the government's economic role, both embarked on a period of rapid growth. At the same time, however, unfettered capitalist growth often has benefited only a portion of the population, leaving the poor behind.

India illustrates this point well. The changeover to a predominantly free-market economy turned that nation into one of the world's fastest-growing major economies. Yet, so far, less than one-third of the population has benefited from that growth—essentially city dwellers employed in the modern economy, especially the expanding middle class. To be sure, those beneficiaries comprise some 350 million people, certainly no small accomplishment. But, nearly two-thirds of India's population—primarily the barely educated rural poor—have gained little from the boom. Many of the country's most rapidly expanding industries are in the high-tech or tech-support sectors, which primarily hire people with more advanced educations. Furthermore, many of the other new industries (such as auto manufacturing) are capital-intensive and generate comparatively few jobs. Thus, despite India's rapid economic growth, almost one-half of all children under five suffer from stunting, a form of malnutrition in which children are shorter than normal for their age.* Indeed, the childhood malnutrition rate has remained fairly unchanged since the 1990s and is about the same as impoverished Bangladesh and Burkina Faso and over five times as high as in China. Currently, over 1 million Indian children die of malnutrition every year.[11]

Elsewhere, as in India, the benefits of economic growth have not reached a significant portion of the population and in many countries wealth and income have become more concentrated. For example, Argentina had once enjoyed one of the more equitable income distributions in Latin America, but this has changed drastically. In the mid-1970s, the most prosperous 10 percent of the population had average incomes that were twelve times higher than the poorest 10 percent. But by the mid-1990s, following structural adjustment, this ratio had risen to 18:1, and by 2002, the richest 10 percent of the population earned forty-three times as much as the poorest 10 percent.[12]

In addition to its tendency to widen income inequality, neoliberal economics has been strongly criticized by environmentalists. From their perspective, even a modified policy of laissez-faire that acknowledges some

---

* Poor sanitary conditions also contribute to this, resulting in high rates of parasitic infection and gastrointestinal disease.

state responsibility for the environment, is inadequate. As Richard Albin noted,

> The idea that private interest, operating within unfettered markets, will tend to produce a close approximation of the socially optimal allocation of resources, was close to the truth when output (population, too) was so much smaller.[13]

But, he argues, as the world's population and associated pollution have reached dangerous levels, society can no longer afford to let free-market mechanisms allocate penalties for pollution. Such remedies would come far too late. Further discussion of economic growth and its impact on the environment follows later in this chapter.

Finding a Proper Role for the State

Political scientists and economists will continue to debate the state's proper role in less developed economies. As time goes on, new models will undoubtedly arise. Still, some areas of agreement have emerged in recent decades.

On the one hand, the level of government intervention in both command economies and Latin American statism now seems excessive. On the other, the extremely limited government role advocated by the neoliberals appears to be unrealistic and inadequate in most developing countries. Indeed, the World Bank—once regarded as a leading advocate of neoliberalism—today increasingly emphasizes the continued importance of state action. Good governance and effective government policies are necessary, it suggests, to provide social welfare for the most vulnerable, implement anti-poverty programs, and protect the environment.

East Asia's developmental state model has been the most successful. But, it is unclear whether it can be replicated elsewhere. Indeed, a model that succeeds in one country or region will not necessarily work in another. Countries vary greatly in size, human capital, and natural resources. Thus, cookbook formulas for growth will likely fall short in many countries. As we have noted, the strong hand of the stereotypical developmentalist state—in Japan, South Korea, Singapore, and Taiwan— would have to be modified to meet current trade regulations under the WTO. Finally, new crises—such as the Latin American and African debt crises in the 1980s, the 1997–98 Asian financial crisis, and the world's deep recession during 2008–10—have forced planners to alter and adapt their development models.

TRADE AND INDUSTRIALIZATION STRATEGIES

Since the time of Britain's industrial revolution, governments have equated economic development and industrialization with national sovereignty and military strength. Starting in Latin America during the 1930s, industrial growth has been the centerpiece of economic development for many developing nations.

Neoliberal economists criticize industrialization programs in many developing countries, arguing that every country should specialize in economic activities for which it has a "comparative advantage." That is, it should produce and export those goods it can provide most efficiently and cheaply relative to other nations. On the basis of this argument, neoliberals maintained that many less developed nations should abandon plans for industrialization and concentrate, instead, on the production and export of raw materials or agricultural products. Rather than manufacture goods such as cars, washing machines, or fertilizers, they insisted, countries such as Sri Lanka and Kenya would be better off increasing tea or coffee exports—products for which they have a comparative advantage—so they could use those earnings to import manufactured products.

Similarly, they contended that it made little sense for Nigeria to build steel mills or for Uruguay to produce refrigerators. Still, many developing countries have been reluctant to depend fully on revenues from the export of primary goods (agricultural products and raw materials such as coal, iron, and petroleum), because their prices are so volatile. One possible solution (easier said than done) is to pursue balanced growth, including some industrial development (presumably manufacturing products that draw on local natural resources and can be exported), while still stressing production of primary goods for export. For example, Brazil has supplemented its traditional agricultural and mineral exports with extensive manufactured exports, including products such as autos and aircraft.

Until now, industrializing nations have generally pursued one of two alternate strategies: **import-substitution industrialization** (ISI) and **export-oriented industrialization** (EOI).* In the first case, as we have seen, developing countries try to reduce their dependency on manufactured imports by producing more goods, especially consumer goods, at home. Like Latin America, Asian nations began their industrial development by producing for their own consumption. However, unlike Latin American ISI, which focused on consumer goods for the home market for an extended period of time, East Asian nations soon turned to EOI, linking their industrial development to manufactured exports. Although EOI has been most closely associated with East and Southeast Asia, it is a strategy now widely

---

* A third strategy would be that of **autarky**, where a state severely limits trade and investment, and emphasizes self-reliance—often for reasons that are as much political as economic. Albania (until the fall of communism there in the early 1990s), Myanmar (until reforms in the early 2000s), and North Korea would be rare examples of this. As these cases suggest, it is not proven an effective way of achieving economic and social development.

embraced in Latin America and other parts of the less-developed world as well. Having started that strategy later, Latin America and other developing areas have yet to catch up with Asia's export capabilities. Consequently, shirts, blouses, electronics, and running shoes sold in Western department stores are still more likely to be manufactured in China, Vietnam, Sri Lanka, Indonesia, or Thailand than in Brazil, Colombia, or Honduras.

Import-Substitution Industrialization

National economic policies are partly the product of deliberate choice and partly the result of political and socioeconomic opportunities and constraints. As we have seen, ISI emerged as a development strategy in Latin America during the 1930s as the worldwide depression sharply reduced international trade. Because North America and Europe reduced their purchases of primary goods (Uruguayan wool, Argentine beef, and Brazilian coffee, for example), Latin American nations no longer were able to earn enough foreign exchange to import the manufactured products that they needed. So, the region's early industrialization was designed, in part, to produce consumer goods that Latin American countries could no longer afford to import.

But although ISI began as a response to an international economic crisis, economic planners subsequently transformed it into a long-term strategy for industrial development. With substantial unemployment at home and an urban population pressing for economic growth and additional jobs, government leaders faced a political imperative to industrialize. Nationalist presidents such as Argentina's Juan Perón and Brazil's Getúlio Vargas forged populist political coalitions of industrialists, blue-collar workers, and the urban middle class, all committed to industrialization.

As previously noted, Latin American governments imposed quotas and tariffs on imported consumer goods in order to protect emerging national industries from international competition. But, planners also wanted to facilitate other types of imports, namely capital equipment (primarily machinery) and raw materials that domestic manufacturers needed. To reduce the cost of those imports, governments often overvalued their own currencies. Eventually, most Latin American countries established multiple currency exchange rates, with differing rates for transactions tied to imports, exports, and other financial activities. To further encourage industrial development, governments also offered domestic industries tax incentives, low-interest loans, and direct subsidies.

Because of ISI's impressive record in Latin America from the 1940s into the 1970s, the strategy was emulated in many parts of Africa and Asia as well, sometimes with comparable success. Turkey, for example, enjoyed strong ISI growth before shifting to EOI during the 1980s. Even East Asia began its industrial development using ISI. By the 1970s, however, the

ISI strategy was undermining Latin America's economies. As John Sheahan notes, "It fostered production methods adverse for employment, hurt the poor, blocked the possible growth of industrial exports, [and] encouraged high-cost consumer goods industries."[14]

To understand how poorly Latin America's newly industrialized countries (NICs) fared in international trade compared to their East Asian competitors, it is useful to compare Mexico (one of Latin America's major industrial powers) with East Asia's four **Asian tigers** (South Korea, Taiwan, Hong Kong, and Singapore). Mexico has a substantially larger population than the combined total of the four Asian countries. It also has a considerable geographic advantage over them in the export market, being located closer to Western Europe and thousands of miles closer to the United States, the world's largest importer. Yet, as of the mid-1980s (prior to the North American Free Trade Agreement, NAFTA), the combined value of manufactured exports of the four Asian tigers was twenty times higher than Mexico's. Since NAFTA, the gap has narrowed.[15]

In many Latin American countries, export taxes and overvalued currencies put traditional primary goods exporters at a competitive disadvantage, thereby depriving the country of badly needed foreign exchange. At the same time, because local consumer-goods industries could import their needed capital goods (machinery and other manufactured products used to manufacture other products) cheaply, the region never developed its own capital-goods industry and, instead, imported manufacturing technologies that were often inappropriate to local needs. Subsidized imports of machinery and heavy equipment also encouraged capital-intensive production (i.e., using more advanced technologies and machinery while employing fewer workers) rather than the labor-intensive production that predominated in Asia. The ISI model of industrialization benefited a small, relatively well-paid "labor elite" (i.e., skilled, unionized workers employed in more capital-intensive factories). But it failed to provide enough jobs for the region's workforce, leaving too many Latin Americans unemployed and underemployed.

Ironically, although ISI was originally designed to make Latin America more economically independent, in the end, it merely replaced dependence on consumer-goods imports with dependence on imported capital goods, foreign technologies, and credit. Traditional primary exports often languished, while deficits contributed to Latin America's spiraling foreign debt, leading eventually to a major debt crisis and a recession in the 1980s. This crisis, in stark contrast to East Asia's rapid growth at that time, induced Latin American governments to abandon their inwardly oriented economic policies as they tried to emulate East Asia's export-driven model. The NAFTA treaty between Mexico, Canada, and the United States is the most dramatic manifestation of that region's move toward EOI. Since that time, Latin American nations have established several regional trade associations, including Mercosur (a trade agreement involving two economic powers—Brazil and Argentina—and two smaller countries in the southern part of South America) and the Latin American Integration Association. In 2018, Mexico, Peru, and Chile joined with eight other countries in signing the new Comprehensive and Progressive Agreement for Trans-Pacific Partnership, which seeks to promote liberalized trade across the Asia-Pacific region.*

Export-Oriented Industrialization

East Asia's NICs began their industrialization drive through import substitution, just as their Latin American counterparts had done years earlier. Soon, however, they diversified into manufacturing for export. As governments phased out their early protectionist measures, they forced local companies to become more competitive in the world market. State planners shaped the market, pressuring industries and offering them incentives to export. By 1980, manufactured goods constituted more than 90 percent of all South Korean and Taiwanese exports but represented only 15 percent of Mexico's and 39 percent of Brazil's.[16] Fueled by their dynamic industrial export sectors, East Asia's booming economies became the envy of the developing world. More recently, India has enjoyed very impressive growth tied to the export of services.

There are a number of reasons why East Asia decided to stress manufactured exports early in its industrialization drive, while Latin America failed to do so for decades. For one thing, East Asian industrialization began in a period of unprecedented expansion in world trade, inspired by the West's enormous postwar economic boom (from the mid-1940s through early 1970s) and the broad assault on trade barriers in the years following the General Agreement on Trade and Tariffs (GATT) in 1947.[†] The opportunities offered by outward-oriented growth were obvious to Asian policy makers by the 1950s. Conversely, the expansion of Latin American industrialization started during the Great Depression of the 1930s, a period of greatly restricted world trade. Indeed, it was their very inability to export traditional products at that time that inspired Latin American nations to turn initially to ISI. In retrospect, Latin America should have moved to EOI after the Second World War, but ISI seemed to be working so well until the 1980s that there was little incentive to

---

*The original Tran-Pacific partnership negotiations were started by the United States in part as a way to offset growing Chinese economic power. The Trump administration later withdrew from the talks and was therefore not included in the new trade bloc, which also includes Canada, Australia, Japan, New Zealand, Vietnam, Malaysia, Singapore, and Brunei.
†In 1995, the WTO replaced the GATT.

change. Ironically, another reason why East and Southeast Asian countries chose EOI was that their economic opportunities seemed more limited than Latin America's. Because of their smaller populations, Hong Kong, Singapore, and Taiwan (though not South Korea) did not believe that ISI, which relied upon the domestic market, was a feasible strategy for them as it had been for larger countries such as Mexico, Argentina, Brazil, and Colombia. Furthermore, with fewer agricultural goods or raw materials to export, East Asians turned their weakness into strength by emphasizing manufactured exports. As the signing of the Comprehensive and Progressive Agreement for Trans-Pacific Partnership underscores, this is an approach that many Latin American and other countries have increasingly embraced too.

GROWTH WITH EQUITY

Until this point, our discussion has focused on the size of the national economy. Indeed, production is the primary measure of economic development used in popular and scholarly analysis. Typically, a country is thought to be performing well when its GDP (or its GNP) grows rapidly. Analysts focus less frequently on how equitably this growth is distributed. It is to this important dimension that we now turn.

Early debate on development often pitted mainstream social scientists against left-of-center analysts, with the first group primarily interested in the prerequisites of growth and the second focusing on the fairness of economic distribution. For example, while many mainstream economists were impressed with Brazil's rapid economic expansion in the late 1960s and early 1970s, critics pointed out that the country's extremely unequal income distribution meant that few benefits of that growth reached the poorest half of the population. On the other hand, although Cuba's income redistribution policies and social welfare programs have favorably impressed some observers, conservative critics criticize its generally weak record of economic growth since the late 1960s.

Many market-oriented economists insist that increased inequality is unavoidable, indeed desirable, in the early stages of economic development in order to concentrate capital in the hands of entrepreneurs, who can then invest more in the economy, expand their enterprises, and create jobs. Their critics counter that development of that sort did little to help the majority of the people. In many developing countries, they maintained, the bottom half of the population would benefit more from meaningful redistribution of wealth and income, even with less growth, than from strong economic growth without redistribution.

In time, however, analysts of varying ideological persuasions have concluded that there is no intrinsic contradiction between these two goals.

In fact, a proper development strategy entails "growth with equity"—a point reflected in the current UN Sustainable Development Goals, in which world leaders pledge themselves to reduce inequality and address greater attention to the needs of poorer citizens.

One study indicates that since the 1960s, countries with higher income equality have developed faster than those with highly concentrated patterns. East Asia's economic takeoff since the 1970s and 1980s demonstrates that point. For example, Taiwan and South Korea have coupled spectacular economic growth rates with relatively equitable income distributions. Indeed, widely based purchasing power in both those countries has helped stimulate their economic growth. In South Korea, almost all rural families own television sets, a feat hardly conceivable in Africa or Latin America. During the Korean television industry's takeoff, these domestic purchases supplemented exports in stimulating that industry's growth.

What accounts for the higher level of economic equality in East Asia compared to Africa or Latin America? One important factor is the pattern of land distribution in the countryside. For a number of reasons, farmland has historically been more equitably distributed in Asia (especially East Asia) than in Latin America. While the size of Latin America's largest landholdings has declined in recent decades, estates of several thousand acres still exist and were common in the recent past. Today, large landowners still dominate the countryside in nations such as Brazil and Colombia. While the largest farms in Africa are not nearly as big, land ownership is still very concentrated in countries such as South Africa, Kenya, and Ethiopia. On the other hand, the largest holdings in Asia, where there is much heavier population pressure, are rarely more than one- or two-hundred acres and they are far smaller in countries such as South Korea.

Landholding patterns reflect both historical legacies and contemporary government policies. Spanish colonialism established an agrarian structure in Latin America and the Philippines dominated by **latifundia** (large estates). In Africa, landholding is most concentrated in countries that had substantial numbers of white settlers (who carved out large agricultural estates) during their colonial period. These include Kenya, Mozambique, and Namibia. On the other hand, Japanese colonial authorities in Korea and Taiwan encouraged smallholder farming. Although European colonial regimes established large export-oriented plantations in Southeast Asia, land ownership there was still never as concentrated as in Latin America. It is surely not coincidental that the Philippines, the only country in East Asia to share Latin America's Spanish colonial heritage, also has the region's most concentrated land and income distribution. In the twentieth century, South Korean and Taiwanese agrarian reform programs led to even more egalitarian land distribution in those countries, just as the American-imposed reform had done in Japan after the Second World War.

By reducing rural poverty, land reform contributed to greater income equality (see chapter 8).

Another major component of national income distribution is the relationship between rural and urban living standards. Although city dwellers enjoy higher incomes and greater social services throughout the developing countries, the urban-rural gap is particularly marked in Africa and Latin America. Residents of Mexico City, for example, have incomes averaging four to five times higher than those in the countryside, while in China the ratio of urban to rural population nationally is over 3:1. There are many reasons for such discrepancies, but government policy often plays an important role. In chapter 8, we will see that, until recently, governments in both regions often kept the prices of basic food crops below their market value in order to provide their urban political constituencies with cheap food. By contrast, East Asian farmers generally have received the free-market price for their crops or even obtained subsidized prices above market value.

Industrial policy also affects income distribution. Latin America's ISI strategy encouraged the importation of capital equipment for domestic industries. Such capital-intensive development created many relatively skilled and well-paid industrial jobs, but left behind a far larger number of poorly paid, "unskilled" urban workers and rural peasants. Conversely, East and Southeast Asia's EOI strategy benefited from the region's large labor force, thereby producing a great number of low-wage jobs in emerging industries.

By initially using labor-intensive methods that utilized their pools of cheap labor, Hong Kong, Taiwan, and South Korea successfully exported cheap low-tech goods such as textiles, toys, and footwear. Over time, as these industries needed increasing numbers of workers, two changes took place. First, greater demand for labor in low-end export industries caused factory wages to rise; second, rural-to-urban migrants seeking factory jobs reduced the supply of rural labor, thereby driving up wages for farm workers in the countryside. What had begun as a policy exploiting cheap labor eventually sponsored strong economic growth, higher wages, and greater income equality.

As factory wages rose substantially in the region's "tigers," those countries shifted from low-tech manufactured products to more sophisticated exports such as electronics, commercial services (most notably in Singapore), computer software, computers, and automobiles (South Korea). Production of apparel and other low-wage items passed to lower-income Asian nations such as Malaysia, Thailand, Indonesia, Bangladesh, and Sri Lanka. China, which first became an industrial giant by manufacturing low-priced consumer goods and parts for foreign brands, is now also producing higher-end products, including some under Chinese brand names.

ECONOMIC DEVELOPMENT AND THE ENVIRONMENT

Throughout the world, economic development has inevitably caused environmental degradation. For example, prior to European settlement, the East Coast of the United States was covered with thick forest. Since then, increased human population, urban sprawl, and farming have destroyed almost all of that growth. Today, industrial and auto pollution in the United States and Europe contaminate the surrounding air and water, sometimes affecting areas thousands of miles away. In the developing countries, rapid population growth, natural-resource extraction, and industrialization have also damaged the environment. In Indonesia, for example, foreign-owned mines have dumped health-threatening waste into nearby water systems, while logging firms harvested vast tracks of jungle timber, bringing birth defects in mining areas and flooding in timber regions in their wake. Massive dams in China have flooded archaeological treasures, farmland, and vacated villages. Since the 1970s, environmental groups in advanced industrialized nations have questioned the trade-offs between economic growth and the conservation of natural resources. Most ominously, the consequences of global warming may soon threaten living standards and lives throughout the planet. Some of the more radical environmentalists in the United States and Europe have proposed zero-growth strategies for highly developed nations. This could require limiting population growth (already on the decline in those countries) and creating a less consumer-oriented society.

But the option of zero growth, or even of reduced economic growth, which has never attracted significant support in the developed world, is totally unacceptable in the developing world. In countries such as Bangladesh, Brazil, Egypt, Indonesia, and Nigeria, where a substantial portion of the population lives in abject poverty, it would be politically suicidal and ethically questionable for government leaders to propose limiting economic growth. Unless and until the environmental consequences of economic growth can be mitigated, the trade-off between growth and environmental decay presents a difficult ethical dilemma. It would be unconscionable to tell poor Pakistanis or Ethiopians that they should not hope for a higher standard of living. But barring major technological and political breakthroughs, achieving an acceptable standard of living for all people could easily overtax the planet's natural resources.

Environmental regulations and controls are also far weaker in the developing world, because of their urgent desire for economic growth and because their "green" (ecology) movements developed much later than in the West and lack the political influence of their American and European counterparts. Moreover, less developed countries often lack the government infrastructure to enforce environmental controls. Finally, polluting industries (both foreign and domestic) often bribe public officials responsible for enforcing environmental laws.

The Costs of Growth

The world's industrialized nations continue to be the major consumers of natural resources, the leading polluters of air and water, and the greatest contributors to global warming, depletion of the ozone layer, and other looming environmental disasters. Yet, ironically, it is those same developed countries that now insist that the developing countries become better environmental citizens. In response, developing countries often point out that the United States, with less than 5 percent of the world's population, annually consumes roughly 20 percent of the planet's energy.[17] Hence, many of them bristle at the suggestion that developing nations make special efforts to protect the environment. Even so, because of their more fragile economic and ecological conditions, a number of developing nations face daunting environmental challenges. In African countries such as Sudan, Nigeria, and Burkina Faso, wood fires produce 75 percent or more of all energy, forcing peasants hungry for firewood to deplete the forests. Each year, rich cattle ranchers and poor peasants in Brazil burn vast areas of the Amazonian jungle to clear the land for ranching, agriculture, or logging. "During the past 40 years, close to 20 percent of the Amazon rain forest has been cut down—more than in all the previous 450 years since European colonization began."[18] In Malaysia and Indonesia, Japanese-owned logging firms cut down large tracts of rain forest. In places such as Central America and sub-Saharan Africa, rains and waterways wash off topsoil, rainfall patterns shift, and both droughts and floods occur more frequently. In many parts of the developing world, the arable land area is declining and deserts are growing.

Cities such as Shanghai, Cairo, New Delhi, Nairobi, and São Paulo have grown tremendously in recent decades (chapter 8), producing enormous quantities of raw sewage, auto emissions, and industrial waste. As cars and buses (most without proper emission controls) choke the streets, air quality rapidly deteriorates. Elsewhere, mines, oil fields, chemical plants, and factories, operating with few environmental safeguards, pollute their surroundings. The consequences for local populations are often tragic—including infections, respiratory illnesses, birth defects, and loss of farmland. Other environmental costs—such as destruction of rain forests, which contributes to global warming—have consequences that extend far beyond the developing countries.

Environmental Decay as a Developing World Problem

The difficult trade-off between economic growth and environmental conservation is probably most starkly illustrated in China, home to almost one-fifth of the Earth's population. From the time its government introduced free-market economic reforms in the 1980s, that country has enjoyed one of the world's highest rates of economic growth, averaging about 8 percent annually. Living standards have tripled, and millions of Chinese citizens have moved out of poverty. The number of people spared from hunger, disease, and early death is staggering. Balanced against those gains, however, are enormous increases in air and water pollution and extensive destruction of the country's farmland, raising the danger of future famine just when China has finally managed to feed its population adequately. Moreover, as the country has built an average of two new coal-burning, electric power plants annually, added over 6.5 million motor vehicles every year, and vastly expanded its industrial production, it has surpassed the United States as the world's largest producer of greenhouse gases (emissions that trap the Earth's heat in the atmosphere and contribute to global warming, principally carbon dioxide and, to a lesser extent, methane).

Seeking a better life, over 100 million Chinese peasants have migrated to the cities, often abandoning farms in productive agricultural regions. In addition, substantial quantities of farmland have been paved over for highways, factories, and urban sprawl. Since the late 1950s, the country's total arable land has decreased by somewhere between 15 and 55 percent (depending on what estimate one accepts), while the nation's population has grown by some 80 percent. Though China's rate of population growth is currently relatively low (1 percent annually), loss of farmland caused by economic development continues to accelerate at an alarming rate. As this enormous country needs to import increasing amounts of food, it will likely drive up prices of grains and other foods in the world market, with serious consequences for the poor throughout the developing countries.

The Shared Challenge of Climate Change

Not only does environmental decay pose dangers to the developing countries themselves, but it threatens developed countries as well. And, of course, the developed world's environmental sins similarly endanger developing countries. Of all the environmental threats currently facing the world, the most menacing is surely **climate change**. Although there are still some who feel that the future risks of global warming have been exaggerated, there is now an overwhelming consensus within the scientific community and among most of the world's political leaders that the Earth has been warming over the long term, that the causes are in large part man-made, and that the consequences will be horrendous if nothing is done to stop it. As the Intergovernmental Panel on Climate Change notes, "Continued emission of greenhouse gases will cause further warming and long-lasting changes in all components of the climate system, increasing the likelihood of severe, pervasive and irreversible impacts for people and ecosystems."

Coal-fired power plants in Datong, China. Air and water pollution, global warming, and other environmental problems pose a serious challenge to developing and developed countries alike. *Source*: Jia Zheng—Imaginechina/Associated Press.

Moreover, the costs and risks associated with this are "unevenly distributed and are generally greater for disadvantaged people and communities."[19]

Specific environmental consequences of warming, if current trends continue, may include more droughts in some regions, more frequent floods in others, declining food production, widespread hunger and starvation, intensified hurricane and typhoon activity, and flooding of coastal cities and low-lying rural areas.[20] Many countries in Africa would be among the hardest hit because they already are subject to frequent drought and severe food shortages and have the fewest economic resources to address the problem. The World Bank has warned that "without urgent action to reduce vulnerability, provide access to basic services, and build resilience, climate change impacts could push an additional 100 million people into poverty by 2030."[21]

Shortages of food, water, and other adverse effects of global warming could also have implications for conflict and security.[22] Environmental scarcity could aggravate tensions within and between states. Somalia, Ethiopia, and Sudan have already fought wars linked, in part, to water and land rights. In many of the most poverty-stricken countries, economic disasters and internal violence may cause states to fail, opening up the way for militias and roving bands, as has already happened in Somalia. Finally, the combination of hunger, warfare, and internal violence would almost certainly intensify population movement from stricken areas to more affluent ones, including intensified migration from Africa to Western Europe and from Latin America to the United States and Canada.

Moreover, there is an additional problem in combating global warming. All countries, less developed countries and advanced industrial nations alike, would benefit from a significant reduction in the emission of carbon dioxide and other greenhouse gases. But for each individual country (say, Indonesia), the cost of reducing emissions is substantial, while their own country would only reap limited advantages because the benefits are spread around the entire world (since air flows freely across borders). Therefore, Indonesia (or any country) has incentives to "free-ride," that is, to let other countries (such as China and Germany) pay the costs of reducing their own emissions while every country, including Indonesia, would reap the benefits.

For the most part, then, developed countries are the primary sources of global warming, while developing nations—particularly in Africa and Asia—are potentially its greatest victims. At the same time, rapid industrialization in Asia and Latin America has sharply increased the developing countries' share of greenhouse gas emissions in recent years. As noted previously, China has surged past the United States as the world's largest source of these gases, while India now ranks third. Those two nations correctly respond that, since each of them is home to more than 1 billion people, they each pollute far less than the Western industrial giants on a per capita basis.* Still, the additional gases produced by these two new industrial powers alone are cause for great concern. In the fifteen-year span between 1992 and 2007, emissions rose by nearly 40 percent worldwide. While emissions actually declined during that period by almost 2 percent among the members of the European Union and grew by only 11 percent in Japan, emissions grew by 20 percent in the United States and jumped 103 percent in India and 150 percent in China.

THE SEARCH FOR SUSTAINABLE DEVELOPMENT

Discussion of the environmental consequences of economic growth often focuses on the objective of **sustainable development**, defined as economic development that "consumes resources to meet [this generation's] needs and aspirations in a way that does not compromise the ability of future generations to meet their needs."[23] Whenever feasible, it involves the use of renewable resources (such as wind and water power for generating electricity)

---

*In recent years, the United States has emitted over ten times as much greenhouse gas per capita as India has and twice China's emissions per person.

in place of resources that cannot be replaced (e.g., coal and petroleum) or that are being consumed at a faster rate than they can be replaced (such as tropical rain forests and ocean fishing grounds). It also embraces consumption of resources in ways that least pollute the environment: limiting auto and industrial emissions, finding sustainable substitutes for pesticides and other agricultural chemicals that pollute the soil and the water system, and reducing the use of products that destroy the world's ozone layer.

In theory, these are goals to which all nations—rich and poor alike—can aspire. Even so, developed and developing nations have long debated which of them should take the lead and which should bear the greatest economic costs. At the groundbreaking international conferences and UN summits since the 1990s, tensions between the developed and less developed countries were obvious. As one analyst observed,

> The conflicts between the rich and poor [have become] evident. The Northern [industrialized] countries, which [feel] vulnerable to global environment problems such as climate change and biodiversity loss, [have] attempted to extract commitments on environmental conservation from the South [the developing countries]. However, the South, which [feels] more vulnerable to perceived underdevelopment, has been concerned with extracting [economic] transfers from the North.[24]

The difficult trade-off between growth and environmental protection was vividly brought home to one of the authors at a meeting in Jamaica with local social scientists. After one US scholar stressed the importance of preserving the island's ecology, a Jamaican economist sarcastically replied, "You Americans raped your environment in order to develop your country and raise your standard of living. Now we Jamaicans reserve the right to do the same." While such feelings are counterproductive, they are understandable. Many developing countries note that industrialized nations ask NICs such as China and Mexico to reduce smokestack emissions and beseech Thailand and Brazil to sustain their rain forests. But it is the developed countries that have wreaked the greatest havoc on the environment and have offered the developing world little help to defray the costs of environmental controls.

US policies created further problems. Favoring immediate economic interests at the costs of longer-term global environmental damage, the United States (which alone produces almost 20 percent of greenhouse cases) has often been reluctant to curb emissions. During the eight years of the George Bush administration (2001–9), and again during the Trump administration (2017–), the US government even questioned whether there was actually a danger of global warming.

In 1997, worldwide negotiations produced the Kyoto Protocol, which envisioned a global contract binding industrialized nations to reduce their emissions of six greenhouse gases by 2012 to 5.2 percent below their 1990 level. This would be 29 percent below what they had been expected to reach without an accord. In 2001, 178 nations agreed in Bonn, Germany, to meet objections from Japan and other nations by modifying the Kyoto agreement so as to lower the targeted 5 percent reduction to only 2 percent. In spite of these modifications, the United States upset its allies in the European Union and much of the world community by announcing that it would not ratify the Kyoto treaty or the Bonn modifications. The Bush White House—supported by a large segment of the business community and congressional Republicans—had two major objections to the treaty: first, the Protocol called for no reduction in greenhouse gas emissions in the developing nations (including high-growth countries in Asia); second, it believed that Kyoto's mandatory environmental targets would undermine American economic growth.

In 2015, a new climate change treaty—the **Paris Agreement**—was signed by 195 countries. This aims at keeping the global rise in temperatures below 2.0 degrees Celsius (and preferably below 1.5 degrees) through a series of national commitments to limit and reduce greenhouse gas emissions. Critics expressed concern that these commitments would not be binding, and that states might set insufficiently ambitious goals. Monitoring of national performance would, however, be obligatory. While more developed and less developed countries alike were required to set national commitments, the Paris Agreement recognized that the capabilities and responsibilities of states varied, depending on their level of industrialization among other factors. It also reiterated earlier calls for $100 billion per year in climate-related financing to be made available to assist developing countries in limiting emissions.

While the United States played a key role in negotiating the Paris Agreement during the then Obama administration, in June 2017, President Trump announced that America would withdraw from the accord—a move that received worldwide criticism. Under the terms of the Paris Agreement, a US withdrawal would not take official effect until 2020.

Some Signs of Progress?

Despite these obstacles, there are some hopeful signs of progress. Most governments around the world recognize the dangers of global warming. Governments of developing countries and international development agencies have also become more conscious of the growth-environmental trade-off. Together many of them have begun searching for ways to achieve development that reduces damage to the environment. Many developing countries have come to realize that sustainable development is in their own interest. Conversely, most of the world's most developed nations have acknowledged that, to date, they have contributed the most to global warming and other environmental dangers and that they will have to help poorer nations pay the costs of future environmental protection. The European Union in particular has taken new, more vigorous initiatives to reduce greenhouse gas emissions. China has undertaken an ambitious program to adopt "greener" technologies. While it still depends heavily on highly polluting coal-fired power plants, immense problems of air pollution have generated significant domestic, as well as international, pressure for change.

Ultimately, even if developing countries applied strict environmental measures, these still would not fully reconcile the tension between economic growth and environmental protection. Furthermore, environmental controls are generally expensive and often reduce productivity. If the world's industrial powers want the developing countries to make such sacrifices, they will probably have to underwrite much of the cost. This might involve debt forgiveness, subsidized technology transfers, and direct grants.

Which of the economic models discussed earlier in this chapter is best equipped to handle the environmental challenge? The answer is not clear. It seems certain that preserving the environment requires significant state intervention. For example, since it is unrealistic to expect industrialists to monitor and control their own pollution or to hope that all drivers will voluntarily purchase fuel-efficient cars, most analysts feel that some government regulation is needed. Consequently, the neoliberal model, which severely limits government economic intervention and depends heavily on free-market mechanisms, seems ill-suited to protect the environment. Still, there are some approaches that use market-based mechanisms to influence economic behavior. Carbon taxes, for example, force polluters to bear some of the costs of their pollution—thereby creating an incentive for companies and consumers to use cleaner energy. Cap-and-trade systems permit companies or countries that successfully limit carbon emissions to "sell" these savings to other polluters—thereby creating a carbon market that rewards more environmentally sustainable economic activity.

In theory, command economies seem particularly well suited to defend the environment because the state controls the means of production and can self-regulate. In fact, however, communist governments from the Soviet Union and Poland to China and North Korea have had very poor environmental records. For one thing, directives to managers of state enterprises usually demand that they maximize production, with little thought given to environmental consequences. At the same time, absent a free society and a free mass media, citizens are unable to organize environmental pressure groups or even to know the extent of ecological destruction.* Thus, it appears that if developing nations are to have any chance at sustainable

---

* The Chinese government has become more sensitive to environmental issues and sometimes responds to grassroots protest demonstrations in that area. But, it still has a long way to go.

development, they must combine an honest, effective, and responsible state with a free democratic society where green activists can mobilize popular support.

FINDING THE RIGHT MIX

It has often been easier to recognize what has not worked in developing countries than to identify what has. The dependency theorists' assumption that economic development was only possible if developing countries reduced their ties to the capitalist core has been shattered by the success of East Asia's export-oriented growth and the failures of protectionism in Latin America. Similarly, command economies, while often able to reduce economic inequalities, generally have had poor records of economic growth and modernization beyond the early stages of development. North Korea's dismal communist economy, in stark contrast to South Korea's prosperity, demonstrates that model's failures. And, China was able to stage its breathtaking economic expansion only after it had moved away from a command economy. On the other hand, the neoliberal minimal state can hardly address the deep inequities, societal cleavages, and looming ecological nightmares plaguing so many developing countries. The challenge for developing economies is to establish a strong and effective, but not overbearing, state—one that can promote growth, equitable income distribution, and a healthy environment, while avoiding crony capitalism, political repression, and unwarranted interference in the market.

Many developing countries have now embraced East Asia's export-oriented industrial model. Beyond the previously mentioned problem of transferability, however, there are at least two other fundamental concerns about universalizing the East Asian experience. The first concerns the extent to which the world economy can continue to absorb mounting industrial exports. East Asia launched its EOI strategy during a period of unparalleled economic expansion in the First World. International trade was expanding rapidly, and developed countries could absorb a rising tide of industrial exports. Since the 1970s, however, First World economic growth has slowed down due, in part, to factors such as periodic spikes in energy costs and the transfer of industrial jobs to the NICs. Even should the Japanese and Western European economies recover their former dynamism, some analysts question whether the international market can absorb an ever-enlarging flow of industrial exports, most notably from China, the world's emerging industrial giant, or whether this will provoke a protectionist backlash.[25] For many in the industrialized and developing world alike, the Trump administration's willingness to impose tariffs on imports have pointed to an erosion of the principles of trade liberalization—principles that havegenerally contributed an expansion of the global economy.

Supporters of EOI counter that there is no sign of a looming ceiling on industrial imports, particularly since the larger NICs have become major importers themselves. The evidence so far suggests that developing countries hoping to industrialize need to develop some type of export sector and to participate actively in the global economy. But they would be wise to also diversify their economy and to build protections against the negative aspects of globalization. At the start of the 2008 global economic crisis, many developing countries that are highly dependent on the developed world for trade and investment suffered sharp economic declines as demand for their exports waned. However, to the surprise of many economists—and unlike previous global recessions—less developed economies bounced back impressively by 2010, growing by nearly 8 percent that year.

Policy and Politics

In examining the economic policy choices made by governments across the developing world, it is essential to recognize that these are not simply technical decisions. On the contrary, they are fundamentally political.

Growing involvement in the economy by many governments in the immediate aftermath of decolonization illustrates the point. Many countries in Africa and Asia responded to large-scale foreign ownership by nationalizing key firms, making them state-controlled enterprises or parastatals. Lacking a cadre of trained technicians and bureaucrats, and eager to reward and maintain the loyalty of their supporters, the government put these oil, mining, and agricultural firms in the hands of people who had been active in the independence struggle, loyalists in the ruling party, or members of the ethnic group that dominated the new governments. At the lower levels, jobs were allocated on the basis of patronage, rather than merit. Higher-ranking government and parastatal officials quickly took the opportunity to skim off profits and extort bribes from foreign or domestic companies that needed to do business with the state firms. Since any transfer of power to a new government would deprive government officials of these cash cows, most African governments limited political party opposition and avoided free elections. Similarly, independent groups in civil society—including trade unions, professional associations, and farmers' organizations—were often co-opted into the ruling party and ceased operating as independent watchdogs monitoring government corruption. Because control of the government was the surest road to personal enrichment, military officers in some countries were motivated to stage military coups.

This fundamental connection between economic policy and political power can be seen in other respects too. Command economies have arisen, for example, where political leaders have sought to use state power to radically redistribute societal wealth, enhance their own control, and break the power of the capitalist class. Latin American statism and the East Asian developmental state reflected particular patterns of connection between governments and business interests, with the former often seeking the support of the latter in the form of trade protectionism or investments in strategic sectors of the economy. Land reform has usually been driven by a desire to address rural grievances and weaken the power of landed elites.

Democratic governments must consider how the economic policies they adopt will affect not only economic growth but also popular support across constituencies with potentially differing economic interests. They need to pay careful attention to the situation of working-class and middle-class voters if they wish to be reelected.

Even authoritarian leaders must consider the preferences of groups upon whom they rely for support. Political parties and leaders enjoying backing from particular ethnic groups will be sensitive to how economic policies affect their constituents. Cutting military spending could be fatal for a regime that relies on military support. In Venezuela, years of mismanagement, low oil prices, poorly designed populist programs, and corruption under Presidents Hugo Chávez (1999–2013) and Nicolás Maduro (2013-) have devastated the country, causing the economy to shrink by up to 20 percent per year. Shortages and hyperinflation (of over 4,000 percent in 2017, predicted to reach as much as 1 million percent by the end of 2018) have aggravated widespread misery and caused millions to emigrate. However, as a report by the widely respected International Crisis Group notes:

> Maduro's increasingly repressive government rejects economic reform, fearing such measures would threaten its grip on power and resources. Current economic policies—including price and currency controls, state subsidy and rationing of food, and expropriation of commercial assets—directly benefit key constituencies in the regime, above all the military. Reversing those policies would threaten these interests.[26]

As noted in detail in chapter 8, policies aimed at improving rural social conditions or addressing the needs of the urban poor are intimately tied up with the political interests of governments, and the imperative of maintaining or expanding political support (or dampening down grievances that threaten the position of the government or regime). In democracies (discussed in chapter 3), elections provide the most immediate feedback mechanisms, with decision-makers mindful of how voters will respond.

Governments must also carefully weigh short-term (political) and long-term (economic) effects. Trade protectionism, for example, can be wrapped in nationalist rhetoric to mobilize supporters, but in the future can lead to price increases, retaliation by trading partners, and reduced economic growth. Similarly, increased government spending enables the expansion of services provided to the population, but needs to be balanced against the state's fiscal ability to support such expenditures in the year ahead.

THE EFFECTS OF GLOBALIZATION ON
THE DEVELOPING WORLD

Perhaps the most important and hotly debated economic development affecting developing countries in recent years is **globalization**. The mass media and social scientists both define globalization in related, but somewhat distinct, ways. In its most fundamental sense, the term refers to the increasing interdependence of national economies throughout the world. It is characterized by rising world trade in goods and services, increasing flows of cross-national finance (including banking, stock market transactions, and corporate acquisitions), greater legal and illegal labor migration, accelerated international transfers of advanced technologies, expansion of MNCs, and mounting influence of global economic institutions such as the IMF, the World Bank, and the WTO. All of these changes enhance the interdependence of national economies. In short, globalization involves the free flow of information, goods, services, and capital across national borders. Beyond this, the term is often also understood to include the spread of culture, consumer tastes, and technology from the West (particularly the United States) to the rest of the world.

Scholarly debate over globalization has centered on several questions: Is this really a new phenomenon or merely a continuation of economic trends that have existed for centuries? If it is new, when did it begin? And, most important for our purposes, has globalization improved or harmed less developed economies? Some scholars who claim that globalization is not a particularly new or dramatic development actually trace the first wave of economic globalization back to the Roman Empire. Some date it to the rise and spread of Western European capitalism in the sixteenth century, while others trace it to the last decades of the nineteenth century.[27] Others question whether there is anything uniquely global about the present era, arguing that the present level of economic interdependence was matched or exceeded in earlier times. Thus, for example, the level of trade as a percentage of the world economy is no higher today than it was in the early years of the twentieth century.

Still, the speed and breadth of today's information technology (IT) revolution have greatly accelerated the interconnectedness of national economies. The effects of debt default in Russia very quickly spill over to Argentina and Brazil. A sharp drop in China's rate of economic growth or its stock market or a liquidity crisis in a major French bank has quickly brought down prices on the New York Stock Exchange. And most recently, world financial markets responded quickly and dramatically when US Treasury bonds ratings were downgraded and when Greece, Ireland, Italy, and other European nations were in danger of defaulting on their external debt. To be sure, skeptics point out that the volume of world trade grew only modestly from 1980 to 2000. However, as we have seen, certain regions of the developing world—Asia and, to a lesser extent, Latin America—increased their manufactured exports substantially. Furthermore, financial globalization escalated dramatically during that period. For example, in the last two decades of the twentieth century, direct foreign investment rose by 250 percent worldwide and by 400 percent in the developing world.[28] The daily turnover of international currency exchanges increased more than tenfold during that same twenty-year period. Moreover, other indicators of globalization—such as the volume of foreign travel, international phone calls, and cross-border use of the internet—have exploded. As one analyst has put it, recent globalization is fundamentally different from earlier forms of international trade and commerce because "national markets are fused transnationally rather than [merely] linked across borders."[29]

If we accept that globalization is an important and, in some respects, a recent development, particularly as it affects developing countries, when did this process begin? Some analysts trace it to the resurgence of world trade after the Second World War. In the 1960s, the term "globalization" acquired its present meaning. But, it was in the 1970s and 1980s, aided by the IT revolution, that the process took off and it is since then that the phenomenon has become the focus of intense scrutiny by scholars, journalists, and political leaders.

One of the most contentious debates regarding globalization focuses on its economic consequences for the developing countries. Neoliberals and other supporters of free trade often see globalization as a panacea, able to stimulate the economies of developed and developing nations alike. They point to the benefits that export-led growth has brought to East Asia, Chile, and India. By allowing for the most rational allocations of investments, labor, and natural resources across national borders, they argue, globalization creates the most efficient and productive economic outcome. The IT revolution, for example, has permitted India's educated and technologically proficient middle class to provide tech support to the world. Foreign direct investment, moreover, tends to prefer countries that exhibit rule of law, political stability, good infrastructure, and an educated, healthy, and productive labor force—thus creating incentives for governments to improve governance and invest in social development.

Critics of globalization see its impact very differently. They view it as a force that has imposed greater Western economic control and cultural dominance over developing countries. Moreover, they insist, it has widened income gaps between industrialized and less developed countries—as well as within the developing countries—has caused environmental decay, and has extended poverty. Competition among governments to attract FDI could lead to weak labor or environmental protection, or tax breaks for multinational corporations. Moreover, the least developed countries are unlikely to attract much investment outside the resource sector.

One of the most influential analyses of these issues is Joseph Stiglitz's *Globalization and Its Discontents*.[30] Unlike many critics, Stiglitz—a Nobel-Prize–winning economist, former chair of President Bill Clinton's Council of Economic Advisers, and former chief economist for the World Bank—is the most respectable of establishment figures. Yet, his writings severely criticize the US government, the World Bank, and, especially, the IMF for pressuring less developed nations to adopt free-trade and privatization policies that have inflicted substantial pain on their populations and made their economies more vulnerable to shifts in the global economy.

While we cannot explore all aspects of this debate, we will focus on what may be the most important question: Has recent globalization deepened or alleviated poverty in the less developed world? Much of this discussion, in turn, has centered on the issue of economic equality and inequality: Has globalization intensified or reduced the economic gaps within individual developing countries and between those countries and the world's wealthier nations? There seems to be general agreement that between 1945 (when the latest wave of economic integration began) and 1980, the gap between rich and poor nations widened. Evidence since the 1980s, when globalization accelerated, suggests that this economic gap may have begun to narrow.

Supporters of globalization argue that rapid industrialization in countries such as China, India, South Korea, and Brazil, and expansion of the international service industry by countries such as India have allowed the developing countries, or at least some of them, to begin catching up with the developed world. Further examination, however, suggests a more complex picture. Since the 1970s, the income gap between the developed and developing countries has narrowed. But this was entirely the consequence of East and Southeast Asia's economic surge. Advocates of globalization point out that the countries in which living standards have most improved and where poverty has most sharply declined in the past two to three decades—including China, Chile, Indonesia, India, and South Korea—are precisely the nations that are most intensely integrated into the global economy. At the same time, the poorest nations in the world and those that, until recently, were falling furthest behind are the countries of sub-Saharan Africa, which have had the least globalized economies. Moreover, as a number of that region's countries have opened up their economies to world trade since 2000, sub-Saharan Africa, though still poor, has had some of the world's fastest-growing economies.

If we turn to the issue of inequality within developing nations, the evidence is somewhat ambiguous. As countries such as Chile and China have entered the global economy more intensely, the gap between their poor and the middle and upper classes has widened. Looking more systematically at data from sixty-five countries from 1995 to 2001, economist Almas Heshmati found that income inequality was somewhat greater in more globalized economies. However, he also observed that globalization was but one of many factors contributing to inequality, explaining only about 10 percent of the difference between nations.[31] Furthermore, depending on how they analyze the data, some economists have argued that income inequality has intensified as a result of globalization in recent decades, while others contend that it has diminished. But, even if there were a consensus that inequality has increased, would that mean that standards of living for the poor are declining on an absolute basis (i.e., the poor are actually getting poorer)? It might, but it could also mean that all income groups have benefited from globalization but the upper and middle classes have gained the most.

The most serious charge leveled against globalization is that it has intensified poverty in developing countries. Case studies describe multinational factories that pay their workers shockingly low wages (at least by Western standards) and peasants who were pushed off their land by foreign-owned plantations and logging operations. But, while case studies often provide useful insights, we cannot know how representative they are of the general population. That is, while a careful case study may demonstrate how MNCs reduced economic opportunities in Nuevo Laredo, Mexico, or how free trade impoverished sugar plantation workers in Malaysia, we do not know whether these situations are typical of Mexico or Malaysia, much less of the developing world as a whole. Moreover, assessing the impact of such investment requires consideration of the situation that would have existed otherwise. In other words, while earnings might be low and working conditions poor, many workers might consider them as an improvement over unemployment and greater poverty.

Indeed, if we examine more systematic statistics from the United Nations and the World Bank, we find that, contrary to globalization's critics, poverty in the developing world has actually declined significantly since globalization accelerated in the early 1980s. For example, according to World Bank statistics, the percentage of the developing countries' population living in "absolute poverty"—defined as those living on less than

$1.90 a day (PPP) has fallen from 35 percent in 1990 to 10.7 percent in 2015 (controlling for inflation). Since the start of the twenty-first century, when many countries in sub-Saharan Africa inserted themselves more vigorously in the global economy, not only has that region enjoyed substantial economic growth, but life expectancy grew from under fifty years (in 2000) to sixty years (in 2016).

A host of factors helped reduce absolute poverty and increase life expectancy (such as reducing the death rate from HIV/AIDS), and it would be an oversimplification to attribute all of this improvement to globalization. But, at the very least, the progress in recent decades does challenge allegations that rapid globalization has further impoverished the developing world. Furthermore, the most dramatic declines in absolute poverty have occurred in China, other parts of East Asia, and India, the regions most intensely linked to the global economy. As its economies have become more globalized, poverty rates in sub-Saharan Africa have declined somewhat more modestly.

At the same time, while extreme poverty fell sharply during this period, a large share of the world still struggles to survive with very low incomes. The World Bank estimates that some 2 billion people live on less than $3.20 a day (PPP), with 60 percent of these in South Asia and sub-Saharan Africa. Furthermore, even if the effect of globalization has generally been benign, it has also produced its share of losers. Even in a wealthy nation such as the United States, many textile mill employees and other workers in the manufacturing sector have seen their jobs disappear when their employer moved operations to Asia or Mexico. In developing countries, where workers and peasants are not protected by Western-style unemployment compensation or other safety nets, the consequences of economic dislocations are far more severe. During the Asian financial crisis in the late 1990s, an unintended consequence of globalization, millions lost their jobs, at least for a period of time. Elsewhere, reduced trade barriers in Latin America have allowed an influx of cheap foreign imports that destroys many local industries and put their employees out of work. This has led analysts such as Stiglitz to argue that since continued globalization seems inevitable, governments must take steps to mitigate its negative consequences on the biggest losers.[32]

Opponents of globalization maintain that the recent world economic recession showed ways in which it may be perilous for developing nations to link their economies to the world's advanced industrial nations. As the economy of developed nations declined in 2008–11, **remittances** by the developing countries' workers employed abroad (money sent home to families or friends) fell as fewer people were able to find work overseas.[33] The World Bank estimated that total remittances to developing countries, though rarely discussed in the West, exceeded $300 billion at the start of the 2008 recession, substantially higher than the value of all foreign aid by developed countries.* In countries such as Haiti, Lebanon, and Honduras, these remittances accounted for more than 20 percent of the GDP at that time.

But, while globalization has in some respects worsened the effects of the recent financial crisis on the developing world, its effects in the long run seem more benign. For example, it is true that this crisis reduced overseas remittances. But the vast cross-national movement of workers thus far in the century (a product of globalization) had caused those remittances to multiply from $116 billion in 2002 to $440 billion in 2015. More importantly, the fact that the developing countries rebounded so quickly and impressively from the initial shock of the most recent global recession, puts into question some of the doomsday predictions from critics of globalization.

CONCLUSION: DEMOCRACY AND ECONOMIC DEVELOPMENT

Earlier in this chapter, we observed that in the second half of the twentieth century, the most dynamic developing economies were often governed by authoritarian regimes, at least at the start of their economic booms. Almost all of Asia's most impressive early economic performances—in Taiwan, South Korea, Thailand, Malaysia, Indonesia, China, and Vietnam— emerged from authoritarian or semiauthoritarian, developmental states or modified command economies. Chile initiated Latin America's most successful transition from ISI to export-led growth under General Pinochet's military dictatorship. On the basis of such evidence, some have argued that authoritarian governments are better equipped to start economic development because they can control workers' wage demands and can impose long-term development plans on business.

On the other hand, for every authoritarian success story, there have been several economic disasters. Corrupt dictatorships throughout Africa, the Middle East, and Latin America have plundered their country's limited wealth, created inefficient private or state monopolies, and used the economy to reward themselves and their political allies. That is, for every South Korea, Chile, or Singapore, there has been a Congo, Tajikistan, and Iran, all of them authoritarian regimes that experienced negative average annual growth rates from 1975 to 2004 (i.e., their economies lost ground). While Chile's bureaucratic-authoritarian regime performed well economically, its

---

* This figure only includes formal remittances made through banks. Some experts estimate that an equal amount of funds or more are transferred informally through friends and relatives who bring the money home personally to avoid bank fees.

counterparts in Argentina and Uruguay were much less successful. Overall, statistical analyses of the developing countries' economic growth rate in recent decades reveal that authoritarian governments do not perform any better than democratic ones do. And one study indicated that dictatorships perform less well. Bruce Bueno de Mesquita et al. ranked hundreds of specific governments worldwide for the second half of the twentieth century and compared the 179 most autocratic governments with the 176 most democratic ones (over that fifty-year span, every country had multiple governments; each of those governments was counted as a different case). During that period, democratic administrations achieved an average real annual growth rate (adjusted for inflation) of 3.04 percent, while autocratic governments had only 1.78 percent, a substantial gap. Moreover, the authors argue convincingly that the difference in performance has a logical explanation, one that reflects the point we made earlier about the political imperatives of economic policy. Governments that need to appeal to a broad coalition of voters (democracies) are more inclined to pursue policies that promote broadly based economic gains. On the other hand, governments that owe their incumbency to a small coalition of strategic allies (dictatorships) are far more likely to be corrupt and to pursue policies designed to keep themselves in power, no matter what the cost is to the national economy.[34] In recent years, India, the world's most populous democracy, has also created one of the world's fastest-growing economies. Of course, the list of democratic governments includes both strong economic performers and weak ones, as does the list of authoritarian governments. But these findings, along with many others, offer hope that democratic governments and the worldwide movement toward democracy eventually may produce faster economic growth as well as greater political justice.

> **Practice and Review Online at**
> http://textbooks.rowman.com/handelman9e

KEY TERMS

apparatchiks

Asian tigers

autarky

climate change

command economy

developmental state

export-oriented industrialization (EOI)

globalization

growth with equity

import-substitution industrialization (ISI)

International Monetary Fund (IMF)

laissez-faire

latifundia

neoliberal

parastatal

Paris Agreement

political economy

remittances

state-led industrialization

structural adjustment program (SAP)

sustainable development

World Bank

World Trade Organization (WTO)

DISCUSSION QUESTIONS

1. What do you consider the major advantages and disadvantages of globalization? What measures might be implemented to alleviate those disadvantages?
2. Under what circumstances has substantial state intervention into the economy been helpful and in what cases has it had negative effects?
3. Any country must resolve trade-offs between economic growth and environmental losses. If you were the leader of a developing country, what criteria might you use to determine whether or not the economic benefits of a particular development project or private-sector investment were worth the environmental costs?

NOTES

1. A. Hewett, ed., *Reforming the Soviet Economy: Equality versus Efficiency* (Washington, DC: Brookings Institution, 1988), 38.

2. Harry Harding, *China's Second Revolution* (Washington, DC: Brookings Institution, 1987), 30–31.

3. John Sheahan, *Patterns of Development in Latin America* (Princeton, NJ: Princeton University Press, 1987), 85.

4. Howard Handelman and Werner Baer, eds., *Paying the Costs of Austerity in Latin America* (Boulder, CO: Westview Press, 1989); Stephan Haggard and Robert

R. Kaufman, eds., *The Politics of Economic Adjustment* (Princeton, NJ: Princeton University Press, 1992).

5. Extrapolated from Sinichi Ichimura and James W. Morley, "The Varieties of Asia-Pacific Experience," in *Driven by Growth*, ed. James W. Morley (Armonk, NY: M. E. Sharpe, 1992), 6; Steven Chan, *East Asian Dynamism* (Boulder, CO: Westview Press, 1990), 8; UNDP, *Human Development Report, 1997* (New York, NY: Oxford University Press, 1997), 21–22.

6. Robert Wade, *Governing the Market: Economic Theory and the Role of Government in East Asian Industrialization* (Princeton, NJ: Princeton University Press, 1990); Stephan Haggard, *Pathways from the Periphery* (Ithaca, NY: Cornell University Press, 1990).

7. Chalmers Johnson, *MITI and the Japanese Miracle* (Stanford, CA: Stanford University Press, 1982).

8. Chan, *East Asian Dynamism*, 47–48.

9. Ibid., 49.

10. Robert Wade, "Industrial Policy in Asia: Does It Lead or Follow the Market?" in *Manufacturing Miracles: Paths of Industrialization in Latin America and East Asia*, eds. Gary Gereffi and Donald L. Wyman (Princeton, NJ: Princeton University Press, 1990), 231–66; Wade, *Governing the Market.*

11. "A New Approach to Fighting Child Malnutrition in India," Knowledge@Wharton (University of Pennsylvania), July 25, 2014.

12. *New York Times*, "A Widening Gap Erodes Argentina's Egalitarian Image," December 25, 2006.

13. Richard Albin, "Saving the Environment: The Shrinking Realm of Laissez-Faire," in *International Political Economy* (2nd ed.), eds. Jeffrey A. Frieden and David A. Lake (New York, NY: St. Martin's, 1991), 454.

14. Sheahan, *Patterns of Development*, 86–87.

15. Wade, *Governing the Market*, 34, 36.

16. Gary Gereffi, "Paths of Industrialization: An Overview," in *Manufacturing Miracles*, 15. But, Brazil's proportion grew steadily from 8 percent in 1965 to 45 percent in 1987.

17. U.S. Energy Information Administration (EIA), *International Petroleum Monthly*, October 6, 2009, http://www.eia.doe.gov/ipm.

18. Scott Wallace, "Farming the Amazon," *National Geographic*, http://environment.nationalgeographic.com.

19. Intergovernmental Panel on Climate Change, *Climate Change 2014: Synthesis Report Summary for Policymakers*, http://www.ipcc.ch/pdf/assessment-report/ar5/syr/AR5_SYR_FINAL_SPM.pdf.

20. Andrew Guzman, *Overheated: The Human Costs of Climate Change* (New York, NY: Oxford University Press, 2013), 54–131.

21. World Bank, *Climate Change Overview*, http://www.worldbank.org/en/topic/climatechange/overview.

22. Michael Klare, "Global Warming Battlefields: How Climate Change Threatens Security," *Current History* 106 (November 2007): 357. This section of the chapter draws heavily on that article.

23. Bhaskar Nath and Ilkden Talay, "Man, Science, Technology and Sustainable Development," in *Sustainable Development*, eds. Bhaskar Nath, Luc Hens, and Dimitri Devuyst (Brussels, Belgium: VUB University Press, 1996), 36.

24. Andrew Blowers and Pieter Leroy, "Environment and Society: Shaping the Future," in *Environmental Policy in an International Context: Prospects*, eds. Andrew Blowers and Pieter Glasbergen (New York, NY: John Wiley & Sons, 1996), 262.

25. Robin Broad and John Cavanaugh, "No More NICs," *Foreign Policy* 72 (Fall 1988): 81–103.

26. International Crisis Group, "Misery as Strategy: The Human Cost of Conflict," May 31, 2018, at https://www.crisisgroup.org/global/misery-strategy-human-cost-conflict.

27. Malcolm Waters, *Globalization* (New York, NY: Routledge, 1995).

28. Mauro F. Guillén, "Is Globalization Civilizing, Destructive or Feeble?" *Annual Review of Sociology* 27 (August 2001): 235–60.

29. S. J. Kobrin, "The Architecture of Globalization," in *Governments, Globalization, and International Business*, ed. J. H. Dunning (New York, NY: Oxford University Press, 1997), 148. Cited in Guillén, "Is Globalization Civilizing . . . ?"

30. Joseph E. Stiglitz, *Globalization and Its Discontents* (New York, NY: W. W. Norton, 2002).

31. Almas Heshmati, *The Relationship Between Income Inequality and Globalization* (Helsinki, Finland: The United Nations University, 2003).

32. Joseph E. Stiglitz, *Making Globalization Work* (New York, NY: W. W. Norton, 2006).

33. *The Global Financial Crisis and Developing Countries* (London: Overseas Development Institute, June 2009).

34. Bruce Buena de Mesquita et al., "Political Competition and Economic Growth," *Journal of Democracy* 12, no. 1 (2001): 58–72.

3

The Surge and Partial Retreat of Democracy

◆ ◆ ◆

A Tunisian voter dips his finger in indelible ink to indicate he has voted in the country's first democratic municipal elections since the 2011 revolution. This technique is used in many developing countries to reduce voter fraud. *Source*: CrowdSpark/ Alamy Stock Photo.

IN THE CLOSING DECADES OF THE TWENTIETH CENTURY, a wave of democracy swept over much of the developing world (and the communist bloc), the so-called Third Wave.[1] Never before had so many countries replaced dictatorships with democratic regimes. Since then, although some new democratic transitions have occurred, the wave of change has diminished to a trickle. To be sure, the overthrow of dictatorships in Tunisia, Egypt, Libya, and Yemen in 2011 (known as the **Arab Spring**) gave hope that democratic transitions were at hand in the region that historically had been the least hospitable to democracy. However, that hope was soon crushed when everywhere but in Tunisia, those uprisings eventually either failed, brought chaos, or led to renewed dictatorships.

Since the overthrow in 1974 of Portugal's long-standing, fascist dictatorship, authoritarian regimes in southern Europe, the former Soviet bloc and the developing world have fallen in the face of democratic movements. Most Westerners considered the demise of Soviet and Eastern European communism to be democracy's most renowned triumph in this era. But in the developing nations, equally dramatic events also deserve our attention. In 1990, Nelson Mandela, the world's most revered political prisoner, left his cell in Pollsmoor Prison and was transported triumphantly to South Africa's capital, Pretoria, ending twenty-seven years of incarceration. There, he and other freed black leaders of the newly legalized political party, the African National Congress (ANC), eventually negotiated an end to white minority rule. President Mandela's triumph accelerated Africa's "second independence"—a wave of political liberalization (easing of repression) that has often led to either electoral or liberal democracy.*

In Asia, Corazón Aquino succeeded her assassinated husband as the result of Filipino "people's power"—massive prodemocracy demonstrations by students, shopkeepers, professionals, businesspeople, and others. Her supporters, backed by the Catholic clergy, took to the streets day after day, peacefully challenging government troops. Ultimately, when the nation's dictator, Ferdinand Marcos, tried to deny Ms. Aquino her apparent victory in a hastily called presidential election (1986), the commander of the armed forces along with the defense minister joined the opposition, forcing Marcos to step down. Soon after, student-led demonstrations against South Korea's military regime (partially inspired by events in the Philippines) accelerated that country's transition to democracy. In 1998, "people's power" demonstrations in Indonesia toppled the thirty-year dictatorship of President Suharto. And, since 2011, international pressure has induced Myanmar's military rulers to substantially reduce repression and give the political opposition a limited voice.

---

* Electoral democracies are countries that have free and fair elections, but may violate their citizens' civil rights and liberties and are, therefore, not fully democratic. Liberal democracies are fully democratic political systems that enjoy both competitive elections and broad civil liberties.

But the most sweeping democratic changes took place in Latin America (1978–90), affecting most countries in the region. Whereas all but a few countries (Colombia, Costa Rica, and Venezuela) had authoritarian or semiauthoritarian governments in the mid-1970s, twenty-five years later, only Cuba and Haiti had failed to establish functioning electoral democracies (though since that time civil liberties have eroded in a few countries, most notably Venezuela). Unlike Asia and Africa, Latin America's democratization process generally lacked charismatic heroes in the molds of Mandela, Aquino, or Burmese Nobel Peace Prize winner Aung San Suu Kyi. Nor did it typically feature mass demonstrations. Instead, democratic transitions often grew out of extended negotiations between the authoritarian government (which had become very unpopular) and opposition leaders, culminated by a relatively peaceful, gradual transfer of power.

Latin America enjoyed two important advantages over Africa and Asia. First, prior to its surge of military takeovers in the 1960s and 1970s, the region had enjoyed the developing world's strongest democratic tradition, most notably in Chile, Costa Rica, and Uruguay. Furthermore, Latin American countries were among the first developing countries to achieve the levels of literacy and economic development that are generally associated with stable democratic governments. Predictably, then, the region's democratic wave has been more sweeping and more successful, ultimately affecting virtually every country in the hemisphere.

In many developing countries, the early years of the twenty-first century were difficult for dictators and quasi-dictators. Augusto Pinochet, Chile's military ruler for nearly seventeen years (1973–90), fought to avoid a human rights trial in Chile after returning from a humiliating house arrest in England. Former Argentine military dictator Jorge Videla was sentenced to life in prison in 2010 for ordering the torture and execution of political prisoners some thirty-five years previously. Indonesia's long-term dictator, General Suharto, also faced possible detention after he was driven from office by mass demonstrations. Like Pinochet, this aged, once all-powerful leader hid behind the humiliating court plea that he was physically too weak and too mentally incapacitated to stand trial.

Of course, not all democratic movements have been successful. In China, army tanks crushed student demonstrations in Beijing's Tiananmen Square (1989). Similarly, massive prodemocracy street demonstrations in 2009 failed to dislodge Iran's authoritarian government. And even when democracy was installed, it failed to last long in some developing countries.

However, despite these setbacks, most notably in the Arab states, the upsurge of political freedom in the developing world since the 1970s, coupled with the breakdown of communism in the Soviet bloc, has produced history's greatest democratic transition. By the end of the twentieth century, the surge of democratization had largely ended, but many of the new democracies have endured. If this progress can be maintained, it will likely influence many of the aspects of politics discussed in this book. For example, by definition, consolidation of democracy reduces military rule. It also lowers the likelihood of revolutionary movements. Democracy generally contributes, at least eventually, to a better quality of political and economic life for women, peasants, and the urban poor. It is also a form of government to which many people aspire. Public opinion studies conducted by the World Values Survey (2010–14) in forty-seven different developing countries (ranging from Algeria to Zimbabwe) found that 82 percent of respondents felt that democracy is a "very good" or "fairly good" political system.[2]

This chapter will examine what democracy is and the challenges of achieving and sustaining it in the developing world. It will look at the local and international factors that seem to encourage democratic change. Finally, it will end by discussing how democratic governance might be improved.

DEMOCRACY DEFINED

Discussions of democratic transformations have frequently been complicated by disagreements over the meaning of democracy. Currently, most political scientists characterize democracy procedurally. That is, democracy is measured by the transparency and fairness of the essential procedures governing the election and behavior of government officials. The least-demanding definition focuses almost exclusively on elections. It simply defines democracy as a political system that holds fair, contested elections on a regular basis, with universal (or near-universal) adult suffrage. Political scientists call countries that only meet this minimal standard **electoral democracies**. Although this bare-bones definition seems reasonable (most Americans think of democracy in terms of free and fair elections), it allows a number of rather questionable governments to be labeled democratic. For example, while they are electoral democracies, recent governments in Colombia and Sri Lanka have widely violated human rights while battling armed insurgencies. In countries such as Thailand and Bangladesh, electoral democracy has been episodic, interrupted periodically by military intervention, often overriding decisions made by elected officials. In Turkey, elections have not prevented President Recep Tayyip Erdoğan from jailing political opponents and intimidating the media.

As the norm of open elections became widely accepted in recent decades, the number of electoral democracies worldwide tripled from 1974 (39 nations) to 2000 (120) and has fluctuated near that level since then.[3] But many of these governments still manipulate the mass media and violate their citizens' civil liberties. This chapter sometimes uses the term "**semi-democracy**" to refer to those electoral democracies whose governments regularly repress civil liberties and breach the principles of a free society. Their elections may be relatively free and fair, but their societies are not. These currently include such countries as Pakistan and Haiti. Finally, some semi-democracies have competitive elections but lack adequate mechanisms for holding the government accountable to its citizens between elections. The terms "**illiberal democracy**" and "**hybrid regime**" are also commonly used by scholars to discuss such political systems.

Consequently, a more stringent definition of "full" democracy (also known as **liberal democracy**) involves more than competitive elections. Instead, it can be defined as a political system that conforms to the following conditions: most of the country's leading government officials are elected;* there is universal or near-universal suffrage; elections are largely free of fraud and outside manipulation; opposition-party candidates have a realistic chance of being elected to important national offices; and civil liberties—including minority rights—are respected, with guarantees of free speech, free assembly, free press (media), and freedom of religion. All these conditions help guarantee that democratic governments are accountable to their citizens in a way that authoritarian regimes are not.[4] Moreover, liberal democracy also includes the rule of law, civilian command over the armed forces, and a vigorous **civil society**.† This definition suggests that competitive elections mean little if unelected individuals or groups who are not accountable to the public (such as military officers, organized crime bosses, business elites, or foreign powers) direct elected officials from behind the scenes. And, free elections do not bring full democracy if elected officials violate their citizens' civil liberties or arbitrarily arrest opposition leaders.

Finally, some observers offer an even more demanding standard for democracy. They argue that any purely procedural definition of democracy, no matter how exacting, is incomplete. Instead, they insist, real democracy requires not only fair elections and proper government procedures, but also fair and just government policy outcomes (**substantive democracy**). For example, substantive democracy requires that citizens have relatively equal access to public schooling and health care regardless of their social

---

* Of course, even in some liberal democracies, high-ranking officeholders are appointed, not elected. In the United States, these include Supreme Court justices and cabinet members. But these positions are appointed by a popularly elected president and are subject to congressional confirmation. But, prior to the 1960s, the United States was not a fully liberal or even a full electoral democracy because large numbers of African Americans were effectively barred from voting in the southern states. And, until the early twentieth century, women also were denied suffrage.
† Civil society is the array of voluntary organizations—including churches, unions, business groups, farmers' organizations, and women's groups—whose members often influence the political system, but are free of government control. Most authoritarian governments weaken civil society, so that it cannot generate a challenge to their rule. Consequently, rebuilding and strengthening civil society are essential tasks for establishing and consolidating democratic governments.

class or ethnicity. Similarly, they insist, any procedural democracy—such as Iraq or South Africa—that tolerates gross economic inequalities, ethnic conflicts, or other social injustices is not truly democratic.

These authors make an important point. Procedural democracy alone does not guarantee a just society; it is merely a step in the right direction. But it is a far more important step than its critics acknowledge. Because governments in procedural democracies are accountable to the people, they are less vulnerable to revolution and other forms of civil unrest. They are also very unlikely to make war against other democracies (to be sure, war between two liberal democracies is virtually unknown). Prodded by a free press and public opinion, they are more responsive to domestic crises such as famines (in fact, there has never been a prolonged famine in any procedural democracy), and while some (electoral) democracies have violated their opponents' civil liberties, most of them do respect their citizens' rights.

Mindful of the fact that democratic societies cannot easily correct all social injustices—the United States, for example, has long endured racial discrimination, poverty, and a high degree of economic inequality—this book defines democracy strictly procedurally. Issues of substantive democracy (reducing poverty, racism, sexism, and the like) are obviously important, but they are a separate matter.

DEMOCRATIC TRANSITION AND CONSOLIDATION

In the discussion that follows, the term "**democratic transition**" means the process of moving from an authoritarian to a democratic regime. The transition period begins when an authoritarian government shows the first observable signs of collapsing or of negotiating its departure from power. It ends when the first freely elected government takes office. Thus, for example, in South Africa, the democratic transition began in 1990 when the white minority government of President Frederik de Klerk decided to free Nelson Mandela and open negotiations with his ANC party. It concluded four years later when Mandela was inaugurated as the country's first president to be elected through universal suffrage. Even after their transitions are completed, however, many new democracies remain fragile, with a real possibility that they will falter.

Only when democratic institutions, practices, and values have become deeply ingrained in society can we say that a country has experienced **democratic consolidation**. This consolidation is a process through which democratic norms ("rules of the game") become accepted by all politically influential groups in society—including business groups, labor unions, rural landlords, professionals, the church, and the armed forces—and no important political actor contemplates a return to dictatorship. Or, as Juan Linz and Alfred Stepan have put it, democracy is consolidated when it becomes

A 2016 election rally in Accra, Ghana. Ghana is one of several countries in the area that have made full or partial transitions to electoral democracy since the early 1990s, making West Africa the most democratic region on the continent. *Source*: Pacific Press/Alamy Stock Photo.

"the only game in town," even in the face of severe economic or political adversity.[5] Consolidation may begin after the democratic transition ends and is completed only when democracy is securely entrenched.

Unfortunately, since 1960 less than half of the transitions to democracy were subsequently consolidated. Many countries have reverted to dictatorship or have remained mired in political disorder. Thus, Kapstein and Converse found that between 1960 and 2004, there were 123 cases in which countries changed from authoritarian to democratic government, of which 98 (nearly 80 percent of the total) were developing countries. A number of nations created democratic governments multiple times only to see them fail. For example, Pakistan established democracy four times in that forty-four-year time span, each of which failed. Of the ninety-eight democratic transitions in the developing world during that period, less than half (46 percent) survived until 2004. In fact, one-fourth of the democratic governments created during that period collapsed within two years.[6]

Most recently, Egypt enjoyed a transition to democracy when mass demonstrations toppled the Hosni Mubarak's thirty-year dictatorship followed by the first democratic election in the nation's history (2012). But that democracy was never consolidated and the following year the armed forces ousted President Mohamed Morsi to install a military dictatorship that is now more repressive than Mubarak's. Elsewhere during the Arab Spring, the overthrow of the long-standing (1969–2011) Muammar Qaddafi dictatorship in Libya and the Ali Abdullah Saleh regime in Yemen resulted in attempted democratic transitions that collapsed into civil war. Scholars have identified several internal factors that increase the likelihood that a new democracy will fail, including ethnic divisions and a failure to build strong political institutions, including institutional checks on the president's powers.

In successfully consolidated democracies, democratic values predominate among politically relevant individuals and groups. Even previously antidemocratic political parties and groups, such as the armed forces, former guerrilla groups, and far-right and far-left political parties, have come to accept democracy as the only game in town. This does not mean that consolidated democracies will never break down. "Never" is a long time, and in the past, consolidated, developing world democracies have given way to authoritarian forces, as we see happening in Turkey today. However, consolidated democracies are secure for the foreseeable future. And they will probably endure unless some deep societal divide (such as class or ethnic conflict) emerges to tear them apart.

AUTHORITARIAN BEGINNINGS

With the surge in democratic transitions in recent decades, a global consensus has been emerging in support of democratic government. But this has not always been true. In the decades after the Second World War, as numerous African, Asian, and Middle Eastern countries achieved independence, many leaders of developing countries as well as foreign observers believed that these emerging nations were not ready for democratic government. Others argued that democracy was not even desirable at that stage of their socioeconomic development. To be sure, a number of newly independent countries—particularly former British colonies—established democratic political institutions modeled after their former colonial rulers. But only in a few, such as India, did democracy take a firm hold.

Since that time, Middle Eastern nations generally have been ruled by monarchs, all-powerful single parties, or dictatorial strongmen. Many new sub-Saharan nations also created political systems dominated by a single party, while others established military dictatorships or suffered one-man rule. Democracy fared somewhat better in Asia, but the military in this region frequently aborted the process. Communist revolutionaries toppled corrupt and inept governments in China and Vietnam. Benefiting from greater socioeconomic development and from more than a century of self-rule, Latin America had the most prior experience with democracy. Indeed, during the 1950s, relatively democratic governments predominated in this region. But the armed forces continued to meddle in national politics and in the 1960s and early 1970s a new wave of military takeovers swept the region, often as a result of political and economic instability. Only since the 1980s has democracy again become the norm in Latin America.

Justifying Authoritarian Rule

In view of democracy's recent broad appeal, it seems hard to believe that many observers once considered freely elected government unattainable or even undesirable in the developing countries. Some modernization theorists believed that the newly emerging African and Asian states were insufficiently economically or socially developed to sustain democracy. Many dependency theorists declared that democracy was unlikely to emerge because powerful industrialized nations and multinational corporations had allied with elites in less developed countries to bolster unrepresentative governments.

At the same time, other scholars like Samuel Huntington worried that levels of mass political participation in democratic or semidemocratic states often exceeded their governments' capacity to accommodate all the new political demands. Unless developing world political institutions were strengthened, they warned, political unrest threatened to derail economic and political development. Concerned about the dangers of substantial disorder, some justified authoritarian rule as a necessary stopgap. Only after developing countries experienced sufficient socioeconomic modernization, they argued, could their citizens learn how to peacefully and effectively participate in politics. At the same time, modernizing societies needed to establish political institutions capable of accommodating the people's expanding demands. Developing countries have usually been able to establish stable, democratic governments only when they have raised their per capita incomes and have reached a literacy rate of 50 percent. In addition to raising literacy, modernization also enlarges the size of the middle class and the organized working class, both essential for a more stable and inclusive democracy.

But if socioeconomic modernization was necessary to establish democracy, what type of government could initiate economic and social development? Some experts believed that only a strong and stable authoritarian government—such as General Pinochet's dictatorship in Chile (1973–90) or South Korea's several military governments (1961–87)—could jumpstart economic modernization and growth. Only authoritarian regimes, they maintained, could limit workers' wages and control labor unrest in order to attract needed multinational and domestic private-sector investment. In East Asia, for example, several repressive governments that had brought about significant economic growth (Indonesia, Singapore, and South Korea) insisted that dictatorial governments could better impose rational, long-term development plans. Thus, the father of Singapore's authoritarian political system and its spectacular economic growth, former president Lee Kuan Yew, stated, "I believe what a [developing] country needs to develop is discipline more than democracy. . . . Democracy leads to indiscipline and disorderly conduct, which are inimical to development."[7] Only later, others said, when a country was "ready," would dictatorships give way to democracy.*

Using some combination of these justifications, many governments in the developing countries insisted that democracy was inappropriate for countries in the early stage of social and economic development. In Africa, leaders in the struggle for independence often created single-party systems, banning or restricting opposition political parties. Some warned that competitive elections would only encourage candidates to organize along ethnic or tribal lines, thereby further polarizing their country (see chapter 6). In Africa and other developing countries, some founding fathers, influenced by the Marxist-Leninist ideology, asserted that their nations needed an all-powerful state, led by a "vanguard party" (i.e., one that claimed to know what was in the best interests of the masses), if they hoped to combat severe poverty, dependency, class tensions, or ethnic divisions. By 1964, roughly two-thirds of the independent African countries had become single-party states. Subsequently, after many of these governments had failed miserably, military dictators took their place, claiming that civilian rulers were too corrupt or too weak to govern effectively (chapter 10). In the Middle East, similar justifications were used to defend one-party or military rule.

In contrast, many Latin American nations had enjoyed democratic or semidemocratic governments in the 1950s and 1960s. But, the 1970s and 1980s witnessed the rise of right-wing military dictatorships in much of the region. The new leaders justified their rule by pointing to perceived leftist threats and the need to reinvigorate the economy. Meanwhile, a number of authoritarian rulers in East Asia clung to power long after their countries had surpassed the thresholds of economic and social modernization normally associated with democratic transitions. In Singapore, South Korea, and Taiwan, the governments claimed that their dictatorships were needed to ward off external threats (from Indonesia, North Korea, and China,

---

* Of course, even defenders of authoritarian governments had to concede that most dictatorships are not efficient modernizers. Far from it! The developing world has had more than its share of corrupt dictators who have stolen millions, run their country's economy into the ground, and awarded the most lucrative business opportunities to relatives and cronies. What many observers do claim, however, is that efficient capitalist dictatorships such as Taiwan's or Singapore's were able to achieve economic modernization. Similarly, supporters of revolutionary dictatorships (such as Cuba and China) believe they are necessary for greater social equality, along with improved literacy and health care.

respectively). Others felt that their Confucian cultures saw political opposition groups as being disruptive to social harmony.

Indeed, in the 1960s and 1970s, democracy was in retreat in the developing world, as countries such as Chile, Nigeria, and the Philippines succumbed to dictatorships. By the mid-1970s, only about thirty-nine of the world's nations were functioning democracies and almost all of those were prosperous, industrialized countries in North America, Europe, and Australia-New Zealand. Thus, Larry Diamond observed,

> The mid-to-late 1970s seemed a low-water mark for democracy and the empirical trends were reified by intellectual fashions dismissing democracy as an artifice, a cultural construct of the West, or a "luxury" that poor states could not afford.[8]

THE THIRD WAVE AND ITS EFFECT ON THE DEVELOPING WORLD

Since that time, however, developing countries have played a notable role in history's most sweeping transition from authoritarianism to democracy. Writing shortly before the 1991 dissolution of the Soviet Union, Samuel Huntington counted twenty-nine countries throughout the world that had democratized in the fifteen years alone prior to 1991. Of these, twenty were developing countries.[9] Although some of the countries on his list had weak democratic credentials and some subsequently slid back to authoritarian rule, there can be no denying that the global trend toward democracy since the late 1970s was palpable.

He noted that the recent surge of democracy is actually the third such wave that the world has experienced since the early 1800s. In each case, democratic ideals and movements in key countries spread to other nations. The first democratic wave (1828–1926), by far the longest, began under the influence of the American and French Revolutions and ended with the Great Depression of the 1920s–1930s. Democratization during that wave was largely confined to Europe and to former British colonies with primarily European populations (the United States, Canada, New Zealand, and Australia). The second, much shorter, wave (1943–62) was precipitated by victory over fascism during the Second World War and the subsequent demise of European colonialism in Africa, Asia, and the Middle East. In that wave, democratic governments emerged in a number of less developed countries, though most of these only met the standards of electoral democracy (competitive elections).

It is the **Third Wave** (from 1974 until about 2000) that most draws our attention because of its pervasive and seemingly lasting reverberations in less developed nations. Of course, the most dramatic Third-Wave transitions were in the Eastern and Central European communist bloc, which brought the Cold War to an end. Pictures of young Germans breaking off

Table 3.1   The Global Growth of Democracy

Year	Free Countries (%)	Partly Free Countries (%)	Countries Not Free (%)	Number of Countries Rated
1972	29	25	46	151
1985	34	34	33	167
1998	46	28	26	191
2010	45	31	24	194
2018	45	30	25	195

Source: Freedom House, *Freedom in the World 2018.*

pieces of the Berlin Wall and of Boris Yeltsin facing down a military coup in Moscow were among the most powerful political images of the late twentieth century. But in developing nations as diverse as South Africa, the Philippines, and Brazil, years of authoritarian or semiauthoritarian rule also came to an end. Huntington noted that the first two democratic waves were followed by periods of backsliding—reverse waves—during which a number of those countries reverted to authoritarian rule.

For over forty years, perhaps the most widely used and respected evaluations of global democracy have been published annually by Freedom House, a nongovernmental, research, and advocacy group. Each year, its panel of experts evaluates the world's nations on two dimensions of democracy: first, their level of political rights (including the extent of electoral competition and citizen participation); and, second, the quality of civil liberties (such as free speech and freedom of religion) and the prevalence of the rule of law. On the basis of their evaluations, Freedom House's annual reports classify all countries as Free, Partly Free, or Not Free.* As table 3.1 indicates, in 1972 less than one-third of the world's 151 countries (29 percent) enjoyed fully democratic government and nearly one-half (46 percent) were not free. During the remainder of the twentieth century, the Third Wave swept over Latin America and other parts of the developing world, with the percentage of full democracies (free countries) increasing fairly steadily. Some of the major advances came from the mid-1980s to 2000. These included the fall of the Soviet bloc and the overthrow of extended dictatorships in Chile and the Philippines. While table 3.1 presents the percentage of free countries in the entire world, developed and developing alike. In fact, the developing countries had a lower percentage of free countries. But it is precisely in developing countries that the Third Wave spread most rapidly.

Table 3.1 suggests that the proportion of free countries remained fairly constant for the past two decades or so. However, Freedom House

---

* The panel of experts rates each country's level of political rights and civil liberties on a scale of one (most free) to seven (least free). Using the combined score for these two ratings, each country is categorized according to its degree of freedom.

Table 3.2   Democracy by Region

Region	Free Countries (%)	Partly Free Countries (%)	Countries Not Free (%)
Latin America and the Caribbean	64	30	6
Asia and the Pacific	44	36	20
Sub-Saharan Africa	18	41	41
Middle East and North Africa	11	22	67

Source: Freedom House, *Freedom in the World 2018.*

has recently warned that democracy may now be facing its "most serious crisis in decades." They note that some 113 countries have suffered some decline in civil and political liberties between 2006 and 2017 (although not necessarily large enough to yet result in a change of category), while only sixty-two have showed improvement.

Table 3.2 reveals that democratization has expanded at different rates in the various regions of the developing world. Latin America and the Caribbean now have the highest percentage of free countries (64 percent) and the lowest not free (6 percent). It is followed by Asia and the Pacific (44 percent free), sub-Saharan Africa (18 percent free), and, well behind the others, the Middle East and North Africa (11 percent free).

INTERNATIONAL CAUSES AND CONSEQUENCES OF THE THIRD WAVE

Obviously, widespread political changes of this magnitude are inspired and influenced by broad currents that transcend the politics of particular states. A number of factors contributed to the Third Wave's democratic transitions. For one thing, the economic crises that devastated so many developing countries in the 1980s revealed that most authoritarian regimes were no more effective and no less corrupt than the elected governments that they had contemptuously swept aside (indeed, they were frequently less efficient and more dishonest). Furthermore, because dictatorships lack the legitimacy that free elections bestow on democratic governments, their support depends much more heavily on satisfactory job performance. So when authoritarian governments in countries such as Argentina and Nigeria dragged their country into war (including civil war), economic decay, or rampant corruption, their support rapidly eroded. In Africa, the gross mismanagement and dishonesty of both military and single-party regimes caused their already poor economies to implode, as the continent's per capita GNP declined by some 2 percent annually throughout the 1980s. Within Latin America, the economic record of military rulers was relatively strong in Chile and Brazil, but military regimes performed poorly elsewhere. By the 1980s, almost all of that region's authoritarian governments were undermined by a major foreign debt crisis.

By contrast, many East Asian dictatorships (most notably South Korea, Taiwan, Indonesia, and Singapore) enjoyed spectacular economic success from the 1960s through the late 1990s. However, rather than produce wider support for those governments, growth and modernization often generated a burgeoning middle class with democratic aspirations and the political skills to pursue them. As the number of politically informed citizens grew, they increasingly resented government repression, state corruption, and the lack of meaningful political participation.

Throughout the world, no sooner had democratic upheavals occurred in one nation than they spread quickly to neighboring countries. In Eastern Europe, Poland's Solidarity movement inspired democratic challenges in Hungary, East Germany, and Czechoslovakia. Students in South Korea watched television coverage of anti-government demonstrations in the Philippines and took the lessons of Philippine "people's power" to heart. Such **demonstration effects** can be an important factor in political change, with populations in one country learning lessons and gaining inspiration from similar struggles elsewhere.

As the democratic tidal wave swept forward, some authoritarian leaders began to get the message. Generals in Ecuador and Paraguay watched neighboring military dictatorships fall and decided to abdicate while the going was still good. After more than forty years of authoritarian rule by the Kuomintang Party, Taiwan's government opened up to authentic electoral competition and political freedom. In Africa, a number of single-party states liberalized their political systems, allowing greater freedom and more political space for opposition groups, while a smaller number established liberal democracies.

The demise of communist regimes in Eastern Europe exposed the deficiencies of their ideology. As Marxism-Leninism was discredited, even among many of its once-fervent adherents, democracy assumed greater international legitimacy. And, the end of the Cold War permitted the United States to be more consistent in its advocacy of political freedom. That is to say, the United States no longer had any reason to coddle allied developing world dictators—including authoritarian regimes in prerevolutionary Iran and the Philippines—whose friendship it had previously cultivated to thwart the spread of communism.*

The "Arab Spring," which brought democracy to Tunisia in 2011, also seemed to promise another wave of democratizing change, with protests

---

*There have remained, however, notable exceptions, as the United States has retained close ties with repressive but strategically important regimes such as Egypt and Saudi Arabia.

spreading across much of the Arab world. In the Middle East, demonstration effects were given further impetus by shared Arabic language and culture, regional broadcast media, and the internet. However, as noted earlier, the overthrow of dictatorships in Egypt, Libya, and Yemen resulted in renewed authoritarianism, or widespread political violence. Syria too collapsed into a brutal civil war, while protests were crushed in Bahrain.

The regional neighborhood matters too in shaping political outcomes. In Europe, the European Union played a key role in supporting democratic transition and consolidation in ex-communist regimes in Eastern Europe and the Balkans in the 1990s. In Africa, the Economic Community for West African States (ECOWAS) pressured President Yahya Jammeh of Gambia to give up power after losing elections in 2016. The Organization of American States today stresses the importance of democracy and human rights. Conversely, in the Middle East most regional states have shown little interest in supporting democratization. Indeed, Saudi Arabia and other members of the Gulf Cooperation Council have acted to support fellow authoritarian monarchies under threat, notably in Bahrain where GCC forces intervened in 2011 to support the regime against protesters calling for reform.

PREREQUISITES OF DEMOCRACY?

While international influences can be catalysts, providing developing countries with incentives and chances to democratize, not all developing countries took advantage of these opportunities. More than thirty years after the start of the Third Wave, some developing countries remain mired in dictatorship, with no openings in their political system. Others either have failed to complete their democratic transitions or have alternated between authoritarianism and weak democracy. But, some fortunate countries have consolidated democracy.

What accounts for these differences? What determines whether or not a particular country embarks on the road toward democracy, whether it completes that voyage successfully, and whether it eventually consolidates democratic values, practices, and institutions? In other words, how do we know whether or not democracy will take root and survive in Brazil, Indonesia, or Madagascar? Finally, why has democracy advanced further in some regions, such as Latin America, than in other regions, such as sub-Saharan Africa and the Middle East?

There are no simple answers. But scholars have debated these issues for decades and have identified a number of historical, structural, and cultural variables that help account for democracy's presence in, for example, India and Uruguay, and its absence in countries such as Sudan or Laos. However, political scientists still disagree about the relative importance of those variables. In the discussion that follows, we examine a number of factors that have been widely identified as prerequisites for democracy.

Social and Economic Modernization

Nearly sixty years ago, Seymour Martin Lipset observed that democracy was far more prevalent in industrialized countries such as the United States and Sweden than in poorer nations—a finding congruent with moderniza-tion theory (chapter 1).[10] Subsequent political science research has largely supported that claim. The reasoning behind this relationship was that

> industrialization leads to increases in wealth, education, communication and equality; these developments are associated with a more moderate lower and upper class and a larger middle class, which is by nature moderate; and this in turn increases the probability of stable democratic forms of politics.[11]

Social scientists have since identified more precisely the particular aspects of modernization that promote democracy. Philips Cutright determined that when other factors are held constant, there is a strong correlation between the extent of a country's mass communications and its degree of democracy, stronger even than the correlation between economic development and democracy.[12] A free and active mass media and opportunities for citizens to exchange ideas promote a free society. And, Axel Hadenius, examining the influence of dozens of independent variables, found that democracy correlates most strongly with higher levels of literacy and education.[13] Also, educated citizens are more likely to participate in politics and to defend their interests. From 1990 to 2011, the developing world's adult literacy rate rose from 68 percent to 80 percent.[14] This bodes well for democracy in developing countries because, as we have noted, in the recent past, countries whose populations are more than half literate are far more likely to sustain (consolidate) democracy than those that fall below that mark. Today, only about ten countries in the world are less than half literate.

Many analysts have also shown that countries with higher per capita incomes are more likely to be democratic than poorer ones, a finding cor-responding to Lipset's observation. Today, for example, most developing countries with per capita incomes that exceed $2,500 (in constant dollars) are democracies of some sort, while those with incomes under that figure usually are not.*

This does not mean that countries inevitably become more democratic as their economies develop. In fact, middle-income countries are frequently less stable and more prone to dictatorship.[15] For example, even though the

---

* All dollar figures in the study were expressed in constant dollars, meaning that they are adjusted for inflation, so that per capita "real incomes" of $1,000 in 1960 and in 1990 are equivalent in terms of what they could buy at those times.

World Bank ranked South America's most industrialized countries (Argentina, Brazil, Chile, and Uruguay) as upper-middle-income nations, their democratic governments all fell to repressive, military dictatorships in the 1960s and 1970s. On the other hand, India—a low-income nation—has enjoyed one of the developing countries' strongest records of sustained democracy. But, while these exceptions are important, there is still generally a correlation between economic development and democracy. Although poor countries are as likely as richer ones to make the transition to democracy, they are less likely to sustain democratic government. East Asia's rapid economic growth, higher literacy, and expanding middle classes promoted democratic consolidation in South Korea and Taiwan. In Latin America, where levels of modernization are high by LDC standards, the democratic wave since the close of the 1970s has seemingly established consolidated democracies in most of the region. Conversely, Africa, which is home to most of the world's poorest nations, has suffered a number of failed transitions.

Class Structure

Some scholars contend that it is not economic growth per se that induces and consolidates democracy but rather the way in which that growth affects a country's social structure. Specifically, they reason, economic development supports stable democracy only if it induces appropriate changes in the country's **class structure**.

Since the time of Aristotle, political theorists have linked democracy and political stability to the presence of a large and vibrant middle class. The middle class, they suggest, tends to be politically moderate and serves as a bridge between the upper and lower classes. Its members also have the political and organizational skills necessary to create political parties and other important democratic institutions. An independent and influential business class (bourgeoisie) also seems essential for developing democracy. So, in those countries where economic growth has failed to create a politically independent and influential bourgeoisie and middle class, modernization does not necessarily buttress democracy and may even weaken it. To be sure, the political independence and the influence of the emerging middle classes have varied among different world regions, depending on the historical period in which those areas industrialized. For example, industrialization and urbanization produced a larger, more powerful, and more independent middle class and bourgeoisie in Northern Europe than it did a century later in Latin America. In the latter case, wealth and income were more concentrated and the middle class was correspondingly weaker and more dependent. Predictably, democracy did not take hold as readily in Latin America as it had in Northern Europe.

Barrington Moore, Jr., in his widely acclaimed study of economic and political change, *The Social Origins of Dictatorship and Democracy*, identified three discrete paths to modernization, each shaped by the relative power of the state and the strength of the major social classes. In one path, typified by nineteenth-century and early-twentieth-century Germany, modernization was led by a strong state allied with powerful and antidemocratic agricultural landowners and a bourgeoisie that was dependent on the state. There and subsequently in developing countries with similar class configurations, that combination ultimately resulted in the rise of fascist and far-right authoritarian regimes. A second path to modernization, found in countries such as China, was characterized by a highly centralized state, a repressive landowning class, a weak bourgeoisie, and a large and eventually rebellious peasantry. The end result of that alignment was a communist revolution fought by the peasantry.

Finally, Moore's third path, identified most closely with Britain, featured a weaker state and a strong bourgeoisie at odds with the rural landowning elite. Only this alignment of forces, distinguished by the middle class's powerful and independent political role, has led to liberal democracy. "No [strong and independent] bourgeoisie," Moore famously noted, "no democracy."[16] Similarly, in developing nations today, a vibrant middle class and an influential business class have been critical ingredients in the establishment and consolidation of democracy. It should come as no surprise, then, that in countries as diverse as Chile, Indonesia, the Philippines, South Korea, and, most recently, Iran, middle-class citizens, including university students, have been on the front lines in the struggles for democracy.

Very poor countries, such as Haiti and Afghanistan, whose middle classes are small and dependent on the state, are far less likely to achieve or consolidate democratic governments. But it is also important to remember that even though a strong middle class and bourgeoisie are necessary for democracy, these sectors are not always democratically oriented. For example, in pre-Nazi (Weimar) Germany and in Argentina and Chile during the 1970s, when the middle class felt threatened by social unrest from below, many of its members supported fascist or other far-right-wing dictatorships.

On the other hand, Rueschemeyer, Huber Stephens, and Stephens have focused attention on the role of organized (unionized) labor in building democracy. They argue that while the bourgeoisie and the middle class generally fostered democracy in Western Europe, Latin America, and the Caribbean, these groups not only tended to favor a restricted form of democratic government that enhanced their own political strength (vis-à-vis the upper class and the state) but also limited the political influence of the lower class. Consequently, countries have achieved comprehensive democracy only when they also have had a politically potent, unionized working class that has pushed for broader political representation and increased social justice.[17]

In summary, democracy tends to flourish best where economic development produces a politically influential and independent bourgeoisie/middle class and where labor unions effectively defend the interests of the working class. When any of these classes are small, weak, or politically dependent on authoritarian actors, such as rural landowners, democracy is less likely to emerge.

Political Culture

In the final analysis, neither a country's level of socioeconomic development nor its class structure can fully explain whether or not it has been able to create or sustain democracy. For example, during the early decades of the twentieth century, Argentina was one of the most affluent nations on Earth, with substantial middle and working classes. Yet, the country failed to develop into a liberal democracy. Instead, it embarked on a half-century of recurring coups and military dictatorships. Subsequently, Singapore, South Korea, and Taiwan retained authoritarian governments long after they had reached the normal social and economic thresholds for democracy.* And, as we have just seen, economic wealth has not brought democracy to petroleum-rich states such as Kuwait and Saudi Arabia. On the other hand, India has sustained democracy for decades despite its extensive poverty and low literacy rate.

Many scholars have argued that, aside from its level of economic development and its class structure, a nation's democratic potential is also influenced by its political culture—that is, its cultural beliefs, norms, and values relating to politics. A country's constitution may call for contested elections, a free press, and the separation of powers, but unless the people value these objectives, constitutional protections are unlikely to have great weight. Some of the most important values needed to sustain democracy include a belief that the vote and other forms of individual and group political participation are important and potentially productive; trust in government institutions and in fellow citizens; tolerance of opposition and dissenting political opinions and beliefs, even when those views are very unpopular; accepting the outcome of free and fair elections as definitive, regardless of who wins; viewing politics as a process that requires compromise; rejecting violent political action or other circumvention of democratic institutions; and committing to democracy as the best form of government, regardless of how well or poorly a particular democratic administration performs. Obviously, there are no countries in which every citizen

---

* South Korea and Taiwan have subsequently democratized, but Singapore still has not.

subscribes to these values or beliefs, but democracy normally is sustainable only if a large portion of the population supports them.

The recent wave of successful democratic transitions has renewed interest in how a country's political culture affects consolidation of democracy. Robert Dahl, a leading democratic theorist, observed that all political systems eventually confront major crises such as economic decline, ethnic violence, or political stalemate. At those times, many political leaders in unconsolidated democracies are tempted to seek authoritarian solutions such as imposing martial law or restricting civil liberties.* If, however, a broad segment of the population (including members of the political and economic elites) shares democratic values, democracy can survive a crisis intact. Dahl stresses two particularly important democratic values: first, that the armed forces and police must willingly submit to the command of democratically elected civilian authorities; second, government and society must tolerate and legally protect dissident political beliefs.

The first value (civilian control of the armed forces) is taken for granted in industrialized democracies, but not in countries such as Guatemala, Thailand, and Bangladesh, where the armed forces have frequently exercised veto power over the policy decisions of elected officials and have often ousted civilian governments. Dahl's second cultural standard—tolerance of dissent—also presents a challenge to many developing nations, where even freely elected governments sometimes silence critics and muzzle opposition leaders. The crucial question, then, says Dahl, is, "How can robust democratic cultures be created in countries where they previously have been largely absent?"[18] He responds that there is no easy answer, but that developing a democratic culture is a gradual process in which socioeconomic modernization and political development need to reinforce each other.

External forces may play a role in shaping political culture. US occupation of Japan, for example, had major effects on that country's postwar political development. On the other hand, US intervention in Iraq and Afghanistan has hardly produced flourishing democracies.

Many African and Asian countries were first introduced to modern politics by the colonial powers that ruled them. Analysis shows that having been a British colony, for example, increased the chances that a country would become a democracy in the postcolonial era, compared to areas that had been colonized by France, Belgium, the Netherlands, Spain, or Portugal. Of course, not all former British colonies became democracies; in fact, during the twentieth century, most of those in Africa and many

---

* Even in a deeply consolidated democracy such as the United States, civil libertarians charge that post-9/11 fear of terrorism led to government infringements on civil liberties, such as eavesdropping, surveillance, and the treatment of prisoners at Guantanamo Bay.

in Asia did not. But was this because Britain more successfully inculcated democratic values in its colonies than did other European powers, or might it be for other reasons? Britain often co-opted local elites during colonial rule, which may have made decolonization less disruptive. It also often established legal and other institutions that survived into the postcolonial era. Was political culture the key factor, or—as institutionalists would suggest—the political, legal, and administrative structures that were put in place, which then shaped societal attitudes? As we can see, establishing causality is difficult.

A country's political culture influences its political system in a number of ways. For example, communities with high levels of mutual tolerance and a politically informed population are more hospitable to democracy than are less tolerant or less knowledgeable societies. But how fixed in a nation's psyche are such values? Is there something inherently more democratic or more authoritarian about Norwegian or Egyptian cultures? Are some religions or philosophies, such as Christianity, more conducive to democracy than, say, Confucianism? Here, scholars disagree strongly. Cultural stereotypes are inherently controversial and often prejudiced. But is it possible that objective analysis could show that countries with certain religions or cultural traditions are more likely to support democratic values, while others are more prone to authoritarianism?

In fact, the data suggests that predominantly Christian nations, particularly Protestant ones, are the most likely to be democratic, even when other causal factors (such as economic development and literacy) are held constant. That is to say, Protestant nations are more likely to be democracies than are countries that have similar levels of economic development but different religious beliefs. "Protestantism is said to foster individual responsibility and is thereby also more skeptical and less fundamentalist in character."[19]

On the other hand, Islamic countries have had a low level of democracy, especially in the Arab states. Some maintain that Islamic beliefs do not readily support democratic institutions because they fail to separate religion and politics.[20] And, when impressive economic growth and increased educational levels during the 1970s and early 1980s were slow to bring democracy to China, Singapore, South Korea, and Taiwan, many experts concluded that cultural (religious) beliefs must have been overriding the positive influences of economic modernization. They argued that Confucian culture promotes rigidly hierarchical societies and encourages excessive obedience to authority, values that are antithetical to democracy.[21]

Not surprisingly, cultural explanations such as these are highly controversial. They are difficult to prove and may simply reflect their proponents' prejudice and ethnocentrism. Catholics may feel uneasy with theories that contrast the traditional strength of democracy in the United States, Canada, and the English-speaking Caribbean with Latin America's authoritarian tradition, leading many analysts to conclude that Catholic values offer less support for democracy than Protestant norms do. Similarly, most Muslims and Confucians reject theories that depict their religions as authoritarian. But do the facts support these hypotheses, however unpleasant some people may find them?

Although Protestant nations are more likely to be democratic than are Buddhist countries and even though democracy has fared poorly in most Islamic nations, it is difficult to ascertain how much these disparities are the result of differing religious values and how much they result from innumerable other historical, economic, and cultural factors that are not easily statistically controlled. We know that several Islamic nations—including Turkey, Lebanon, and, most recently, Indonesia—have achieved some degree of democracy. Moreover, Alfred Stepan and Graeme Robertson demonstrated that while Arab countries, even wealthier ones, have rarely achieved electoral democracy, non-Arab Muslim nations are somewhat more likely to be democracies than a matched sample of non-Muslim countries with comparable levels of economic and social development.[22] Confusing the picture still further, opinion surveys show individual citizens in Arab and Muslim countries are just as favorably oriented toward democracy as a political system as are populations elsewhere in the world.

Furthermore, if Catholic and Islamic religious beliefs inherently promoted nondemocratic values, one would expect that American Catholics and Muslims would be less democratically inclined than their Protestant counterparts are. In the same way, we would predict that Bosnian Muslims would be less committed to democracy than Bosnian Serbs (Christians) and Indian Muslims would be less likely to have democratic values than Hindus. But there is no evidence to support any of these expectations.

Finally, we need to remember that religious beliefs and political cultures are not monolithic within any given society, are capable of change and reinterpretation, and do not permanently mire a country or region in a particular value system. For example, during the Second World War, the Japanese and German political cultures were considered militarily bellicose and authoritarian. Today, however, these countries are highly consolidated democracies. In the United States, intolerant attitudes to certain minorities—while still far too common—have declined sharply over the last generation. According to Gallup surveys, only 25 percent of American whites accepted interracial marriage in 1973, compared to 84 percent in 2013. In 1977, one-third of all Americans believed that the rights of LGBT+ (lesbian, gay, bisexual, transgender) citizens should be restricted, yet by 2015 attitudes had changed to the point that the right of same-sex couples to marry had been upheld by the US Supreme Court. In the case of East Asia, some scholars viewed Confucian values as obstacles—yet

Confucianism has apparently not impeded South Korea's and Taiwan's democratic transitions. Nor did the fact that Catholic societies were less hospitable to democracy in the past hinder their democratic transitions during the closing decades of the twentieth century. Indeed, from Portugal and Spain to Argentina, Brazil, and Mexico, democracy has taken root in Catholic nations that not long ago were depicted as culturally authoritarian. Moreover, in recent decades, the church hierarchy itself has been a pivotal voice for democratic change in Catholic countries such as the Philippines and Brazil. In Tunisia, it was an Islamist political party, Ennahda, that won the country's first free elections. It thereafter played a key role in shepherding the country toward full democratic transition. In short, political cultures appear to be more complex and malleable than once recognized.

We also need to keep in mind that institutions shape culture, just as culture shapes institutions. As Larry Diamond notes, often "democratic culture is as much the product as the cause of effectively functioning democracy."[23] Just as democratic values support democratic consolidation, therefore, sustained democratic institutions and behavior help inculcate democratic values. Many first-time democracies initially lack a healthy democratic political culture. In countries such as Russia (where citizens generally accept Vladimir Putin's authoritarian leadership), this has helped cut short democracy in its infancy. But other nations have overcome this obstacle and the longer they continue democratic practices, the better are their chances of acquiring democratic values. In fact, if a country can sustain it for two decades, democracy is unlikely to ever collapse. For example, Robert Dahl's examination of fifty-two countries in which democracy had failed identified only two (Chile and Uruguay) that had enjoyed democracy for more than twenty years prior to that failure.[24] And even these two exceptions subsequently reinstituted democracy more successfully than did neighboring countries such as Bolivia and Ecuador, which lack comparable democratic traditions.

The Oil Curse

The prevalence of authoritarian regimes in the Middle East and North Africa raises the question of why that region has been so inhospitable to democracy.[25] Many scholars of the region have suggested the answer to this puzzle may lie in political economy rather than political culture. Noting that the economies of many countries in the region are heavily dependent on oil exports, they have argued that abundant petroleum production may boost economies yet have a pernicious influence on the political system. The distorting effects of excessive economic dependence on oil exports (the **oil curse**) have obstructed democracy in countries as diverse as Iran, Russia, and Saudi Arabia. Indeed, almost all countries whose exports and government revenues are dominated by petroleum have been woe-fully unable to democratize.[26] Larry Diamond has identified twenty-three nations—twenty-one of them in the developing world—that have received 60 percent or more of their export earnings from the petroleum sales. Yet, only two of these twenty-one countries have enjoyed a period of liberal democracy in recent decades (Nigeria and Venezuela) and these two have regressed to being only Partly Free.[27]

Why has oil wealth been such an obstacle to democracy? Ana-lysts have suggested a number of reasons. For one thing, currently the petroleum industry in most oil-rich, developing countries is owned or largely controlled by their governments. Consequently, the new oil wealth strengthens the power of the state, providing funds for the armed forces and police and funding large government bureaucracies that offer patronage jobs to government supporters. Also, these countries do not produce the independent bourgeoisie that has historically been crucial for democracy. Similarly, the middle class—another bulwark of liberal democracy—also fails to challenge state power because so many of its members have jobs in the government bureaucracy (including the state petroleum company). And, with little industrialization, a large portion of the working class is employed in the oil industry, making them depen-dent on the state and, like the middle class and bourgeoisie, unlikely to challenge state power.

Armed with substantial oil and gas revenues, these petroleum regimes (**rentier states**, so called because they survive off the economic rents from oil wealth) can lower taxes and offer private companies and the general public inexpensive services and goods such as subsidized credit, food, and housing. Although these obviously have their attractions, the consequence is that "people become clients and not citizens," that is, they turn into virtual wards of the state who are not active in the political system.[28] With low taxes and an array of government benefits, the average citizen has little incentive to question government corruption, mismanagement, or repres-sion. To reverse a battle cry of the American Revolution, "No taxation—no representation."

Another curse of oil dependency is massive corruption. Expanding bureaucracies and state enterprises give politicians opportunities to sell jobs. At the same time, businessmen seeking subsidized financial credit from the government and those in the hunt for state contracts routinely bribe public officials. High-level government officials often plunder the national treasury. In the worst example, a former military dictator of Nige-ria, General Sani Abacha, is believed to have stolen some $3–$4 billion of government funds prior to his death. Indeed, according to the watchdog organization Transparency International, less developed, oil-centered coun-tries (most of them in the Middle East and Africa) have particularly high rates of government corruption. All of these factors—heavy concentration of economic power in the hands of the state, clientelism, bourgeois and middle-class dependency, and corruption—have effectively impeded the growth of democracy.

DEMOCRATIC CONSOLIDATION EXPLAINED

It is important to recall that although the breadth of democratic transitions in the developing world has been impressive, political change can occur in both directions. Many countries that have achieved electoral or liberal democracy have seen their new governments fail, followed by a return to authoritarian rule. In 2012, a military coup in Mali ended twenty years of democratic government. Recent examples of renewed authoritarianism include Burundi, Bangladesh, and Thailand. Between 1980 and 2000, democracy collapsed in twenty-six countries, though a number of these (such as Ecuador) subsequently returned to being free or partly free.[29] What makes democracy endure or falter? Which of the new democracies have the qualities needed to consolidate democracy?

To answer these questions, Adam Przeworski and his associates analyzed data for 135 countries over a forty-year period. Democracy, they found, is most fragile in poor countries (with per capita incomes of less than $1,000 in constant dollars), and it becomes more stable as national income rises: "Above $6,000 [per-capita real income], democracies are impregnable and can be expected to live forever; no democratic system has ever fallen in a country where per-capita income exceeds $6,055 (Argentina's level in 1976)."[30] Several factors explain why richer democracies are more likely to last. For one thing, they normally have a crucial foundation for democratic government—high educational levels.* For another, class conflict over the distribution of economic rewards is typically less intense in more affluent societies.

Contrary to what many political scientists had believed, Przeworski et al. also found that the faster a nation's economy grows, the more likely it is to sustain democracy. Conversely, democracy is less likely to survive in countries suffering economic decline, high inflation rates, or other forms of economic crisis. However, important as domestic economic factors are, the authors discovered that international political conditions exert a more powerful influence on democratic survivability. Specifically,

---

* In other words, countries that are more economically advanced normally have higher literacy and education rates, and countries with higher literacy rates are more likely to be democratic. There are several petroleum-producing countries (such as Saudi Arabia and Angola) that, although wealthy, do not have particularly high literacy rates. None of these are democracies.

the more prevalent democratic government becomes in other nations, the more likely any particular less developed country is to sustain its own democracy, regardless of its per capita income, literacy rate, or economic growth rate. In other words, as many analysts had suspected, democracy is contagious.

Other scholars have noted that developing and maintaining effective political institutions—including representative and responsible political parties, a broad array of interest groups, a representative and influential legislature, a strong but not unlimited executive branch, an honest and independent judicial system—are absolutely critical for sustaining stable and effective democracy. Too often, judicial systems lack independence from the executive branch, do not have adequate legal training, and are corrupt. Consolidating democracies must strengthen their judiciary systems, so that they can stand up to power-hungry presidents or prime ministers and so that court decisions are respected by the electorate. A related problem in many new and reestablished democracies is executive-branch dominance over the national legislature. In Latin America, Russia, and elsewhere, democratically elected presidents have sometimes interpreted their electoral victories to mean that the voters had delegated absolute authority to them. For example, even though they were initially elected democratically, once in office, Presidents Carlos Menem (Argentina) and Alberto Fujimori (Peru) ran roughshod over their nation's congress and court system.

HOW DO DEMOCRACIES PERFORM? PUBLIC POLICY COMPARED

Some of the benefits of democracy are obvious: protecting personal freedom and holding governments accountable to the governed, to name but two. Nonetheless, academics have long debated whether democratic governments also better provide for the economic and social welfare of their citizens. As we noted earlier, during the closing decades of the twentieth century, many international agencies, journalists, and scholars maintained that certain dictatorships—in countries such as Chile, Indonesia, Singapore, and South Korea—had imposed the efficiency and discipline necessary to generate rapid economic growth.[31] The dramatic economic growth these authoritarian regimes produced into the 1990s was often compared to the less impressive performance at that time of democratic governments in countries such as India and Uruguay.

However, the passage of time and a closer examination of more than one hundred developing nations have dispelled such claims. Those who have insisted that authoritarian rule is likely to produce economic development have usually based their argument on the accomplishments of a few successful authoritarian cases. But for every authoritarian regime that has had an impressive economic record—including Chile, China, South Korea, Singapore, and Taiwan—there were far more cases of authoritarian governments with disastrous economic records—such as Myanmar, Haiti, North Korea, Tajikistan, and Zimbabwe. In fact, "between 1960 and 2000, 95 percent of the world's worst economic performances . . . were overseen by nondemocratic governments."[32] Furthermore, prior to its market-oriented reforms begun in the late 1980s, China's communist regime had a much more erratic record of economic growth. Chile's rate of growth was generally strong under its military dictatorship, but growth improved when the country restored democracy. Finally, in recent decades, the once-stagnant economy of India—the world's largest democracy—became one of the most dynamic in the world.

Analyzing annual economic growth data from more than 150 countries during each year from 1960 to 2001, Halperin, Siegle, and Weinstein compared the performance of democratic nations with those of autocracies (dictatorships). They found that in every one of the more than forty years studied, the democratic nations as a group grew faster than the autocracies. Furthermore, "citizens of democracies live longer, healthier lives, on average, than those in autocracies [with comparable per capita incomes]."[33] It is true that when they examined only the world's poorest nations, they observed no difference in the economic growth rate of democracies versus dictatorship. Still, even among the poorest countries, economic growth was less volatile in democracies than in autocracies (less subject to sharp ups and downs).

Similarly, Dani Rodrik used regression analysis to examine data for more than eighty countries over a span of twenty-four years (1970–94). He found that there was no appreciable difference between the long-term economic growth rates of democracies and authoritarian governments. But, democracies outperformed authoritarian regimes on several other important economic indicators. Their economies were less volatile, were more predictable, paid better wages to workers, and could "handle adverse shocks [like the Asian financial crisis or severe jumps in oil prices] much better."[34] Finally, another recent study comparing democracies with nondemocracies found that democratic countries spent more on public education, had higher school enrollments, higher literacy rates, and greater public access to health-care services.[35]

Democratic governments are not necessarily superior in all areas of governance. In theory, freely elected government officials should be less corrupt than authoritarian administrators because they are held accountable in the next election. But in countries that have simultaneously switched from command economies to capitalism, in nations that have enormous sources of natural-resource wealth (such as oil revenues) linked to the government, and in countries with a historical tradition of corruption, democratization may not improve government honesty and may actually make things worse. Thus, for example, Russia's transition to capitalism and to democracy in the 1990s opened up the floodgates for corruption. In Cambodia, the communist regime has been replaced by a government of competing "mafias."

IMPROVING THE QUALITY OF DEMOCRACY

More than three decades after the start of the Third Wave, its reach has become far broader than the previous two waves. In all, the number of countries categorized as "free," "partly free," and "not free" has remained fairly steady since the turn of the century.* As noted earlier, democracy is now widely accepted as a desirable form of government.

On the other hand, as noted earlier, Freedom House has worried about the dangers of democratic slippage. Noted democracy scholar Larry Diamond has gone so far as to warn of an ongoing **democratic recession,** characterized by declining faith in democratic institutions in many countries, and the continued prevalence of illiberal and hybrid regimes in which elections mask more authoritarian political dynamics.[36] In many developing countries, democratic governments have failed to meet the needs of their citizens. Free and fair elections, improved civil liberties, and civilian command over the armed forces are important achievements. But too often the public has been disappointed by the failures of democratic rule: continued or increased economic inequality, an unjust judicial system, and widespread corruption (which may actually be less pervasive than during authoritarian rule, but is now more visible because of a free press).

Consequently, many political scientists have turned their attention from studying the consolidation of democracy to examining the quality of democracy and are looking for ways to improve it.[37] Public opinion surveys in both advanced industrial democracies and developing world democracies have indicated that citizens are becoming more distrustful of government and suspicious of political parties and politicians. Frequently, they consider government officials corrupt and self-serving. Thus, any search for higher-quality democratic governments has two important objectives: first, it is a moral imperative (fair, effective, and honest governments are obviously a desirable objective); second, more effective and honest democratic governments normally increase support for democracy and, thereby, increase democracy's longevity. Slightly modifying Larry Diamond and Leonardo Morlino's model, we can evaluate the quality of democracy in

---

* That is because the number of countries that ceased to be free has about equaled the number of countries that became free.

terms of seven dimensions, which, in turn, can be grouped into three broad categories:[38]

1. Procedural Dimensions. The procedures used to elect government officials and the procedures that public officials use to govern must be honest, fair, and equitable. These procedures can be divided into four categories:

    a. Participation. All (or nearly all) adult citizens must have the right to vote as well as to participate in the political system in other ways. Powerful groups should not intimidate the poor or ethnic minorities about participating. A politically aware citizenry should not allow apathy to restrict their own participation.

    b. Competition. There should be free and fair elections between competing political parties, and the incumbent party should not have any built-in advantage in gaining access to state funds or to the media. The electoral system should not give any party a built-in advantage.

    c. Accountability. A democratic electoral system must guarantee that government officials are fairly elected. But officials must also be held accountable for their actions between elections. Vertical accountability refers to procedures that allow citizens or independent groups to challenge or criticize a government official's behavior. Horizontal accountability refers to the ability of one government body to check the power of another branch, such as the Supreme Court overruling a decision by the president or the parliament removing a prime minister.

    d. The Rule of Law. The legal system must apply equally to all citizens and all laws must be publicly known and clear. The judiciary must be neutral and independent.

2. Substantive Dimensions. Beyond adhering to proper procedures, quality democracies must pursue policies that advance:

    a. Respect for Civil Liberties and the Pursuit of Freedom. This includes respect for individual liberty, security, and privacy; freedom of information, expression, and religion; and due process.

    b. Reductions in Political, Economic, and Social Inequalities. In order to attain political equality, where there is substantial social and economic inequality, governments need to reduce sharp income gaps. Scholars such as Terry Karl and Dietrich Rueschemeyer maintain that political equality and democracy have been difficult to achieve in the face of glaring income inequalities in

Latin America and parts of Africa.[39] Different analysts, however, disagree on how much equality is possible or perhaps even desirable.

3. Result Dimensions. This final category includes only a single dimension—responsiveness. A democratically responsive government is one in which "the democratic process induces the government to form and implement policies that the people want."[40] In order to achieve this, there needs to be a stable political party system, with parties that offer coherent and distinguishable programs.

CONCLUSION

Too frequently, democratic transitions have produced unfulfilled economic aspirations, corrupt governments, and widespread dissatisfaction with government institutions. Hence, even though most citizens in the developing countries have an abstract preference for democracy as a form of government, many of them are cynical about the performance of democratic regimes. In a 2013 survey of eighteen Latin American nations by Latinobarómetro, 56 percent of those polled agree with the abstract statement that "democracy is preferable to any other form of government," but only 40 percent were satisfied with the actual way that democracy was working in their own country.[41]

A recent Afrobarometer survey of thirty-four sub-Saharan African nations revealed that despite the scarcity of democratic governments in that continent, about 70 percent of those surveyed agreed that "democracy is preferable to any other form of government." But only about half considered their own country a democracy. A similar percentage favored limits to presidential terms.

If the citizens of current democracies become more critical of their government's performance in the future, it does not necessarily mean these countries will revert to authoritarian rule. In countries where the political and economic elites continue to support democratic regimes, those governments may be able to survive considerable grassroots discontent. Furthermore, even if there is considerable support for a return to military rule, the armed forces may not be interested. In fact, in many countries, most notably in Latin America, the failures of recent military governments caused the armed forces so much internal discord and loss of prestige that the generals were reluctant to seize power again. Moreover, despite growing citizen discontent with democratic performance, in only a small number of cases have many people supported revolutionary or other authoritarian alternatives. Still, in many fragile democracies, the elites' commitment to democracy is soft and should there be substantial mass discontent over the government's performance, those democratic regimes might collapse.

To date, it appears that even among the many inhabitants of the developing countries who have been dissatisfied with their government's performance under democracy, most have unwittingly accepted Winston Churchill's argument that "democracy is the worst form of government except for all the others that have been tried." However, without future improvement in social and economic conditions, democratic governments may cease commanding widespread support. In Latin America, where income inequality is higher than in any region of the world, the gap between the "haves" and "have-nots" has widened since its transition to democracy. Likewise, income inequality has soared in postcommunist Eastern Europe and the former Soviet Union. From Colombia to the Philippines and from Pakistan to Peru, the poor suffer from highly unequal land and income distribution, pervasive poverty, rising crime rates, inadequate public health service, and corrupt police and judicial systems. Until such injustices are addressed, democracy will remain incomplete and often precarious.

> **Practice and Review Online at**
> http://textbooks.rowman.com/handelman9e

KEY TERMS

Arab Spring
civil society
class structure
democratic consolidation
democratic recession
democratic transition
demonstration effects
electoral democracy

hybrid regime
illiberal democracy
liberal democracy
oil curse
rentier state
semi-democracy
substantive democracy
third wave (democratization)

DISCUSSION QUESTIONS

1. Discuss the differences between electoral democracy, liberal democracy, and substantive democracy. In what way does each of these definitions provide a useful measure of democracy in a range of countries?
2. In what ways do economic factors shape the prospects for democratic transition and consolidation?
3. Discuss the arguments for and against political culture playing an important role in democratization.
4. How does the "Arab Spring" of 2010–11 illustrate the difficulty of getting from democratic transitions to democratic consolidations?

NOTES

1. Samuel P. Huntington, *The Third Wave: Democratization in the Late Twentieth Century* (Norman, OK: University of Oklahoma Press, 1991).
2. Data from World Values Survey website, http://www.worldvaluessurvey.org.
3. These figures come from Freedom House (discussed later in the chapter).
4. There has been a long, ongoing debate over what conditions, and how many of those conditions, a country must meet in order to be called a democracy. The definition offered in this textbook draws from several sources, including Philippe C. Schmitter and Terry Lynn Karl, "What Democracy Is and Is Not," *Journal of Democracy* 2, no. 2 (Summer 1991): 75–88; Robert A. Dahl, *Democracy and Its Critics* (New Haven, CT: Yale University Press, 1989).
5. Juan Linz and Alfred Stepan, "Toward Consolidated Democracies," in *Consolidating the Third Wave Democracies*, eds. Larry Diamond, et al. (Washington, DC: The Johns Hopkins University Press, 1997).
6. The statistics cited here are drawn from Ethan B. Kapstein and Nathan Converse, *The Fate of Young Democracies* (New York, NY: Cambridge University

Press, 2008), 39–40. We have adjusted Kapstein and Converse's statistics to remove European countries.

7. Quoted in Morton H. Halperin, Joseph T. Siegle, and Michael M. Weinstein, *The Democracy Advantage* (New York, NY: Routledge and the Council on Foreign Relations, 2005), 25.

8. Larry Diamond, "Introduction: In Search of Consolidation," in *Consolidating the Third Wave Democracies*, Volume 1, eds. Larry Diamond et al (Baltimore: Johns Hopkins University Press, 1997), xv.

9. Huntington, *The Third Wave*, 271.

10. Seymour Martin Lipset, *Political Man* (Garden City, NY: Anchor Books, 1960).

11. Dietrich Rueschemeyer, Evelyne Huber Stephens, and John D. Stephens, *Capitalist Development and Democracy* (Chicago, IL: University of Chicago Press, 1992), 14.

12. Philips Cutright, "National Political Development: Measurement and Analysis," *American Sociological Review* 28, no. 2 (April 1963): 253–64.

13. Axel Hadenius, *Democracy and Development* (New York, NY: Cambridge University Press, 1992).

14. UNESCO Institute for Statistics, May 2013.

15. Huntington, *Political Order in Changing Societies* (New Haven, CT: Yale University Press, 1968). On the rise of repressive authoritarian regimes in Latin America's most industrialized nations, see Guillermo O'Donnell, *Modernization and Bureaucratic Authoritarianism* (Berkeley, CA: Institute of International Studies, 1973).

16. Barrington Moore Jr., *The Social Origins of Dictatorship and Democracy* (Boston, MA: Beacon Press, 1955), 418.

17. Rueschemeyer, Huber Stephens, and Stephens, *Capitalist Development and Democracy*.

18. Robert Dahl, "Development and Democratic Culture," in *Consolidating the Third Wave Democracies* (Baltimore: Johns Hopkins University Press, 1997), 34.

19. Hadenius, *Democracy and Development*, 118–19. Of course, there are many branches of the Protestant religion and some of them are quite fundamentalist.

20. Amr G. E. Sabet, *Islam and the Political* (Ann Arbor, MI: Pluto Press, 2008), 251–52.

21. Samuel P. Huntington, *The Clash of Civilizations and the Remaking of World Order* (New York, NY: Simon & Schuster, 1996).

22. Alfred Stepan with Graeme B. Robertson, "An 'Arab' More than 'Muslim' Electoral Gap," *Journal of Democracy* 14, no. 3 (July 2003): 30–44.

23. Larry Diamond, "Three Paradoxes of Democracy," in *The Global Resurgence of Democracy*, eds. Larry Diamond and Marc F. Plattner (Baltimore, MD: The Johns Hopkins University Press, 1993), 104.

24. Robert A. Dahl, "The Newer Democracies: From the Time of Triumph to the Time of Troubles," in *After Authoritarianism: Democracy or Disorder?* ed. Daniel N. Nelson (Westport, CT: Greenwood Press, 1995), 7.

25. For more on this debate, see Rex Brynen, Pete Moore, Bassel Salloukh, and Marie-Joëlle Zahar, *Beyond the Arab String: Authoritarianism and Democracy in the Arab World* (Boulder, CO: Lynne Rienner Publishers, 2012).

26. Michael Ross, "Does Oil Hinder Democracy?" *World Politics* 53 (April 2001): 328–56.

27. Larry Diamond, *The Spirit of Democracy* (New York, NY: Times Books, 2008), 74–79.

28. Ibid., 75.

29. Halperin, Siegle, and Weinstein, *The Democracy Advantage*, 71.

30. Adam Przeworski et al., "What Makes Democracies Endure?" in *Consolidating The Third Wave Democracies* (Baltimore: Johns Hopkins University Press, 1997), 297.

31. See, for example, M. G. Quibria, *Growth and Poverty: Lessons from the Asian Economic Miracle* (Asian Development Bank, Working Paper No. 33, 2002); more broadly, Huntington's *Political Order in Changing Societies* argues that countries in the early stages of development often need authoritarian government.

32. Halperin, Siegle, and Weinstein, *The Democracy Advantage*, 13.

33. Ibid., 35. See also, 29–43. Data were collected from the Polity IV project, an interuniversity project that collects a wide range of data on all of the world's nations with populations exceeding five hundred thousand. Polity ranks each country on a scale of 1–10 based on its degree of democracy.

34. Dani Rodrik, *Democracy and Economic Performance* (Cambridge, MA: Unpublished Paper, Harvard University, December 14, 1997), 2.

35. Iñias Macías-Aymar, "Does Income Inequality Limit Democratic Quality?" in *An Unequal Democracy?* eds. Carlo Benetti and Fernando Carillo-Flórez (Washington, WA: Inter-American Development Bank, 2005), 84–85.

36. Larry Diamond, "Facing Up to the Democratic Recession," *Journal of Democracy* 26, no. 1 (January 2015).

37. For example, Maxwell Cameron and Eric Hershberg, eds., *Latin America's Left Turns: Politics, Policies and Trajectories of Change* (Boulder, CO: Lynne Rienner, 2010).

38. This section is based on Larry Diamond and Leonardo Morlino, eds., *Assessing the Quality of Democracy* (Baltimore, MD: The Johns Hopkins University Press, 2005). We have combined their "vertical and horizontal accountability" into one category.

39. Terry Lynn Karl, "Economic Inequality and Democratic Instability," *Journal of Democracy* 11 (January 2000): 149–56; Dietrich Rueschemeyer, "Addressing Inequality," in *Assessing the Quality of Democracy* (Baltimore: Johns Hopkins University Press, 2005), 41–61.

40. G. Bingham Powell Jr., "The Chain of Responsiveness," in *Assessing the Quality of Democracy*, 62.

41. *The Economist*, November 2, 2013.

4

Corruption as an Obstacle to Development

Brazilians protesting government corruption in March 2016. President Dilma Rousseff was impeached the following August. While democracy in Brazil has allowed citizens to mobilize against wrongdoing, corruption has proven to be deeply rooted in the political system and difficult to eradicate. *Source*: Wilson Dias/ Agência Brasil.

ON AUGUST 31, 2016, THE BRAZILIAN SENATE, having found President Dilma Rousseff guilty of breaking budget laws, voted to impeach her and remove her from office. The irony of her impeachment was that Rousseff's illegal activities—using funds from government banks to cover budget deficits—had not stolen any funds for herself, while a large number of the senators who voted to remove her were knee-deep in self-enriching corruption.

Numerous officials of the national oil and gas company, Petrobras, have been convicted of taking substantial bribes in return for awarding lucrative contracts to private companies. High-ranking government and Petrobras officials took millions in bribes and kickbacks. Among these was former president Luiz Inácio Lula da Silva, who was convicted of receiving a beach-front apartment in exchange for helping an engineering company secure contracts with Petrobras.

At the time of President Rousseff's impeachment, 60 percent of the members of Brazilian Congress had been accused of criminal activities, including bribery and corruption, illegal deforestation, even kidnapping and murder.[1] Indeed, the man who replaced Rousseff as president, Michel Temer (Rousseff's vice president), for many years had been suspected of corruption when he was a congressman. And less than a year after he took office, a leading Brazilian newspaper disclosed secretly recorded tapes of Temer discussing hush money to be paid to a Brazilian businessman in return for his silence in a major anti-corruption investigation.

Government corruption, like private-sector corruption, blemishes most, if not all, countries in the world, both rich and poor. Thus, while countries, such as the United States, enjoy relatively honest political systems, even the most affluent and politically advanced nations have notable examples of borderline or blatant corruption. On the whole, levels of political corruption tend to be lowest in advanced industrial democracies, with stable political institutions (including a strong legal system), higher levels of literacy and education, and political cultures that value government honesty.

Transparency International (TI) publishes an annual *Corruption Perception Index* that rates most of the world's political systems according to experts and opinion surveys. Its latest annual index, published in early 2018, rated New Zealand and Denmark as the least corrupt countries in the world. Singapore was the only developing country in the top ten, and even it is a country with a well-developed economy and strong public administration. The United States ranked 16th, the United Arab Emirates 21st, Uruguay 23rd, and Chile 26th.[2]

At the other end of the TI ratings, none of the one hundred most corrupt countries are high-income economies. It is clear that economic and political underdevelopment are major contributors to government corruption—and, equally, that corruption itself hampers development in many important ways. Indeed, the issue highlights the complex interplay of politics and economics that is at the very heart of the development process. In the discussion which follows, we will look at the types, costs, and causes of corruption in the developing world. We will also look at how this scourge can be combatted.

DEFINITION AND TYPES OF CORRUPTION

While corruption at the top of government draws the most headlines, **corruption** exists at all levels of public life. This includes mayors who demand payoffs from construction firms seeking contracts to build municipal public works; building inspectors who take bribes to overlook safety violations in newly built buildings; Chinese village officials who confiscate peasant farm plots and sell them to real estate developers; and school principals who demand bribes from parents trying to get their children into better schools. What all of these examples have in common is that they involve government officials (from governors to traffic police) using their positions for private gain, rather than the public good. Corrupt officials may be elected officials (including politicians in non-democracies who have won sham elections) at any level, or they may be government administrators, bureaucrats, or civil servants.

Most commonly the "private gains" which public officials accrue involve monetary gains: taking or extorting bribes; or skimming government funds (such as appropriating millions for building roads or housing, when only half of that amount is actually spent and the rest is siphoned off). In other instances, the rewards may be political, such as votes as when political candidates reward voters with gifts, or political leaders who bribe legislators to vote positively on important legislation.[3]

Corruption can occur at all levels of government. Most media coverage of political corruption, and much of the scholarly analysis, focuses on higher-ranking government officials, such as the Brazilian corruption scandals discussed earlier in the chapter. However, average citizens may also experience every day, lower-level corruption as they seek the most elemental and important government services such as medical care, police protection, and education for their children. Here the bribe-takers are not powerful elites but police officers, bureaucrats, and others. This sort of endemic corruption is not simply the illegal behavior of a few greedy individuals, but rather points to serious structural problems of governance, public administration, and underdevelopment.

While most developing nations suffer from some degree of political corruption, such illicit activity is far more likely to be exposed and punished in relatively more politically developed countries such as Brazil, South Korea, and India than it is in the least developed countries such as Afghanistan, South Sudan, Libya, and North Korea.

High-Level Corruption

For more than one-half century the South Korean national government has worked extremely closely with big business in economic policy-making. In the 1960s, the military regime of General Park Chung-hee (South Korean president 1963–79) decided that Korea, then a relatively poor country still recovering from the devastation of the Korean War (1950–53), could best advance economically through close cooperation between the government and the nation's largest industrial corporations.*

The government enacted economic policies—including protective tariffs for major manufacturers, low-cost government loans, and favorable taxes—that would allow the country's emerging corporate giants to flourish. These policies helped generate huge, interlocking corporations, known as *chaebols*.† In return, these conglomerates have followed government economic directives such as concentrating on manufactured exports.

A *chaebol* is a family-controlled corporation that includes dozens of companies in a wide range of activities. For example, Samsung, headed by the Lee family for three generations, consists of fifty-eight interlocking subsidiaries. Another giant, LG, makes smartphones, televisions, electronic components, chemicals, and fertilizers, while also owning professional baseball and basketball teams. Hyundai not only manufactures the Hyundai and Kia automobiles, but also makes elevators, services container shipping, and manages a chain of hotels and department stores. In all, the ten largest Korean chaebols account for about 80 percent of the country's gross domestic product (GDP). Just one of those giants, Samsung Electronics, a world leader in the manufacture of televisions and smartphones (as a major supplier of parts for the Apple iPhone), by itself accounts for one-fifth of South Korea's exports.

While close ties between the Korean government and the chaebols have been a key contributor to the country's astonishing economic growth (it now is the world's 13th largest economy), it has also opened the doors to widespread, high-level corruption. Six of the ten giant conglomerates have had leaders who have been convicted of white-collar crimes, often without subsequent punishment. For example, Lee Kun, the long-time chair of Samsung, has twice been convicted of bribery and tax evasion, but has never served a day in jail, being pardoned by the government both times.‡ In early 2017, his son, Lee Jae-yong—Samsung's vice chair, but the effective leader of the company since his father's illness a few years earlier—was arrested on charges of bribing the nation's president, Park Geun-hye. Park had been

---

* The war started with North Korea's invasion of the South in June 1950 and subsequently brought the United States and allied United Nations forces to defend South Korea, while the North Koreans were joined by the Chinese military.

† The word *chaebol* roughly translates as "rich clan."

‡ In Korea, as in most East Asian nations, the family name comes before the given name.

impeached by the National Assembly (the country's parliament) in December 2016 and was removed from office three months later. In short order, she was put on trial and formally charged with abuse of power, bribery, and coercion.*

In perhaps the world's most infamous individual case of high-level corruption, Nigeria's General Sani Abacha is believed to have stolen at least $1 billion and likely over $4 billion during his military dictatorship (1993–98). Much of his ill-gotten gains came from skimming the military's budget, which undoubtedly weakened the armed forces in the fight against Islamist terrorists (Boko Haram). "Nigerian authorities believe[d] that up to $450 million [was] deposited by Abacha, his family, and associates in some of London's leading banks."[4] Only after the ouster from office and then death of Abacha did the Nigeria government begin to recoup some of that money. Abacha's son, Mohammed,

> admitted that his father had given him $700m in cash over a period of two years in bags and boxes. At times, he said, he had up to $100m in his house in the capital Abuja. A few weeks after Abacha's death, his widow was detained while trying to depart for Saudi Arabia with 38 suitcases full of foreign currency.[5]

While Nigeria's return to democracy may have ended such egregious cases of corruption, it by no means brought an end to widespread illicit activity. Once corruption has become part of politics and business, it is difficult to clean up.

A recent government audit indicated that over $15 billion of the funds that the state oil giant, the Nigerian National Petroleum Corporation (NNPC), was supposed to turn over to the central government in 2014 was missing.[6] For many years, government oil profits have been siphoned off by NNPC officials, state governors, and other government officials. In addition, the company's failure to properly maintain or protect oil pipelines has meant that an estimated 150,000 barrels of oil are siphoned from those lines daily. While some of that oil is stolen by average citizens, the vast majority is stolen by criminal gangs that sell it abroad. Although oil revenues account for an estimated 75 percent of the nation's GNP, no accurate records exist on how much petroleum is actually produced.

While current Nigerian president Muhammadu Buhari was elected on a pledge to clean up the NNPC and other government institutions, it is not

---

* It should be noted that the Park scandal emerged in the headlines because South Korea is a relatively open society with a free press, independent judiciary, and political system that allows mass anti-corruption demonstrations. The country ranks in the middle of TI's corruption index (51st) and, with the exception of Singapore and Hong Kong, ranks as the least corrupt government in Asia.

clear that he will be able to do so. A number of high-level officials, both within the NNPC and in other branches of government, have been arrested, but recent Nigerian history suggests only a few offenders will be convicted. Some officials enjoy legal or de facto immunity. Judges are routinely paid off. In all, the web of government corruption is so widespread that most experts doubt whether current efforts will be able to scratch far beneath the surface.

The tiny African country of Equatorial Guinea (with a population of only 1.2 million) is the continent's third-largest oil producer. Consequently, its per capita income of nearly $39,000 is the highest in Africa and 45th in the world, just behind Japan and ahead of New Zealand, Spain, and Italy.[7] Yet, most of its population lives in abject poverty. Indeed, the country has a Human Development Index (HDI) ranking 135th in the world (behind Egypt and India) and 20 percent of its children die before the age of five. The reason for the discrepancy between the country's natural wealth and the dire poverty of its population is that most of the oil wealth is stolen by its president Teodoro Obiang, who has ruled the country with an iron hand since he seized power in a coup against his uncle in 1979.

Since the country's oil boom began in the 1990s, he, his family, and his cronies have accumulated most of their country's wealth. In 2006, *Forbes*, a leading American business magazine, estimated Obiang's personal wealth at approximately $600 million, and it has undoubtedly grown since then. In 2017, French authorities began a corruption trial of Obiang's son, Teodorin, who, despite being Equatorial Guinea's vice president, had spent much of his time in Paris and other European locations. He is accused of stealing $115 million while serving as his country's minister of agriculture (2004–11). Previously, Dutch, Swiss, and French authorities had seized portions of his holdings, including his 800-foot yacht and a Paris mansion worth some $200 million.

Corruption in Everyday Life

While periodic exposures of high-level government corruption get national and international attention, more infuriating to average citizens (especially the poor) are the day-to-day bribes they must pay to policemen, low-level government bureaucrats, and service providers.

In many developing nations, police routinely demand bribes in simple shakedowns or in return for "protection." One of the authors had the opportunity to witness this type of police corruption, while living for a few months in Guadalajara, Mexico. When arranging to rent a house, the owner noted that, at the beginning of every month, a local policeman would come to our home to take payment for "protecting our home against theft." When that policeman arrived at our door the next month, he looked somewhat amused when I initially did not remember our landlord's instructions. Both of us were relieved when I quickly remembered the reason for his visit and paid him the designated monthly "contribution." I was well aware that if I did not make the payment, my home would surely be burglarized in short order. On another occasion, I stood on a busy intersection in the downtown area and watched as an officer routinely flagged down vehicles for an imagined traffic offense. Rather than write a ticket, the officer accepted a cash payment from the driver. During the half-hour that I watched this happening, the only cars to pass the intersection without making a payoff were those that drove through while the policeman was occupied taking his bribe from another driver. Since police are almost always paid a low salary, throughout the developing world, the temptation to extort money is often irresistible.

In many developing countries, average citizens must pay bribes before receiving the most basic government services. For example, in India, patients at many public hospitals or clinics must bribe doctors before receiving treatment. Since middle- and upper-class Indians pay for private medical care, these bribes fall on the shoulders of people who are least able to afford them, the poor. In Peru, deprived villagers routinely have to bribe local officials before their children can be enrolled in school. In Kenya, "getting a place at a good school; getting permission to build on land you own; starting a business: all can involve paying people off," which "makes life miserable for ordinary people."[8]

The precise extent and scale of such everyday corruption is impossible to know. But, in a 2014 TI survey of twenty-eight sub-Saharan African countries, 22 percent of respondents reported having paid a bribe in the previous year—a number that rose to 43 percent in Nigeria and 69 percent in Liberia.[9] It should be noted, however, that several African nations had low levels of corruption. In the TI survey, only 1 percent of the respondents in Botswana and Mauritius indicated that they had paid a bribe in the previous year. Indeed, these countries fare better on TI's corruption index than some much more developed countries like Italy, Greece, and Hungary. According to a similar study by the World Justice Project, 43 percent of respondents in South Asia reported having paid a bribe to a police officer, 25 percent to secure a permit, and 10 percent to access hospital services. The rate of bribe paying varied substantially, being much more common in Afghanistan, Pakistan, India, and Bangladesh than it was in Sri Lanka or Nepal.[10]

In some instances, rather than being forced to pay a bribe, average citizens receive a bribe or other rewards as when candidates for office, political parties, or political machines give voters gifts to support their candidacy or candidates. Where there are organized political machines, individuals who campaign or organize for the winning candidates may be rewarded with government jobs for which they are not particularly qualified.

THE COSTS OF CORRUPTION

The most immediate cost of corruption is its injustice. Rather than awarding government services such as medical care at public clinics and hospitals to those in greatest danger, treatment goes to those able to pay bribes. Those students whose parents are able to pay the biggest bribes, rather than those with the most academic ability, gain entrance to the best schools. Thousands of Chinese peasants whose plots of land are on potential urban development sites, such as shopping malls, have their land seized (for little or no compensation) by local Communist Party officials, who then sell them to developers at a huge profit. Similarly, even though developing economies need innovative, small and mid-sized businesses, talented entrepreneurs are often unable to start or maintain them because the bribes needed to secure permits and operating licenses are too high. In other cases, government officials monopolize certain business activities and keep competitors out.

At the same time, widespread corruption causes citizens to be cynical of their entire political system, making them less likely to vote, contact their political representatives, run for office, or otherwise participate in politics. Union, business, and farmers associations are also likely to be corrupted, reducing civil society's ability to hold public officials, police, and civil servants accountable. As citizens come to expect little from bureaucrats and elected officials, their cynicism becomes a self-fulfilling prophesy, since honest people are uninterested in government service.

Widespread corruption also extracts a tremendous toll on economic development. Businesses paying substantial bribes have to divert funds that could be used for further investment or for improving the salaries of managers and other employees. Managers of large government corporations make decisions based on what can enrich themselves, rather than on what is best for their enterprises.

Besides these systemic evils, corruption can also greatly harm many specific areas of government policy. For example, by reducing the quality and quantity of health care, corruption often negatively affects public health. Government officials and private contractors may collude to skim off funds that should have been spent building public clinics and hospitals. In other cases, suppliers may bribe health officials so that they can provide less medicine than they are paid to deliver. In an exhaustive analysis of child mortality in 178 countries, Matthieu Hanf et al. found that—even when other relevant factors, such as per capita income and educational levels, are controlled for—"more than 140,000 annual children deaths [world-wide] could be indirectly attributed to corruption."[11]

At the same time, many of the buildings that have collapsed during earthquakes in developing countries have either been built by corrupt government agencies that skimped on proper construction or in privately owned buildings where the owners had bribed government construction inspectors. For example, China has experienced some of the world's highest number of earthquake deaths in recent years. While many factors account for these grim statistics (not least of which is the country's dense population), government corruption added to the toll. The 2008 earthquake in Sichuan province killed over 69,000 people.

> Following the [that] quake, relatives of the victims wondered aloud why the town's schools had collapsed while the sturdier government buildings remained standing. The uproar—soon squelched by the government—touched upon a number of broader controversies in China: government privilege, official corruption, and the yawning gap between rich and poor. . . . [The problem is particularly acute when schools are built in impoverished neighborhoods.] Contractors feel pressure to complete projects ahead of schedule and cut corners. Builders substitute cheap materials in order to cut costs. And then, you have the omnipresent specter of bribery and corruption.[12]

Corruption—usually involving builders who have bribed government officials to evade construction codes—has also contributed to earthquake high death tolls in Haiti, Turkey, and dozens of other developing countries.

An anti-corruption sign in Uganda. Substandard building construction coupled with corrupt building inspectors have contributed to many deaths in the developing world. *Source*: Future Atlas (www.futureatlas.com).

Nicholas Ambraseys and Roger Bilham found that some 83 percent of earthquake deaths (worldwide) over a thirty-year period (1980–2010) had occurred in countries with high levels of government corruption. They estimated that during that time, an additional eighteen thousand people *per year* died in quakes because buildings had not been built to code as a result of corruption.[13]

In Bangladesh, owners of the country's many export-oriented clothing and textile factories regularly payoff government inspectors to overlook substandard construction or inadequate safety precautions. As a consequence, during periods of heavy rain, many of these buildings have collapsed, leading to the death of many poorly paid workers (mostly women).

Altogether, the World Bank has estimated that some $1.5 trillion in bribes are paid every year, representing about 2 percent of the world's total GDP. This amount, they note, is around ten times the total amount of development aid that goes to less developed countries.[14]

THE CAUSES OF CORRUPTION

As we have noted, even in the United States and other highly advanced democracies, there is a degree of public and private-sector corruption. In May 2018, for example, Spanish prime minister Mariano Rajoy was forced to resign following a scandal involving kickbacks paid to a secret campaign fund. It is also worth noting that during its early history, when the United States was still a relatively underdeveloped country and poverty was widespread, politics was far more corrupt than it is today. Up until the latter half of the eighteenth century, secret ballots were not widely used in American or British elections—in part, so that candidates could be assured that vote buying had paid off. During the first half of the nineteenth century, it was legal for Congressmen to accept payoffs.

But, why does government corruption occur so much more widely in developing nations? There are usually several interrelated factors at work, including poverty and lack of opportunity; efforts by powerful economic elites to influence public policy; the use of patronage and corruption as a political strategy; the impact of conflict; and political attitudes and culture. The degree of democracy in a political system can also be an important factor.

Poverty and Corruption

In most developing countries, civil servants and policemen are paid very low salaries that make it difficult for them to support their families. Consequently, there is a tremendous temptation to augment their income by demanding bribes from the public. That temptation becomes even greater when most of their fellow workers are corrupt, when the chances of being caught and punished are low, and when the public views paying bribes as an unavoidable burden. Indeed, in countries with per capita incomes of below $2,700 (in 2010 dollars), "corruption can be seen as a survival strategy" for those officials taking bribes.[15] In Egypt, the World Bank has noted that in most cases where officials have been caught taking bribes, either nothing has been done, or the investigation would be opened but never concluded. As a result, petty bribery had very much become part of the system, with "the vast majority of Egyptians believed that paying a bribe—or even a tip for services rendered—virtually guaranteed the delivery of a public service or resolved a problem they had with the government, particularly in urban areas."[16]

Indeed, in some cases governments—faced with limited budgets or fiscal austerity measures—may underpay public employees with the expectation that they will supplement their incomes, whether by moonlighting on the job or by taking bribes. As one review of the academic literature on corruption has noted:

> Evidence from ethnographies and qualitative case studies provides support for the contention that corruption emerges when salaries are below a basic living wage. Corruption has been particularly prone to flourish when austerity measures or other crises of state capacity force wage cuts for civil servants . . . in part because bribes may be perceived as morally acceptable when civil servant wages are below the poverty threshold.[17]

Government corruption is not only more prevalent in lower income countries, but also tends to be more common in countries with higher economic inequality and higher levels of "social exclusion"—that is, where poor people receive disproportionately fewer government services. Indeed, social exclusion is a better predictor of corruption levels than is per capita income.[18]

The Private Sector and Corruption

Corruption is not simply a product of poorly paid or greedy public officials trying to supplement their meager incomes through petty bribe-taking. Much of it is also driven by the private sector. Business owners may seek greater profit by avoiding taxes and fees. Entrepreneurs may try to overcome or avoid government regulation by paying bribes to junior officials, or secure favorable government policies and decisions by influencing senior politicians. In cases where economic change has seen, some groups grow in economic wealth, corruption represents a way to translate such newfound riches into greater political influence. South Korea's *chaebols*, discussed earlier, represent one such example.

Research shows that private-sector bribe paying is most likely in those areas where government regulation and licensing is most substantial (such as mining and property development), or where the government is a major purchaser of goods and services (such as public works and defense). Political scientist John Waterbury has termed this as **"developmental corruption,"** arising as it does from the interaction of economic entrepreneurship, development, and the role of the state in the economy—thus distinguishing it from low-level, routine **endemic corruption** discussed in the previous section.

Foreign as well as domestic companies may also pay bribes in order to secure contracts, gain mineral rights, or influence policy in developing countries. According to a "bribe payers index" developed by TI, Chinese, South Korean, Taiwanese, Italian, and Malaysian companies are perceived as most likely to engage in such unethical business practices abroad, followed by Japan, France, and Spain.

One of the most notorious examples of this is in the mining sector, especially in poor and conflict-affected countries in West and Central Africa. In the Democratic Republic of Congo (also known as Congo—Kinshasa), corrupt foreign investors and corrupt local officials involved in the sale of mining rights are estimated to have cost the country more than $1.3 billion in missing revenues between 2010 and 2012.[19] Foreign companies were only too willing to turn a blind eye to illegal activity and pay bribes to secure mining rights. Some Congolese officials simply pocketed the proceeds, while others were used to finance political patronage and slush funds.

Defense sales are another example.[20] British arms makers, for example, may have paid as much as £6 billion ($8 billion US dollars) to members of the Saudi royal family to secure various weapons sales between 1985 and 2007. In Malaysia, the sale of French submarines to the country was reportedly accompanied by €146 million ($170 million) in "commissions."

These, of course, are only the cases we hear about. Bribe paying by Chinese companies abroad is much less likely to ever be reported, both because of the authoritarian nature of China's political system and because investment by Chinese public and private firms may be linked to Chinese foreign policy. In one notable case, Chinese companies investing in Sri Lanka's Hambantota Port Development Project are known to have paid at least $7 million in questionable political contributions to associates of then Sri Lankan president Mahinda Rajapaksa.[21]

Corruption and Neopatrimonial Politics

Political **patronage**—providing rewards or favors to supporters and loyalists—has long been a key aspect of politics. Politicians, after all, need to build and maintain political coalitions to succeed. When such patronage is maintained with the aid of public resources, it is often referred to as **neopatrimonialism**.* The resulting chain of patron-client relations can stretch from

---

* *Patrimonial* political systems, by contrast, are those where public and private positions overlap, such as might be the case with a hereditary chief, king, feudal lord, or political-religious leader. In such a system, loyalty is maintained less with public resources and incentives (as in neopatrimonialism) and more by traditional attitudes to authority and legitimacy.

the very top of the political system down to the urban neighborhoods and rural villages, with support flowing upward, and rewards flowing down.

Patronage politics is not necessarily illegal. In the United States, for example, each change of presidential administration brings with it several thousand new political appointees to the government. Some may be appointed because of their qualifications or ideological support for the president's agenda, while others may be party activists, fund-raisers, and contributors receiving rewards for their past loyalty.

In developing countries, where political institutions and the rule of law tend to be weaker, neopatrimonialism tends to be an especially important tool for mobilizing and maintaining support. It is also a tool that lends itself easily to corrupt activity. Funds may be siphoned from the state budget or private-sector bribe paying into political slush funds, which are then used to reward political loyalists. Political allies may be given preferential access to government contracts and other opportunities. A large state role in the economy, whether through regulation, state spending, or state-owned enterprises, increases the ability of leaders to secure support through employment and economic incentives.

In countries with elections, candidates and political parties may offer gifts, money, or favors to voters to secure their votes, whether individually or to secure electoral endorsement of influential figures within family groups, clans, tribes, or religious and ethnic groups. The 2012 *Americas Barometer* survey of several Latin American countries found that between 13 percent (Argentina, Paraguay) and 34 percent (Guatemala) of respondents reported that they had been made such an offer by a candidate in exchange for their vote. A recent study of low-income voters in the Philippines found that virtually all had been offered something for their vote. Almost all accepted the offer, and most had voted for the candidate concerned.[22]

The use of patronage politics to manage ethnic diversity is another factor that can contribute to corruption.[23] As we will see in chapter 6, many developing countries—especially in Africa and Asia—are composed of multiple, nonintegrated, ethnic groups. Often one of those groups leads the anticolonial struggle and dominates the new, independent government. Not surprisingly, the new government tends to favor the dominant ethnicity or tribe when appointing bureaucrats and civil servants. Not only is this a form of corruption, but it tends to entrench the notion that background and connections—not competency or institutions—is what matters. It can also contribute to greater ethnic polarization, fueling the grievances of disadvantaged groups.

The state may also deliberately overlook illegal activity by its supporters. In this case, turning a blind eye is itself a reward for continued political loyalty. From the regime's point of view, the tolerance of corruption has the added advantage that is both cheap (clients are generating their own payoffs through illegal activities) and easy for the political patron to withdraw should the corrupt client prove to be insufficiently loyal. Waterbury termed this **planned corruption**, where corruption itself forms part of a neopatrimonial strategy of political control.

Corruption and Conflict

Corruption is also rife when wars or economic disasters greatly weaken the political system. Countries torn by civil wars—such as Afghanistan, Libya, Somalia, Syria, and Yemen—have some of TI's highest corruption perception scores. To an Afghan or Somali citizen, fighting corruption is a distant hope amid their daily struggle for survival. Weak government capacity and rule of law provides an opportunity for illegality to flourish.

Governments and rebels alike may also turn to illegal means—smuggling, extortion, bribe taking—to raise revenue and finance their struggle. In keeping with our previous discussion on planned corruption, they are likely to also overlook abuses by their allies. In Afghanistan, former president Hamid Karzai (2001–14) was notorious for overlooking corruption among his supporters, including members of his own family: his half-brother Ahmed Wali Karzai was a famously corrupt politician and powerful warlord in the Kandahar district until his assassination in 2011.* Similarly, Syrian president Bashar al-Asad, embroiled in years of bloody civil war, clearly has little interest in reining in the thuggish and corrupt behavior of the militias and military commanders who support him.

In some cases, a particular nexus may develop between illegal economic activities, conflict, and violence in the form of illicit drug production and distribution. In Afghanistan, poor farmers have turned to opium as a way of making additional income. The Taliban, other militant Islamist groups, and Afghan government officials alike have become involved in protecting and facilitating opium production in exchange for cash payoffs. The United Nations estimates that the amount of land in Afghanistan cultivated for opium poppies grew from 74,000 hectares in 2002 to 328,000 hectares in 2017. The drug economy not only fuels the war, but also contributes to bribery and payoffs, from local police to more senior officials.[24]

In Colombia, cocaine production gave rise to powerful drug cartels in the 1990s, who used both bribery and violence against the state to protect their criminal enterprises. The leftist revolutionary FARC (*Fuerzas Armadas Revolucionarias de Colombia*) also turned to the drug trade to finance its insurgency. While some of the most powerful drug cartels were broken up, and a peace agreement was reached between the Colombian

---

*While diplomats and aid officials frequently criticized Ahmed Wali Karzai for corruption, US military and intelligence officials found him to be a useful ally against the Taliban—again highlighting the ways in which conflict creates conditions under which corruption flourishes.

government and the FARC in 2016, the cultivation of coca (the plant from which cocaine is produced) has become deeply entrenched. Drug production in Colombia and other Andean countries has, in turn, been a major contributor to crime and corruption in both Central America and Mexico, where local gangs grew as Colombian cartels weakened. High crime rates have contributed to Central American migration to the United States, while in Mexico drug gangs have been implicated in thousands of killings as well as bribery of police officers and politicians alike.

Corruption thus contributes to conflict, while conflict creates fertile grounds for corruption to flourish—yet another example of the "conflict trap" noted in chapter 1. Of the ten countries ranked by TI as suffering most from corruption, seven (Somalia, Sudan, Syria, Afghanistan, Yemen, Sudan, Libya) have experienced civil war or other violent conflict in recent years.

Attitudes to Corruption

Public attitudes to corruption may vary. In some cases, activities that were once considered traditional and appropriate are gradually considered to be wrong and illegal. Vote buying, for example, was a regular part of politics in many Western countries until the latter half of the nineteenth century, but today would land a candidate in jail. Up until 1871, military commissions were purchased in the British military, with higher ranks and more prestigious regiments costing more. If one were to offer a British Army recruiter money to become an officer today, however, the response would be very different. In a similar way, offering tribute to tribal chiefs, sheikhs, or monarchs was once an accepted, even desired, part of social and political interaction across Africa or the Middle East. Increasingly, however, gifts to politicians are seen as corruption.

Where corruption is linked to neopatrimonial politics, clients may not see the benefits they receive as corrupt, but rather as evidence that politicians are doing their job. In much of the Middle East, surveys show that most people feel that *wasta* (family, group, and political "connections") is a form of corruption—yet many use it to secure employment or assistance. In the case of the Philippines, research shows that vote buying is not seen in a negative way by poor recipients, but rather as a form of constituency service and evidence that candidates are engaging with their community—thereby strengthening the patron-client relationship. In short, it may be *other politicians* that are seen as corrupt, but not the local leader from one's neighborhood, family, tribe, or ethnic or religious group. Not surprisingly, corruption tends to be strongest in countries with long histories of patron-client politics. Where corruption is widespread, some may come to accept it as simply part of the way things are—as "the norm rather than the exception," as one scholar of Afghanistan put it.[25]

Conversely, a shift in public attitudes against corruption can provide impetus to reform, and even threaten the stability of regimes. The popular protests that toppled the dictatorship in Tunisia in 2011, for example, were driven in part by public anger at corruption, including the growing enrichment of members of the President Ben Ali's extended family. However, public outrage itself is not enough. Many Tunisians claim that corruption has actually worsened since their revolution. In Brazil, protests spurred the introduction of new anti-corruption measures, but many argued that the effectiveness of these had been limited by politicians and corrupt officials.

Corruption and Democracy

Corruption is more common in the authoritarian countries than in democracies. Determining the exact connection between the two is rather complicated, however.

On the one hand, greater transparency in democracies increases the risks and costs of engaging in corrupt behavior. In corrupt dictatorships like Syria or Equatorial Guinea, the government controls or intimidates the media, there is no independent judiciary, and there are not independent groups in civil society strong enough to rally the public against corrupt officials. On the other hand, when corruption arises in democracies such as Brazil and South Korea, the free press was able to expose corruption at the highest level, the public responded with protests, independent prosecutors took on the corruption, and autonomous courts convicted high-ranking government officials. Electoral competition in democracies also created a strong incentive for politicians to expose the corruption of their political rivalries. It is for such reasons that TI itself stresses the key role played by a free media and empowered civil society in its reports and recommendations.

On the other hand, electoral competition may itself provide an incentive for corruption in some democratic systems. In countries like Kenya and Lebanon, a combination of identity politics (tribal and religious, respectively) and closely fought elections means that parties and candidates have a strong incentive to mobilize support within their key constituencies through vote buying and patronage. Similarly, we have seen how vote buying is widespread in elections in the Philippines and found in some parts of Latin America too. Once elected, governments may funnel some state resources to their supporters to reward their political loyalty.

COMBATING CORRUPTION

Once corruption is widely entrenched in a political system, it becomes extremely hard to root out. Civil servants who see many of their colleagues demanding bribes may feel that it would be foolish to be honest. They may also feel pressure from their coworkers to accept bribes, not least of all because any honest bureaucrat is a potential whistle-blower. Similarly, poor voters feel they would be foolish not to take payoffs for their vote and businesspersons observe that they cannot get government contracts while being honest. Politicians may be reluctant to give up vote buying and slush funds if they feel it would put them at a political disadvantage. In countries where planned corruption is used to consolidate support, moving away from such a system might imperil regime stability.

Nevertheless, the serious adverse effects that corruption has on development do create an incentive for countries and leaders to address the problem. Aid donors and international financial institutions have placed growing emphasis on such reforms too, as part of broader efforts to promote good governance in developing countries.

Anti-corruption initiatives can take many forms. These typically aim at detecting and punishing existing corruption, as well as deterring it in future. They may seek to strengthen anti-corruption groups, whether in the media or civil society. Finally, they may attempt to change attitudes among the public and officials alike.

Greater transparency in government finances is essential, so that diversion of funds can be detected in the first place. Oversight by legislative committees or specialist auditing institutions can serve to spot and deter certain types of corrupt behavior. In Nigeria, audits of the Nigerian National Petroleum Corporation not only revealed the scope of fraud and corruption there, but also led to the recovery of $2.4 billion in missing funds.

Prosecution of offenders is important not only to punish those engaged in corrupt activities, but to send a broader signal to others in government, the business sector, and across society. In Pakistan, for example, in 2017 the Supreme Court barred Prime Minister Nawaz Sharif from holding political office after leaked documents showed he and his family were linked to several offshore companies and undeclared property holdings. A year later, he was also sentenced to ten years in jail. Interestingly, some of the evidence in the case hinged on the use of the Calibri typeface in a falsified document—while the document was dated 2006, Microsoft did not introduce the font until 2007.*

An unusual example of joint local and international effort to investigate and prosecute illegal activity is the International Commission against Impunity in Guatemala (CICIG), a partnership between the United Nations and Guatemalan police and prosecutors. In 2015, CICIG and local prosecutors uncovered evidence of systematic tax and customs duty fraud ring ("La Línea") involving President Otto Pérez Molina and Vice President Roxana Baldetti. Molina was impeached, Baldetti resigned, and both were

---

* Some observers of Pakistani politics also suggest that the charges against Sharif were encouraged by the country's powerful armed forces, as a way of removing him from the political arena.

immediately charged with corruption. However, such investigative determination proved disquieting to Molina's successor, President Jimmy Morales. When CICIG began to investigate allegations of illegal campaign financing by the new president and his associates, Morales sought to bar the head of the Commission from entering the country and end CICIG's mandate.

Procedural and technical mechanisms may be used to make financial flows easier to trace. In Palestine, for example, the Palestine Authority largely eliminated the problem of "ghost" employees in the police and security services (i.e., employees who do not really exist) by switching from cash payment of salaries to electronic fund transfers to employee bank accounts. In India, biometric smartcards were distributed to 19 million poor villagers as part of a rural development and employment project, to reduce the risks of welfare fraud.

Regulatory reform can be an important tool. Excessive regulation can, as we have seen, spur corruption as businesses try to bribe their way out of a legal and bureaucratic maze. By streamlining and rationalizing the process for obtaining, say, a business license, the incentive to bribe officials to facilitate paperwork is reduced.

As we have seen, low wages and poor working conditions in the police and public service can contribute to endemic corruption. Research suggests that higher wages might reduce corruption in very low-income countries where accepting bribes has become an economic survival strategy, although at higher income levels it may have little effect.

High-level corruption often involves the transfer of large amounts of illicit funds. Indicative of the scale of this problem, the African Union and United Nations estimate that Africa loses more than $50 billion a year to illicit financial flows.[26] Banking reforms and anti-money laundering efforts can make it easier to detect illegal activity. As part of this, national banking systems and financial crimes units today cooperate more closely with their international counterparts. This also makes it more difficult for wealthy individuals to avoid taxation by hiding their assets.

International and corporate responsibility is important too, since foreign firms may play a major role in high-level corruption and tax evasion. Such efforts often involve a partnership between developing countries, business, and the industrialized world. The *Kimberley Process Certification Scheme* is one such initiative. It established a process of government certification of legal diamond exports so as to reduce the trade in illegal "blood diamonds" from war-torn countries. The *Extractive Industry Transparency Initiative* is another global initiative, which calls upon energy and mining companies, as well as governments, to report revenues from extractive industries so as to contribute to great transparency. Western countries have also taken other measures of their own to limit their corruption in developing countries, such as tighter banking regulations and anti-corruption legislation.

> **Practice and Review Online at**
> http://textbooks.rowman.com/handelman9e

KEY TERMS

anti-corruption initiatives

chaebol

corruption

developmental corruption

endemic corruption

neopatrimonialism

patronage

planned corruption

DISCUSSION QUESTIONS

1. What effects does corruption have on political and economic development?
2. What are the various types of corruption, and what are their causes?
3. Imagine you are an advisor to the government of a developing country. What sort of initiatives would you recommend to address the challenge of corruption? What sort of obstacles might these reforms face?

NOTES

1. Simon Romero and Vinod Sreeharsha, "Trying to Oust Brazil's Leader, but Facing Own Graft Charges," *New York Times*, April 15, 2016.

2. Transparency International, *Corruption Perception Index 2017*, https://www. transparency.org/news/feature/corruption_perceptions_index_2017.

3. Ray Fisman and Miriam A. Golden, *Corruption: What Everyone Needs to Know* (New York, NY: Oxford University Press, 2017), 27–53.

4. David Pallister and Peter Capella, "British Banks Set to Freeze Dictator's Millions," *The Guardian*, July 7, 2000.

5. Ibid.

6. "Nigeria's NNPC 'Failed to Pay' $16bn in Oil Revenues," *BBC News*, March 15, 2016; "Nigerian State Oil Firm 'Withheld $25bn Over Five Years," *BBC News*, March 22, 2016.

7. Central Intelligence Agency (CIA), *The World Factbook, 2016*. That ranking is based on gross domestic product adjusted for the cost of living—GDP per capita (PPP).

8. "The Scale of Corruption in Africa," *The Economist*, December 3, 2015.

9. Ibid.

10. World Justice Project, *The Rule of Law in Pakistan* (2017), https://worldju sticeproject.org/our-work/wjp-rule-law-index/special-reports/rule-law-pakistan.

11. Matthieu Hanf et al., "Corruption Kills: Estimating the Global Impact of Corruption on Children Deaths," *PLOS*, November 2, 2011, https://doi.org/10.1 371/journal.pone.0026990.

12. Matt Schiavenza, "Why Earthquakes in China Are So Damaging," *The Atlantic*, July 15, 2013.

13. Nicholas Ambraseys and Roger Bilham, "Corruption Kills," *Nature* 469 (January 13, 2011), 153.

14. World Bank, "Combatting Corruption," September 26, 2017, http://www.worldbank.org/en/topic/governance/brief/anti-corruption.

15. Alina Mungiu-Pippidi, *The Quest for Good Governance: How Societies Develop Control of Corruption* (Cambridge, MA: Cambridge University Press, 2015), 215. Evidence for the importance of that income cut-point was presented in Paul Collier, *Wars, Guns, and Votes: Democracy in Dangerous Places* (New York, NY: HarperCollins, 2010).

16. World Bank, "Egypt: Too Many Regulations Breed Corruption," December 11, 2014, http://www.worldbank.org/en/news/feature/2014/12/09/egypt-bureaucracy-regulations-and-lack-of-accountability-inspire-corruption.

17. Jordan Gans-Morse et al., "Reducing Bureaucratic Corruption: Interdisciplinary Perspectives on What Works," *World Development* 105 (May 2018).

18. Finn Heinrich, "Corruption and Inequality: How Populists Mislead People," *Transparency International*, January 25, 2017, https://www.transparency.org/news/feature/corruption_and_inequality_how_populists_mislead_people.

19. "Congo's Secret Sales," *Global Witness*, May 13, 2014, https://www.globalwitness.org/en/campaigns/oil-gas-and-mining/congo-secret-sales/.

20. Data drawn from the Global Arms Trade and Corruption project, Tufts University, https://sites.tufts.edu/wpf/global-arms-trade-and-corruption/.

21. Maria Abi-Habib, "How China Got Sri Lanka to Cough Up a Port," *New York Times*, June 25, 2018.

22. Tristan Canare, Ronald Mendoza, and Mario Antonio Lopez, "An Empirical Analysis of Vote Buying Among the Poor: Evidence from Elections in the Philippines," *South East Asia Research* 26, no. 1 (2018).

23. Mungiu-Pippidi, *The Quest for Good Governance*. Such correlations only show tendencies and there are important exceptions to their rule. For example, Botswana, which has a multiethnic population, is regarded as the least corrupt country in Africa. Similarly, Chile has a very low level of corruption even though it has high-income inequality.

24. United Nations Office on Drugs and Crime and Afghan Ministry of Counter Narcotics, *Afghanistan Opium Survey 2017*, https://www.unodc.org/documents/crop-monitoring/Afghanistan/Afghan_opium_survey_2017_cult_prod_web.pdf.

25. Weeda Mehran, "Neopatrimonialism in Afghanistan: Former Warlords, New Democratic Bureaucrats?" *Journal of Peacebuilding & Development* 13, no. 2 (2018): 94.

26. African Union and United Nations Economic Commission for Africa, *Illicit Financial Flow: Report of the High-Level Panel on Illicit Financial Flows from Africa* (2015).

5

Religion and Politics

A Christian member of the Iraqi security forces lights a candle in a church in Qaraqosh after it was freed by government forces from Daesh (ISIS) control in 2016. Despite its dramatic use of brutal violence and social media to promote its cause, surveys show the radical Islamist group is viewed unfavorably by the vast majority of Muslims in the Middle East and beyond. *Source*: Aurelie Marrier d'Unienville/Alamy Stock Photo.

EARLY MODERNIZATION THEORISTS PREDICTED that developing countries would become increasingly secularized, limiting the role of religious ideas and institutions in the political process. As one scholar suggested, "Political development includes, as one of its basic processes, the secularization of politics, the progressive exclusion of religion from the political system."[1] Indeed, perhaps religion itself would become less prominent in society as a whole, a trend that has been evident in much of Europe and the West over the past century. For their part, dependency theorists barely noted any role for religion in their analysis. Instead, they were far more interested in issues of class struggle and political economy—religion was little more than a marginal factor, that was either irrelevant or reflected underlying structural aspects of society.

Certainly, the postcolonial era has seen states across the developing world assert themselves in many areas that were once under strong religious influence or control. In Latin America, the Catholic Church no longer exercises nearly as much control over education or reproductive rights as it once did. Following independence, the Indian government tried to ameliorate the injustices of the caste system, a cornerstone of Hindu religious practice. Some Muslim countries such as Turkey established relatively secular political systems, while almost everywhere in the Middle East education, health care, and social services that were once provided by local religious institutions have been supplanted by government schools, hospitals, and welfare. Similarly, religious courts and law have given way to secular courts and criminal law in most countries.

Yet, contrary to the expectations of modernization theorists, religion continues to be a powerful force in many parts of the developing world, and in some cases has grown in importance. The World Values Survey shows that around 90 percent of (Muslim) Egyptians, Malaysians, and Moroccans, (Catholic) Filipinos, and (Muslim or Christian) Nigerians report religion to be "very important" in their lives.* In some instances, such as prerevolutionary Iran, rapid and destabilizing modernization has even stimulated a militant religious backlash. As David Little has observed, "Modernization was supposed to mean the gradual decline and eventual disappearance of religion from public life, but, as we know, that hasn't happened. Religion is very much alive as a part of politics."[2] At the same time, even the most conservative religious-political groups have incorporated elements of modernity, using modern technology (including videos and social media) to recruit new members and disseminate propaganda.

---

* Conversely, under 10 percent of Chinese, Estonians, Japanese, or Swedes report that religion is "very important" to them. Around 40 percent of Americans consider religion to be very important to them, a rate much higher than most Western countries and more similar to countries like Rwanda or Peru.

At the moment, the importance of religion is nowhere more apparent than in the growth of **Islamist** politics in the Middle East and parts of Africa and Asia. Islamist groups are those that claim a religious basis for their political program. Some of these are **fundamentalist,** in that they seek to return society to what they see as the fundamentals of religion and an idealized past. An even smaller minority of Muslim fundamentalists are violent radicals, exemplified by al-Qa'ida (responsible for the 9/11 terrorist attacks in the United States, among others) and Daesh (also known as the "Islamic State" or ISIS), which temporarily seized control of areas of Iraq and Syria. Many more Islamists are much more moderate, promoting conservative religious values while condemning violence and seeking change within the system. Although not necessarily liberal in their view of women or religious minorities, many support democratic reforms as a way of empowering the Muslim masses. There are also Islamist groups that embrace pluralism and democracy.

It should be remembered that most Muslims do not necessarily support Islamist political parties, any more than most Germans, Swiss, or Chileans necessarily vote for the parties in their own countries that describe themselves as "Christian" or "Christian Democratic." Moreover, while Islamist politics in the Muslim world receives the most attention, the most successful religious-political party in the world is arguably a Hindu nationalist one: the Bharatiya Janata Party (BJP) in India, the world's largest democracy. The BJP was first elected to government in 1996. In the 2014 elections, it won 171 million votes, representing almost one-third of the electorate. It is also the case that all religions have sometimes produced extremists who promote violence against others, and tensions between various religious groups have been the basis for civil conflict. In Myanmar, for example, radical Buddhist groups have encouraged violence against the Rohingya (Muslim) minority. Thousands of Rohingya have died in the crisis, and over half a million have fled the country.

Herein we will discuss the major religious groups in the developing world, and how they might shape politics. We will discuss the puzzle of religion, modernity, and secularization, looking in particular at the changing role of the Catholic Church in Latin America, the Iranian Revolution, and religious fundamentalism in the Middle East and elsewhere.

RELIGION IN THE DEVELOPING WORLD

According to one recent demographic study, Christianity is the largest religion in the world today, with approximately 2.3 billion adherents in 2015 (out of a world population of over 7 billion).[3] Of these, around half are Catholics, and the remainder split between various Protestant and

Orthodox churches, and others. The global spread of Catholicism was intimately tied to Spanish and Portuguese colonialism, as evidenced by the historic dominance of the Church in Latin America and the Philippines. However, in recent decades, Protestantism—especially Pentecostalism and other forms of evangelical Protestantism—has found many new followers in the developing world. In Africa and Latin America, such groups have grown from around 77 million adherents in 1970 to perhaps 460 million today.[4]

Europe and North America account for a declining share of the world's Christians, with the proportion expected to drop from 36 percent in 2015 to around 23 percent by 2030. By 2060, two-thirds of Christians will live in Africa or Latin America. This demographic shift has implications for major churches, and it is perhaps not surprising that the Catholic Church selected an Argentine Cardinal, Jorge Mario Bergoglio, as Pope in 2013. Pope Francis (as he is now called) is the first non-European head of the Catholic faith since Pope Gregory III, a Syrian, in the eighth century.

Islam is the second-largest religion in the world, with 1.8 billion adherents. It is also the fastest-growing faith and is expected to become the world's largest religious group in the latter half of this century. Like Christianity, Islam is far from monolithic. In particular, the split between **Sunni** Muslims and **Shi'ite** Muslims dates back to the early years of the faith and today is reflected in a number of differences regarding religious practice. Around 85–90 percent of Muslims are Sunnis, while Shi'ites account for around 10–15 percent.

Although many associate Islam with the Middle East, the region where the religion was born and where all countries except Israel have a large Muslim majority, only 20 percent or so of the world's Muslims live there. Indeed, the countries with the largest Muslim populations today are Indonesia (with a population 260 million), followed by Pakistan, (predominantly Hindu) India, Bangladesh, and (approximately half Muslim, half Christian) Nigeria. Significant Muslim minorities are found in countries as far-flung as the Philippines, Senegal, Ethiopia, Tanzania, Trinidad and Tobago, and elsewhere. Shi'ism is the majority faith only in Iran, Iraq, and the small nations of Azerbaijan and Bahrain, but its adherents are significant minorities (10–35 percent of the population) in Afghanistan, Kuwait, Lebanon, Pakistan, Saudi Arabia, Syria, Turkey, Yemen, and elsewhere.

Of the world's 1.1 billion Hindus, most are found in South Asia, in India and Nepal (where they form majorities), as well as Sri Lanka and Bangladesh (where they are much smaller minorities). Hindus also form a slight majority in the island republic of Mauritius, off the east coast of Africa, and comprise significant minorities in Guyana, Fiji, Trinidad and Tobago—a legacy of British colonialism, and the use of indentured Indian laborers across the British Empire.

Approximately half a billion Buddhists live in South, South East, and East Asia, and elsewhere. They form a majority in Cambodia, Thailand, Myanmar, Bhutan, Sri Lanka, Laos, and Mongolia.

To be sure, not everyone in the developing world belongs to one of these major religions. Confucianism (perhaps more a philosophy and way of life than a religion) still influences Chinese society (even after the communist revolution), as well as Japan, South Korea, and Taiwan. Tens of millions of Africans adhere to various traditional, animist belief systems. The impact of these religions on politics, however, is generally limited. Consequently, this chapter restricts its analysis to the four global religions just discussed, particularly emphasizing Catholicism and Islam.

Church, Mosque, Temple, and State

Many preconceptions about religion and politics emerge from misinterpretations, both of American politics and of political systems elsewhere. Americans accept a constitutional separation of church and state as the normal state of affairs (though some wish to blur this line). In his classic work, *Democracy in America*, the French author Alexis de Tocqueville suggested that this separation was a linchpin of American politics:

> I learned with surprise that [the clergy] filled no public appointments . . . [and] I found that most of its members seemed to retire from their own accord from the exercise of power, and that they made it the pride of their profession to abstain from politics. . . . They saw that they must renounce their religious influence if they were to strive for political power.[5]

However, many Western European democracies, though generally less religious than the United States, lack legal walls between religion and politics. In the United Kingdom, for example, the last successful prosecution for blasphemy took place in 1977, and the Church of England (the Anglican Church) remains the official state religion. Norway's government funds the (Lutheran) Church of Norway, the status of which is enshrined in the constitution. Even in the United States, religious organizations and beliefs continue to influence political behavior. Black Baptist churches and ministers like Martin Luther King, for example, were in the forefront of the American civil rights movement. Since the 1980s, the so-called Christian right has been an influential force within the Republican Party. Indeed, in recent decades, conflicts over issues such as abortion led one expert to observe that "far from rendering religion largely irrelevant to politics the structure of [American] government may actually encourage a high degree of interaction."[6]

Today, many analysts still believe that maintaining the pluralist values and the tolerance underlying democracy requires limiting the influence of religion on politics. But others reject the notion that democracy can exist only under a strict separation of church and state. In their book, *Religion and Democracy*, David Marquand and Ronald Nettler insist,

> Even in the absence of a . . . bargain keeping church and state apart, religion and democracy can coexist. Communities of faith do not necessarily imperil the foundations of pluralist democracy by seeking to pursue essentially religious agendas through political action.[7]

But, they add, there is a necessary restriction if this intermingling of religious political action and democracy is to work. "A degree of mutual tolerance, or at least of mutual self-restraint, is indispensable. Religious groups have to accept the right of other religious groups—and . . . the right of the nonreligious—to abide by their own values."[8]

Religion is even more firmly embedded in many cultures in the developing world, and its impact on politics is correspondingly more pronounced than it is in the West. In India, for example, the BJP has carried the torch of Hindu revivalism with considerable political and electoral success.

The blending of religion and politics is most apparent in (admittedly, very rare) **theocratic states**, where political systems are formally dominated

Supporters of the (Hindu nationalist) Bharatiya Janata Party celebrate their party's victory in India's 2014 general elections. *Source*: AP Photo/Rajesh Kumar Singh.

by religious leaders and institutions. One such example is Iran, where the Shi'a clergy have been the final arbiters of public policy since that country's 1979 Islamic revolution. Similarly, when the Taliban ruled Afghanistan (1996–2001), their government became an extension of the fundamentalist clergy. But the close integration of religious officials into governance is also significant in some American allies, most notably Saudi Arabia.

Precisely because of their potential social and political influence, religious leaders may be intimidated or co-opted by authoritarian regimes. Haynes's explanation of why most local Christian religious leaders, from the 1960s through the 1980s, failed to speak out against Africa's authoritarian rulers applies equally well to other religions in the developing countries:

> Church and state developed mutually supportive relationships. . . . . [Frequently] it was in . . . the interests of both Church and state for there to be social and political stability, even if it required authoritarian rule to achieve it.[9]

Speaking out against a dictator, at the very least, would cut off government financial support for the church and, at worst, would subject the clergy and perhaps their parishioners to persecution. In the 1970s and 1980s, for example, then Congolese dictator Mobutu Sese Seko first exiled (Catholic) Cardinal Joseph Malula for criticizing his policies and then allowed him to return—and gave him a mansion to live it—in exchange for his political silence. Mobutu subsequently gave a Mercedes to every Catholic and Protestant bishop in the country.[10] While there were also some prominent clergymen who demanded social justice and criticized government repression and corruption, it was not until the 1990s that the Congolese church became a prominent voice for democracy.

Later, and most notably in Latin American nations like Brazil and Nicaragua, a "Theology of Liberation" espoused by radical Catholics motivated many priests and nuns to mobilize the poor in their struggle against economic and political injustices. Although not a "liberationist" himself, Pope Francis's strong commitment to the underprivileged, to social justice, and toward protecting the environment has been strongly influenced by that theology.

Two factors have particularly important implications for a religion's political involvement. The first is its theological views regarding the relationship between temporal and spiritual matters. The second relates to religious institutionalization and the degree to which its clergy are hierarchically organized and centrally controlled.

More than any other major religion, Catholicism has a well-defined and hierarchical ecclesiastical structure that enables it to have a considerable impact on the political system. At the church's apex is the pope, whose religious authority is unchallenged and whose official pronouncements on matters of faith and morals are accepted by believers (in theory, if not always in practice) as infallible. Consequently, papal declarations can carry considerable political importance. For example, note the great controversy over Pope Francis's recent pronouncements indicating the obligation of Catholics to combat climate change. Within each country, the church hierarchy is headed by cardinals or bishops, who often have substantial political influence in Latin America and in other Catholic developing countries such as the Philippines.

Catholicism once was the state religion in a number of Latin American countries. Today, however, countries in the region either have ended official state religions or have rendered that link unimportant. Still, church doctrine has generally supported the established political regime and helped legitimize it. This does not mean, however, that the church has always supported the government. There have been periodic clashes between the two, particularly when the state has challenged church authority in areas such as education or when the state has violated human rights. Thus in the Philippines, church support of Corazón Aquino's democratic reform movement helped topple the dictatorship of Ferdinand Marcos. Similarly, Catholic authorities opposed conservative military dictatorships in Brazil and Chile during the 1970s and 1980s.

From its inception in seventh-century Arabia, Islam has been a "religio-political movement in which religion was integral to state and society."[11] Today, the bond between religion and politics remains strong in most Muslim societies, though there is considerable variation. Turkey has been the most notable secular state in the Islamic world. In the early 1920s, Mustafa Kemal Atatürk ousted the sultan (the political and religious leader of the Ottoman Empire), emancipated women, and starkly limited the power of religious institutions. In recent years, the governing Justice and Development Party (better known by its Turkish abbreviation, AKP) is increasingly Islamist and has rolled back a few of these measures, but key elements of the secular state remain in place. At the other end of the spectrum, a few Muslim-majority states base their governing philosophies on the Koran and Islamic law. Iran and Saudi Arabia are among the best-known examples. But, these regimes can be quite distinct from each other. These states may be Sunni (Saudi Arabia) or Shi'a (Iran), anti-Western (Iran and Sudan), or pro-Western (Saudi Arabia).

The division within Islam between the Sunni and Shi'ite branches has its historical origins in a dispute over the very issue of political and religious leadership, following the death of the Prophet Muhammed in 632CE and the consequent need to choose a successor (Caliph) as leader of the rapidly growing Muslim community. Shi'ites supported the leadership claim of Ali ibn Abi Talib, his cousin and son-in-law. Sunnis argued that the choice should be made by wider consultation and supported the candidacy of the

Prophet's companion, Abu Bakr. The schism eventually erupted into several periods of open conflict between the two groups, and the emergence of two separate lineages of political leadership. Sunnis generally recognized a line of temporal and religious leadership extending through the Umayyid (661–750 CE) and Abbasid (750–1517 CE) caliphates, and continuing to the Ottoman (Turkish) Empire, until the Caliphate—or, at least, the Turkish claim to lead it—was abolished by Atatürk in 1924. Shi'ites, on the other hand, attribute religious and political authority to a line of Imams that descends from Ali and his sons Hasan and Husayn. The largest group of Shi'ites ("Twelvers") believe that the 12th Imam vanished, but will reappear shortly before the Day of Judgment.

As is often noted, classical Sunni Islam recognized no separation of religion and politics, in that the Caliph was expected to serve as political leader of the Muslim community and the Muslim religion. In practice, however, the authority of the Caliph was far from unchallenged, and—as with European kings, popes, and emperors—intrigue and conflicts were commonplace. The religious authority of the Caliph also weakened over time, especially during the Ottoman Empire, and the position often seemed little more than a way of legitimizing temporal rule. Today, while some fundamentalist Muslims hope for a reestablishment of the caliphate, most view it as a bygone historical institution or distant theological notion of little or no relevance to their modern daily lives.

Ironically, while Sunni Islam theoretically recognized a religious-political leader at its helm, the practice of faith is much less hierarchically organized, and indeed rather decentralized. Not one but several schools of Islamic religious law (sharia) emerged. These, moreover, have been increasingly supplanted by state-constructed legal systems in Muslim countries, although sharia courts may continue to operate, especially in issues related to family, inheritance, and personal status law. Mosques, religious endowments, and centers of religious learning have largely been independent, although governments—recognizing their social influence—have often sought to bring them under some degree of control. Unlike most Christian faiths, there is no formal process whereby one is ordained as a religious leader (imam). Rather, any pious and religiously learned person can lead the community in prayers or issue a religious opinion (fatwa).

By contrast, Shi'ism is much more hierarchically organized. During the classical era, the leaders of the Shi'ite community rarely exercised political control over populations and territories the way Sunni Caliphs had. Instead, they were revered as providing moral and religious leadership. The main centers of Shi'ite religious learning (in Karbala and Najaf in Iraq, and Qom in Iran) encouraged a degree of institutional hierarchy and doctrinal cohesion, and the most senior and respected Ayatollahs (high-ranking Shi'ite scholars) are considered to be legal authorities and sources of emulation for the faithful to follow. In Iran, Grand Ayatollah Ali Khomeini serves as Supreme Leader of the country, the source of both religious authority and political authority. However, this particular fusion of political power and Shi'ite religious authority is very much an innovation introduced by his predecessor, revolutionary leader Ayatollah Ruhollah Khomeini. Other Shi'ite religious figures, such as Iraq's influential Ayatollah Ali al-Sistani, prefer a less public and more subtle role, focusing on the interests of the Shi'ite community rather than public statecraft. Some are not politically involved at all.

Unlike the Catholic Church, Asia's major religions—Hinduism and Buddhism—have a weak or nonexistent religious hierarchy. Hence, the clergy are relatively unorganized as an institution and are, therefore, less directly involved in politics than have been the clergy in Catholicism and Islam. To be sure, India's BJP is a major political force—but the party has no linkage to a formally organized Hindu "clergy."

Buddhism grew out of the Hindu religion in the sixth century BC, emerging from the teachings of a Nepalese prince, Siddhartha Gautama, the Buddha (Enlightened One). Though greatly influenced by Hinduism, Buddhism rejects one of its basic tenets, the caste system. It also differs from Hinduism in that it does have an organized ecclesiastical organization, its monastic orders. And in some countries, such as Myanmar, each religious community has its own leader, providing a hierarchical structure. Still, when compared to the Roman Catholic Church or to Shi'ite Islam, Buddhism's religious structure is much less centralized. Fundamentalist activism among Buddhist clerics tends to be associated with particular factions, rather than the religion overall.

In discussing the influence of religious doctrine and institutions on contemporary politics, it is important to keep in mind that attitudes change with time and context, and that neither clerics nor the faithful are uniform in their views. The infallibility of the pope within Catholic doctrine, for example, does not prevent many Catholics from holding personal views at odds with their church's teachings. The Canadian province of Quebec is one of the most Catholic jurisdictions in the Americas, with three quarters of the population identifying as members of the Catholic faith—yet, surveys there also show very high rates of support (typically over 80 percent) for access to contraception, abortion services, and same-sex marriage. Similarly, Muslims vary widely from country to country in their views on whether religion should play a major role in politics: while almost half of Pakistanis strongly believe that religious authorities should play a key role in interpreting law in a democracy, fewer than 20 percent of Algerians, Iraqis, or Palestinians share that view.[12] In some parts of the Middle East, almost half the population report that they have no trust at all in religious leaders, and between half and two-thirds typically prefer that religious leaders not interfere in election choices or government policy—hardly evidence of a population waiting to slavishly follow religious edicts in their personal or political lives.[13]

RELIGION, MODERNITY, AND SECULARIZATION

We have already observed that social and economic modernization does not necessarily reduce religious observance, at least not in the short run. What about the reverse side of this relationship? That is, what is the impact of religion on modernity? Here again, most early analysts felt they were largely incompatible. "It is widely, and correctly, assumed," said one scholar, "that religion is in general an obstacle to modernization."[14] In the realm of politics, this interpretation suggested that the intrusion of religious institutions into government impedes the development of a modern state. At times, other analysts linked Catholic, Islamic, and Hindu beliefs to authoritarian values.

Subsequently, political scientists have developed a more nuanced understanding. Religious institutions may inhibit development in some respects, while encouraging it in others. For example, all of the great religions have legitimized the state's authority at some point in their history, a necessary step for state building. No longer facilely dismissing organized religion's contributions to development, some scholars now credit Confucianism—more specifically, work ethic and its spirit of cooperation—with facilitating East Asia's rapid modernization in the second half of the twentieth century.

The argument that political modernization requires **secularization** (the separation of religious and political institutions) has two bases—one empirical and the other normative. The empirical component notes that as Western societies became more literate, urban, institutionally organized, and industrialized, their political systems invariably became more secular. In effect, modern, Western societies developed a specialization of functions. Increasingly, the state-controlled politics, while the church oversaw religion, and each usually has refrained from interfering in the other's realm. Political scientists anticipated that as the developing countries modernized, they would experience the same division of responsibilities. The related normative argument holds that secularization is not only a common trend, but it is also desirable because it increases religious freedom, reduces the likelihood of state persecution of religious minorities, and permits the state to make more rational decisions free of religious bias.

We have noted the weakness of the first assumption. To be sure, modernization has induced political secularization in many developing countries, such as Turkey (at least until recently) and Mexico. But elsewhere economic and social change has sometimes precipitated a religious backlash when pursued too rapidly. Religious fundamentalism—a desire to address the perceived corruption and moral crisis of modern society by returning to the real or imagined roots of religious belief—can be one manifestation of this.

At an individual level, many people in Africa, Asia, and the Middle East have defied the notion that more educated and professionally trained citizens will be less religiously orthodox. For example, Hindu activists in India are frequently professionals, not uneducated peasants. In the Middle East, Islamist groups draw support from all social classes, and from men and women alike. Most of the terrorists who attacked the Pentagon and the World Trade Center on September 11, 2001, were relatively well educated and middle class. So too are many current recruits and leaders of Daesh. Religion-state relationships are more varied and complex than early development theory had assumed.

Some religious influences contradict accepted norms of modernity, as when they induce political leaders to violate the rights of religious minorities (or majorities). Similarly, many religiously inspired restrictions on women are clearly antithetical to modernization. But need there always be a strict wall between politics and religion or between clerics and politicians? Sometimes, analysts offer contradictory answers prompted by their own political ideologies. Many of those who lamented the political activities of leftist priests in Nicaragua may have cheered political involvement by Reverend Jerry Falwell in the United States.

Three examples can be used to illustrate the complex relationship between religion, politics, and social change. The first is the evolution of the Catholic Church and its role in politics from the 1960s until today, especially in Latin America. The second is the 1978 Iranian Revolution, as a reaction against rapid modernization. Finally, we can examine the rise of recent religious fundamentalisms, especially within Islam but in other religions as well.

The Evolution of the Catholic Church in Latin America

During the era of Spanish and Portuguese colonialism, the Catholic Church had supported the conquest and religious conversion of native populations in the Americas, providing the conquistadores with ideological and religious backing. Thereafter and through the first half of the twentieth century, the church had supported the political and economic status quo, thereby legitimizing Latin America's elite-dominated governments. Provoked by the anticlerical positions of the French Revolution and of European and Latin American liberals, the Catholic hierarchy allied with conservative political parties and factions in Europe and, especially, in Latin America. Many church leaders were also profoundly anti-communist, a view they shared with oligarchs and military dictators alike.

In the decades after the Second World War, however, many Catholic clergy, particularly at the parish level, began to abandon the church's former conservatism. This accelerated in the 1960s, when Pope John XXIII moved the "Church universal" in a more liberal direction, placing greater emphasis on social concerns. The Second Vatican Council (convened by Pope John between 1962 and 1965) moved international Catholicism from a "generally conservative and sometimes authoritarian position to one that was more concerned with democracy, human rights, and social justice."[15] Catholics were encouraged to address pressing social issues and to begin a political dialogue with liberals.

In 1968, the Latin American Bishops Conference (CELAM) met in Medellín, Colombia, to apply the lessons of Vatican II to their own region. Challenging the status quo, their ideas reflected the influences of reformist theologians from the so-called progressive church. The clergy, said the bishops, must heed the "deafening cry . . . from the throats of millions asking their pastors for a liberation that reaches them from nowhere else."[16] To do so, the church must "effectively give preference to the poorest and the neediest sectors." In short, an institution historically allied with the region's power elite was in some ways becoming the church of the poor.

The CELAM conference must be understood in the broader context of political change that was shaking Latin America at the time. In 1959, the triumph of the Cuban Revolution highlighted the poverty and oppression afflicting so many Latin Americans. Cuba's far-reaching educational, health, and land reforms impressed and radicalized many Catholics. Although left-leaning Catholic priests almost universally rejected violence, many accepted elements of Marxist political and economic analysis, while they identified with the plight of their underprivileged parishioners and helped organize and politicize peasants and slum dwellers.

Though always a minority within the church, leftist clergy had an important influence in Central America during the 1970s and 1980s, most notably in Nicaragua, El Salvador, and Guatemala. Many Nicaraguan priests and nuns supported the Marxist-leaning Sandinista Revolution in the 1970s. So, when the Sandinistas came to power, the president's cabinet contained four priests, more than any other government in Latin America.

For most of Latin America, however, the 1970s and 1980s were not years of revolution. Instead, much of the region came under the control of right-wing military dictatorships. Reacting to a perceived radical threat, repressive military regimes replaced civilian democracies in Argentina, Brazil, Chile, and Uruguay. At the same time, the rule of armed forces continued in much of Central America and the central Andes, where democratic traditions had never been strong. Ironically, right-wing repression spurred the growth of the progressive church more effectively than the Cuban or Nicaraguan revolutions had.

Many radical clergy and laity were outspoken in their criticism of the military regimes and, consequently, suffered severe reprisals. Dozens of priests and nuns were murdered and many more persecuted in countries such as Brazil, El Salvador, and Guatemala. In El Salvador, for example, a far-right death squad called the White Warriors distributed handbills stating, "Be a Patriot, Kill a Priest."[17] But such repression only radicalized many moderate Catholics. "When committed Catholics were imprisoned, tortured, and even killed, bishops in a significant number of cases then denounced the state, setting off a spiral of greater repression against the Church, followed by new Church denunciations of authoritarianism."[18]

In Chile, Brazil, El Salvador, and Peru, the church became a leading critic of government human rights violations. The most celebrated example was El Salvador's archbishop Oscar Romero, its highest-ranking cleric, who had begun his tenure as a conservative. Increasingly appalled by the military's widespread human rights abuses, in 1980, he wrote President Carter asking him to terminate US military aid to the ruling junta until human rights violations had ended. Later, he broadcast a sermon calling on Salvadorian soldiers to disobey orders to kill innocent civilians. "No soldier is obliged to obey an order against God's law," he declared. "In the name of God and in the name of this suffering people, I implore you, I beg you, and I order you—stop the repression."[19] The following day Romero was assassinated as he said a requiem mass, murdered by a death squad linked to the military. In 2018, Pope Francis declared his canonization as a saint.

A number of the bishops' pronouncements originated with a radical Peruvian priest, Gustavo Gutiérrez, the father of "liberation theology." Writings by him and other liberation theologians influenced the progressive church in Latin America and other parts of the world. The Theology of Liberation calls on Catholic laity and clergy to become politically active and to direct that activity toward the emancipation of the poor. Drawing on Marxist analysis, Gutiérrez preached the notion of nonviolent class struggle. The poor, liberation theologians argued, should organize themselves into Ecclesial (or Christian) Base Communities (CEBs) where they can recognize the need to transform society through their own mobilization. CEBs spread through much of Latin America, most notably in Brazil along with Chile, Peru, and Central America.

Since the early 1980s, the influence of Latin America's progressive church has diminished considerably. One cause, ironically, was the region's transition from military dictatorships to democracy. Absent massive human rights violations and open assaults against the poor, Catholic clergy have generally been less motivated to enter the political arena. Furthermore, without a common foe, moderate and radical priests no longer have a common cause. And, many political activists who had used the church as a protective "umbrella" during the military dictatorships (since those regimes had been less likely to persecute church-affiliated radical groups) were now able to participate in politics through other political organizations.

Perhaps, more importantly, for some thirty-five years (1978–2013), the Vatican under Popes John XXIII, Paul II, and Benedict XVI was quite unsympathetic to political activism among priests and nuns, particularly when related to the CEBs and liberation theology. However, although Pope Francis (2013-) has not encouraged that theology itself, he has been a major force in promulgating many of its ideas and reviving the ideas of the progressive church as he passionately calls for the Catholic Church to be "the church of the poor." His views, however, have generated some opposition among Vatican conservatives, concerned that he is straying too far from doctrinal orthodoxy.

The Iranian Revolution

The 1978 revolution in Iran offers a good example of religiously based reaction to rapid social and economic change—in this case, a swing to social conservatism. Starting with the reign of Shah Reza Pahlavi (1925–41), the imperial government antagonized the Shi'ite clergy with a series of modernizing reforms that included unveiling women, mandatory Western dress, and transferring control over various economic, educational, and political resources to the state. The Shah's son, Mohammed Reza Pahlavi, ruled from 1941 to 1979 as a close ally of the United States. Indeed, when the Shah's power was threatened in the 1950s by Prime Minister Mohammad Mosaddegh—a popularly elected prime minister, who had nationalized the Iranian oil industry over British and American objections—the US Central Intelligence Agency helped organize a coup to drive Mosaddegh from power and confirm the Shah's absolute rule.

The Shah's so-called White Revolution of the 1960s and 1970s expanded women's rights, extended general literacy, and promoted a land reform program that included the transfer of land from Islamic institutions to the peasants. As a result, land was redistributed to some 3 million peasants, educational levels rose substantially, and oil wealth doubled the size of the middle class.[20] By 1976, Iran had the highest GNP per capita in the developing world. However, the gap between the rich and the poor widened, widespread government corruption alienated the population, and many suspected opponents of the government were brutally suppressed.

At the same time, the Shi'ite clergy and other devout Muslims objected to the secularization of society and the intrusion of Western values and customs, not to mention a long history of foreign meddling and intervention in the country. As political tensions grew, a religious leader, the Ayatollah Ruhollah Khomeini, emerged as one of the Shah's leading critics. In 1964, Khomeini was sent into exile for nearly fifteen years, but that only bolstered his popularity as he continued to criticize the Shah's regime. In January 1979, with much of Iran's urban population involved in strikes and demonstrations against the regime, the Shah went into exile, and Khomeini returned to Iran.

Three interrelated developments set the tone for the Islamic revolution. First was the merger of the country's religious and political leadership. The new "Islamic republic," declared the Grand Ayatollah, is "the government of God."[21] While nonclerical figures have held important government posts—including the presidency—ultimate power resides in the hands of the Supreme Leader (currently Ayatollah Ali Khamenei)—a cleric to whom all government officials are beholden—and the Guardian Council (dominated by clerics and conservatives), which screens candidates for political office and has the power to overrule parliamentary votes.

The second important development was the revival of traditional Islamic observances. Women now must be veiled in public and are strongly encouraged to wear the chador, the shapeless shroud that conceals all parts of the body. The state actively polices possible violations of "correct" Islamic behavior. However, the government also doubled the female literacy rate from 36 to 72 percent in its first two decades in office.

Finally, Iran's radical revivalism has embraced an assertive foreign policy that has supported kindred Islamist groups abroad—such as Lebanon's Hizbullah—and has been highly antagonistic toward countries that it perceived as enemies—especially Israel and the United States. Currently, it is one of the major military backers of the repressive Syrian regime of Bashar al-Asad.

Yet, there is much more to Iranian politics than religion alone. Despite government censorship, Iranians are quite eager to share political views on issues ranging from religion to the economy to foreign policy. The country also holds regular parliamentary and presidential elections. While these can hardly be considered free or fair—candidates are all prescreened for adherence to the principles of the Islamic Republic, and those deemed unacceptable are barred from holding office—they are competitive among those candidates permitted to run. This has sometimes resulted in the election of more reform-oriented presidents, notably Mohammad Khatami (1997–2005) and Hassan Rouhani (in office since 2013). During these periods, the regime has periodically been less repressive at home and has sometimes moderated its foreign policy—agreeing, for example, to forgo developing nuclear weapons.*

Religious Fundamentalism

In recent years—indeed, since the Iranian Revolution—the growth of Islamic fundamentalism has drawn increasing attention from the media,

---

*Iran signed the Joint Comprehensive Plan of Action (JCPOA) with the United States, European Union, France, Germany, the United Kingdom, Russia, and China in 2015, agreeing to temporarily suspend certain civilian nuclear activities and forever forgo the development of nuclear weapons, in exchange for relief from economic sanctions. Despite Iranian compliance and the objections of its European allies, the United States later withdrew from the deal.

governments, and scholars. With the 9/11 terror attacks, conducted by the radical Sunni Muslim fundamentalist group al-Qaida as part of a broader global campaign of violence against both the West and Muslim regimes alike, fundamentalism came to be seen as a major security challenge. This was followed by the emergence of Daesh and its 2014 declaration of a new "caliphate" in parts of war-torn Syria and Iraq—all accompanied by campaigns of horrific violence against (and even enslavement of) Shi'ites, Christians, Yezidis, and other religious minorities, and encouragement of worldwide terrorism by sympathizers and supporters.

As previously noted, Islam is not alone in having fundamentalist movements within it. The precise meaning of fundamentalism varies somewhat from religion to religion, and—like much of the terminology in this chapter—can be contentious. But its adherents do share certain points of view across religious lines. To begin with, they wish to preserve their traditional worldview of religion and resist the efforts of religious liberals to reform it. They tend to view many outside influences as a threat to traditional values. They also want to revive the role of religion in private and public life, including politics, lifestyle, and dress. In the developing world, such revivalism often appeals particularly to people who are angered by the inequalities and injustices in their country's political and economic systems.

It is important to note that not all fundamentalist movements are violent—indeed, most are not. The Amish, for example, peacefully adhere to what they see as a more authentic version of Christianity, including traditional views of gender roles and rejection of some forms of modern technology. Similarly, many ultra-Orthodox (Haredi) Jews also regard their practices as adhering more closely to Jewish law than those of others of their faith.

In the Muslim world, those Sunnis who harken back to what they see as a purer form of Islam as practiced in the time of the Prophet Muhammad and his companions are often known as **Salafists** (from the term for "predecessors"). Most Salafist movements do not seek to confront political authorities, but rather preach to fellow Muslims and encourage them to return to what they see as the fundamentals of the faith. They are also often active with various charitable initiatives. Some reject democracy as setting the popular will above that of God, but others have actively participated in elections, believing that Islamic values might best be promoted through political representation. In Egypt, for example, various Salafist parties won over a quarter of the vote in the 2011–12 (democratic) elections.

A minority of fundamentalist movements can be more radical and even violent, however. Within the Sunni Muslim world, these groups are often referred to as Salafist jihadists—although here too, the terminology can be problematic.*

While it was far from the first such group, al-Qaida became the most prominent because of its success in using high-profile terror attacks to garner international attention. The organization had its roots in the 1979 invasion of Afghanistan by the Soviet Union. Soviet occupation led to the growth of armed local resistance, the Afghan mujahideen. It was also a struggle that attracted religiously motivated volunteers from elsewhere in the Muslim world, especially the Arab countries. Some of these were organized by Osama bin Laden, a Saudi construction tycoon and entrepreneur. Among those joining him was an Egyptian medical doctor, Ayman al-Zawahiri, who had been among the founding members of (Egyptian) Islamic Jihad—the group that has assassinated Egyptian president Anwar al-Sadat in 1981. Zawahiri would later take over leadership of al-Qaida following the assassination of Bin Laden in Pakistan by US forces in 2011.

Al-Qaida was formally established in the late 1980s. After Soviet forces withdrew from Afghanistan in 1989, al-Qaida forged close links with the fundamentalist Taliban movement that ultimately took control of much of the country by 1996—establishing training bases for its foreign volunteers.

Unlike many radical jihadist groups, al-Qaida emphasized the battle not just against the "near enemy" (i.e., the Muslim regimes it opposed) but also the "far enemy"—the United States, and its Western allies. Indeed, the 9/11 terror attacks were intended in part to provoke America to overreact, in the hopes of sparking a broader confrontation between Islamic fundamentalism and the West that would radicalize and polarize the Muslim world. To the extent that al-Qaida terrorism sparked US intervention in Afghanistan in 2001, contributed to the atmosphere in Washington that led to American intervention in Iraq, and set the stage for years of a "global war on terrorism," it was remarkably successful in heightening the profile of the radical jihadist cause.

Largely driven out of Afghanistan and forced into hiding by the US riposte, al-Qaida adopted a new "franchise" model for its operations. Rather than organize these centrally, it would lend its name and political support to Sunni fundamentalist insurgencies elsewhere.

It would be in Iraq that al-Qaida's most active affiliate would emerge, mobilizing Sunni grievances against the post-2003 American occupation

---

* In Arabic, the term "jihad" simply means a noble struggle, and in a religious context can refer to any struggle on behalf of faith—for example, against the temptations of sin. In the West, however, it has (incorrectly) become synonymous with violence. Muslim governments are understandably reluctant to apply a word with possible positive connotations (jihad) to a violent phenomenon (terrorism), and hence tend to use other terms. They also object to the formulation "Islamic terrorism" favored by some Western politicians as too broad and counterproductive—noting that terms like "Christian terrorism" are rarely applied to, say, religiously motivated attacks on abortion clinics in the West.

there. Al-Qaida in Iraq not only targeted US and other coalition forces but also engaged in widespread violence against Sunni rivals and Shi'ite Muslim majority—to the point of earning them a rebuke from al-Zawahiri. Atrocities committed by al-Qaida in Iraq would contribute greatly to sectarian polarization in the country, with ramifications felt to the present day.

From al-Qaida in Iraq would ultimately emerge another Salafist jihadists group, Daesh. While al-Qaida had argued that the global struggle against faithless Muslim regimes and the Western world would eventually lead to the reestablishment of a worldwide caliphate, Daesh argued that the time to build a new "Islamic state" had already come. Amid the chaos of the Syrian civil war (2011 onward), it seized control of areas of eastern Syria from government forces and rival opposition groups. It then took control of several Sunni towns in western Iraq, exploiting widespread Sunni dissatisfaction with the Shi'ite-dominated Iraqi central government. The capture of Iraq's second-largest city, Mosul, by Daesh in June 2014 signalled its growing influence. Soon thereafter the movements' leader, Abu Bakr al-Baghdadi, declared the reestablishment of the caliphate, with himself as caliph.

This declaration was treated by scorn by the vast majority of Muslims worldwide, who were appalled by the brutal violence of Daesh. Thousands of Sunni Muslim scholars and institutions denounced its actions. Daesh did, however, attract the support of some Salafist jihadist groups elsewhere (in the Egypt, Libya, Yemen, Afghanistan, and even the Boko Haram insurgency in Nigeria), as well as rallying and radicalizing individual supporters in countries around the world. Thousands of foreign fighters traveled to Syria and Iraq to join Daesh, whether attracted by its religious appeal, anger at the equally brutal (secular) Syrian government, or a search for adventure and sense of belonging.

Ultimately the self-proclaimed caliphate would be vanquished. The United States, Canada, European countries, and others provided support to the Iraqi government (and Kurdish Regional Government in northern Iraq) as it pushed back Daesh forces. Iran, alarmed at the emergence of a Sunni jihadist movement with a near-genocidal antipathy to Shi'ites near its borders, also was a major backer of the Iraqi government. Mosul was recaptured by Iraqi government forces by July 2017, after months of bitter fighting. In Syria, local Kurdish and Arab militias, backed by US and other coalition forces, ultimately drove Daesh from its "capital" of Raqqa later that same year.

American media coverage, understandably, tended to emphasize the American contribution to these military victories. It is important to remember, however, that of the many thousands who gave their lives fighting against Daesh and its self-styled "caliphate," 99 percent were Muslims.

As a final observation, it should be noted that not all Islamist groups that have taken up arms in pursuit of a political cause are entirely sustained by fundamentalism. In Lebanon, for example, Hizbullah has been involved in attacks against Israeli targets and even, on occasion, Lebanese rivals. It has close ties to Iran, with which it shares political and religious views. However, it enjoys widespread support from its Shi'ite constituency not necessarily because of theology or attachment to fundamentalist views of religion, but because of its long-standing opposition to Israel (which occupied south Lebanon from 1982 to 2000, and which many Lebanese still view as a threat), the social services it provides, and its reputation as an effective protector of Shi'ite interests within Lebanon's flawed but vibrant democratic political system (with thirteen members in Lebanon's current parliament). Similarly, the Palestinian Hamas movement—which has also engaged in terrorism and other acts of violence against Israel—developed from the local branch of the Muslim Brotherhood, but also wins support for its Palestinian nationalist credentials. It does not impose a particularly stringent view of Islam in the Gaza Strip where it currently holds power and has vigorously suppressed any effort by Daesh to organize support there. Indeed, surveys show that personal religiosity is a poor predictor of whether Palestinians support Hamas, or instead support its (more secular, pro-peace process) rival, Fateh.

THE FUTURE OF RELIGION AND POLITICS IN THE DEVELOPING WORLD

The hold of religion on the human heart and spirit, and its consequent impact on the political process, has been frequently misunderstood by Western observers. As we have seen, the initial error of both modernization and dependency theorists was to undervalue the significance of religion. Several factors account for the unanticipated resurgence of fundamentalism and other forms of religiously based politics in recent decades. In many countries, rapid modernization has left people alienated and searching for their cultural identity. The breakdown of village life and the erosion of traditional customs and values often create a void not filled by the material rewards of modern life. In the Middle East, the indignities of colonialism and neocolonialism, resentment against Israel and the West, and dismay over decades of failed development since independence have all contributed to the region's religious revival.

Turning to Latin America, the progressive church offered a shield against political repression and a voice for the poor. As vastly different as they are, Islamic revivalism and the progressive Catholic church have a few similarities. For example, both were grounded in revulsion over poverty and over government repression and corruption. Thus, the resurgence of religion often was linked to a yearning for social and political justice, even if that vision of justice is sometimes unpalatable to those outside the movement. Other religious movements, not discussed in this chapter, have different worldviews. The rapidly growing Pentecostal and other evangelical

Christian churches in Latin America tend to be conservative politically and in their lifestyles.

Having previously underestimated the impact of religion on politics in the developing world, analysts now risk overstating its importance. To begin with, the political weight of the movements that have attracted the most attention—Islamic revivalism and progressive Catholicism—must be put into perspective. Influential as they have been, they are not representative of the religions from which they have sprung. This point requires particular emphasis in relation to Islam, because a militant minority has left some Westerners with a negative image of the entire Muslim world. They consider Islam to be backward and intolerant when, actually, like all religions, it encompasses a range of outlooks, some reactionary and some progressive. It is worth remembering that seven Muslim-majority countries—Bangladesh, Indonesia, Kosovo, Mali, Pakistan, Senegal, and Turkey—have had female prime ministers or presidents, something the United States has yet to achieve (as of the writing of this book).

It is also important to recognize that the realities of practical politics shape the behavior of political actors, religious and secular alike. When religiously-based parties (Muslim or Hindu) have assumed power, no matter their original intentions, their behavior in office has often been moderated by their need for parliamentary coalition partners, their desire to appeal to a wide range of voters (if facing elections), and the dangers of offending powerful nonreligious actors, such as the army.

Indeed, in many cases, religious identification may act more as a marker of social identity than it does a philosophy of politics. In Lebanon, for example, competition between Sunni, Shi'ite, Druze (another Muslim sect), and Christian-based political parties is much more about the distribution of power and resources between the groups, and the patron-client networks associated with them, than it is a theological dispute. Fluid political alliances reflect this jockeying for position. Thus, (Shi'ite semi-fundamentalist) Hizbullah is closely allied with the (Shiite but non-Islamist) Amal party and (Christian) Free Patriotic Movement, while Hizbullah's chief rival is the (Sunni but non-Islamist) Future Movement and various other Christian parties. The (secular, Druze) Progressive Socialist Party variously remains neutral or tilts against Hizbullah, depending on the political context. In this sense, religious-sectarian politics may largely be another type of ethnic politics, as explored in chapter 6.

When evaluating the current religious revival, we cannot assume that current trends will continue long into the future. History reveals that "religious resurgence is a cyclical phenomenon."[22] Religious movements may arise where more secular political movements have failed, offering an alternative approach and view of the challenges of development. So too, the failure of religion-based mobilization may spur more secular political actors. For the foreseeable future, however, religion will continue to be an important influence in the politics of many developing nations.

Practice and Review Online at
http://textbooks.rowman.com/handelman9e

KEY TERMS

fundamentalist
liberation theology
Islamist
secularization

Salafist
Shi'ite (Muslim)
Sunni (Muslim)
theocratic (theocratic states)

DISCUSSION QUESTIONS

1. Why did early analysts of religion in the developing countries think that modernization would lead to a diminished political role for organized religion? Has this happened and, if not, why not?
2. What factors caused the growth of the progressive church in Latin America, and what is distinct about its followers' beliefs? Why has the progressive church lost so much of its influence in recent times?
3. What factors have led to the resurgence of Islamic fundamentalism in Afghanistan, Iran, Syria, and other parts of the Muslim world?

NOTES

1. Donald Eugene Smith, *Religion and Modernization* (New Haven, CT: Yale University Press, 1974), 4.

2. Quoted in Timothy D. Sisk, *Islam and Democracy* (Washington, DC: United States Institute of Peace, 1992), 3.

3. Pew Research Center, *The Changing Global Religious Landscape*, April 5, 2017, http://www.pewforum.org/2017/04/05/the-changing-global-religious-landscape/.

4. "Why Is Protestantism Flourishing in the Developing World?" *The Economist*, November 9, 2017.

5. Alexis de Tocqueville, *Democracy in America*, ed. Alan Ryan (London: Everyman's Library, 1994), 309–12.

6. Kenneth D. Wald, "Social Change and Political Response: The Silent Religious Cleavage in North America," in *Politics and Religion in the Modern World*, ed. George Moyser (New York, NY: Routledge and Kegan Paul, 1991), 240.

7. David Marquand and Ronald L. Nettler, "Forward," in *Religion and Democracy*, eds. David Marquand and Ronald L. Nettler (Oxford: Blackwell Publishers, 2000), 2–3.

8. Ibid., 3.

9. Jeff Haynes, "Religion and Democratization in Africa," in *Religion, Democracy and Democratization*, ed. John Anderson (New York: Routledge, 2006), 68.

10. Ibid., 69.

11. John L. Esposito, *Islam and Politics*, 2nd ed. (Syracuse, NY: Syracuse University Press, 1987), 1.

12. Data derived from World Values Survey data (http://www.worldvaluessurvey.org), counting those who scored strong agreement (nine or ten on a ten-point scale).

13. Data derived from Arab Barometer surveys (http://www.arabbarometer.org).

14. Donald Eugene Smith, *Religion and Political Development* (Boston, MA: Little, Brown, 1970), xi, italics added.

15. Paul Sigmund, *Liberation Theology at the Crossroads* (New York, NY: Oxford University Press, 1990), 19.

16. Ibid., 29–30.

17. Jennifer Pearce, "Politics and Religion in Central America: A Case Study of El Salvador," in George Moyser, ed., *Politics and Religion in the Modern World* (New York: Routledge, 1991), 234.

18. Scott Mainwaring and Alexander Wilde, eds., *The Progressive Church in Latin America* (Notre Dame, IN: University of Notre Dame Press, 1989), 13.

19. Philip Berryman, "El Salvador: From Evangelization to Insurrection," in *Religion and Political Conflict in Latin America*, ed. Daniel Levine (Chapel Hill: University of North Carolina Press, 1986), 58–78, 114.

20. Cheryl Bernard and Zalmay Khalilzad, *The Government of God: Iran's Islamic Republic* (New York, NY: Columbia University Press, 1984), 12–13.

21. Robin Wright, *In the Name of God: The Khomeini Decade* (New York, NY: Simon & Schuster, 1989), 65.

22. Donald Eugene Smith, "The Limits of Religious Resurgence," in *Religious Resurgence and Politics in the Contemporary World*, ed. Emile Sahliyah (Albany: State University of New York Press, 1990), 34.

6

The Politics of Cultural Pluralism and Ethnic Conflict

A makeshift refugee camp in Bangladesh for members of the Rohingya minority fleeing persecution in Myanmar. Of the more than 65 million refugees and forcibly displaced persons around the world, most have fled ethnic or religious violence. *Source*: Associated Press.

FOR MANY YEARS, MUCH OF THE DEVELOPING WORLD has suffered from ethnic, racial, and religious clashes periodically punctuated by outbreaks of brutality and carnage. Progress in one location has repeatedly been followed by deterioration in another. In some cases, that conflict has taken on international ramifications.

Appalling ethnic confrontations are not new. A century ago (1915–17), in the midst of the First World War, Turkey's embattled Ottoman government launched a genocidal campaign against the country's (Christian) Armenian population that left perhaps 1–1.5 million dead. Some thirty years later, as Britain relinquished power over India, it divided its former "jewel in the [imperial] crown," into two nations—largely Hindu India and mostly Muslim Pakistan. But the religious communities in each country then savagely turned on each other, with a resulting death toll of approximately 1 million. Millions of Hindu and Sikh refugees fled Pakistan to India, while millions of Muslims fled India to Pakistan. In 1994, Hutus militias in the African nation of Rwanda massacred some eight hundred thousand of their Tutsi countrymen. During the twentieth century, religious clashes (e.g., in India, Iraq, and Lebanon), tribal animosities (e.g., Nigeria and Rwanda), racial prejudice (e.g., in South Africa), and other forms of ethnic rancor frequently produced violent riots, civil wars, and genocidal brutality. Continuing ethnic clashes and tensions in the first two decades of the twenty-first century—for example, in Syria, Yemen, South Sudan and Myanmar (Burma)—seem to confirm the prediction—that wars between "peoples" (ethnic, religious, racial, or cultural groups) will continue to far outnumber wars between states.

> Classic accounts of modernization, particularly those influenced by Marx, predicted that the old basis for divisions, such as tribe and religion, would be swept aside. As hundreds of millions of people poured from rural to urban areas worldwide, during the nineteenth and twentieth centuries, it was expected that new alliances would be formed, based on social class in particular.[1]

However, significant as class conflict has been, no cleavage in modern times has more sharply and oftentimes violently polarized nations than has ethnicity. "Cultural pluralism [i.e., ethnic diversity]," notes Crawford Young, "is a quintessentially modern phenomenon." It has been closely linked to the growth of the middle class and the emergence of politicians who articulated nationalist or other ethnic aspirations, while mobilizing workers and peasants behind that ideal.[2] Scholars point out that hostility toward other ethnic groups is far older and often more entrenched than modern principles of tolerance or equality under the law. "No matter how we may wish for it otherwise, we did not leave violence against outsiders behind us as our nations became modern and democratic."[3] To be sure, ethnic minorities have been victimized for hundreds of years. So, such struggles are not new. One need only look to the nineteenth-century frontier wars between white settlers and Native Americans in the United States and Chile.

Still, the level of ethnically based internal conflict has grown since the 1980s, in marked contrast to the dramatic decline in wars between states in the same period. Indeed, the most frequent settings for violent confrontation over the past fifty years have not been wars between sovereign states, but rather internal strife tied to cultural, tribal, religious, or other ethnic animosities. Between 1989 and 2004, there were 118 military conflicts in the world. Of those, only 7 were between states and the remaining 111 occurred within a single state, a large portion of which involved ethnic conflict.[4] According to another recent estimate, "nearly two-thirds of all [the world's] armed conflicts [at that time] included an ethnic component. [In fact], ethnic conflicts [were] four times more likely than interstate wars."[5] Another study claimed that 80 percent of "major conflicts" in the 1990s had an ethnic element.[6]

Any contemporary listing of the world's most bloody wars would include ethnically based internal warfare or massacres in Syria, Rwanda, Congo, Ethiopia, Sudan, Lebanon, Sri Lanka, and Indonesia. Between 1945 and 1998, an estimated 15 million people died worldwide as a result of ethnic violence (much of that total from war-related starvation and disease).[7] In the years since then, ethnic battles in Congo (Kinshasa)* alone resulted in millions of additional deaths (directly from violence—or, much more so, indirectly from displacement, hunger and disease), while many thousands more have died in Sudan, Ethiopia, Iraq, Syria, and elsewhere.

Warfare between Serbs, Croats, Bosnian Muslims, and Kosovars in the former Yugoslavia, along with separatist movements by French-speaking Québécois, racially based riots in Los Angeles, Basque terrorism in Spain, and Protestant-Catholic clashes in Northern Ireland, all demonstrate that ethnic friction and violence can erupt in developed countries. But such battles have been particularly widespread and cruel in Africa, Asia, the Middle East, and other regions of the developing world—in part because developing countries tend to be more ethnically diverse, in part because a sense of shared national identity may be less established, and part because their political systems frequently lack the institutions needed to resolve such tensions peacefully. One study has determined that at the start of this century there were approximately 275 "minorities at risk" in the world (i.e., ethnic groups facing actual or potential repression), with a total population

---

* Congo (Kinshasa) is used to distinguish the current Democratic Republic of Congo (formerly known as Zaire) from the neighboring Republic of Congo, referred to here as Congo (Brazzaville).

exceeding 1 billion people (about one-sixth of the world's populations at that time) scattered in 116 countries. Approximately 85 percent of the at-risk population lived in the developing countries. Although Asia has the highest absolute population of such minorities, sub-Saharan Africa has the highest proportion of its population at risk (about 36 percent), followed by the Arab World (26 percent).[8]

The intensification of ethnic, racial, and cultural hostilities during the twentieth and twenty-first centuries undercut several assumptions of modernization theory; it also contradicted an influential social psychology theory called the "contact hypothesis." This hypothesis predicted that as people of different races, religions, and ethnicities came into greater contact with each other, they would better understand the other groups' common human qualities, causing prejudice to decline. Although the contact hypothesis frequently describes individual-level attitudes and behavior (i.e., as individuals of different races or religions come to know each other better, their prejudices tend to diminish), increased interaction between different ethnic groups—occasioned by factors such as migration—often intensifies hostilities. Moreover, in some cases such as Rwanda and Bosnia, despite years of close interethnic contact and intermarriage, neighbors and even relatives by marriage viciously turned against each other once group violence had taken on a momentum of its own. This is particularly true when the political and economic systems are biased in favor of one ethnic group or when ethnic leaders play on their followers' prejudices to advance their own political agendas.

Neighboring ethnicities that lived peacefully side by side for decades may also confront each other when new, valuable natural resources are discovered on their common lands. Thus, for example, in Nigeria, the upsurge of oil production in the Niger Delta sparked unrest by tribal minorities in the region, who perceived that great wealth was being extracted from the delta while the local population was left in poverty. Similar ethnic violence has arisen in the neighboring country of Niger after the discovery of substantial uranium deposits.

Regional and global politics can play a role too. Internal conflict in Congo (Kinshasa) in 1996–97 and again in 1998–2003 was exacerbated by the involvement by nine neighboring African countries, each supporting local allies and proxies to further their political and economic interests. Similarly, the ongoing civil wars in Syria and Yemen, while arising from domestic sectarian and political tensions, have been fueled by the outside involvement of Iran, Turkey, Saudi Arabia, the United Arab Emirates, Russia, the United States, and others.

This chapter focuses on the most protracted and intense ethnic group conflicts in the developing world. In doing so, it runs the risk of conveying the erroneous impression that all developing countries are aflame with violent ethnic clashes. In truth, most ethnic tensions do not lead to violence and many developing nations have been comparatively free of such conflict. Indeed, some research suggests that ethnic diversity does not really contribute greatly to the risk of insurgency or civil war, when other factors (such as economic development) are taken into account.[9]

Ethnic warfare is most pronounced in the Indian subcontinent, the Middle East, Southeast Asia, and much of Africa. It is less common in Latin America and the Far East. A number of developing countries—Uruguay and Korea, for example—are fairly ethnically homogeneous, eliminating the possibility of such struggle. Others have developed a fairly stable, if not necessarily just, relationship between ethnicities, including Ghana and Taiwan. A number of Latin American countries are multiracial and have varying degrees of racial discrimination and tension. But rarely do those conflicts now become violent. So, although this chapter focuses on the most difficult and vicious cases in order to illustrate the obstacles that ethnic confrontations may present to political and economic development, it does not imply that most developing countries are riddled with ethnic violence.

DEFINING ETHNICITY

Many scholars have maintained that human beings have a deeply rooted social and psychological need to identify with a group that protects them from outsiders and gives them a sense of belonging (i.e., to create an "us" to protect ourselves from "them"). Although it is challenging to define **ethnicity** precisely, certain common qualities set ethnic groups apart. Most analysts agree that ethnic identity is usually a social construction—a way that certain groups have come to view themselves over time as distinct from others—rather than an inherent or primordial characteristic. Each ethnicity "share[s] a distinctive and enduring collective identity based on a belief in a common descent and on shared experiences and cultural traits."[10] While they frequently have some basis in fact, these identities and histories are typically created or embellished by entrepreneurial politicians, intellectuals, and journalists who gain some advantage by "playing the ethnic card." The real or imagined common history, tradition, and values not only unite the group, but also distinguish it from neighboring ethnicities, sometimes giving rise to ethnic conflict. Thus, J. E. Brown's cynical definition of a "nation" can be applied to ethnic identities generally: "A group of people united by a common error about their ancestry and a common dislike of their neighbors."[11] In times of great uncertainty or crisis, intellectuals and politicians are likely to create historical myths that give their ethnic group a sense of security in the face of perceived external challenges. In the words of Vesna Pesic, a Serbian peace activist, ethnic conflict is caused by the "fear of the future, lived through the past."[12]

Chinese in Malaysia, Hmong in Laos, and indigenous peoples in Peru often form their own political organizations or business groups. However, ethnic groups are usually not socially homogeneous or politically united. Frequently, class, ideology, or religion divides them. For example, Indian Muslims and Nigerian Ibos are internally divided by class. South Koreans may be Buddhist or Christian (or both). Still, the factors that bind these ethnic groups are more powerful than elements that divide them. Thus, Ibo peasants normally identify more closely with businesspeople from their own ethnicity than they do with fellow peasants from the Hausa or Yoruba communities. Indeed, Cynthia Enloe notes that "of all the groups that men [or women] attach themselves to, ethnic groups seem the most encompassing and enduring."[13]

Often, outside observers erroneously assert or assume that certain contemporary ethnic identities and ethnic clashes are deeply rooted in history. For example, during the bitter civil war between Bosnian Muslims and Serbs (in the former Yugoslavia), many Western journalists and political leaders claimed that violence could be traced to centuries-old religious tensions and conflicts (dating to the Middle Ages) between Orthodox (Christian) Serbians, Muslim Bosnians, and Catholic Croatians. But actually, prior to the breakup of Yugoslavia in the early 1990s, the three groups had lived together in harmony for many years, and intermarriages were common. With the collapse of communism, however, nationalist politicians (particularly Serbs) used ethnic appeals to mobilize political support. As conflict grew, people were forced to choose an ethnic identity.

Some ethnic classifications were initially imposed by outsiders. During the era of the white minority regime in South Africa, the classification of "Colored," was used to denote those of racially mixed or Asian backgrounds, as part of a broader policy of state-enforced racial segregation (known as Apartheid). And although Mexicans may feel little in common with Cubans, Ecuadorians, or Nicaraguans when they live in their home countries, all of these nationalities have become an ethnic group called "Latinos" or "Hispanics" after they immigrated to the United States—viewed as a homogeneous mass by their "Anglo" neighbors. Once individuals begin to accept the group label imposed on them, however, even artificially created ethnic classifications become politically relevant.

Ethnic groups may have their own social clubs, soccer teams, schools, or cemeteries. For an insecure Peruvian Indian recently arrived in Lima from her rural village, or a Hausa migrant seeking a job in Lagos, ethnically based social clubs are invaluable for finding employment, housing, and friendships in an otherwise cold and inhospitable city. In the threatening environment associated with modernization and social change, "fear, anxiety, and insecurity at the individual level can be reduced within the womb of the ethnic collectivity."[14] At the same time, however, ethnic consciousness normally creates barriers between groups. Relatives, friends, and neighbors tend to frown upon interreligious or interracial marriages, for example. When two or more ethnic groups live in close proximity to each other, there may be some tension or apprehension. But the way in which society handles these relationships varies considerably from place to place. Countries such as Canada, Malaysia, and Trinidad and Tobago have managed ethnic divisions fairly amicably and peacefully. In other cases, however, ethnic divisions lead to tensions or even conflict.

ETHNIC AND STATE BOUNDARIES

If the world were composed of fairly homogeneous countries such as South Korea or Iceland, ethnically based wars might continue between nation-states, but there would be little ethnic tensions or strife within individual countries. In other words, one underlying cause of some internal ethnic conflict is that boundaries for nations or ethnic groups—distinct cultural-linguistic groups such as the Kurds—frequently fail to coincide fully with boundaries for states (self-governing countries). Indeed, the world's nearly two hundred countries are home to approximately five thousand ethnic groups, most of whom do not have their own nation-state and some of whom seek that goal. For example, Sikh militants in the Indian state of Punjab have demanded the creation of a Sikh nation-state. Kurds in Iraq, Syria, Turkey, and Iran have had similar aspirations. When ethnic groups feel that they have been denied their fair share of political and economic rewards, they will frequently mobilize to demand their rights.

At least 80 percent of the world's countries today contain two or more ethnic groups. Furthermore, in at least one-third of the world's countries, no single ethnic group accounts for even half of the total population. This pattern is most striking in sub-Saharan Africa, where nearly every country is composed of several ethnic (tribal) groups. For example, it is estimated that Nigeria, the most populous African state, has more than two hundred linguistic (tribal) groups.

Many Africans attribute their continent's legacy of tribal conflict to the European colonizers who divided the region into administrative units little connected with ethnic identities. In some cases, antagonistic groups were thrown together into a single colony, while elsewhere individual ethnic groups were split between two future countries. Borders were often drawn along rivers or as straight lines across deserts—convenient for colonial cartographers, but in no way reflecting patterns of social belonging and interaction on the ground. In Africa, Asia, and the Middle East, colonial powers regularly exacerbated ethnic tensions by favoring certain groups over others and by using "divide-and-conquer" strategies to control the local population. Yet, colonialism was but one of many factors contributing to ethnic discord. Given the thousands of tribal groups in Africa, even if the European powers had shown greater ethnic sensibility, postcolonial states would still have to address the challenge of multiple group identities.

At the same time, however, the breakdown of European colonialism also led to a number of extremely unhappy ethnic marriages. When the Portuguese withdrew from the small Southeast Asian colony of East Timor in 1975, neighboring Indonesia annexed it against the local population's will. In its efforts to crush the organized Timorese opposition, the Indonesian military killed or starved approximately 150,000 people (about 25 percent of the region's population). Elsewhere, following years of Italian colonial rule and a brief British occupation, the East African colony of Eritrea was forcibly merged with Ethiopia in the early 1950s. The Eritrean people resented the Ethiopian takeover and soon embarked on a long struggle for independence. Three decades of civil war resulted in thousands of deaths. The collapse of the Ethiopian military dictatorship in 1991 allowed Eritrea to finally achieve independence. But the two countries fought a bloody border war during 1998–2000 and relations between them remain tense.

TYPES OF ETHNIC AND CULTURAL DIVISIONS

In order to better grasp the range of ethnic tensions that currently pervade much of the developing world, we will classify all types of ethnicities into a set of somewhat overlapping categories: nationality, tribe, race, and religion.

Nationality

In ethnic analysis, the term "**nation**" has a specialized meaning distinct from its more common usage designating a sovereign country. It refers, instead, to a population with its own language, cultural traditions, historical aspirations, and, sometimes, its own geographical home. Frequently, nationhood is associated with the belief that the interests and values of that nation supersede any competing interests.

Unlike other types of ethnic groups, nationalities usually claim sovereignty over a specific geographic area. But, as we have seen, these proposed national boundaries frequently do not coincide with those of sovereign states (independent countries). For example, India and Sri Lanka are both sovereign states that encompass several distinct nationalities (cultural identities). In each case, members of at least one of those nationalities—Muslim Kashmiris (India) and mostly Hindu Tamils (Sri Lanka)—have waged long struggles for independence. On the other hand, the Chinese are a nationality that, through migration, has spilled over to several East Asian countries and to other parts of the world. The approximately 30 million Kurds are one of the largest ethnic groups in the Middle East, residing primarily in

Turkey, Iraq, and Iran. Unlike the Chinese, however, so far they have been a nation without a state of their own.

As with other types of ethnicity, the political significance of national identity is related to a number of subjective factors. Nationality becomes politically important only when its members believe that their common history and destiny greatly distinguish them from other ethnicities in their country. The most critical basis for national identification is the preservation of a distinct spoken language. Because French Canadians, Turkish Kurds, and Malaysian Chinese have maintained their "mother tongues," their national identities remain politically relevant. Chinese speakers in Southeast Asia have maintained their own cultural and political organizations and feel strong emotional ties to China. On the other hand, because most immigrants—including Chinese, Italians, and Germans—to countries such as the United States, Canada, and Australia have largely assimilated into their new language and culture, usually dropping their language of origin after one or two generations, their original national identity loses much of its political and social impact.

When multilingual countries throughout Africa and Asia gained their independence from the 1940s through the 1970s, they needed to choose which language or languages would be their official state language. In some of these countries—such as, Cameroon, India, Indonesia, and Nigeria—hundreds of different languages are spoken. As we will see in Sri Lanka, the choice of the official language(s) or a change in the official language is often very contentious and may become the source of intense ethnic conflict. This is particularly true if the government chooses the language of the political-economic elite rather than the most widely spoken tongue. One way that many multilingual countries have tried to avoid such conflict is to pick a language that is not native to any of the language groups, but is widely known across ethnic groups, as a means of interethnic communication (a **lingua franca**). Frequently, the choice is the language of the former colonial power (such as English or French).[15] In other cases, it is a language or dialect that is used for commercial purposes (such as Tagalog in the Philippines or Swahili in Kenya and Tanzania).

In their more limited manifestations, nationalist movements simply seek to preserve the group's cultural identity and promote its economic and political interests. For example, the large Lebanese community in Brazil, East Indians in Guyana, and Irish-Americans in the United States take pride in their distinctive cultures, but none has entertained visions of self-governance. On the other hand, nationalist movements become more provocative when they seek to create a separate nation-state of their own. Such separatist movements can arise when an ethnic minority is concentrated in a particular region of the country and represents a majority of the population in that area. Those conditions exist in Sri Lanka, where the Tamil-speaking population is concentrated in the country's northern and eastern provinces, particularly the Jaffna Peninsula region in the far north. Even before the intrusion of European colonizers, the Tamils kept themselves apart from other ethnicities inhabiting Ceylon. The British conquest and colonization of the entire island produced a nationalist reaction among the majority Sinhalese (Sinhala-speaking) population, which, in turn, provoked friction between them and the Tamil minority.

Since independence in 1948, political power has been concentrated in the hands of the Sinhalese (who constitute about three-quarters of the country's population). As in most nationality-based ethnic clashes, language issues were at the heart of the conflict. Eight years after independence, Sinhala replaced English as the country's official language, giving the Sinhalese population a significant advantage in securing government jobs. As one Tamil political leader put it, "Not until 1956 did we really believe that we were second-class citizens. Until then all we engaged in were preventive measures, which we thought would hold."[16] From that point forward, however, the battle for Tamil self-rule intensified. Conversely, when Tamil acquired equal legal status in 1978, many Sinhalese felt victimized. Religious differences between the largely Hindu Tamils and the predominantly Buddhist Sinhalese augmented their language and cultural divisions, though religious issues remained secondary.

Since independence, Tamil leaders (representing around one-sixth of the population) have demanded a federal system that would grant their regions substantial autonomy (some degree of self-rule) within Sri Lanka. Sinhalese nationalists, in turn, tried to impose their language on the entire nation. In 1958, Sinhalese mobs attacked Tamils in various parts of the country, and in 1964, the central government signed an agreement with India calling for the eventual return to India of 525,000 Tamils whose families had migrated from that country. Faced with these threats, Tamil nationalism became increasingly strident and violent. Early calls for autonomy were superseded by demands for secession and the creation of a sovereign Tamil state. By the early 1980s, the most powerful political force in the country's predominantly Tamil areas was the Liberation Tigers of Tamil Eelam (also known as the Tamil Tigers or the LTTE), a secessionist force engaged in guerrilla warfare, terrorism, and, ultimately, conventional war.

In 1987, following a major national government offensive against the LTTE, India (concerned about demands for autonomy from its own Tamil minority) intervened militarily in Sri Lanka. The resulting Indo-Lanka Peace Accord called for a multiethnic, multilingual Sri Lankan state with increased regional autonomy for the Tamil areas. Though signed by the Indian and Sri Lankan governments, the accord was rejected by many Sinhalese, particularly the ultranationalist National Liberation Front (JVP). From 1987 to 1989, the JVP launched its own campaign of strikes, boycotts, and terrorism, resulting in thousands of deaths. A brutal government campaign eventually crushed the JVP, but the war against the Tamil Tigers continued. Although many Tamils welcomed the Indo-Lanka accord, the Tigers rejected it as inadequate. Instead, they expanded their guerrilla war, first against India's sixty-thousand-man military force and then, after the 1990 withdrawal of foreign troops, against the Sri Lankan government and moderate Tamils.

The Tamil Tigers were responsible for the 1993 assassination of the country's president and hundreds of suicide bombings. By 2000, about sixty-two thousand people had been killed in the civil war, out of a total Sri Lankan population of only 21 million. Although a cease-fire temporarily halted the fighting, by 2005, the truce broke. Soon, the armed forces launched a major offensive against the LTTE stronghold in the northeast, driving them into an increasingly smaller area. Many thousands of civilians died while the government shelled and bombed the enclave with little concern for civilian lives. In May 2009, the rebels were forced to abandon their twenty-five-year struggle. With the war's end, up to three hundred thousand Tamil civilians, who fled the war zone, were held for months (or, in some cases, for years) in "displacement camps," often in deplorable conditions. Since then, efforts to promote national reconciliation have made little headway, and many Tamils continue to feel disadvantaged.

Tribe

The very use of the category **tribe**—especially when applied to African cultures—is quite controversial. Many anthropologists and political scientists find it arbitrary and unhelpful. Instead, they prefer the terms "ethnicity" or "ethnolinguistic group." This chapter, however, still refers to "tribes" or "tribal groups" because this term is familiar to most readers and has long been used by many scholars of ethnic politics and by numerous political leaders in Africa and Asia. It describes subnational groups that share a collective identity and language and believe themselves to hold a common lineage.

Tribal conflict has frequently sparked violence in sub-Saharan Africa, affecting more than half the countries in that region at one time or another. Ethiopia, Rwanda, Burundi, Uganda, Sudan, Congo, and the Central African Republic, among others, have been torn apart by civil wars that were primarily or partially ethnically based. In Liberia, Angola, and Mozambique, conflicts begun about other issues were aggravated by tribal divisions.

From the time of its independence, Nigeria experienced enmity between the Muslims in the north and the populations of the south and east. With approximately half the country's population, the Hausa-Fulani (primarily

Muslim) and other northern tribes were a dominant political force, resented by southerners and easterners such as the Ibo (largely Christian), who considered themselves more advanced than northerners. Northerners, in turn, feared the influence of the more modern and commercially success-ful Ibo people. Each of the three major ethnic groups (Hausa-Fulani, Ibo, and Yoruba) prevailed in one region of the country, casting a shadow over smaller tribes in their area. Each major group, in turn, feared domination by the others. Two coups in 1966 intensified friction between military offi-cers of differing ethnic backgrounds and sparked violence against the large number of Ibos who had migrated to the North. As many as thirty thou-sand Ibos were killed, while 1–2 million more, fearing for their lives, fled back to their homeland. In May 1967, Colonel Chukwuemeka Ojukwu, an Ibo military leader, declared that eastern Nigeria was withdrawing from the country to become the independent nation of Biafra. But the Nigerian national government was determined to prevent the secession and was able to cut off food deliveries to the area. As many as 1 million Ibo civilians died of starvation before the war ended in 1970. Since that time, the Ibos have been successfully reintegrated into Nigerian society, but intertribal tensions and periodic religious violence between Christians and Muslims persist.

Unfortunately, these events were followed by a large number of ethni-cally based civil wars that have plagued the African continent since that time. Some of the most intense and prolonged tribal conflicts took place in the former Belgian colonies of Burundi and Rwanda in the Great Lakes region of central Africa. Since they gained power in the early 1970s, Burundi's ruling Tutsi minority has crushed a series of uprisings by the Hutus—who constitute about 85 percent of the population—massacring some one hundred thousand people in 1972 alone. In 1993, when a Tutsi soldier assassinated the country's first freely elected president, a Hutu, new bloodshed erupted. One year later, in the neighboring country of Rwanda, a Hutu president's death in a plane crash set off an orgy of violence. A government-directed massacre led by Hutu extremists was aimed at the minority Tutsis and, to a lesser extent, at moderate Hutus. During the next hundred days, local Hutu militia and allied villagers hacked or beat to death approximately 750,000 Tutsis and 50,000 Hutus. Eventually, a well-trained Tutsi revolutionary army, supported by neighboring Uganda, gained control of the country and jailed thousands of Hutus. An additional several hundred thousand fled to nearby Congo (Kinshasa), where many of them starved to death or were massacred by the anti-Hutu regime of then-president Laurent Kabila. Under President Paul Kagame, the Rwandan government has sought—vigorously and often with a rather authoritarian hand—to overcome ethno-tribal divisions and impose a common Rwandan identity.

Race

We have noted that cultural identity involves a common set of values and customs and a shared sense of history and destiny. Race, while normally the most visible of ethnic distinctions, is a more recent source of group identity. Only when people live in multiracial settings do individual racial groups use race to define themselves and distinguish themselves from "others." Indeed, Crawford Young indicates that "there was no common sense of being 'African,' 'European,' or 'Indian,' prior to the creation of multiracial communities by the population movements of the imperial age."[17] Many scholars stress that race itself is a rather fuzzy and often dubious scientific concept, a category often imposed by others on the basis of apparently shared physical characteristics.

South Africa was the most notorious example of race-based political conflict. From its colonization by the British until its 1994 transition to majority rule, the country was ruled by a white minority constituting only about 15 percent of the population. The country's Apartheid system created official racial classifications for the entire population assigned everyone to a racial category and rigidly segregated employment, public facilities, housing, marriage, and more. Non-whites were denied fundamental civil liberties, including the right to own property. Blacks, by far the largest racial group, constituted 70–75 percent of the national population and were subjected to the greatest amount of legal discrimination. Coloreds—mostly people of mixed race—totaled about 10 percent of the population, primarily concentrated in Cape Town and Cape Province. Asians (mostly Indians and Pakistanis) represented another 3 percent. Both coloreds and Asians enjoyed a higher socioeconomic status and greater legal and political rights than blacks did, but still ranked considerably below whites. Finally, whites (some 15 percent) dominated the political and economic systems.

Despite international disapproval, South Africa's minority government was determined to maintain apartheid indefinitely. In time, however, the country came under intense domestic and international pressure to end white domination. South Africa became an international outcast—particularly after several massacres of peaceful black protesters—subject to diplomatic, economic, and cultural isolation. Though slow to take effect, these sanctions eventually impaired the country's economic growth. Growing protest and unrest in the black townships (outlying urban slums) added to the country's international isolation. Finally, a growing number of powerful voices within the white economic, legal, and intellectual elites pressed the government for racial reform.

By the start of the 1990s, President F. W. de Klerk's government, recognizing that Apartheid was no longer viable, legalized the ANC, the leading black opposition group, after decades of banishment. The ANC's legendary leader, Nelson Mandela, the world's most celebrated political prisoner, was released from jail (after twenty-seven years of imprisonment) along with hundreds of other political prisoners. In December 1991, the Convention for a Democratic South Africa (CODESA) brought together the government, the ANC, and seventeen smaller groups for discussions of the new political order. In a 1992 national referendum called by de Klerk, nearly 70 percent of all white voters endorsed negotiations with the ANC and other black groups. The following year, the government and the ANC agreed to the election of a constitutional assembly that would create a new political system with equal rights for all South Africans. Universal suffrage ensured an ANC parliamentary majority and in 1994 that body elected Nelson Mandela president of the new, majority-ruled South Africa.

In the years since that time, South Africa has established itself as one of the most democratic nations on the continent. However, significant challenges to democratic consolidation remain. Although majority rule has established greater social justice and human dignity, many black South Africans remain mired in poverty. To be sure, government housing programs have benefited numerous urban slum dwellers and the black middle class has swelled. On the other hand, with most farmland still owned by whites and limited funds available for schools and clinics in the countryside, the black rural population remains impoverished. Faced with high unemployment, high crime rates, and one of the world's greatest incidences of AIDS, the urban poor also continue to struggle. Until now, at least, the government has pursued moderate economic policies to reassure the white business community. These policies have brought economic growth but have been slow to alleviate poverty. This, coupled with a series of corruption scandals, has increasingly tainted the ANC's reputation, although it still remains the most popular political party in the country.

Religion

Because it involves deeply felt values, religion has frequently been the source of bitter "communal strife" (i.e., conflict between ethnic communities). In chapter 5, we examined the influence of religious beliefs on political attitudes and behavior, particularly those of fundamentalists and others favoring close links between church and state. We saw that a group's religious orientation often shapes its political beliefs and behavior.

In this chapter, we look at a related but distinct aspect of religion, namely the degree to which coreligionists identify strongly with each other and try to enhance their political and economic power relative to other religious groups. In other words, we are concerned here, not with the political ramifications of religious beliefs but with conflict between religious groups (defined here as one type of ethnic community). Such discord may pit one religion against another or may involve conflict between two branches of the same religion. Two factors influence the likelihood of tensions between religious groups: first, the extent to which one religious community feels ill-treated by another; and second, the degree to which any religion regards itself as the only true faith and rejects alternate theologies. Thus, Catholics and Protestants coexist rather harmoniously in the United States and Germany because neither of those conditions applies. On the other hand, in Northern Ireland, where Catholics have resented the Protestants' political and economic powers and Protestants have feared political domination by the Catholic community, paramilitary groups representing both sides engaged in decades of armed struggle until "the Troubles" finally came to an end in the late 1990s with the Good Friday Agreement.

In 1992, thousands of Hindu fundamentalists destroyed a sixteenth-century Muslim mosque in the northern Indian town of Ayodhya. Like many such clashes, the incident grew out of centuries-old beliefs and hostilities. Many Hindus believe this to be the spot where their god Ram had been born ages before. To the BJP, the leading Hindu political party, and to the more militant World Hindu Council, the mosque was a symbol of Islamic domination during the three hundred years of Mogul rule prior to the British colonial era. Within days of the 1992 assault, rioting in northern and central India left about two thousand dead. Ten years later, Hindu mobs in the city of Ahmedabad murdered over one thousand Muslims, burning some of them alive. In neighboring Islamic countries, Pakistani crowds attacked Hindu temples and Bangladeshis assaulted Hindu-owned shops.

In fact, India and Pakistan were born of communal violence, and neither has been free of it since. Although both countries had been part of a single British colony, when negotiations for independence advanced in the late 1940s, the Muslim League insisted on the creation of a separate Muslim state. Using language that classically defines an ethnic group, League leader Mohammed Ali Jinnah declared, "We are a nation with our own distinctive culture and civilization, language and literature . . . customs . . . history and tradition."[18] In 1946, as independence approached, political tensions between the Muslim League and the dominant Congress Party (a nonreligious party led largely by secular Hindus) touched off communal violence that left thousands dead. Finally, the British reluctantly divided their most important colony into two countries: India, with roughly 300 million Hindus and 40 million Muslims; and Pakistan, with approximately 60 million Muslims and 20 million Hindus, at that time. No sooner had independence been declared (August 15, 1947), when horrendous religious massacres began in both countries. Whole villages were destroyed, twelve million refugees of both faiths fled in both directions across the border, more than seventy-five thousand women were abducted and raped, and somewhere between five hundred thousand and one million people were killed in one of the twentieth century's worst ethnic conflagrations. Two decades later, Pakistan itself split in two, as geography, language, and cultural differences rather than religion divided its population. With support from India, the Bengali-speaking eastern region broke away from the dominant, primarily Urdu-speaking, west to form the country of Bangladesh.

In recent years, Muslim separatists in the Indian-controlled portion of Kashmir have waged guerrilla warfare aimed either at Kashmiri independence or at unification with Pakistan. In 2001, Islamic fundamentalists attacked the Indian parliament, once again bringing India and Pakistan (both of them nuclear powers) to the brink of war. Since early 2004, the two countries have engaged in a series of peace talks and confidence-building measures. But basic differences over Kashmir and ingrained suspicions keep that region volatile, as have terrorist attacks on India. In November 2008, an Islamist terrorist group named Lashkar-e-Taiba or LeT ("Army of the Pure") launched a deadly attack on the center of Mumbai (formerly Bombay, one of India's largest cities and its financial capital), killing nearly two hundred people and wounding more than three hundred. Based in Pakistan, that group is committed to "liberating" the Indian-controlled portion of Kashmir. Like the Afghan Taliban, the LeT and other Islamist groups have received assistance from Pakistan's intelligence service (the ISI), and they likely still receive help from ISI hard-liners.

Of all the major world religions, Buddhism has generally been regarded as the most-nonviolent and tolerant. However, in recent years, extremist Buddhist priests in Myanmar have led violent attacks against the Muslim minority, known as Rohingya, a population of about one million persons who have largely emigrated from Bangladesh. The military dictatorship that ruled Myanmar from 1962 to 2015 refused to recognize Rohingya born in the country as citizens and redistricted most of them to refugee camps.* It was hoped that the victory of Aung San Suu Kyi's National League for Democracy party in the 2015 election would lead to better treatment of the Rohingya since Sui Kyi was a widely respected fighter for democracy who had won the Nobel Peace Prize in 1990. But, her government has failed to protect the Muslim minority. Indeed, "the Rohingyas have often been called the most persecuted minority in the world."[19] In 1982, the government passed legislation making them stateless (i.e., they don't have the rights of Myanmar citizens). In recent years, they have been attacked in riots led by radical Buddhist monks and by the

---

* The military dictatorship officially came to an end in 2011, but the armed forces continued to exert its control until the 2015 general elections. The military continues to have considerable political influence until today.

Burmese (Myanmar) military. In those attacks thousands of Muslims have been driven from their homes.

In the Middle East, recent years have seen growing tensions between Sunni and Shi'ite Muslims. These are not entirely new—they have long been characteristic of politics in Lebanon (where politics is largely organized along sectarian lines) and Bahrain (where a Sunni royal family rules over a largely Shi'ite population). However, the wars in Iraq, and later in Syria, contributed greatly.

In Iraq, the repressive regime of former dictator Saddam Hussein and his Ba'th Party officially embraced secular principles, but in practice often favored fellow Sunnis connected to president's family and home region. The Iran-Iraq War (1980–88) also led the regime to grow suspicious of those (Shi'ite) Iraqis who might harbor sympathies for (Shi'ite) Iran. After Saddam Hussein was toppled in 2003 by American intervention, and elections subsequently held, many politicians used religious (Sunni, Shi'ite) and ethnic (Arab, Kurdish) appeals to mobilize support. With Shi'ites comprising around 60 percent of the population, Shi'ite parties and politicians benefited.

Many Sunni grew resentful of this shift in political power. This, coupled with nationalist anger at foreign occupation, resulted in a predominantly Sunni insurgency against American forces. Purges of (predominantly Sunni) Ba'th Party members from the Iraqi military and bureaucracy contributed further to Sunni feelings of marginalization.

Later, after US troops withdrew, feelings of alienation and discontent with the Shi'ite-dominated government in Baghdad would grow still further. Prime Minister Nouri al-Maliki used widespread patronage to reward and empower his Shi'ite supporters while paying little heed to Sunni grievances. As a result, some Sunnis initially acquiesced in, or even supported, the growth of Daesh. Subsequently, Haider al-Abadi (who replaced al-Maliki as prime minister in 2014) made some attempt to address Sunni concerns. At the same time, however, his government's military campaign depended heavily on Shi'ite volunteer militias, organized into the (Iranian-backed) Popular Mobilization Forces (PMF). While the central government defeated Daesh forces in Mosul and elsewhere, continued Sunni grievances, the temptations of Shi'ite majoritarianism, and years of religious politics and violence all mean that Iraq will not quickly or easily escape from its current sectarian tensions.

The growth of sectarian politics in the region was given further impetus by the eruption of civil war in neighboring Syria in 2011. Syria, like Iraq, had been ruled by the Ba'th Party—albeit a rival wing, under President Bashar al-Asad. In theory, the party emphasized the common Arab identity of most Syrians, rejecting religious differences. In practice, however, President Asad (like his predecessor and father, Hafez al-Asad) depended heavily for support from among their own Alawite community, a small offshoot of Shi'ism comprising around 11 percent of the population. Alawis make up a disproportionate share of elite military units, the Syrian officer corps, and other senior positions.

When the Arab Spring led many Syrians to protest economic conditions and call for political reforms, the Asad regime replied with brutal force. This in turn sparked a full-scale uprising and civil war. The rebels tended to be from the Sunni majority (representing around 70 percent of the population), especially rural and poorer urban Sunnis. Christian and other minorities, like the Alawi community, tended to support the government—sometimes enthusiastically, but often reluctantly, fearing the increasingly Sunni fundamentalist orientation of many rebel groups.

Years of bloodshed have followed, with up to half a million killed. The Syrian regime has used chemical weapons against its own population. Millions have been forcibly displaced, either within Syria or to neighboring countries and beyond, contributing to the worst global refugee crisis since the Second World War. Such violence has only contributed to further sectarian polarization and radicalization, which has been exploited by extremist groups. It was in this context that Daesh was able to take control of areas of eastern Syria, until largely defeated by a coalition of Syrian forces (both government and opposition), Kurds, and external support.

External intervention has been a key characteristic of the sectarianization of politics in Iraq, Syria, and beyond. US overthrow of the Saddam Hussein dictatorship resulted in Sunni-Shi'ite tensions becoming a defining characteristic of recent Iraqi politics. Iranian support for the Baghdad government also angered many Iraqi Sunnis, whether on sectarian or Arab nationalist grounds. In Syria, Saudi Arabia, Qatar, Turkey, and the United States, all lent varying degrees of support to Syrian opposition, while Iran, Hizbullah, and Russia rallied to President Asad's side. The deep-seated rivalry between (fundamentalist Sunni) Saudi Arabia and (fundamentalist Shi'ite) Iran has had particularly important ramifications for the region. This hostility is only partly religious and ideological in character—it is just as much a geostrategic rivalry between two major powers seeking influence in the Gulf* and the broader Middle East.

Yemen is another casualty of this regional competition. During the Arab Spring, popular protests forced President Ali Abdullah Saleh to resign, and the country embarked on a difficult process of political reform. This was aborted, however, when Houthi rebels seized the capital of Sanaa in

---

* Reflecting this rivalry, many Arab States in the area strenuously object to the term "Persian Gulf," preferring "Arab Gulf" instead. Iran, not surprisingly, prefers "Persian Gulf." While the latter is the term generally used in the West, outside scholars and politicians visiting the region often just call it "the Gulf" to avoid controversy.

2014–15, forcing the transitional government of Abdrabbuh Mansur Hadi from power.

The Houthis are a Zaydi (Shi'ite) fundamentalist movement that drew their initial support from Yemeni tribes in the northwest of the country. They enjoyed some support from Iran, and from former president Saleh. Iranian meddling led Saudi Arabia and its allies (somewhat reluctantly supported by the United States) to launch a major military intervention in 2015 in support of Hadi—to which Iran then responded by stepping up support for the Houthis. The situation was further exploited by the local al-Qaida affiliate (which has fought against the Houthis as well as loyalist forces) and by South Yemeni secessionists. The result of all this has been a bloody stalemate, with many thousands killed, hundreds of thousands displaced, and the very poor country facing destruction, epidemic disease, and widespread hunger.

Before the crisis, religious tensions between Sunnis and Shi'ites were not the predominant characteristic in Yemeni politics, which tended to revolve more around region, tribe, ideology, and patron-client relations. However, the dynamics of the civil war, aggravated by outside involvement by Saudi Arabia and Iran, have heightened religious differences in the country.

DEPENDENCY, MODERNIZATION, AND ETHNIC CONFLICT

Western analysts once assumed that improved education and communications would diminish ethnic tensions. Because of their country's experience as a "melting pot" for immigrant groups, Americans in particular have supposed that socioeconomic modernization enhances ethnic integration and harmony.* Yet, in Africa and Asia, early modernization has frequently politicized and intensified ethnic antagonisms. In fact, Crawford Young observes that "cultural pluralism [and ethnic strife] as a political phenomenon" was not significant in traditional societies but, rather, emerged "from such social processes as urbanization, the revolution in communications and spread of modern education."[20] Early modernization theorists, who were quite optimistic about the positive effects of literacy, urbanization, and modern values, clearly underestimated the extent to which these factors might mobilize various ethnic groups and set them against each other. Dependency theorists, on the other hand, provided a rather superficial analysis of ethnic issues, tending to blame these conflicts on colonialism or neocolonialism.

---

* Yet, even America's image as a successful melting pot has often been overstated. Racial inequality remains high: on average, white families in America have eight to ten times the net assets that Hispanic and black families do, while one-third of Hispanics and almost half of African Americans report experiencing workplace discrimination.

During the era of European colonialism, ethnic divisions in Africa and Asia were often kept in check by the struggle for independence, which encouraged a common front against the colonial regime. After independence, however, previously submerged ethnic rivalries frequently rose to the surface. In the new political order, religious, racial, tribal, and nationality groups competed for state resources such as roads, schools, and civil service jobs. Furthermore, rural-to-urban migration brought previously isolated ethnic groups into closer contact with each other for the first time. Indeed, urbanization, increased education, and the spread of mass communications have frequently mobilized sectors of the population along ethnic lines. The spread of higher education, rather than generating greater harmony, sometimes produces a class of ethnically chauvinistic professionals and intellectuals, who become the ideologists of ethnic hostility. Eventually, as these groups come to know each other, these tensions may diminish.

LEVELS OF INTERETHNIC CONFLICT

Although most countries are ethnically heterogeneous, there are wide variations in how ethnicities relate to each other. In some cases, different ethnicities or religions interact amicably; in others, deep resentments inspire shocking atrocities. Having examined the various types of ethnic communities, we will now consider the nature and intensity of relations between them. In theory, these relationships can be measured by the frequency of interethnic friendships and marriages, by the degree to which political parties, trade unions, and other civic organizations are either heterogeneous or ethnically based, and by the extent to which ethnic divisions are reinforced by other social cleavages such as class. In any particular country, relations between ethnic communities may range from minimal levels of conflict (Brazil) to systematic violence (Sudan).

Minimal Conflict

As we have seen, modernization frequently intensifies ethnic antagonisms in the short run, but usually ameliorates them in the longer term. Consequently, affluent democracies are more likely than developing countries to enjoy amicable ethnic relations. Although First World countries are not exempt from racial, religious, or linguistic conflict, such tensions are more likely to be resolved calmly. In Switzerland, for example, German-, French-, and Italian-speaking citizens have lived together peacefully for centuries. In Brazil and the island nations of the Caribbean, relations between blacks and whites are generally more harmonious than in the United States. For instance, interracial dating and marriages are quite common, particularly among lower-income groups. Still, this harmony is relative, because even those countries have maintained a social hierarchy between races.

For example, although there are many people of color in the Dominican, Brazilian, and Panamanian middle classes, most blacks remain mired in the lower class, and few make it into the political and economic elites.

In short, even the countries classified as harmonious are only categorized that way relative to other, more sharply divided societies. In Brazil and Cuba, for example, despite a long history of interracial marriages and more recent government efforts to promote racial equality, blacks have yet to attain their proportional share of government leadership positions. But ethnic tensions are limited and rarely lead to violence.

Uneasy Balance

In countries such as Trinidad and Tobago and Malaysia, relations between the principal ethnic groups are somewhat more strained. Although still generally peaceful, ethnic relations are in an uneasy balance, in which different groups predominate in specific areas of society. For example, in Malaysia, the Muslim Malay majority dominates the political system, including the parliament and the government bureaucracy, while the Chinese minority dominates the business community. Ethnic riots in 1969 led the Malaysian government to introduce new policies designed, in part, to redistribute more of the country's wealth to the Malays. Fearful of Chinese economic domination, the Malays have received ethnic preferences in education and the civil service. Since 2009, however, the government has begun to eliminate some ethnic quotas.

The Caribbean nation of Trinidad and Tobago offers another example of uneasy balance. During the second half of the nineteenth century, British colonial authorities encouraged the migration of indentured plantation workers from India who joined the black (Afro-Trinidadian) majority and small white elite. Contrary to the normal Caribbean practice of extensive racial mixing, there were fewer interracial marriages. Each of these groups currently constitutes about 40 percent of the population, with the remaining 20 percent made up of Chinese, whites, Arabs, and others. Following Trinidad's independence in 1962, ethnic frictions increased as blacks and East Indians competed for state resources. Most of the important political, civil service, military, and police positions since that time have been held by blacks, who predominate within the urban middle and working classes. Whites still predominate in the upper ranks of the business community. Traditionally, most East Indians have been small- to medium-sized businesspeople or poor farmers and farmworkers.

Trinidadian politics do not feature the same overt ethnic appeals that characterize many developing countries, but most of its political parties and unions have primarily represented one race. During the first parliamentary elections after independence, each of the major parties received 80–90 percent of its votes from a single ethnic group. For twenty-four years (1962–86), the People's National Movement (PNM), the party that led the independence movement, headed the national government. While drawing votes from various races, the PNM's leadership and base have been mostly Afro-Trinidadian. During that time, the opposition was led by various Indian-dominated parties. Only in 1986 did the newly formed National Alliance for Reconstruction (NAR) finally dislodge the PNM from power by forging the first electoral alliance between the two dominant ethnic groups. In 1995, Trinidad's first prime minister of East Indian origin was elected. At the same time, however, the two communities continued to maintain their social, political, and economic distance. And, in 1990, a radical black Muslim movement, the Jamaat al Muslimeen, briefly captured the parliament building and held the prime minister and members of parliament hostage for six days while many poor blacks rioted in the capital. Jamaat's manifestos reflected the resentment toward East Indians, but their violent behavior was an aberration in the nation's racial relations. In 2015, the PNM once more returned to power.

Enforced Hierarchy (Ethnic Dominance)

One important factor permitting ethnic balance in countries such as Malaysia and Trinidad and Tobago has been the division of political and economic powers between the competing ethnicities. Typically, one ethnicity predominates in the political arena and the other is more influential in the economy. But, in enforced hierarchies, both forms of power are concentrated in the hands of the ruling ethnic group. South African apartheid represented the most blatant example of such a relationship.

Latin American nations with large indigenous (Amerindian) populations*—including Guatemala, Bolivia, Ecuador, and Peru—have a less overt, but still significant, form of hierarchy. Since the Spanish conquest, most Indians in those countries have been poor peasants at the bottom of the social and political ladder. Even today, despite important recent gains in Indian rights, most positions of political and economic influence remain in the hands of whites or mestizos.† At the same time, however, unlike the United States, racial classifications in Latin America tend to be culturally rather than biologically defined. Consequently, they are more flexible and open up opportunities for at least some people of color. If a young Indian villager moves to the city, adopts Western dress, and speaks Spanish, he or she becomes a mestizo (or cholo), a higher social status. And in the rural highlands of Ecuador and Peru, entire peasant communities that spoke

---

*Different terms for indigenous populations are used across the Americas, with the social acceptability of each varying from country to country. Here we use Amerindian, Indian, and indigenous interchangeably.

†Persons of mixed Amerindian and white racial origin, also often applied to an Indian who adopts much of white culture.

Quechua a generation ago have switched to Spanish and changed to Western clothing in a process. This, more flexible, cultural definition has obvious advantages, but an important disadvantage as well. Although it facilitates individual upward social mobility, until now it only affords that mobility to Indians who largely abandon their own culture.

Since the 1980s, however, indigenous peoples have begun to assert their cultural rights and political influence in several Latin American countries through grassroots political movements and through the election of government officials, sometimes at the highest levels. In Bolivia, where 60 percent of the population is indigenous, Indian social movements organized mass protests against the government's free-market (neoliberal) economic policies. These protests brought down the nation's president and subsequently led to the 2006 election of Evo Morales, the country's first indigenous president. Peru elected its first president of Indian descent in 2001 and Ollanta Humala, a former army colonel of partial Indian extraction, took office in 2011. Finally, in the Mexican state of Chiapas, a group known as the Zapatistas staged a 1994 peasant rebellion in behalf of Indian rights. Though it never had a chance to seize national power (nor did it intend to), the group received a remarkable amount of national support from Mexicans of all ethnicities and social classes.

In all these cases of enforced hierarchy, racial and class distinctions are closely intertwined. Those higher up the social ladder tend to be lighter skinned; those at the lower ranks of society are generally darker. Unlike South Africa's old apartheid system, Latin America's racial hierarchy is enforced informally, not legally, and is far less repressive. Even so, during some forty years of revolutionary upheaval and intense government oppression, the Guatemalan armed forces viewed rural Indian communities as breeding grounds for Marxist guerrillas. Consequently, successive military regimes massacred tens of thousands of Indian peasants in a policy bordering on genocide. Fortunately, since the 1990s, a peace treaty with the guerrillas has curtailed such violence.

Systematic Violence

In the worst-case scenario, deep ethnic resentments have led to mass violence or even civil war. As we have seen, in a number of countries—including India, Bangladesh, Ethiopia, Rwanda, and Sudan—systematic violence has resulted in thousands or hundreds of thousands of deaths and huge numbers of displaced refugees and rape victims. Often, violence develops when ethnic divisions are reinforced by class tensions. In Bahrain, the Shi'ite majority chafes under the domination of the Sunni monarchy, which has responded to demands for reform with arrests and repression.

Ethnic bloodshed also occurs when one ethnicity seizes political power and then takes reprisals for real or imagined past indignities. Thus, when

General Idi Amin seized power in Uganda, he ordered the slaughter of Langi and Acholi soldiers who were identified with the regime of ousted president Milton Obote. In both Rwanda and Burundi, the deaths of Hutu presidents opened the floodgates to violence between Hutus and the long-dominant Tutsis.

In times of crisis and conflict, political leaders may have an interest in fanning the flames of ethnic tension in order to rally their supporters, as seen in Iraq and Syria. In turn, increasing insecurity and polarization forces may force people to choose a "side" for reasons of self-protection or to access scarce resources. During the breakup of Yugoslavia, extremist leaders—such as then Serbian president Slobodan Milosevic—promoted ethnic hatred and mass murder in order to build their own political power base. In the end, Milosevic brought both Bosnia and Serbia to ruin. Similarly, the 1994 massacres in Rwanda were orchestrated from above. Government officials pressured Hutu villagers to attack their Tutsi neighbors, with whom most of them had been living peacefully for years.

At its worst, systematic violence may involve **ethnic cleansing** (when one group tries to drive another from disputed territory through widespread intimidation, killings, and sexual assault) or even **genocide** (when a group tries to eliminate some or all of another), as seen in the Bosnian and Kosovo wars and Rwanda respectively.

OUTCOMES AND RESOLUTIONS

Whether ethnic antagonisms arise from competition over government resources, resentment over the division of political and economic powers, or an ethnic community's demands for greater autonomy, there are a number of possible results. Although some outcomes are peaceful, others may spawn intense violence. And while some resolutions are successful, others do not endure. In seeking a peaceful and lasting resolution, government and ethnic leaders are constrained by the history and intensity of their ethnic cleavages, by the degree of previous ethnic cooperation, and by the country's political culture. Nonetheless, within these constraints, the creativity and statecraft of national leaders and outside mediators can contribute to successful solutions. Thus, political elites may seek reasonable, negotiated solutions or they may choose to play on ethnic tensions for their own advantage.

When political elites are willing to resolve bitter ethnic conflicts through negotiations, they may arrive at one of several types of resolutions. In the next section, we examine those possible outcomes and also look at several options that have been tried when negotiations have failed. Although the alternatives presented here are not exhaustive, they cover a wide range of experiences.

Power Sharing: Federalism and Consociationalism

Power-sharing arrangements seek to create stability by dividing political power among major ethnic groups. These settlements generally follow protracted negotiations and constitutional debate. If power sharing is introduced into the constitution at the time of independence, it may head off ethnic violence before it gets started. Unfortunately, however, many such arrangements later break down. **Federalism** and **consociationalism** are two such systems, although their use is not confined to situations of potential ethnic tension.

Federalism, the primary form of power sharing, is "a system of government [that] emanates from the desire of people to form a union without necessarily losing their various identities."[21] It may involve the creation of autonomous or semiautonomous regions, each of which is governed by a particular ethnicity. But it is only possible in situations where contending ethnic groups are concentrated in different regions of the country. For example, prior to its collapse, Yugoslavia consisted of six autonomous republics mostly governed by individual nationalities, including Serbs, Croats, and Slovenes. The constitution mandated power sharing between the various republics at the national level. But, this compromise began to unravel in the 1970s following the death of Marshal Joseph Broz Tito, the country's long-term strongman. It collapsed completely in the early 1990s when the Communist Party lost its grip on several republics.

Industrialized democracies have had greater success with ethnically based federalism. Each of Switzerland's twenty-two cantons is dominated by one of the country's three major language groups, with German-, French-, and Italian-speaking cantons coexisting harmoniously. Canada's federalism, though not based on ethnic divisions, has allowed the primarily French-speaking province of Quebec a substantial amount of autonomy regarding language and other cultural matters. Although the country's constitutional arrangement has not satisfied Québécois nationalists, it has accommodated many of their demands and convinced the province's voters to reject independence in two separate provincial referendums.

In the developing world, power sharing has been less successful. Following independence, Nigeria tried to accommodate its ethnic divisions through federalism. As we have seen, the country's north was dominated by the Hausa and Fulani, the east by the Ibos, and the west, to a lesser extent, by the Yoruba. This union came apart when the Ibos tried to secede. Although the Biafran War took a terrible toll, a new federal solution has subsequently taken hold. On the other hand, Pakistani federalism failed to overcome the antipathy between the country's more powerful western region (populated largely by Urdu speakers) and the Bengali-speaking east. In 1971, relations between the two regions broke down completely, resulting in the massacre of five hundred thousand Bengalis by western Pakistani troops. When India went to war with Pakistan, the eastern region was able to secede and form the new nation of Bangladesh.

Consociationalism offers another potential solution to ethnic conflict. It is frequently used where major ethnic groups reside in close proximity and lack distinct "homelands," making a federalist solution impossible. Its power, designed to protect the rights of all participants, involves the following components:

1. The leaders of the major ethnic groups form a ruling coalition at the national level.
2. Each group has veto power over government policies that affect them.
3. Public employment, such as the civil service, is divided between ethnicities, with each receiving a number of posts roughly proportional to its population. Often the most important government positions—such as prime minister, president, and parliamentary leader—are reserved for specific ethnicities.
4. Each ethnic group is afforded a high degree of autonomy over its own affairs.[22]

Flags of the (Christian) Free Patriotic Movement mingle with those of the (Shi'ite) Hizbullah movement as the two celebrate the election of FPM leader Michel Aoun as president of Lebanon in 2016. Lebanon uses an uneasy system of consociational power sharing to manage its otherwise deep sectarian divisions. *Source*: ZUMA Press, Inc./Alamy Stock Photo.

Thus, consociational democracy consciously rejects strict majority rule. Instead, it seeks to create a framework for stability and peace by guaranteeing minorities a share of political power—even veto power—to protect them against the majority. It has been tried in several developing nations, including Cyprus (where it failed), Lebanon (where it has twice collapsed into civil war, only to be reestablished) and Malaysia (where it has generally succeeded). Some mutual trust and cooperation between the leaders of contending ethnic groups is the key to effective consociational arrangements. Sadly, trust is difficult to establish in times of ethnic hostility and becomes ever more problematic after that hostility has erupted into bloodshed.

Secession
When power sharing or other forms of compromise do not succeed, disgruntled ethnic minorities may attempt to secede (withdraw) from the country in order to form their own nation or join their ethnic brothers and sisters in a neighboring state. As one author put it, "Secession, like divorce, is an ultimate act of alienation."[23] It offers a potential way out of a "failed marriage" between ethnic groups within a nation-state. Unfortunately, however, like divorce, secession or the threat of secession frequently provokes bitterness and hostility. It is possible only when the group seeking to secede predominates in a clearly defined territory.

Given the large number of ethnically divided developing countries, we should not be surprised to find many secessionist movements. Central governments, faced with such breakaway efforts, almost always try to repress them because they are unwilling to part with some of their country's territory or resources, just as the United States was unwilling to part with the Confederate states. This chapter has previously discussed secessionist movements in southern Sudan, by Tamils in Sri Lanka, Eritreans in Ethiopia, and Sikhs in northern India. Other secessionist movements have included the Moros in the Philippines, Muslims in Indian Kashmir, and the Karen in Myanmar (Burma). In 2015, a cease-fire agreement largely ended the civil war between the Karen and the Burmese government.

Although many aggrieved nationalities would like to secede, few have accomplished this goal. In Africa, we have noted that Eritrea attained independence from Ethiopia in 1993 after three decades of civil war and South Sudan has recently seceded from Sudan following a twenty-one-year-old struggle. While in Asia, Bangladesh (formerly East Pakistan) withdrew from Pakistan in 1971 with the help of the Indian armed forces and East Timor finally gained independence from Indonesian occupation in 2002. But successful secession movements have been few and far between in the developing world and they have been achieved at a tremendous cost in human lives. During East Timor's struggle for independence, one-fourth or more of its total population (about six hundred thousand people) were killed or starved to death. Estimates of the number of lives lost in Bangladesh and South Sudan run into the millions. Elsewhere, the best outcome that secessionist movements have achieved is greater autonomy and many (like Tibet) fail to gain even that.

The number of secessionist wars has actually declined significantly since the start of the 1990s. From 1991 to 1999, sixteen such wars were settled and eleven others were held in check by cease-fires or continuing negotiations. Thus, as this century began, only eighteen secessionist wars continued worldwide, fewer than at any time since 1970.[24] Often, leaders in the developing world are concerned that redrawing colonial-era boundaries or breaking up existing states could destabilize the postcolonial political order.

The case of the Kurds illustrates this. Following the two Gulf Wars, the world briefly focused its attention on Saddam Hussein's persecution of Iraq's Kurdish population. A decade later, Kurdish militias supported American-led coalition forces in the war to topple Saddam. However, Kurdish separatism in Iraq and elsewhere dates to the collapse of the Ottoman Empire at the close of the First World War. Residing in a mountainous region that they call Kurdistan, perhaps 30 million Kurds live in adjacent areas of Turkey (home to about half of all Kurds), Iran, and Iraq, with a smaller community in Syria. Over the years, the Kurds have been persecuted in all of those countries. As a result of America's two wars with Iraq, that country's Kurds achieved virtual autonomy and currently exercise considerable influence in that country's national government.

In September 2017, Kurds in Iraq held a referendum on secession, which passed overwhelmingly.* However, Kurdish independence was strongly opposed both by the Iraqi central government in Baghdad and by neighboring states (fearful of its impact on their own Kurdish population). The Iraqi military took control of some disputed areas, and the prospects for a Kurdish state quickly receded.

Outside Intervention
We have already seen how involvement by other African states in Congo (Kinsaha) aggravated past conflict in that country, and how regional rivalry between Iran and Saudi Arabia intensified current conflicts in Yemen, Syria, and Iraq. In fact, some degree of external involvement in civil wars is quite common, as neighboring states and great powers seek to advance their interests, back their allies or co-ethnics, or try to topple their opponents.

---

*Reflecting the use of ethnic appeals for political purposes discussed earlier, the referendum was called, in part, to distract from the growing unpopularity of the Kurdish Regional Government.

At times, however, the international community might also seek to address the devastating costs and destabilizing effects of ethnic conflict. In considering this, they face a moral and practical dilemma. On the one hand, they may feel morally compelled to somehow intervene on behalf of a victimized minority. Such intercession can span the gamut from simply agreeing to take in refugees all the way to armed intervention aimed at putting a stop to the bloodshed. At the same time, however, outside countries are constrained from interference by international laws regarding national sovereignty, or international power alignments, or lack of public support at home. Even the nonaggressive act of offering refuge to the victims of ethnic strife may seem too costly or too risky. Indeed, the outside world has stood by as millions died in ethnic massacres in such countries as Indonesia, Congo (Kinshasa), Rwanda, and Sudan. Today, most developed countries have been reluctant to provide refuge to the millions fleeing civil war in Syria, preferring that developing countries like Turkey, Uganda, Pakistan, Lebanon, and Iran shoulder the burden.

In recent years, the international community has partly accepted the principle of a **responsibility to protect,** whereby national sovereignty may be overridden if necessary to protect civilians or deal with the consequences of state collapse. However, "R2P" faces problems of great power politics—there is no agreement on what to do with regard to Syria, for example, where the Russians are closely allied to the Asad regime and willing to use their veto in the United Nations Security Council to protect it (e.g., when Syria has been caught using chemical weapons against its own population).

Governments contemplating humanitarian interventions have to weigh their own national interests and the costs of intervention against their commitment to sustaining human rights abroad. Most nations are reluctant to risk their soldiers' lives for humanitarian purposes. A fairly small number of American soldiers (eighteen) brutally killed in 1993 during a mission to restore order and distribute food in war-torn Somalia shocked US public opinion and caused President Bill Clinton to withdraw the remaining American troops. Only a year later, government leaders in Washington, Paris, and other Western capitals were warned that an ethnic massacre was likely to unfold in Rwanda. Sobered by the recently failed intervention in Somalia and unsure of how well they could prevent genocide, they decided against interference. Some analysts insist that the United Nations or the United States or France could have saved thousands of lives if they had quickly sent a military force to quell the violence.[25] Indeed, President Clinton subsequently said, after he left office, that his greatest regret of his presidency was his failure to take preventive action in Rwanda. Others disagree, arguing that the Rwandan genocide took place so quickly (most of the deaths occurring within a few weeks) that intervention could not have arrived in time to save that many victims.[26]

Thus, there are also pragmatic questions regarding the likely effectiveness of intervention. Under what circumstances does outside interference (including military involvement) prevent ethnic persecution and impose a durable solution, and when is it futile or counterproductive? In 2011, there was a rare international consensus to support intervention against Muammar Qaddafi in Libya when it appeared he would brutally suppress a popular uprising. NATO and Arab forces lent their support to the rebels, backed by a United Nations Security Council resolution. Qaddafi was overthrown (and killed), and elections then held in the country. Soon thereafter, however, Libya collapsed into a new cycle of civil conflict as local militias vied for power.

The difficulties encountered by the United States in Afghanistan and Iraq also show the limits of military intervention. Of course, these actions were not motivated by a desire to resolve local conflicts, but rather by retaliation for the 9/11 terror attacks (Afghanistan's Taliban regime was a strong supporter of al-Qaida) and geopolitics (Washington saw Saddam Hussein as a regional foe). However, the fact that the strongest military power on the planet could spend thousands of lives and trillions of dollars (with even greater losses suffered by the Afghans and Iraqis themselves)—and yet fail to bring political stability or impose its political will—is a reminder of the costs of overconfidence.

It is important to note that while military interventions like these tend to garner the most attention in the media, they are not the way in which the international community usually assists in resolving ethnic and other conflict. Although far less dramatic, United Nations and other multilateral **peacekeeping operations** can play a critical role in helping to secure or implement a peace agreement among warring parties. As of 2018, there were fourteen UN peacekeeping missions around the world (and eight other small special missions undertaking mediation efforts) involving more than ninety thousand peacekeepers. The African Union has also deployed some twenty thousand peacekeepers to Somalia, and also jointly operates a mission in Darfur (Sudan) with the United Nations.

Most peacekeeping missions do not try to impose peace on local actors, but rather help to monitor and implement peace agreements, assist with humanitarian and development initiatives, and provide other assistance. They can report human rights violations, protect civilians, and help to reassure and build confidence among the various local parties. While such missions may fail, research suggests that peace agreements backed by such measures are more likely to endure. The question of why such agreements might come about in the first place brings us to our final outcome of ethnic conflict: settlement through exhaustion.

Settlement through Exhaustion

Ethnic conflicts sometimes come to an end through the exhaustion of the warring parties—or, more accurately, what is sometimes termed a **hurting**

stalemate. If an actor believes they can win a conflict through violence, they have little incentive to compromise. Similarly, if they benefit from violence—say, by using conflict to rally support from their ethnic constituency, or through corruption and illegal economic activities (smuggling, drug production, or looting natural resources, such as diamonds in parts of Africa)—they may not wish to end the fighting. However, if they cannot win and also suffer costs from the continuation of violence, they are more likely to seek compromise and it may become possible to negotiate a peaceful resolution of the conflict.

Although the Ugandan government continues to clash periodically with the Acholi and Langi tribes, conflict has been held in check because Ugandans do not want to return to the ethnically based bloodshed of the Amin and Obote eras. In Indonesia, a long-standing conflict between the government and rebels in Aceh Province ended in a peace agreement in 2005, in part because the Indian Ocean tsunami one year earlier had devastated the region and created new incentives to cooperate. In Sudan, a "hurting stalemate" contributed to the end of a twenty-one-year war between the Arab-dominated national government and the black (African, non-Muslim) population of the south—although, sadly, it did not prevent the later emergence of conflict in newly independent South Sudan between rival political leaders.

Toward a Peaceful Resolution of Conflict

If developing countries are to avoid the horrors of civil war, secession, and foreign intervention, they must arrive at legal, political, and economic solutions that can reduce ethnic tensions. This goal, though clearly reasonable, is more easily said than achieved. More difficult still is the task of repairing the damage done to plural societies that have been torn apart by bloody conflict (e.g., Rwanda, Iraq, and Kashmir) or by decades of prejudice and segregation (South Africa). Not long after South Africa's new, multiracial government was installed in 1994, President Mandela's administration created a Truth and Reconciliation Commission, before which perpetrators of racially based violence and injustices were invited to confess their crimes in return for amnesty. The goal of the commission was to further unearth the crimes of apartheid and, more importantly, to allow the nation's races to live together more harmoniously. Yet, as some observers of the commission's hearings have suggested, in countries that have experienced systematic repression or extensive ethnic violence, reconciliation—the creation of harmony between formerly hostile parties—may be too much to hope for. A more realistic goal, they suggest, is establishing the basis for coexistence between these groups.

ETHNIC PLURALISM AND DEMOCRACY

Crafting peaceful scenarios for multicultural societies remains one of the greatest challenges facing leaders in the developing world. During the 1970s and 1980s, increased ethnic violence in the developing world and the former communist states of Eastern Europe frequently coincided with the spread of democratic government. This raised two questions about the relationship between democracy and ethnic politics: First, "Are multiethnic countries less likely to maintain democracy than are culturally homogeneous societies?" Second, "Do the growth of citizen participation and the creation of democratic governments intensify conflict between ethnic communities?"

The first question can be answered quite easily. Democracy can be harder—although far from impossible—to establish and maintain in multiethnic countries. We have seen, for example, how Lebanon, long considered the most democratic Arab country, was devastated by civil war. Looking at democracy's failure to take root in most of Africa and Asia from the 1960s to the 1980s, Rabushka and Shepsle concluded that ethnic antagonisms had created important obstacles to democratization. Democracy, they argued, "is simply not viable in an environment of intense ethnic preference."[27] Here, they referred to societies in which powerful ethnic groups receive special privileges, while others suffer discrimination.

An examination of both developed and developing countries reveals that democracy has fared best in nations that are most ethnically homogeneous (such as Botswana, Uruguay, and Japan) or in countries of "new settlement" (including the United States, Canada, New Zealand, and Australia), populated primarily by immigrants and their descendants who have created a new common culture. In Africa, Asia, and the Middle East, where many countries labor with strong ethnic divides, the growth of democracy and mass political participation may unleash communal hostilities, sometimes intensified by opportunistic politicians who use group fears to build a political base. Today, of the twenty-five most ethnically diverse countries in the developing world, only five are democracies (and "flawed democracies" at that). Eleven are hybrid regimes, while the remaining nine are full-fledged authoritarian states.[28]

Ethnic pluralism poses a particular obstacle to democracy in poorer countries, where various groups must contend for limited government resources in the "politics of scarcity." But although democracy is more challenging to achieve in plural societies, it is not impossible even in very poor nations. Despite its history of religiously based violence, India—one of the world's most ethnically diverse country—has maintained democratic governments for all but two of its more than seventy years of independence. Indonesia—where ethnic Javanese represent less than half the population, and scores of different ethnic groups can be identified—has maintained a flawed but functioning electoral democracy since for almost two decades. Together these two countries alone represent almost 1.6 billion people, or more than a quarter of the entire developing world.

To be sure, the initial transition to democracy frequently intensifies existing ethnic animosities. Newly formed political parties often base their support in competing ethnic communities. Politicians, even those opposed to violence, are tempted to use ethnic appeals as a means of gaining public support. As public resources are distributed through more transparent legislative decisions, ethnically based interest groups and political parties fight for their fair share. Some analysts warn that "the opening of democratic space throws up [so] many groups pulling in different directions, that it causes demand overload, systematic breakdown and even violent conflict," a danger particularly relevant in societies with deep ethnic tensions prior to their democratic transitions.[29] This danger is greatest in strict majoritarian democracies, where a single ethnic group or allied ethnicities can dominate parliamentary or presidential elections without affording constitutional or other institutional protections to minority groups. Thus, the Carnegie Commission on Preventing Deadly Conflict concluded:

> In societies with deep ethnic divisions and little experience with democratic government and the rule of law [a common phenomenon in Africa, Asia and the Middle East], strict majoritarian democracy can be self-defeating. Where ethnic identities are strong and national identity weak, populations may vote largely on ethnic lines. Domination by one ethnic group can lead to a tyranny of the majority.[30]

But this merely indicates the importance of limiting majority rule in democratic, multiethnic societies. It does not suggest that authoritarian government is preferable in such situations. Indeed, in the long run, the only way ethnicities can resolve their differences is through open discussion and bargaining in a reasonably democratic political arena, as long as majority rule is tempered by constitutional guarantees of human rights, consociational arrangements, or other institutional protections for minorities.

Although dictatorships in Yugoslavia and the Soviet Union were able to repress ethnic conflicts for many years, in the long run, they actually intensified these grievances by denying their existence, silencing them, and failing to deal with them. As we have seen, after the fall of Saddam Hussein, long-repressed antagonisms burst to the surface, producing civil conflict. Elsewhere, dictators such as Laurent Kabila (Congo-Kinshasa) and Suharto (Indonesia) presided over ethnic massacres that would have been unthinkable in a democracy monitored by public opinion and a free press.

Conversely, democratic politicians are open to interest group pressure from ethnic minorities and, hence, seem more likely to settle disputes peacefully before they degenerate into violence. Indeed, the recent study of "minorities at risk" throughout the world revealed that democratic regimes are more likely than dictatorships to negotiate peaceful settlements of ethnic warfare. Political discrimination and, to a lesser degree, economic discrimination against ethnic minorities were more likely to decline in democracies than under authoritarian governments.[31]

Practice and Review Online at
http://textbooks.rowman.com/handelman9e

KEY TERMS

consociationalism

ethnic cleansing

ethnicity

federalism

genocide

hurting stalemate

lingua franca

nation

peacekeeping operations

race

responsibility to protect

secession

tribe

DISCUSSION QUESTIONS

1. What are the differences and similarities between ethnic tensions and conflict in the United States (or other industrialized democracies) and ethnic divisions in the developing world?
2. Discuss the effect that modernization has had on ethnic identification and ethnic conflict.
3. How can power-sharing approaches help to address ethnic tensions within a political system? What challenges might such systems encounter?

NOTES

1. Quoted in Yueh-Ting Lee, Fathali Moghaddam, Clark McCauley, and Stephen Worchel, "The Global Challenge of Ethnic and Cultural Conflict," in *The Psychology of Ethnic and Cultural Conflict*, eds. Lee, Moghaddam, McCauley, and Worchel (Westport, CT: Praeger, 2004), 3.

2. Crawford Young, *The Politics of Cultural Pluralism* (Madison, WI: University of Wisconsin Press, 1976), 23.

3. Patrick Inman and James Peacock, "Conclusion: Ethnic and Sectarian as Ideal Types," in *Identity Matters*, eds. James Peacock, Patricia Thornton, and Patrick Inman (New York, NY: Berghahn Books, 2007), 208.

4. Jennifer De Maio, *Confronting Ethnic Conflict* (Lanham, MD: Rowman & Littlefield Publishers, 2009), 23.

5. Monica Duffy Toft, *The Geography of Ethnic Violence: Identity, Interests, and the Indivisibility of Territory* (Princeton, NJ: Princeton University Press, 2003), 3.

6. David Bloomfield and Ben Reilly, eds., *Democracy and Deep-Rooted Conflict: Options for Negotiations* (Stockholm, Sweden: International Institute for Democracy and Electoral Assistance, 1998), 4.

7. "By the Numbers: Ethnic Groups in the World," *Scientific American* (September 1998).

8. Ted Robert Gurr, *Peoples versus States: Minorities at Risk in the New Century* (Washington, DC: United States Institute of Peace Press, 2000), 10–11.

9. James Fearon and David Laitin, "Ethnicity, Insurgency, and Civil War," *American Political Science Review* 97, no. 1 (February 2003).

10. Gurr, *Peoples versus States*, 5.

11. Quoted in Francine Friedman, *The Bosnian Muslims: Denial of a Nation* (Boulder, CO: Westview Press, 1996), 1.

12. Quoted in David A. Lake and Donald Rothchild, "Spreading Fear: The Genesis of Transnational Ethnic Conflict," in *The International Spread of Ethnic Conflict*, eds. David A. Lake and Donald Rothchild (Princeton, NJ: Princeton University Press, 1998), 7.

13. Cynthia Enloe, *Ethnic Conflict and Political Development* (Boston, MA: Little, Brown, 1973), 15.

14. Young, *Politics of Cultural Pluralism*, 20.

15. Amy H. Liu, *Standardizing Diversity: The Political Economy of Language Regimes* (Philadelphia, PA: University of Pennsylvania Press, 2015).

16. Appapillai Amirdhalingam, quoted in Jack David Eller, *From Culture to Ethnicity to Conflict* (Ann Arbor, MI: University of Michigan Press, 1999), 123.

17. Charles W. Anderson, Fred R. von der Mehden, and Crawford Young, *Issues of Political Development*, 2nd ed. (Upper Saddle River, NJ: Prentice Hall, 1974), 21.

18. Cited in T. Walker Wallbank, *A Short History of India and Pakistan* (New York, NY: Mentor, 1958), 196.

19. "The Most Persecuted Minority in Asia," *The Economist*, June 13, 2015.

20. Young, *Politics of Cultural Pluralism*, 65.

21. J. Isawa Elaigwu and Victor A. Olorunsola, "Federalism and the Politics of Compromise," in *State versus Ethnic Claims: African Policy Dilemma*, eds. David Rothchild and Victor Olorunsola (Boulder: Westview Press, 1983), 282.

22. Arend Lijphart, *Democracy in Plural Societies* (New Haven, CT: Yale University Press, 1977), 25–40.

23. Ralph Premdas, "Secessionist Movements in Comparative Perspective," in *Secessionist Movements in Comparative Perspective*, eds. Ralph Premdas, S. W. R. de A. Samarasinghe and Alan Anderson (London: Pinter Publishers, 1990), 12.

24. Gurr, *People versus States*, 276.

25. David Carment and Frank Harvey, *Using Force to Prevent Ethnic Violence* (Westport, CT: Praeger, 2001).

26. For example, Alan K. Kuperman, *The Limits of Humanitarian Intervention: Genocide in Rwanda* (Washington, DC: Brookings Institution Press, 2001).

27. *From Politics in Plural Societies* (Columbus, OH: Merrill, 1972) quoted in Larry Diamond and Marc F. Plattner, eds., *Nationalism, Ethnic Conflict, and Democracy* (Baltimore, MD: Johns Hopkins University Press, 1994), xix.

28. Ethnic diversity was measured using an index developed by James Fearon, while the level of democracy was assessed using the 2018 ratings provided by the Economist Intelligence Unit. The latter categorizes countries as democracies, flawed

democracies (a category into which the United States has now slipped, due to social polarization and lack of trust in political institutions), hybrid regimes, and authoritarian regimes. James Fearon, "Ethnic and Cultural Diversity by Country," *Journal of Economic Growth* 8, no. 2 (2003); Economist Intelligence Unit, *Democracy Index* (2018), at https://infographics.economist.com/2018/DemocracyIndex/.

29. Quoted in Claude Ake, "Why Humanitarian Emergencies Occur: Insights from the Interface of State, Democracy and Civil Society," *Research for Action* 31 (1997), 8.

30. Quoted in Robin Luckham, Anne Marie Goetz, and Mary Kaldor, "Democratic Institutions and Democratic Politics," in *Can Democracy Be Designed: The Politics of Institutional Choice in Conflict-Torn Societies*, eds. Sunil Bastian and Robin Luckham (London and New York: Zed Books, 2003), 43.

31. Gurr, *People versus States*, 152–63, 169, 204.

7

Gender and Development

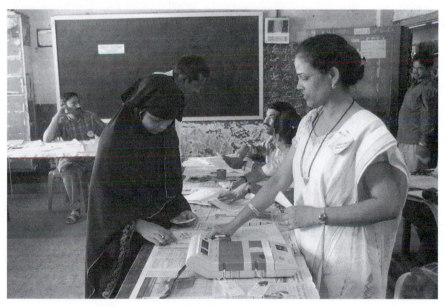

A woman votes during elections in India. Despite universal suffrage since independence in 1947, women make up only 12 percent of members of parliament, and the country continues to suffer from high degrees of gender inequality. *Source*: Dinodia Photos/Alamy Stock Photo.

A CHINESE PROVERB OBSERVES THAT "women hold up half the sky." Yet, for many years, scholars, governments in the developing world, and Western aid agencies seemed oblivious to women's role in the development process. Most early studies of political and economic change in the developing world said little or nothing about gender. Instead, it was either assumed that men were the primary economic actors in society, or it was assumed that men and women experienced development in similar ways. This, in practice, also tended to treat men's experiences as universal.

That, of course, is not the case. **Gender**—that is, the socially constructed roles that are assigned to men and women by society and culture—has a profound impact on living conditions and life opportunities. **Patriarchy** (male dominance) is largely upheld by deeply embedded social attitudes that view men as naturally and appropriately dominant in the **public sphere** (the formal economy and politics), and relegate women to the **private sphere** (as family caregivers). The World Values Survey has found, for example, that 75 percent of Pakistanis, 59 percent of Filipinos, and 18 percent of Chileans believe that, when jobs are scarce, men deserve priority in employment over women. Similarly, 77 percent of Nigerians, 71 percent of Algerians, 52 percent of Indians, and 28 percent of Brazilians believe that men make better political leaders.[1]

As a consequence, women are usually concentrated in certain occupations—including agriculture, domestic service, street vending, and teaching—and face barriers to entering others—such as management and higher-paid professions. Distinctions between "women's work" and "men's work" have obvious economic implications, with women's jobs usually earning lower wages or salaries and wielding less power. Moreover, women are also greatly underrepresented in the political arena. Not only do they hold far fewer government posts than men do, but their share diminishes as one moves up the pyramid of power. To be sure, patriarchy shapes men's role in society too, sometimes with adverse consequences.* However, it is women who predominantly suffer from economic and political disadvantage.

Although gender inequality and exploitation exist in all societies, the problems are more severe in the developing world. In its most horrifying form, the list of injustices includes the sale of child brides for dowries in Bangladesh; domestic abuse in Zambia and Peru; the murders of several thousand Indian women annually by husbands who were dissatisfied with the size of their dowries; courts that condone "honor killings" of women

---

* Men, for example, are more often conscripted into war, and more often targeted for killing during mass atrocities.

suspected of extramarital relations or even dating unapproved partners; and economic deprivations that drive many women into prostitution.

Recently, a village chief in rural West Bengal, India, learned that a young woman had accepted a marriage proposal from a man outside the village. He and the village council ordered her to stop the marriage and fined her and her family the rupee equivalent of a few hundred dollars (a huge amount in that setting). When they refused to pay, he ordered villagers to gang rape her, which a number of them did.[2] Nor are such incidents confined to rural villages. In Delhi, the nation's capital, Bhawna Yadav, a university student, was strangled by her parents for having married outside her caste. In a landmark six-nation survey of ten thousand men in Asia and the Pacific, a UN study reported that nearly one-quarter of those interviewed said they had raped a woman or girl at some time. "Half of those who admitted to rape reported their first time was when they were teenagers."[3] In the Congo (Kinshasa), during its long and unusually brutal civil war, rape was used as a weapon of war designed to force residents of contested villages to flee. Several years ago, the *New York Times* reported that a woman was raped in that country, on average, every minute, for an annual total of over five hundred thousand victims.

Nor is the legal system of any help in many cases and often it adds injury (and insult) to injury. In Saudi Arabia, a woman who was kidnapped and raped by seven men was sentenced to two hundred lashes for having placed herself in a vulnerable position. Until 2006, Pakistani law required a woman to produce four male witnesses to substantiate her claim of having been raped, an obviously impossible task in almost all situations. Worse yet, if she could not produce those witnesses, she could be charged with adultery. If convicted, she might be flogged, imprisoned, or even stoned to death.

Other acts of violence toward women include **female genital mutilation,** primarily practiced in Africa on girls and young women. The World Health Organization estimated in 2014 that about 125 million women then living in twenty-nine countries (mainly in Africa) had suffered this procedure, the aim of which is to reduce female sexual desires. Beyond traumatizing young women, the practice has no health benefits and sometimes results in heavy bleeding or infection, which can be fatal. While a number of countries have officially outlawed this practice, the laws are often unenforced. For example, Guinea outlawed these "female circumcisions" in 1965. But forty years later, 99 percent of that country's women continued to be affected and not a single violation of the law had been prosecuted by the authorities.

Less chilling, but no less significant, examples of gender inequality in many developing countries include divorce laws that greatly favor husbands; barriers to women seeking commercial credit for small businesses; the "double day" that working women typically face (coming home after a day's work and having to do most of the housework and child care); and few opportunities for women in government, the professions, and better-paid, blue-collar jobs.

But the study of women in the developing world is by no means confined to issues of inequality and victimization. After years of neglect, many international agencies and government planners have increasingly focused on the role that gender plays in development. As noted in chapter 1, greater gender equity is a key objective of the current, globally agreed sustainable development goals.

At the same time, increasing numbers of women are refusing to be mere subjects who are victimized or "acted upon." Their political activity has ranged from the quiet resistance common to many oppressed groups to a more vigorous assertion of their political, economic, and social rights. A growing body of scholarly literature now focuses on women's empowerment. Throughout Latin America, for example, women have played a decisive role in independent, grassroots political organizations and have burst upon the scene since the 1970s. Focusing on gender issues, human rights, poverty, and a range of other concerns, these new social movements have provided an important alternative to political parties, labor unions, and other mainstream political organizations that are typically dominated by men. Elsewhere, revolutionary movements in countries such as El Salvador, Nicaragua, and China opened up opportunities for female activism and leadership that had not existed previously. In nations as diverse as Argentina, Bangladesh, Brazil, Chile, India, Liberia, Pakistan, the Philippines, and Thailand, women have headed their national governments. And a growing number of developing countries have reserved seats for women in national, state, and local legislatures, while other nations have introduced more indirect gender quotas governing candidates for these positions. These measures have frequently increased the number of female office holders dramatically.

In addition to the issue of equality for women, there has also been growing attention to the situation of sexual minorities, whose gender identity or sexual orientation differs from that of the majority. **LGBT+** (lesbian, gay, bisexual, transgender, and others) persons have, in many societies, long been subject to discrimination, hostility, legal repression, and even outright violent persecution.

In much of the industrialized world, social attitudes have shifted in recent decades, although homophobic and transphobic attitudes remain. In the developing world, the picture is rather more complex. In many countries in Africa, the Middle East, and parts of Asia, homosexuality is a crime. In a few (like Iran, Sudan, and Mauritania) the possible punishment is death. In sub-Saharan Africa, Nigeria, Uganda and several other countries have introduced draconian new anti-LGBT legislation, often at the urging of (Muslim or Christian) religious conservatives. Even where homosexuality is legal, homophobia can inflict a terrible toll. Brazil, for example, currently holds the world record for known hate-based LGBT murders, with one occurring every 25 hours on average.

On the other hand, there have also been dramatic shifts toward greater tolerance, especially in the Americas, but elsewhere as well. South Africa was the first country in the world to explicitly prohibit discrimination on the grounds of sexual orientation in its (post-Apartheid) constitution. It was also the first country in Africa, and the fifth country in the world, to recognize same-sex marriage. Today, same-sex unions (marriages or civil partnerships) have been legalized in Argentina, Brazil, Chile, Colombia, Ecuador, Mexico, Uruguay, South Africa, and Taiwan, as well as two dozen or so industrialized countries. In India—one of many countries where the criminalization of homosexuality is a legacy of laws dating back to the British colonial era—the Supreme Court ruled in 2017 that "discrimination against an individual on the basis of sexual orientation is deeply offensive to the dignity and self-worth of the individual." It added that "equality demands that the sexual orientation of each individual in society must be protected on an even platform." A year later, the court went a step further, fully decriminalizing gay sex.

After being banned by city officials, Turkish police move against an LGBT+ pride march in Istanbul. Across the developing world, sexual minorities face discrimination—but have also made significant gains in some areas in recent years, notably Latin America. *Source*: Evren Kalinbacak/Alamy Stock Photo.

THE STATUS OF WOMEN IN THE DEVELOPING WORLD

One problem in many less developed countries is that women have fewer educational opportunities than men do. In the most extreme case, Afghanistan's Taliban government (1996–2001) prohibited females from attending school, and today Taliban rebels continue to attack girl students and schools. Because education significantly affects income, health, and political participation, this gender gap influences other important facets of political and economic life. We know, for example, that as women's educational levels rise, birth rates and family size decline.

The first two columns in table 7.1 compare literacy rates for *adult* women and men in the major regions of the developing world as of 1990 and 2015. They show how impressively the rates for both sexes improved in those twenty years, with the sharpest gains coming among women in South and West Asia (from 33.6 to 60.8 percent literate) and in the Arab States (from 47.9 to 71.4 percent). But women in both regions started from a very low base and they are still among the least educated groups. On the other hand, Central Asia and East Asia have essentially eliminated the gender gap, while Latin America and the Caribbean are only slightly behind.

The last column, the **gender parity index** (GPI)—which is calculated from the previous two columns—indicates how the female literacy rate in each region compares to the male rate.* So, for example, the 2015 GPI for South and West Asia is 0.76 and for Latin America and the Caribbean it is 0.99. This means that today the percentage of females in South and West Asia who are literate is only 76 percent as high as the male literacy rate. On the other hand, the current Latin American and Caribbean GPI of 0.99 shows that the two sexes have nearly equal rates of literacy.

Even in the regions that continue to have substantial adult GPI gaps— South and West Asia, sub-Saharan Africa and the Arab World—gender differences are rapidly declining and will continue to do so. For example, in sub-Saharan nations such as Kenya, Mozambique, and South Africa, the GPIs for *youth* (aged 15–24) all now exceed 0.9 (i.e., the female literacy rate for youth almost equals the male rate).

The first column in table 7.2 presents **gender inequality index** (GII) raw scores and ranks for each country. The GII is a composite index comparing men and women on four dimensions—political empowerment, education, participation in the work force, and measures of health. The raw scores can theoretically range from 0.000 (most equality) to 1.000 (least equality).

---

* Note that GPI does not indicate how high literacy rates are for either males or females. Thus, if country A has a male literacy rate of 80 percent and a female rate of 60 percent, its GPI would be 0.75, that is, the female rate is ¾ as high as the male rate. If another country had much *lower* literacy rates for both males and females, say 50 percent for each sex, its GPI would still be much *higher* (1.00) because the female literacy rate equals the male rate.

Table 7.1 Female and Male Literacy Rates

Region	Female Adult Literacy Rate (percent)		Male Adult Literacy Rate (percent)		GPI	
	1990	2015	1990	2015	1990	2015
Arab States	47.9	71.4	67.9	86.6	0.62	0.83
Central Asia	97.0	99.6	99.0	99.6	0.98	1.00
East Asia	74.4	94.0	89.0	97.6	0.84	0.96
Latin America and the Caribbean	84.4	92.4	87.0	93.3	0.97	0.99
South and West Asia	33.6	60.8	58.9	79.7	0.57	0.76
Sub-Saharan Africa	43.2	55.8	63.6	71.6	0.68	0.78

Source: UNESCO Institute for Statistics, Data Centre.

The number immediately after the score (in parenthesis) indicates how that country ranks compared to the 159 nations that have calculated GIIs. Generally, inequality is highest in the less developed countries such as Indonesia, Egypt, and Liberia. However, some developing nations in the table have comparatively low gender inequality, including China and Uruguay (not in the table), which have, respectively, the 37th and 55th least inequality.

The remaining columns compare recent adult literacy rates for women and men in each country. During the last decade or two, the gender gap in literacy has narrowed considerably in most developing countries, as girls have enrolled in primary schools at rates approaching, and occasionally even surpassing, boys. In fact, as the last column indicates, Thailand and China have achieved full or nearly full gender equality in literacy (Indeed, Thai women have a minutely higher level of literacy than do Thai men). On the other hand, women in Egypt and, especially, Liberia not only have

Table 7.2 Gender Inequality Index

Country	Gender Inequality Index (GII) (and global rank)	Female Adult Literacy Rate (percent)	Male Adult Literacy Rate (percent)
Switzerland	0.040 (2)	99.0	99.0
China	0.164 (37)	94.5	98.2
Thailand	0.366 (79)	96.7	96.6
Peru	0.385 (86)	91.7	97.3
South Africa	0.394 (90)	93.1	95.5
Indonesia	0.467 (105)	91.5	96.3
Egypt	0.565 (135)	65.4	82.2
Liberia	0.649 (150)	32.8	62.4

Source: UNDP, *Human Development Reports*; CIA, *The World Fact Book*.

Table 7.3   Measures of Gender Empowerment

Country/Region	Gender-Related Development Index (GDI)	Years of Education		Per Capita Income ($)	
		Women	Men	Women	Men
France	0.988	11.5	11.8	$31,742	$44,776
Arab States	0.856	5.9	7.6	$5,455	$23,810
East Asia	0.956	7.3	8.0	$9,569	$14,582
Latin America and the Caribbean	0.981	8.3	8.3	$10,053	$18,091
South Asia	0.822	4.9	7.8	$2,278	$9,114
Sub-Saharan Africa	0.877	4.5	6.3	$2,637	$4,165

Source: UNDP, *Human Development Report*.

relatively low literacy rates, but their rates are considerably lower than men's. In this respect, they are typical of the countries in their regions.

Finally, table 7.3 offers data on women's socioeconomic status. The first data column presents the country's score for the **gender-related development index** (GDI), which is a composite score that compares female life expectancy (in years), education, and income with those of men. The data row for France allows us to compare the performance of the major regions of the developing world to that of a highly industrialized democracy. The table indicates that Latin America and the Caribbean have the greatest gender equality in the factors just mentioned (life expectancy, etc.) of any LDC region, with a GDI (0.983), a degree of equality comparable to developed democracies such as Belgium or Canada.* On the other hand, the gender gap remains quite large in sub-Saharan Africa, and, especially South Asia.

The next two data columns compare the average years of education attained by women and men in each of these areas. Again, the regions show a similar pattern, with women and men having the same average years of education. Once again, the education gap is greatest in South Asia, next largest in sub-Saharan Africa and, interestingly, slightly less in the Arab World.

What is most striking about the last two data columns is the great income gap between sexes, even in a highly developed country such as France, where men, on average, earn about one and a half times as much as

---

* Again, life expectancy, education, and income would be much lower in Latin America than in Belgium or Canada, the GDI score merely indicates that the gender gap is comparable.

women do. The gender income gap in developing regions is actually lowest in East Asia, where men also earn about one and a half as much as women. Once again, the gender gap is greatest in South Asia, where men earn more than four times as much as women.

It is in the comparatively traditional countryside, rather than in modern cities, where women often play the most vital economic role. A few years ago, the UN Food and Agriculture Organization (FAO) estimated that women constitute over 40 percent of the agricultural labor force in the developing world, with this number reaching about 60 percent in some countries.[4] In time, aid agencies and governments in less developed countries began to recognize women's role in rural development. The percentage of the agricultural workforce that is composed of women ranges from about 20 percent in Latin America and the Caribbean to nearly 50 percent in East and Southeast Asia, Africa, and the Middle East. In parts of Asia and Africa, this percentage has grown in recent decades as many men migrate to find better-paying jobs in the urban economy, leaving their wives behind to work the family farm. While many developing world governments and international development organizations have become more sensitive to the special problems of poor, women farmers, gender blindness persists, farmers have been widely perceived as "male" by policymakers, development planners, and agricultural service deliverers. Therefore, women often find it more difficult to gain access to crucial resources such as credit, agricultural inputs, technology, and training that would enhance their productivity.

During the past half-century in most less developed countries, there has been an enormous population shift from the countryside to the cities (see chapter 8). Modernization theorists had expected that urbanization— often accompanied by increased industrialization, literacy, and exposure to the mass media—would offer women greater occupational and educational opportunities, thereby enhancing their status. In many Latin American nations, the majority of the migrants to urban centers have been women. But while many of them have benefited from their move, others have been left behind. Once settled in the city, most women are only able to secure low-end jobs. Indeed, in many Latin American countries, the most common type of employment among female migrants is as cleaning ladies or maids, for which they generally earn the legal minimum wage or lower. Another major source of employment is the so-called **informal sector**— including street peddling, some small businesses, employment in "sweatshops," and doing "piece-work" at home for contractors. These activities are "unregulated by the institutions of society [most notably the state], in a legal and social environment in which similar activities are regulated" by the government (e.g., safety standards) and taxed. Many men also work in this sector, but the majority of the informal-sector labor force is female (including the vast number of market and street vendors).[5] Although some informal-sector workers earn higher incomes than blue-collar laborers in the modern economy do, many others fall below the poverty line. Finally, in newly industrializing countries, women are often employed in low-wage manufacturing. Over time, as factories become more technologically sophisticated and as wages rise, the percentage of female employees tends to decline.

Since the 1980s, East Asia's industrial boom has created many new jobs for women, particularly in labor-intensive industries such as apparel and electronics. Often these firms prefer hiring young unmarried women for several reasons: the jobs frequently require manual dexterity, a skill that employers associate with women; because they are not the principal breadwinners in their families, young women are frequently willing to work for lower wages; and, finally, women are less likely to join unions or participate in strikes. During economic downturns, women are commonly the first fired because employers believe that men need their jobs more in order to support their families.

Because women in the majority of developing countries have fewer educational opportunities than men (see table 7.1) do and face other forms of discrimination, their occupational prospects are more limited. All too often, poverty and a lack of vocational skills force women into prostitution. Despite Thailand's economic boom since the mid-1960s, continuing rural poverty has driven many young female migrants into Bangkok's thriving "sex tourism" industry. One study of Bangkok and Manila (Philippines) revealed that 7–9 percent of female employment in these two major cities was "prostitution related." Some desperately poor families in that region have sold young daughters to brothels or given them as collateral for loans. A study of Southeast Asia by the International Labour Organization estimated that the number of sex workers in the mid-1990s was 140,000–230,000 in Indonesia and 200,000–300,000 in Thailand, where the number of prostitutes grew tenfold, between the early 1970s and the 1980s. In the economically depressed Philippines, "the estimated 400,000–500,000 prostitutes in the country approximated the number of its manufacturing workers."[6]

While these studies document the severe problems that frequently accompany modernization in the less developed countries, it is important to recognize that long-term economic growth, most notably in East Asia, has improved the incomes of millions of other underprivileged women newly employed in the modern sector of the economy. This is particularly true in the countries where female educational opportunities have also improved. Among middle- and upper-class women, the advantages of higher-class status usually mitigate the educational and career disadvantages of being female. In Asia and Latin America, the number of women professionals and businesswomen has increased rapidly in recent decades. Still, through most of the developing world, women remain underrepresented in positions of political and economic power alike.

GENDER AND POLITICS

The same traditions and prejudices that have undermined women's social and economic positions have also disadvantaged them politically. In Latin America, for example, women won the right to vote considerably later than they did in industrialized democracies. Whereas the United States and most European democracies legalized female suffrage in the first two decades of the twentieth century, only seven of twenty Latin American countries allowed women to vote before the close of the Second World War. Ecuador was the first nation in that region to extend the franchise (1929) and Paraguay the last (1961). In Africa and Asia, the situation was different. Because most of the countries in those regions did not become independent until the decades after the Second World War, when female suffrage was a universally accepted principle, women were normally enfranchised from the start of self-rule. However, the Arab Gulf State of Bahrain enfranchised women only in 2001, while Kuwait did it in 2005. Today, women in the less developed countries generally still vote at a lower rate than men do, but this gender gap is narrowing.

In much of Africa, Asia, and the Middle East, traditional social attitudes have limited both women's political participation and activism, as well as the participation of openly LGBT+ citizens in local or national politics. Lower-income women generally have few educational opportunities, which effectively limit their level of participation. Indeed, social class correlates particularly strongly with female political participation. In some less developed countries, highly educated and Westernized women, many of them born to elite families, are nearly as likely to hold important political offices as women in the West are. For example, although the countries of the Indian subcontinent have some of the world's lowest levels of female literacy and empowerment, Bangladesh, India, Pakistan, and Sri Lanka all have had women prime ministers. The first woman president of the United Nations General Assembly and the first female chair of the Security Council were both from Africa, rather than the industrialized West.

Because developing countries encompass so many cultural traditions, and because social change has impinged so differently on each nation's social classes and sectors, there are no simple generalizations about the way in which modernization has influenced women's political status. Modernization theory would lead us to expect that more socially and economically developed countries would be quicker to grant political rights to women. If we look at Latin America, however, we find little correlation between a country's literacy rate or per capita income and the year in which it granted suffrage to women. Thus, the spread of education alone does not guarantee women greater political equality. At the same time, governments of countries such as Rwanda, Mozambique, South Africa, Argentina, Costa Rica, and Cuba have made conscious efforts in recent times to change traditional values regarding gender. More recently, many countries have increased women's political representation by creating reserved seats and other types of quotas in elected legislatures (discussed later). This has given a number of developing countries a higher percentage of female representatives than many developed nations have. In fact, countries such as Bolivia and Senegal now have much higher proportions of women in their national legislatures than Ireland or the United States do.

Political Activism at the Grassroots

In some cases women have exerted the greatest influence on the politics of the developing world when acting through grassroots organizations in their own neighborhoods and villages. Community-based groups afford them opportunities for participation and leadership which are usually absent at the national or regional level. Furthermore, these organizations typically focus on issues that are of immediate importance to underprivileged women—housing, health care, nutrition, and education. Finally, neighborhood and village organizations are more accessible to poor women, who have no day care for their young children and usually cannot travel far from home. In short, many women who have been excluded from mainstream political parties, interest groups, and government institutions are attracted to community groups because of their accessibility and relevance to their own lives.

In recent decades, a range of grassroots organizations representing poor and middle-class women have emerged in many developing countries. Some represent women exclusively, while others include members of both sexes but are led by women or contain women's wings. Jana Everett examined several Indian community organizations in urban and rural settings, finding important similarities and differences.[7] Both urban and rural groups were first led by politically experienced, middle-class women committed to organizing the poor. But, as low-income women became more involved in community activities, their political awareness and confidence grew, stimulating, in turn, greater participation in the broader political system.

However, the goals and tactics used by these groups varied. For example, Everett found that the rural grassroots groups were more likely than urban organizations to stage demonstrations and other types of protest. They were also more prone to demand redistributive economic remedies such as land reform. In comparison, urban women's groups were generally more moderate in their goals and tactics. Amrita Basu's study of female rural protests in the Indian state of Maharashtra also noted their militancy. In one case, when a woman villager complained that the local police had ignored her charges against a landlord who had beaten her severely, a crowd of 300 women and 150 men "smeared [the landlord's] face with cow dung . . . and paraded him through the surrounding villages."[8] The rural women's greater aggressiveness likely resulted from the more hostile political atmosphere they confronted. Because village political and economic elites are usually less willing than their urban counterparts to redress the grievances of the poor through normal political channels, these women were forced to use more radical tactics.

In Latin America, opposition to the authoritarian military governments that governed much of the region during the 1970s and 1980s was a major catalyst for grassroots political activity. In Argentina, Brazil, Chile, and Uruguay, military dictatorships suspended elections, banned many political parties and unions, and arrested, tortured, or killed suspected "subversives." At the same time, a major debt crisis in the 1980s, coupled with harsh government economic remedies, produced the worst recession in the region since the Great Depression of the 1930s and a precipitous decline in living standards. Women played an important role in antiauthoritarian social movements, which helped pave the way for the restoration of democracy in the 1980s and 1990s.

The women's movement incorporated three types of political organizations, all largely urban-based. First were feminist groups, primarily consisting of middle-class women. They included many professionals who previously had been active in leftist political parties, but had become disillusioned by the left's disinterest in women's issues at that time. A second type, neighborhood organizations, represented women from the urban slums. In the face of the region's severe economic crisis, poor women organized self-help groups to run communal kitchens, infant nutrition centers, and other anti-poverty activities. Though not highly politicized originally, many of these groups radicalized over time as they demanded more equitable distribution of state expenditures and the restoration of democracy.

Finally, a third strand of the women's movement was devoted to human rights. During the 1970s and 1980s, Argentina's "Mothers of the Plaza de Mayo" regularly marched in defiance of government restrictions to demand an accounting of their missing children and grandchildren, who had disappeared at the hands of the police or armed forces. Responding to state-sponsored imprisonments, torture, and assassinations, women's groups in Brazil, Chile, and Uruguay became major components of the human rights movement. This was one of the few instances in which women's organizations had an advantage over similar groups led by men. Because the military governments viewed women as inherently less political than men and, hence, less dangerous, they allowed women's human rights groups greater freedom than they gave other protest movements. Furthermore, this was the most socially integrated branch of the women's movement, bringing together participants from the middle and working classes. In many cases, they also joined forces with other human rights activists in the Catholic Church (chapter 5).

Ironically, the restoration of democracy reduced the need for unity among the disparate wings of the women's movement. Furthermore, as female leaders and militants became increasingly involved in the restored democratic system, many of them returned to party politics and lost their close ties to community groups representing the urban poor. Thus, the return of democratic governments actually demobilized many lower-income women and weakened their movements. More recently, however, the explosion of **nongovernmental organizations** (NGOs) in developing areas worldwide has created new opportunities for women's grassroots political participation. As their name suggests, NGOs are issue-based organizations, independent of government control. Many try to influence public policy in areas such as democratization, human rights, women's rights, environmental protection, housing, health care, and education. The best-known and financed groups operate internationally, including the Catholic Relief Services, Amnesty International, Greenpeace, and Oxfam. On the other hand, most NGOs are limited to the local or, at most, the national level, where many of them try to mobilize popular support and influence government policy. In India, for example, it is estimated that national and local NGOs number in the tens or likely hundreds of thousands. Throughout the developing world, they have contributed enormously to the expansion of civil society, particularly in democratizing societies, where they often provide a political voice to women and otherwise powerless groups seeking reform.

In addition to issues of women's empowerment, grassroots organization and lobbying efforts by NGOs have played a key role in the expansion of LGBT+ rights too. The most visible example of this are large solidarity marches in a growing number of cities around the world. The annual Pride parade in São Paulo, Brazil, for example, attracts more than 3 million participants and is today one of the largest in the world. But activists also play a key role in challenging discriminatory laws in court, engaging in public outreach and education, and promoting legal reform in national legislatures.

Breaking the Glass Ceiling: Women as National Political Leaders*

Women Heads of Government

Throughout the developing world, women are severely underrepresented in political leadership positions, including seats in the national parliament and national cabinets. Slowly this has begun to change. In Asia—especially South Asia—and in Latin America, a number of women have risen to the top of the political ladder in recent decades. Four nations in South Asia have been led by women prime ministers.[†] The most prominent member of this group was Indira Gandhi, who served four terms as prime minister (1966–77 and 1980–84) and dominated Indian politics for eighteen years, until her assassination in 1984. In Sri Lanka, a woman president and a female prime minister controlled the country's politics for many years. And in Bangladesh, one of two women rivals—Begum Khaleda Zia and Sheikh Hasina Wazed—has been prime minister for most of the period since 1991. Elsewhere in Asia, women have been presidents of the Philippines (twice) and Indonesia as well as prime ministers of Thailand and Pakistan.

Nine of the thirty-three countries in Latin America and the Caribbean have elected female presidents or prime ministers, the largest proportion of any region in the developing world. They include the recent presidents of three of the most important countries in the area—Argentina's Cristina Fernández de Kirchner, Brazil's Dilma Rousseff, and Michelle Bachelet in Chile. Previously, Costa Rica, Panama, and Nicaragua all had women presidents.

---

* While this section focuses on the representation of women in formal politics, LGBT+ citizens may face even greater barriers to election or appointment to senior roles. However, since 1997 several countries in Latin America have seen openly gay or lesbian candidates elected to national legislatures. In Nepal, Sunil Babu Pant was elected as an openly gay member of the constituent assembly (and the first such elected national representative in Asia) in 2008, while Geraldine Roman became the first transgender person elected to Congress in the Philippines in 2016. In South Africa, Lynne Brown became Africa's first openly lesbian cabinet minister in 2014. Many more LGBT+ politicians exist, of course, but would be reluctant to reveal their identities for fear of discrimination.

† Many countries have both a president and a prime minister and the relative power of each leader varies from country to country. In Latin America, East Asia, and Africa, the president is normally the more powerful figure. In the rest of Asia, the Caribbean, as well as Europe, the prime minister is usually the major governmental leader.

Although several sub-Saharan parliaments have among the highest percentages of women in the world (discussed later), that region has had far fewer women heads of government or heads of state than either Asia or Latin America. Only recently have two female presidents been elected (in Liberia and Malawi), while women have been prime ministers in at least six African countries.

Several caveats must be raised regarding the political success of women leaders in Asia. First, most of them emerged from the tiny elite of highly educated, upper-class women in powerful families. Thus, they were not at all representative of women's societal status generally. For example, Pakistan's Benazir Bhutto attended Oxford and Harvard Universities, while Corazón Aquino belonged to a powerful, Filipino landowning family.

Second, many of the most influential women leaders everywhere, but particularly in Asia, have been the widows, wives, or daughters of charismatic national leaders: Indira Gandhi was the daughter of India's legendary first prime minister, Jawaharlal Nehru; while former Indonesian president Megawati Sukarnoputri is the daughter of President Sukarno, that country's first president and founding father. More recently, Thailand's prime minister, Yingluck Shinawatra, was, in effect, a stand-in for her brother, a former prime minister. In Latin America and the Caribbean, most of the first women presidents also were all the wives or widows of former presidents.

Indeed, a shocking number of female government leaders in developing countries, most notably in Asia, have been the widows or daughters of assassinated political leaders. Sri Lankan prime minister Sirimavo Bandaranaike was the widow of a slain prime minister, while that country's former president, Chandrika Kumaratunga, endured the political assassinations of both her father and her husband (thirty years apart). Former president Corazón Aquino, hero of the Filipino democracy movement, was the widow of an assassinated opposition leader. The father of former Pakistani prime minister Benazir Bhutto was a former prime minister who was ousted by the Pakistani armed forces and hung. She herself was assassinated in 2007. In Latin America, former Nicaraguan president Violeta Chamorro was the widow of a famed newspaper editor whose assassination sparked the Nicaraguan Revolution.

This does not imply that these women lacked political ability or leadership qualities. Indira Gandhi was recognized as one of the world's most accomplished political leaders, and Violeta Chamorro helped heal the wounds of her country's civil war. After Sri Lanka's Sirimavo Bandaranaike succeeded her assassinated husband as prime minister, she dominated that country's political system for the next three decades.* Still, no matter how highly skilled

---

* On the other hand, some widows who succeed to leadership, such as Argentina's Isabel Perón, were not so capable.

they have been, until recently most female government leaders have been able to reach the top of their political system only as heirs to their fathers or husbands. That blueprint seems to be changing in Latin America and, to a lesser extent, in Africa, where several women have been elected presidents in the twenty-first century (in Chile, Brazil, Costa Rica, Liberia, and Malawi) without having inherited their husband's or father's political following.

Women Cabinet Ministers

Another important gauge of women's political empowerment is the number and type of ministerial posts they hold in their nation's cabinet. In many countries, these are the next most influential government positions after the president or prime minister. Although women continue to hold a low share of cabinet posts in most less developed countries, their numbers have increased from a mere 3.4 percent in 1987 to over 17 percent in 2015. Because cabinet ministers are appointed by the president or prime minister, the percentage of women in that institution (in any particular country) is more volatile than their percentage in parliament. The proportion of women may change from year to year depending on which political party or leader is in office. In general, however, the percentage has grown, and some developing nations now have a substantial portion of women in their cabinets. For example, as of 2017, women comprised around half the ministers in Nicaragua, Rwanda, and South Africa, and around one-third of the cabinet posts in Colombia, Zambia, and Grenada. However, in the majority of less developed countries, women held less than one-fifth of cabinet seats, and the percentages in Vietnam, Turkey, and Nepal were less than 5 percent. A few countries—including Pakistan and Saudi Arabia—had no female cabinet ministers at all in 2017.[9]

Beyond a simple head count of the number of women appointed to ministerial positions, it is interesting to consider the types of cabinet positions that women have held. Frequently they head ministries such as education, women's affairs, and health and social welfare—areas traditionally believed to be suited for women's "nurturing role."[10] At the same time, few women hold such key cabinet ministries such as defense, economics, or foreign affairs. Only since the start of this century have a small number of women held these posts (before she became president, Michelle Bachelet—once a political prisoner of the country's former military regime—served as Chile's defense minister in 2002–4).

Reserved Seats and Quotas: Female Representation in Parliament

The participation of women in national legislatures has been more complex. Since women normally account for approximately half the national population, gender-neutral political systems would presumably produce a corresponding percentage of female representatives in those institutions.

Table 7.4 **Women in National Parliaments: Regional Averages (in percentages)**

Region	1995	2017
Nordic Countries	36.4	41.7
Europe Excluding Nordic Countries	13.2	26.0
Latin American and the Caribbean	12.7	28.2
Sub-Saharan Africa	9.8	23.5
Asia	13.2	19.4
Arab Countries	4.3	17.4
World Average	11.3	23.5

Source: Inter-Parliamentary Union, *Women in National Parliaments* (online).

However, few regions or countries come close to such parity. Table 7.4 shows that, although the percentage of women in parliament worldwide more than doubled from 1995 to 2017—and grew in every world region—women still constitute only 23.5 percent of all MPs (Members of Parliament) today. As the second data column reveals, of all world regions, only the Nordic nations (Norway, Sweden, Denmark, Finland, and Iceland), with 41.7 percent, come close to having women fill half the seats. Within the less developed countries, women MPs advanced at the fastest in the Arab World (increasing by over 300 percent between 1995 and 2017), but still lagged behind the rest of the developing world. Latin America and sub-Saharan Africa both more than doubled their percentage of female MPs.

We might expect women to hold a larger share of parliamentary seats in more modern and more educated countries. But looking at the major regions in the table, we see that this is not necessarily so. While it is true that the Nordic region—with the highest rate of women MPs in the "lower house" of the national legislature—is very socioeconomically advanced, the rest of Europe has a slightly lower percentage of women in that chamber (26.0 percent) than does Latin America and the Caribbean (28.2 percent).* Moreover, of the ten parliaments with the highest percentage of women in the world (all over 40 percent female), seven are less developed countries from either Latin America (Bolivia, Cuba, Nicaragua, and Mexico) or Africa (Rwanda, Senegal, and South Africa).†

---

*In a parliament or congress with two chambers (**bicameral legislature**), the "lower house" refers to the larger chamber, whose entire membership is elected at the same time (usually every two or four years), such as the US House of Representatives. Despite its name, the lower house has greater power than the so-called upper house in most countries (but not in the United States). The upper house (often called "the Senate") is normally a smaller chamber, whose members have longer terms of office and run in staggered years (like the US Senate). Some national legislatures are **unicameral** (they have only one chamber) and in table 7.4 they are grouped together with the lower house of bicameral legislatures.

†As of July 1, 2017. These rankings change when there are new elections.

Thus, a country's or region's percentage of women MPs may be determined as much by its history, culture, and politics as it is by its level of development. Most African and the Middle Eastern countries did not gain independence until the 1940s or later, when the importance of female political participation had greater currency in the world's political culture and practices. Some of the governments with high representation of women in parliament (such as South Africa, Eritrea, Cuba, and Nicaragua) came to power after revolutionary struggles in which traditional values had been open to challenge, and women often played an important part in the struggle. As we have previously seen, the East African nation of Rwanda experienced a genocide in 1994 when five hundred thousand to one million people (mostly men) were killed in approximately one hundred days, depleting the country's male population. After peace was restored, women, by necessity, took on a far greater role in the country's government, including holding more than half the seats in parliament.

Elsewhere, several social, economic, and cultural factors help account for women's underrepresentation in most of the world. Pippa Norris and Joni Lovenduski have argued that the number of women in elected office depends on various factors affecting "supply and demand."[11] Supply refers to the number of women who meet the socioeconomic standards of public officeholders in their country. Because women in many less developed countries have lower levels of education, lower status, and, most important, fewer economic resources than men—all factors closely related to political success—they are able to "supply" fewer viable candidates for office. In fact, Rae Lesser Blumberg's research in several regions of the world indicates that "the most important variable . . . affecting the level of [political] equality [or inequality] between men and women is economic power" as defined by their relative incomes and control of economic resources.[12] On the "demand" side (i.e., society's acceptance of female political leaders), widespread cultural prejudice in some regions against the empowerment of women, most notably in the Islamic world, has also restricted the number of women from holding public office.

In the past two decades, as women's educational levels have risen in most developing countries, as they have entered the professions in greater numbers, and as cultural prejudices have diminished in many places, both the supply of and demand for women officeholders have increased. The most important change in recent years has come from the demand side—the introduction of gender quotas for parliament. Since 1991, the number of countries implementing this electoral mechanism has climbed sharply, and today about one hundred countries, primarily in the developing world, have some form of **gender quota**. Although the intent of all of these gender quotas is to enhance the number of women in parliament, we will see that some countries have made only token efforts and achieved few gains, while others have sharply increased the number of women MPs. Latin America, though often associated with machismo (male chauvinism), has been the world leader in effecting reform measures. Across that region, the number of female representatives has jumped from 12.7 percent in 1995 to over 27 percent in 2015 (a higher percentage than in Canada or the United States).[13]

Legislated and voluntary attempts to raise the proportion of women in national parliaments have taken several forms. The most direct and certain method is to reserve a designated number of parliamentary seats for women. The basic justification for **reserved seats** is that because many societies have deeply ingrained gender prejudices, the only way a significant number of women can gain office is by setting aside a bloc of seats for them. In fact, many of the reserved seat systems were introduced in Arab States, South Asia, and in parts of Africa, where prejudices against women office-holders are generally strongest. Two of the recent countries introducing this form of gender quota are Afghanistan and Iraq, where they have about 25 percent of parliamentary seats reserved.

Unfortunately, in some countries, creating reserved seats seems to have created a "glass ceiling," blocking further electoral gains for women. Although women are allowed to contest parliamentary seats beyond the number reserved for them, the use of reserved seats often signals voters that women have gotten their "fair share" and do not deserve to be elected beyond their guaranteed quota. Also, many political parties in more traditional societies have similar attitudes and see no need to include women in their regular slate of parliamentary candidates.[14]

However, some countries have set aside a substantial number of reserved seats for women and have also elected a significant number of women beyond that quota in contests that are open to both sexes. Thus, in Rwanda, 30 percent of the seats (twenty-four out of a total of eighty) in the Chamber of Deputies are reserved for women candidates. In addition, in the last parliamentary election, women candidates won almost half of the nondesignated seats, which were open to both male and female candidates. This gave them a total of fifty-one seats (i.e., 64 percent of the entire chamber), the highest portion in the world. It is now one of only two lower chambers of parliament in the world where women are in the majority—the other is Bolivia.

Another means of reducing gender underrepresentation is to establish quotas for the slates of parliamentary candidates in general elections. Such quotas may take two forms. First, individual political parties may voluntarily guarantee that their slate of parliamentary candidates will contain a certain percentage of women. In Europe, for example, Scandinavia enjoyed the first major gains in female parliamentary representation when that region's socialist parties (frequently the largest parties in those countries) agreed to gender quotas. In the less developed countries, the most successful example of voluntary quotas has been in South Africa's dominant party, the ANC.

The second type of **candidate quota** is legislated (or sometimes included in the constitution) and is binding on all political parties. Both voluntary and legislated candidate quotas commit political parties to nominate a stipulated percentage of women candidates on their tickets. In many quota systems, women must constitute at least 30 percent of their party's list of parliamentary candidates. This number reflects the **critical mass** of female MPs commonly needed to produce government policies friendly to women's interests. A dozen Latin American countries and a number of other developing nations passed some form of a gender candidate quota during the wave of democratic transitions in the 1990s. Argentina was a pioneer in this area and by 2006 dozens of countries, mostly less developed countries, had some sort of quota system.[15]

The goal of candidate quotas is purportedly to give women a greater opportunity to hold regularly elected seats rather than fill seats specially reserved for them. But candidate quotas, particularly when legislatively imposed, are frequently ineffective because their objective is easily circumvented if major political parties nominate most of their women candidates in races that the party has little chance of winning. Many countries (including Britain and a number of its former colonies) have electoral systems with **single-member districts** (SMD) in which voters elect only one MP in each parliamentary district. This is the system used to elect the US House of Representatives. In such countries, most electoral districts usually lean heavily toward one party or another. So, political parties that want to satisfy the letter of the quota laws, but wish to circumvent their spirit, can simply nominate most of their women candidates in districts where they had little chance of winning the general elections. For example, imagine that the United States had a 30 percent gender quota for congressional candidates and that party officials, rather than voters in primary elections, were the ones who selected the candidates.* If Democratic Party leaders wanted to circumvent the quota law, they could nominate men in districts that are safely theirs and nominate most of their women congressional candidates (30 percent of the total) in heavily Republican states ("Red States"), such as Alabama or Utah, where they would stand little chance of beating the Republican candidates in the general election. Similarly, the Republicans could run their male candidates in Red States, while fielding the women

---

* The United States is one of the few countries in the world that hold primary elections to select party candidates. In most countries, candidates are named by party officials in conventions, caucuses, or other types of meetings.

candidates in Democratic strongholds such as Boston, New York, and San Francisco.

While some developing nations elect their parliaments in SMDs, most use an electoral system called **proportional representation** (PR). To understand how PR works, let us imagine a country with a five-hundred-seat parliament divided into twenty-five electoral districts, each of which elects twenty MPs. The national parties each nominate a "party list" of twenty candidates in each district, with candidates ranked from one through twenty (closed lists). Rather than select a single candidate, as American voters do when they cast their ballots for the House of Representatives, voters in PR elections generally choose an entire party list (e.g., the Christian Democratic Party list of twenty candidates or the Socialist Party list). Seats are then allocated in proportion to the percentage of votes that each list receives. Thus, if the Christian Democrats' list received 40 percent of the votes in "district A," they would win 40 percent of the twenty seats in that district (i.e., eight seats). But which eight of that party's twenty listed candidates would go to parliament? It would be those who were ranked first through eight on the party's list prior to the election. If we further imagine that a quota law requires that at least 35 percent of each party's candidates be women (i.e., at least seven candidates in each district), the number of women who actually are elected would depend on where they had been ranked on the party list. Thus, even with the 35 percent quota requirement, if all of the female candidates had been ranked in the bottom half of the party list, all eight of that party's victorious candidates would still be men.*

To put teeth into a legislated quota system and prevent dumping of women candidates into hopeless positions at the bottom of the party lists (in PR systems) or in districts that the party knows it cannot win (in SMD systems), countries such as Argentina passed electoral laws requiring so-called **zipper quotas**. This means that each party must not only meet its quota of female candidates, but also alternate male and female candidates, according to that quota percentage from the top of the list downward. For example, if a country such as Argentina has a zipper-style gender quota of 33 percent, women candidates have to occupy every third position on the list from the top rank on down. So, if a party won nine of the thirty seats in a particular multimember district, the nine winning candidates would include three women. In general, elections through zipper-style proportional representation with closed lists (i.e., where voters cannot select individual candidates on the list) benefit women candidates more than quotas in SMD elections do.†

---

* There are many varieties of PR elections, and what is described is a simplified, generic version.
† In "open list" PR systems, winning candidates from each party are chosen not in the order they are presented on a party list, but on the basis of the votes they individually receive. This may make zipper quotas impossible, and often favors the male candidates on a list.

Since 1991, the spread of legally mandated quotas, of any type, has been a major factor in the worldwide increase in female MPs. For example, in ten Latin American countries that enacted quotas between 1991 and 1997, the number of women in parliament rose by an average of 8 percent in the very next national election.[16] However, results have been most impressive when electoral laws mandate zipper-style quotas or their equivalent. For example, when Costa Rica's Supreme Court strengthened that country's quota law by insisting that women be proportionally included in competitive races, the percentage of women in Congress rose from 19 percent in 1997 (already higher than in the US Congress at that time) to 35 percent by 2002. Also, when the ANC took power in South Africa and voluntarily adopted a gender quota, the percentage of women MPs rose from 141st in the world in 1994 to 9th highest today.*

Ultimately, the issue of reserved seats and candidate quotas raises another fundamental question. How much difference does increased female representation have on government policy? The evidence suggests that legislatures with significantly higher female membership (in either less developed countries or developed nations) are more prone to address issues such as gender bias, child care, education, rape, domestic violence, and divorce law and are more likely to produce legislation in these areas that is beneficial to women. However, most analysts agree that even a substantial increase in female representation from a very low base—for example, the Arab World's huge jump in female MPs from 4.3 percent in 1995 to 18 percent today—is usually not sufficient to affect government policy on those issues because there are still too few female MPs to influence policy. Indeed, when women hold fewer than 30 percent of parliamentary seats, they tend to be co-opted or are simply ineffective in pressing "women's issues." As female representation approaches that 30 percent level, however, parliaments are more likely to pass "women-friendly" legislation. As of 2017, there were forty-seven countries that had reached that threshold, over half of them developing nations.[†]

Earlier, we noted the growing number of women prime ministers and presidents in the less developed countries, most notably in South Asia. While we might assume that gains for women at the pinnacle of government would either reflect or cause broader political or socioeconomic advances for women generally—as they do, for example, in the Nordic countries—this has not necessarily been true in the less developed countries. Sri Lanka and Bangladesh most glaringly demonstrate that point. Women have served for extended periods as Sri Lanka's president (eleven years) and prime

---

*The African National Congress is the only South African party to impose a gender quota. But since it holds almost two-thirds of the seats in parliament, its quota obviously affects the nature of the entire legislature.

[†]A number of these countries—such as Cuba—are not democracies and in those countries it is unclear how much women MPs exert independent influence on legislation or to what extent all MPs—including women—normally vote as the ruling party dictates.

minister (eighteen years). Yet, they currently constitute only 5.8 percent of that nation's MPs, less than one-quarter of the international average. Similarly, although Bangladesh has been led by either of two female prime ministers for fifteen of the past eighteen years, it still ranks seventy-five among all nations that have recorded GII scores.

Although electoral mechanisms such as quotas and reserved seats are the most important factors responsible for greater female representation in parliament, social, cultural, and historical forces also play a role. At the same time, these factors also help explain why a particular country introduces quotas or reserved seats in the first place.

For example, in Scandinavia, the culture's strong emphasis on gender and class equality produced a very high number of female MPs even before those countries' major parties adopted voluntary quotas. Denmark's parties abandoned gender quotas in 1996 (after enforcing them for nearly two decades) yet, even without the benefit of quotas, women currently hold 37 percent of their country's parliamentary seats, one of the world's highest percentages. In Africa, the countries with the highest proportion of women in parliament are often "post-conflict states," which have come through bloody internal conflicts (Rwanda, Burundi), long wars of independence against their colonial masters (Angola, Mozambique), or struggles against white minority rule (South Africa). While these conflicts took a terrible toll in lives and suffering, they also opened up new opportunities for women who were involved in them. In these countries and others, such as Tunisia or Iraq, the process of post-conflict political reform also opened up new opportunities for legal and constitutional reform—often with the encouragement and support of outside aid agencies.

The Effect of Reaching a Critical Mass on Policy Outcomes

We noted earlier that it seems that in order to be effective agents of change in advanced industrial societies (Europe, North America, Japan etc.), women seem to need to hold at least 30 percent of the legislative seats. What about the less developed countries that have reached that threshold (usually with the help of gender quotas) or come close? Has that helped advance "women's issues," such as medical and nutritional care for mothers and their small children? Mala Htun and Jennifer M. Piscopo have found that, in Latin America, countries with gender quotas (and, therefore, higher percentages of women) are likely to pass gender-related legislation that does not conflict with their countries' cultural values, such as laws that protect women against violence. They are unlikely to change culturally or religiously sensitive laws, such as easing restrictions on abortion.[17]

In Asia and the Arab World, gender quotas are less likely to lead to any kind of gender-friendly legislation. In a number of cases, they have adopted quotas to satisfy the United Nations, Western countries, or other possible aid donors. And in two nations where gender quotas were introduced as a result of American invasions—Afghanistan and Iraq—these quotas are unlikely to produce policies that help women.

Women and Revolutionary Change

Both because of their ideological commitment to gender equality and because they needed military recruits, some revolutionary armies heavily recruited women and offered them greater opportunities for upward mobility. For example, women constituted an estimated 20–30 percent of the revolutionary guerrilla forces in Eritrea and Nicaragua and held high leadership positions in El Salvador's FMLN.

More generally, the political, economic, and social changes brought about by revolutions in the less developed countries often present women with unique opportunities. Revolutionary regimes in countries such as China, Vietnam, and Cuba have tried to transform traditional cultural values through education and propaganda. Combating society's conventional restrictions on women has been a part of that process. When the Chinese communists came to power, they eliminated the last vestiges of foot binding for young girls and prohibited the sale of women and girls as wives, concubines, or prostitutes. New institutions, such as the Cuban Federation of Women (FMC)—officially representing 70 percent of the country's women—and China Women's Federation, were created to mobilize women in support of the revolution and to give them some voice in the political process.

In Cuba, longtime FMC leader, Vilma Espín, was a particularly effective force for gender equality because she was married to (former president) Raúl Castro and was Fidel Castro's sister-in-law. The federation was instrumental in creating the nation's Family Code (the law governing family relations), which requires both spouses to contribute equally to domestic chores (child care, cooking, cleaning, etc.). Today, women make up about two-thirds of all university graduates and a similar proportion of all professionals, including lawyers and judges.[18]

But even revolutionary societies find it difficult to eradicate long-standing patriarchal attitudes and they are no panacea. In many cases, radical rhetoric exceeds actual accomplishments. In China, women generally still hold less-skilled, lower-paying jobs. While women have advanced professionally in both China and Cuba, in neither country do they have a significant share of high-level positions in government or in the Communist Party. Although the Cuban Family Code requires husbands to do half of the house work, few men do.

In rural China (where half the population lives), the country's stringent population control policies limit most families to two children.* While this

---

* Urban families are limited to one child.

program has lowered the nation's birth rate impressively, the policy has had disturbing, unanticipated consequences. Worldwide, the normal gender ratio of babies at birth is around 106 or 107 males to 100 females. But in China the ratio was as high as 121:100 in 2004 and is currently about 117:100. Consequently, males exceed the number of female newborns by well over 1 million each year. China's huge gender gap (the largest in the world) raises the question of "what happened to the missing girls?"

As in many Asian countries, the Chinese—particularly in rural areas—have a strong cultural and economic preference for sons. Because the population control program limits the number of children that they can have, villagers are concerned that one of those be a boy. Therefore, many prospective parents who can afford prenatal gender tests—ultrasounds, though officially illegal, can be rather easily secured for as little as $12—opt for abortions of female fetuses. And in an unknown, but significant, number of cases, girls who are born fall victim to "gendercide," the murder of female babies by parents who want their child to be a boy (though this practice has decreased in recent years). In addition, many newborn girls are sent to orphanages, where more than 95 percent of the children who are put up for foreign adoption have been female. At the same time, the cumulative effect of the one-child policy has made it harder for young men to find women whom they can marry. In recent years, the Chinese government's growing concern over the gender imbalance has led it to relax some population control measures.[19]

MODERNIZATION AND THE STATUS OF WOMEN

Our discussion has revealed that the political and economic status of women in less developed countries varies considerably from region to region and from country to country. Two factors are particularly influential: a country's dominant cultural values and its level of socioeconomic modernization.

Because gender is a social construct, culture—including religious values—sets baseline boundaries for most women, affecting both the opportunities available to them and the restrictions they face. This is most obvious in fundamentalist Islamist countries such as Iran and Saudi Arabia. Political leadership in all these fundamentalist countries is an exclusively male preserve. Cultural restraints are more subtle in East Asia, but even in a relatively modern society such as South Korea women are underrepresented in politics and have a significantly lower income and development indices than do men.

Contrary to modernization theory—but in accordance with much feminist analysis—socioeconomic modernization has often adversely affected women in the less developed countries in the short term. In Africa, for example, the commercialization and mechanization of agriculture have benefited male cultivators disproportionately, frequently at the expense of women farmers. In East and Southeast Asia, rapid industrialization based on cheap labor frequently has given many female laborers higher wages than they earned in their previous jobs, but often has exploited many others. But although such economic development often harms poor women initially, its longer-term effects are mostly positive. A growing middle class, wider educational opportunities, and higher rates of literacy make women more aware of their rights and opportunities, while increasing their capacity to defend any gains. Socioeconomic development also tends to create more egalitarian values within society. It is not coincidental that women in Europe and in more modernized Latin America generally enjoy greater political and economic equality. The feminist movement has also become global, with ideas and inspiration spreading from one country to another through the media and the demonstration effect. In many developing nations, women's rights movements have emerged where none had existed, or were even conceivable, a decade or two earlier.

Given that full gender equality does not exist yet in the most advanced industrialized democracies, it seems unlikely that socioeconomic modernization or the spread of democratic norms will automatically bring gender equality to the developing world. Future economic development can be expected to produce both negative and positive consequences. In countries suffering severe economic downturns, such as the recent global financial crisis, or those experiencing civil conflict, women will doubtless continue to bear a disproportionate share of the burden. And the spread of religious fundamentalism in many parts of the Middle East and Africa bodes poorly for women's rights in those nations. In the long term, however, economic modernization, higher educational levels, and modern values seem to offer women their best hope.

GENDER AND DEMOCRACY

Because democratic ideology endorses equal opportunity and equal rights for all citizens, we might expect the Third Wave of democracy to have advanced gender equity. Yet, our discussion of revolutionary societies revealed that some nondemocratic governments have promoted women's rights more effectively than comparable democracies have. A number of revolutionary regimes have raised the number of women in the national legislature, improved the legal status of women, banned oppressive traditional customs, and, to some degree, infused respect for women's rights into the new political culture. It is also true that the Eastern European transition from communism to democracy brought a precipitous drop in the percentage of women elected to parliament. But most authoritarian governments are neither radical nor committed to women's rights. These rights have fared poorly under both religious fundamentalist regimes and right-wing military dictatorships.

How did women's groups influence the wave of democratization that has swept across the developing world since the 1970s, and how did the emergence of democracy affect women's economic and political standing? In a number of Asian and Latin American nations (such as Argentina and South Korea), women's social movements helped topple repressive regimes. Yet, the return to center stage of male-dominated political parties and interest groups during the subsequent democratic transitions frequently marginalized those grassroots political groups and NGOs in which women had played a major role. Thus, the restoration of democracy had contradictory effects on women's political participation. As Mala Htun has observed,

> The return to civilian rule and the consolidation of democratic governance created many more opportunities for women to be politically active, but also reduced the comparative advantage of gender-specific organizations as conduits for social demands. As a result, many women, who had entered politics during the struggle against authoritarian rule, left gender-specific organizations for political parties and other "traditional" organizations like labor unions.[20]

It is possible, of course, for democratic politics to empower socially conservative groups that hold traditional attitudes to gender—for example, some Islamist parties. Politicians may also exploit homophobia and transphobia to mobilize support, as is evident in some right-wing populist parties and among some current political leaders in Africa. In general, however, it appears that democratic governments tend to have more gender equality than authoritarian regimes do. Respect for sexual minorities also tends to be greater in such countries. No doubt this is because women's and LGBT+ groups in liberal democracies are able to mobilize politically, lobby government officials, and otherwise voice their concerns through democratic channels. At the same time, such advocacy groups are more likely to be heard by a free press and by politicians who want to be reelected. To be sure, some authoritarian regimes, such as Cuba, have a strong record on women's equality. Yet in authoritarian governments, women's rights depend on the will of the (heavily male) political leadership. In most authoritarian governments this will is lacking.

> **Practice and Review Online at**
> http://textbooks.rowman.com/handelman9e

KEY TERMS

bicameral legislature
candidate quota
critical mass
female genital mutilation (FGM)
gender
Gender Inequality Index (GII)
Gender Parity Index (GPI)
gender quota
Gender-Related Development
   Index (GDI)
informal sector

lesbian, gay, bisexual, transgender
   (LGBT+)
nongovernmental organizations
   (NGOs)
patriarchy
private sphere
proportional representation
public sphere
reserved seats
single-member districts
unicameral
zipper quotas

DISCUSSION QUESTIONS

1. What might explain why some governments headed by women made greater progress on "women's issues," while others did not?
2. What are some of the reasons (hopefully including some not mentioned in the chapter) that democracy seems to contribute to greater gender equality? Under what circumstances might greater democracy end up diminishing women's rights in some countries?
3. What factors might contribute to greater respect for the rights of LGBT+ citizens in the developing world (and elsewhere)?

NOTES

1. World Values Survey data, http://www.worldvaluessurvey.org. Results from a WVS survey in the United States shows that 19 percent of Americans and 11 percent of Swedes also believe that men make better political leaders.

2. "Village Council in India Accused of Ordering Rape," *New York Times*, January 23, 2014.

3. UNDP, "UN Survey of 10,000 Men in Asia and the Pacific Reveals Why Some Men Use Violence Against Women and Girls," September 10, 2013, http://www.undp.org/content/undp/en/home/presscenter/pressreleases/2013/09/10/un-survey-of-10-000-men-in-asia-and-the-pacific-reveals-why-some-men-use-violence-against-women-and-girls-.html.

4. Food and Agriculture Organization, *The Role of Women in Agriculture*, Working Paper No. 11–02 (March 2011).

5. Ruth Pearson, "Reassessing Paid Work and Women's Employment: Lessons from the Global Economy," in *Feminisms in Development*, eds. Andrea Cornwall, Elizabeth Harrison, and Ann Whitehead (London: Zed Books, 2007), 202–3.

6. Cited in Alan Gilbert and Josef Gugler, *Cities, Poverty and Development: Urbanization in the Third World*, 2nd ed. (New York, NY: Oxford University Press, 1992), 104, fn. 29. Italics added.

7. Jana Everett, *Women and Social Change in India* (New York, NY: St. Martin's Press, 1979).

8. Amrita Basu, *Two Faces of Protest: Contrasting Modes of Women's Activism* (Berkeley, CA: University of California Press, 1992), 3.

9. Inter-Parliamentary Union, *Women in Politics 2017*, https://www.ipu.org/resources/publications/infographics/2017-03/women-in-politics-2017.

10. Jane Parpart and Kathleen Staudt, "Women and the State in Africa," in *Women and the State in Africa*, eds. Jane Parpart and Kathleen Staudt (Boulder, CO: Lynne Rienner Publishers, 1989), 8.

11. Pippa Norris and Joni Lovenduski, *Political Recruitment: Gender, Race and Class in the British Parliament* (Cambridge, England: Cambridge University Press, 1994).

12. Rae Lesser Blumberg, "Climbing the Pyramids of Power: Alternative Routes to Women's Empowerment and Activism," in *Promises of Empowerment*, eds. Peter Smith, Jennifer Troutner, and Christine Hunefeldt (Lanham, MD: Rowman and Littlefield, 2004), 60.

13. Unless otherwise cited, all of this chapter's statistics on the number of women in the world's parliaments come from two web sites, which are frequently updated: the Inter-Parliamentary Union, Women in National Parliaments, www. ipu.org; and IDEA (the International Institute for Democracy and Electoral Assistance), Quota Project: Global Database of Quotas for Women, http://www.quotaproject.org.

14. All data on reserved seats comes from IDEA, Quota Project: Global Database of Quotas for Women, http://www.quotaproject.org/.

15. Mona Lena Krook, *Quotas for Women in Politics* (New York, NY: Oxford University Press, 2009), 161–206.

16. Mala Htun, "Women and Democracy," in *Constructing Democratic Governance in Latin America*, eds. Jorge Domínguez and Michael Shifter (Baltimore: The Johns Hopkins University Press, 2003), 122.

17. Mala Htun and Jennifer Piscopo, "Presence Without Empowerment? Women in Politics in Latin America and the Caribbean," Paper prepared for the Conflict Prevention and Peace Forum of the (GIGR), originally presented in 2010, updated in 2015.

18. American Association of University Women (AAUW), "Gender Equality and the Role of Women in Cuban Society," (whitepaper online: February 2011).

19. "Why is China Relaxing Its One-Child Policy?" *The Economist*, December 10, 2013; Cristina Larson, "In China More Girls are on the Way," *Bloomberg Business*, July 31, 2014; Gwynn Guilford, "China's Ratio of Boys to Girls is Still Dangerously High," *Quartz*, March 5, 2013.

20. Htun, "Women and Democracy," 125.

8

The Politics of the Rural and Urban Poor

Urban slum and modern high-rise buildings in Mumbai, India. More than half the population of the developing world now lives in urban areas. While rapid urbanization like this is associated with economic growth, it also poses many economic, social, and political challenges. *Source*: Chirag Wakaskar/Alamy Stock Photo.

IN MANY DEVELOPING COUNTRIES, the rural and urban poor are the two largest segments of the population. At the same time, however, they are usually the least influential politically because they lack the power resources—wealth, education, professional skills, organizational ability—available to the middle and upper classes and to skilled workers. To be sure, in times of revolutionary upheaval or even moderate political and economic reform, they may wield considerable influence, but even then they generally need outside leadership and organization. This chapter will begin with a discussion of the rural poor and then examine their urban counterparts, many of whom began life in the countryside. It will focus on the social and economic challenges each group faces, as well as the way their needs and grievances might find political expression.

THE RURAL POOR: THE PEASANTRY IN THE DEVELOPING WORLD

For millennia, most people lived in the countryside. As recently as 1960, two-thirds of the world's population was rural, with a much higher percentage in developing nations. It is in the countryside where some of the worst aspects of political and economic underdevelopment prevail. In nations as distinct as China and Mexico, rural annual incomes are only 20–30 percent as high as average urban earnings. Wide urban-rural gaps also persist in literacy, health care, and life expectancy. Finally, rural villagers are less likely than their urban counterparts to have clean drinking water, electricity, or schools.

While the proportion of the population of the developing world living in the countryside is usually substantially greater than in highly industrialized nations, this percentage varies greatly from country to country: from over 80 percent in Nepal, Sri Lanka, and Uganda to about 10 percent in Argentina and Chile. Almost everywhere, the rural rate of poverty far exceeds the urban rate. Peasants generally suffer from inadequate housing, widespread illiteracy, malnutrition, and high rates of infant mortality.

In most of the developing world, political and economic power are concentrated in the cities. Consequently, government policies—on issues ranging from social expenditures to agricultural pricing—have a predictable urban bias. As noted in chapter 1, modernization theory argued that as countries develop, modern values and institutions would spread from the cities to the countryside, and the gap between the two will narrow. Conversely, dependency theorists maintain that the links between urban and rural areas replicate the exploitative international relationship between the industrialized core (the industrialized world) and the periphery (the less developed countries). What is certain is that resolving the political and economic tensions between urban and rural areas, reducing the vast inequalities within the countryside, and dealing with urban-to-rural migration remain among the most difficult and important challenges facing developing countries today.

RURAL CLASS STRUCTURES

Within the countryside, there are generally substantial disparities in land-ownership. Often, agricultural property is concentrated in a relatively small number of hands. These inequalities have contributed to rural poverty and produced rigid class systems in countries such as Colombia, the Philippines, and parts of India. Landownership is most concentrated in Latin America, while East Asia (excepting the Philippines) has the most equitable distribution of farmland among the less developed regions. Land concentration in Africa varies considerably between countries. In recent decades, the spread of plantations (mostly growing produce for export) has increased agricultural concentration in a number of nations.

At the apex of the **rural class system** stand the large and powerful landowners, sometimes known as "the oligarchy." Major Filipino sugar growers and Argentine cattle barons, for example, have historically exercised considerable political power in national politics. In El Salvador, the most influential coffee producers dominated the country's political system for much of the twentieth century. Land concentration in Latin America dates back to the Spanish colonial era with its tradition of large estates (latifundia). In the Philippines, Sri Lanka, Pakistan, and Bangladesh, along with parts of India, Indonesia, and Thailand, reactionary landed elites have also contributed to rural exploitation and poverty.

Since the middle of the twentieth century, the economic and political powers of rural landlords have declined considerably in numerous less developed countries. In the most dramatic cases, radical revolutions in countries such as China and Vietnam stripped landlords of their property. Revolutionary governments sometimes killed many big landowners and sent others to prison camps for "political reeducation." Elsewhere, non-revolutionary and relatively peaceful agrarian reform undermined the rural elites of countries such as Peru and South Korea.* In industrializing nations such as Brazil and Thailand, the economic importance of agribusiness at the national level has diminished relative to the industrial and commercial sectors. Therefore, numerous wealthy, landowning families have diversified into those economic sectors or have left agriculture entirely.

---

* The terms **"agrarian reform"** and **"land reform"** are often used interchangeably. However, as discussed next, land reform refers only to the redistribution of land to needy peasants or farm laborers. Agrarian reform is a broader process encompassing financial and technical aid, which must support land redistribution if it is to be effective.

At the local and regional levels, however, landlords in much of Latin America, Asia, and Africa continue to exercise considerable power. For example, upper-caste farmers in the Indian state of Bihar and large cattle ranchers in the Brazilian interior retain virtually unchallenged local supremacy. At times, they have intimidated, or even murdered, peasant organizers and union leaders without fear of the legal consequences. Such was the fate of Chico Mendes, the celebrated Brazilian union leader who had organized Amazonian rubber-tree tappers against the powerful ranchers who were clearing the forest and destroying the local habitat. Despite Mendes's impressive international stature and links to influential American environmental groups, local landlords hired gunmen to assassinate him in 1988. Hundreds of lesser-known Brazilians have been killed on orders from powerful landlords—crimes that often go unpunished.

On the rung beneath the landed elite, we find midsized landlords and more affluent peasants. The latter group consists of peasants who, unlike small landlords, still work on the land themselves. However, unlike poorer peasants, they can afford to hire additional peasant labor to work with them. While neither midsized landlords nor richer peasants belong to the national power elite, they usually exercise considerable political influence locally in countries such as India and Pakistan. Indeed, in much of Asia, where the biggest agricultural holdings are not nearly as large as those in Latin America, these two groups are a potent political force. Extended family networks typically magnify their influence.

Finally, at the bottom of the socioeconomic ladder, the rural poor—including peasants who own small plots of land, tenant farmers, and farmworkers—are generally the less developed countries' most impoverished and powerless occupational group. **Peasants** are defined as family farmers who work small plots and maintain a traditional lifestyle that is distinct from city dwellers. Because they are typically poor and poorly educated, peasants often lack the means to transport their crops to market themselves, ready access to credit, and the knowledge or resources to deal with the legal or bureaucratic proceedings that they periodically have to deal with. As a result, they depend on the services of merchants, moneylenders, lawyers, and government bureaucrats, many of whom exploit them. Their links to the world—including the government, the military, the church, and the market economy—are largely dependent upon individuals and institutions outside the peasants' community.[1] Thus, as Eric Wolf has noted, "Peasant denotes an asymmetrical structural relationship between the producers of surplus [peasants] and controllers [including landlords, merchants, and tax collectors]."[2]

We may further subdivide poor peasants into two subgroups: those who own small amounts of land for family cultivation (smallholders) and those who are **landless**. The ranks of the landless, in turn, include tenant farmers (who enter into various types of rental arrangements with landlords) and wage laborers. However, these categories are not mutually exclusive. Smallholders, for example, may also supplement their incomes by working as farm laborers or renting additional land as tenants. Usually, it is the landless who constitute the poorest of the rural poor. While they represent a mere 10 percent of all agricultural families in countries such as Kenya and Sierra Leone, their numbers rise to 50–70 percent in India, Pakistan, the Philippines, and Brazil. Not surprisingly, in Latin America and parts of Africa and Asia, where concentrated landownership and associated peasant landlessness have been particularly notable, the issue of land reform has often been at the center of rural politics.

PEASANT POLITICS

Despite their vast numbers, peasants often play a muted role in the politics of developing countries. Because most less developed countries did not have competitive national elections until recently and because, even where there have been elections, powerful groups have often controlled the peasant vote, the rural poor have not readily converted their numbers into corresponding political influence. The peasantry's political leverage is also limited by poverty, lack of education, dependence on outsiders, and physical isolation from the centers of national power and from peasants elsewhere in the country. Cultural values stressing caution and conservatism may further constrain peasant political behavior. In his classic study of peasants, Robert Redfield argued: "In every part of the world, generally speaking, peasants have been a conservative factor in social change, a brake on revolution."[3]

Indeed, over the years, anthropological writings frequently have depicted peasant political culture as fatalistic and isolated. Hence, it was claimed, most of them doubt that collective political action can better their own fate. Discussing the reaction of Indian villagers to local government authorities, Phyllis Arora describes a sense of powerlessness resulting in political apathy. "Helplessness is . . . evoked by the presence of the district officer. The peasant tends to feel that all he [or she] can do before such authority . . . is petition for redress of grievances. . . . In the ultimate analysis, however . . . the peasant feels at the mercy of the whims of the [political] authorities."[4]

No doubt, peasants typically are wary of radical change and respectful of community traditions. To some extent, this conservatism reflects a suspicion of outside values—distrust frequently grounded in religious beliefs and other long-standing traditions. Indeed, the maintenance of a distinct peasant culture depends, to some extent, on the rejection of external influences. But peasant suspicion of social change is frequently understandable and rational. Struggling on the margins of economic survival, the rural poor have found that the commercialization and mechanization of agriculture, as well as other aspects of rural modernization, have often impacted their lives negatively. In rural Pakistan, for example, the introduction of tractors improved the output and income of the farmers who could afford them. As a consequence, however, many of poorer tenant farmers who could no longer compete were forced off their plots, thereby concentrating land into fewer hands. Political changes may also be threatening. For example, when outside activists have organized the rural poor to challenge local injustices, these peasants have often been ruthlessly repressed. Small wonder, then, that they are frequently suspicious of change, including any challenge to the power structure.

This does not mean, however, that they are incapable of standing up to landlords and government authorities who wrong them. Examples of peasant resistance are commonplace, ranging from the most restrained to the most radical. James C. Scott has demonstrated that peasants in Southeast Asia who appear to accept the established order actually often engage in unobtrusive **everyday forms of resistance**, such as theft and vandalism against their landlords, "foot dragging, and false deference."[5] Elsewhere, peasants have presented their political demands more openly and aggressively. The allegedly conservative peasantry was a critical actor in most twentieth-century revolutions, including communist upheavals in China, Vietnam, and Cuba, as well as in less radical insurgencies in Bolivia and Mexico.[6] More recently, they have been the backbone of guerrilla movements in Colombia, El Salvador, Peru, Cambodia, Nepal, the Philippines, and parts of India. And, in scores of other less developed countries, ranging from India to Ecuador, well-organized peasant groups have also become influential actors in democratic political systems.

We will examine the role of the peasantry in revolutionary movements in greater detail in chapter 9. For now, however, suffice it to say that peasants are neither inherently conservative nor intrinsically radical. Rather, they vary considerably in their ideological propensities and their capacity for collective political action. To understand why peasants so often accept the political status quo, while others choose to resist or even rebel, we must first examine the relationship between the powerful and the weak in the countryside. Although traditional landlords frequently exploit their tenants or neighboring smallholders, mutually understood boundaries usually limit the extent of that exploitation. Links between landlords and peasants are usually grounded in long-standing patron-client relationships involving reciprocal obligations. Despite the landlords' superior power, these relationships are not always exploitative. For example, landowners frequently provide their tenants with land and financial credit in return for labor on their estate. And, they may fund religious festivals or serve as godparents of their tenants' children.

As long as landlords fulfill their obligations, peasants often accept the traditional order despite its many injustices. However, should rural modernization and the commercialization of agriculture induce rural patrons to cease discharging their traditional responsibilities, the peasantry may conclude that the previously existing **moral economy**—the social bargain and economic context that has sustained them—has failed.[7] In some cases, rural modernization may also give landlords (who can afford farm machinery and irrigation pumps) a competitive advantage over peasants (who cannot) and eventually force the smallholders off the land. Eric Wolf has noted that the transition from feudal or semifeudal rural relations to capitalist economic arrangements often strips peasants of the certainty and protection afforded to them by the old order (even an unjust old order). Frequently, the result is rural upheaval. Thus, he argued, revolutions in China, Vietnam, Cuba, Mexico, and other developing nations originated with the threats to the peasants' traditional way of life posed by the rise of rural capitalism.[8]

This in no way suggests that rural economic change and the transition to capitalism always radicalize the peasantry or drive them to revolutionary activity. But when peasants feel that their way of life is threatened, they will resist change or at least try to channel it into forms more beneficial to their interests. How effectively they engage in collective political action and how radical or moderate their demands are depend on a number of factors: the extent to which they perceive themselves to be exploited; how desperate their economic condition is; the degree of internal cohesion and cooperation within their communities; their ability to form political linkages with peasants in neighboring villages or in other parts of the country; the extent to which they forge political ties with nonpeasant groups and leaders; the type of outside groups with whom they ally (be it the Catholic Church in the Philippines or Maoist revolutionaries in Nepal); the responsiveness of the political system to their demands; and the types of political options that the political order affords them.

The last two factors suggest that the probability of radical peasant insurrection depends as much on the quality of the political system as it does on the nature of the peasantry. Given a meaningful opportunity to secure change by working within the existing political system, few peasants will choose to join revolutionary movements, since that would endanger their lives and those of their families. In short, revolution is an act of desperation normally entered into only when other options are unavailable. It is perhaps for this reason that no democratic political system (offering alternatives to radical action) has ever fallen to revolutionary insurgency.

In recent decades, the spread of the mass media throughout the countryside, increased rural educational levels, and the broadening of voting rights in numerous less developed countries (such as extending the vote to illiterates) have greatly increased the political influence of peasant voters in electoral democracies. In countries such as India, Bolivia, and Thailand, politicians must now consider the interests of the rural poor more seriously. Still, voting power is of little use in many nondemocratic nations in Africa, the Middle East, and Asia. And even in competitive party systems, the peasantry's political power is usually not proportional to their numbers.

On the whole, the range of peasant political activity runs the gamut from the far left to the far right, from peaceful to violent. As Samuel Huntington noted, "The peasantry . . . may be the bulwark of the status quo or the shock troops of revolution. Which role the peasant plays is determined by the extent to which the existing system meets his immediate economic and material needs as he sees them."[9] In India, for example, many peasants support the BJP—a conservative, Hindu fundamentalist party (see chapter 5). In Latin America, on the other hand, peasants often vote for moderately left-of-center candidates. And, in countries such as China, Vietnam, Nicaragua, and Colombia, still other peasants have supported revolutionary insurrections. Whatever their political inclinations, the peasants' economic and political concerns usually revolve around four broad issues: the prices they receive for their crops, the prices of goods they buy, taxes, and the availability of land. The issue of land has been the most volatile and the most critical to the political stability of many developing countries, and it is to this issue that we now turn our attention.

THE POLITICS OF AGRARIAN REFORM

In those areas of the less developed countries where landownership is highly concentrated, agrarian reform has long been an issue in the national political debate. **Agrarian reform** is composed of two components. First, the most important element is **land reform**, which involves the redistribution of agricultural land—generally from large landowners or from public property—to land-hungry peasants, either as family plots or as collective farms. Second, in order for land recipients to farm their plots successfully, the government usually must provide them with some mix of technical assistance, credit, improved access to markets, and social services (such as health care). To be sure, the pressure for agrarian reform has waxed and waned and other models of rural development have become more popular in recent years. Still, the issue lingers in numerous less developed countries.

Patterns of Land Concentration
In much of the developing world, especially Asia, landless peasants constitute a large portion of the rural population. For example, about half of Bangladesh's rural population and 40 percent of India's are landless. In addition, millions of peasant smallholders own plots too small to support their families adequately.

Concentrated land ownership is most pronounced in Latin America, where large estates control a substantial proportion of the region's farmland. In Brazil, for example, slightly over 3 percent of the nation's farms, each exceeding 500 hectares (about 1,250 acres),* control 56 percent of the nation's farmland.[10] Since 1995, several government administrations have introduced modest agrarian reforms that have distributed land to thousands of landless or land-hungry peasant families. To some extent, these programs have been a response to the emergence of the MST (the Landless Workers' Movement). Founded in the mid-1980s, the MST represents landless workers throughout the country and, with a membership of some 1.5 million people (the largest social movement in Latin America), it has placed substantial pressure on the government. Since the mid-1980s, through various government land reforms, the MST has won titles to 7.5 million hectares of land, which 370,000 families currently farm. In addition, 150,000 other families live on land whose ownership is contested. But, at the same time, about 90,000 peasant farms are being purchased or grabbed by agribusiness annually, mostly aimed at exports. In fact, government studies suggest that land concentration has actually increased in the last two decades.

With different historical traditions and far higher population density, Asia does not have agricultural units as large as Brazil's or Argentina's. In nations such as Indonesia, India, and Pakistan, farm holdings have rarely exceeded fifty hectares. In Bangladesh, one of the world's most densely populated countries, the largest farms are relatively small, rarely exceeding five to ten hectares. Yet, less than 3 percent of these units controlled more than 25 percent of the country's agricultural land. In the Philippines, similar data showed 3.4 percent of the country's farms accounting for 26 percent of the land.

Patterns of land ownership vary widely in Africa, depending in part on how extensively European colonial rule concentrated land in the hands of white settlers. But, a study of Ethiopia, Kenya, Mozambique, and Rwanda noted that approximately one-quarter of their total farm population was either landless or virtually landless (making them dependent on the landlords for either wage labor or tenancy).[11]

The Case for Agrarian Reform

Facing powerful landed elites and their political allies, who oppose land redistribution, proponents of reform have defended their position on several grounds, including social justice and equity, greater political stability, improved agricultural productivity, economic growth, and preservation of the environment.

---

* A hectare, rather than an acre, is the standard (metric) measurement of farmland area in most parts of the world. One hectare is equivalent to 10,000m2 or 2.47 acres.

Some governments, such as in El Salvador and the Philippines, have redistributed farm land to the rural poor in order to reduce the likelihood of peasant unrest. Huntington starkly linked land reform to political stability:

> Where the conditions of land tenure are equitable and provide a viable living for the peasant, revolution is unlikely. Where they are inequitable and where the peasant lives in poverty and suffering, revolution is likely, if not inevitable, unless the government takes prompt measures to remedy those conditions.[12]

Opponents of agrarian reform maintain that land redistribution lowers agricultural output, thereby diminishing food supplies for the cities and curtailing export earnings. Citing "economies of scale," they argue that large agricultural units are generally more productive than smallholdings because they are more easily mechanized and use rural infrastructure (such as irrigation and roads) more effectively.

Advocates of agrarian reform counter that, in fact, smallholders are more efficient producers of domestic food than larger landlords. Many empirical studies have found that when small and large farm units are compared within Latin American, Asian, and African countries, labor-intensive smallholders (peasants who devote large amounts of physical labor on small land units) usually have higher yields per acre than large-scale, capital-intensive (mechanized) producers.* Peasant landholders tend to farm their plots very intensively because their families' living standards depend on raising productivity. This does not mean that small peasant-run units are always more efficient. Smaller farm units tend to outperform larger farms in growing vegetables and legumes (important components of the local diet), which are best cultivated by hand. But ranching and cultivation of crops suitable for mechanical harvesting—such as sugar, wheat, and rice (grown largely for export)—are usually more efficiently farmed on large plantations.

In underdeveloped rural societies with a surplus of labor (i.e., many underemployed people who are willing to work for low wages), it is often more cost-effective to use family or hired labor intensively rather than invest in machinery. Out of economic necessity, peasant cultivators work hard, exploiting their own family labor. On the other hand, most large, mechanized estates are farmed by hired laborers, who do not gain directly from raising productivity.

Finally, another value for agrarian reform relates to environmental protection. For example, Brazilian ranchers and farmers deliberately burn

---

* If we measure productivity in terms of output per (farm) worker, then large farms are usually more efficient. Advocates of land reform insist, however, that in most less developed countries, where farm land is scarce and labor is abundant and cheap, productivity per acre (or hectare) is the most relevant measure of productivity.

tracts of the Amazonian rainforest to clear land for agriculture, annually destroying a forest area equal to the size of New Jersey. The fires are so vast that they contribute to the greenhouse effect on world climate. Although large landowners create a substantial portion of this burn-off, peasant settlers also contribute. Driven out of the nation's poorest regions by desperation, land-hungry peasants colonize the jungle in search of a better life. Once there, however, they discover that cleared jungle soil quickly loses its nutrients. So, they must soon move on, clearing yet more forest land. Land reform in Brazil's unforested regions would reduce landlessness and give tenant farmers a greater stake in the land they farm, thus reducing migration to the Amazonian basin.

The Decline of Agrarian Reform

Despite these benefits, the number of extensive agrarian programs has remained limited. Usually, the extent of land redistribution is not determined by factors such as agricultural productivity. Rather it is most influenced by the balance of political power between peasants and landlords, by the government's perception of whether land redistribution would help or hurt it. Perhaps the most successful agrarian reform programs were initiated in East Asia in the years following the Second World War. Fearing the spread of Chinese-style peasant revolutions, the US occupation forces introduced far-reaching land redistribution in Japan, and Washington strongly endorsed reform in South Korea and Taiwan, both facing external communist threats from North Korea or China.

In all three of these countries, landlords were in an unusually weak position: Japanese landlords were powerless to oppose the US military occupation; Korean landlords were discredited at home because most had supported the Japanese invasion in the Second World War; and in Taiwan, the former landed elite had just fled from their defeat on the Chinese mainland. All three nations were heavily dependent on the United States, which was pressuring them to implement reform. The resulting agrarian reforms were very extensive and very successful: agricultural production increased, peasant living standards rose, peasant consumption helped fuel industrial growth, and the rural poor became pillars of support for the government.

Many experts as well as institutions such as the (United Nations) Food and Agriculture Organization have continued to support expanded agrarian reform in the developing world.

> While globalization, industrialization, and (often subsidized) commercial agriculture are creating wealth for some, they are also dramatically increasing the socio-economic disparities within and between countries, further exacerbating land concentration. . . . Investment has tended to favor the development of the industrial, urban and service and often military sectors, at the expense of agriculture and rural development.[13]

Yet, there have been few extensive land redistribution programs in recent decades. Often, landed elites have had enough political and economic power to water down reform efforts. At the same time, peasants are usually poorly organized and unable to exert much pressure on their governments. Outside donors have generally lacked the leverage or desire to push for major agrarian reform, as they did in East Asia in the postwar years.

Revolutions and Rural Reform

The most comprehensive agrarian reform programs have been introduced by revolutionary movements and governments. These include Bolivia, China, Cuba, Mexico, Nicaragua, and Vietnam. In all of these, peasants were an important, sometimes dominant, part of the revolutionary struggle. At the same time, the revolutions destroyed the landlord's political and economic powers, thereby eliminating a roadblock that so often has limited or derailed reform efforts. However, the outcome of revolutionary change often was not what most peasants had fought and died for. They had hoped or expected the large estates to be divided into peasant family farms. Instead, the new revolutionary governments pressured or forced the peasantry to join collective farms of some sort—principally cooperatives or state farms. In China, Ethiopia, Russia, and Vietnam, tens of thousands of peasants died resisting collectivization. In fact, in most cases, collective farms were not efficient. Indeed, China's forced collectivization during the Great Leap Forward (1958–61) caused such a sharp drop in food production and distribution that perhaps 25 million people died of starvation.

Eventually, several communist regimes (including China, Vietnam, and, more recently, Cuba) have recognized these failures and have essentially privatized many or all farm units—breaking up communes, collectives, state farms, and other government-imposed production units and returning the land to peasant-controlled family plots. In both China and Vietnam, the de-collectivization of agriculture resulted in greater food production and significant improvements in the standard of living.

THE FUTURE OF THE RURAL POOR

For decades, development policies have emphasized industrial growth and urban modernization, often to the detriment of the rural sector. Frequently, the result has been stagnant agricultural production, growing food imports, rural poverty, and heavy rural-urban migration. Most notably in Africa and Latin America, government bias in favor of urban areas, along with the forces of capitalist modernization, have driven many peasants into the urban slums in a process known as proletarianization. In some instances, rural poverty has led to peasant insurrections. Pessimistic scholars have

Children gather around a communal village pump in Madagascar. Access to a safe and reliable water supply is essential to good public health. Poor rural populations are most likely to rely on water sources that are either distant from home or vulnerable to contamination. *Source*: Travelib Madagascar/Alamy Stock Photo.

predicted the inevitable spread of large, mechanized farms to the detriment of peasant family farming.

More recently, however, research in countries such as Bolivia, Ecuador, and Colombia has revealed that, in at least some regions, innovative peasants have adapted skillfully to the forces of rural capitalism and modernization, taking advantage of new commercial opportunities to compete successfully in the marketplace. In Africa and Asia, peasant smallholders remain an even more important component of rural society. Rather than abandoning the peasantry as a relic of history, governments and international agencies need to promote balanced economic and political development that gives proper weight to the rural poor. Since the 1990s, recurring hunger and malnutrition in the less developed countries have led some important foreign-aid donors to rethink their attitudes toward peasant farming. Despite the large landholders' financial advantages and widespread government neglect of peasant farming, smallholders still produce about 60 percent of the food consumed in the developing world.

The global trend (until recently) for neoliberal reforms within countries and freer trade between them has important, but complex, implications for peasant farmers. In some cases, market liberalization helps small producers, notably in those countries where the state has forced them to sell their produce at lower prices (either to alleviate the urban cost of living, or to allow state-controlled marketing boards to increase their profits by obtaining cheaper produce to sell abroad). In other cases, however, austerity cuts may mean less support for rural development. Freer trade may harm small producers if they have been previously protected from competition by tariffs on foreign food imports. Conversely, it may aid them if they were previously locked out of foreign markets by those countries' own agricultural protectionist policies.

RAPID URBANIZATION AND THE POLITICS OF THE URBAN POOR

Every day, in the villages of Bangladesh, China, Kenya, Egypt, and Brazil, thousands of young men and women pack up their meager belongings and board buses, trucks, or trains for the long trip to, respectively, Dhaka, Shanghai, Nairobi, Cairo, or Rio. Often they travel alone, sometimes with family or friends. They are a part of the largest and most dramatic tidal wave of human migration in world history. Despairing of any hope for a better life in the countryside and seeking new opportunities for themselves and their children, millions of villagers leave the world they have known for the uncertainties of the city. In Africa, refugees fleeing civil wars and famine have augmented the legions of migrants. At the same time, as migration adds to the size of the less developed countries' cities, urban populations are also growing as a result of "natural increase"—the annual total of births minus deaths—among those already living there.

THE DEVELOPING WORLD'S URBAN EXPLOSION

As the world approached a new century (1997), the United Nations Population Fund (UNFPA) predicted that "the growth of cities will be the single largest influence on development in the 21st century." In 2008, the number of people living in cities throughout the world exceeded the rural population for the first time in human history. In developing countries, the proportion of city dwellers exceeded 50 percent by 2017.

Most migrants maintain close links with their rural roots long after they have left the countryside. Some of them intend to accumulate savings and eventually return to their villages. Indeed, in various parts of West Africa and Southeast Asia, more than half of the urban migrants are temporary, including those who repeatedly circulate between village and city. In China, prior to the 1980s, government restrictions made it difficult to migrate. Even now, most urban migrants live in a bureaucratic limbo without assurance of permanence. Known as China's "floating population,"

Table 8.1 Urbanization (in percentages)

	2000	2025 (projected)	2050 (projected)
Developed Countries	74.2	80.1	86.6
Developing Countries	40.1	54.3	65.6

Source: United Nations Population Division, World Urbanization Prospects 2018.

they currently number more than 150 million and this figure is expected to double by 2025.* Some stay permanently, but most do not because of their marginal legal status. Although not officially counted as part of the urban population (because their government supposedly restricts their residence to their home villages), they actually account for about one-fifth of China's urban residents. In Shanghai, China's largest city and its economic hub, 6 million migrants constitute one-third of the population. In contrast, Latin America's cityward migrants tend to settle permanently. Whatever be their initial aspirations, migrants continue to crowd the urban slums and shantytowns that they have come to call home.

Swelled by the influx of migrants and by natural increases, urban populations have ballooned and will continue to grow rapidly in the coming years. Currently, eight to nine of the world's ten largest metropolitan areas are in the less developed countries.† Between 2000 and 2050, the urban population of the world's developed nations is expected to grow by about 230 million, an increase of approximately 26 percent. By contrast, cities in the developing world will expand by 163 percent (from under 2 billion people to almost 5.2 billion). During the first half of this century, urban growth will slow down in both regions, but cities in developing nations will continue to grow about five to six times faster than in industrialized nations. As of 2000, less than one-half of the less developed countries' population (40 percent) lived in cities, but by midcentury, this figure will increase to almost two-thirds (table 8.1).

Such **urbanization** has placed tremendous strains on public services, housing, public health, and personal safety in these large cities. In Latin America, the rate of growth was most rapid in the middle of the twentieth century, when some primary cities such as Bogotá and Lima nearly doubled their populations in a single decade (1950–60). While the rate

---

* In order to reduce further mass, "illegal" migration to China's established cities, the government has begun to create new cities (with projected populations of several million each) in rural areas. These are designed to create jobs for villagers in the surrounding areas.
† Different sources have widely varying populations for the world's largest cities and for their rank. In large part this depends on whether they are measuring just the official population of the city in question or whether they are reporting the much larger population of the "metropolitan areas" ("urban agglomerations") that includes suburbs and more. The urban populations and rankings discussed in this chapter mostly refer to the metropolitan areas.

Table 8.2 Population in Urban Areas (in percentages)

Region	1975	2015	2050 (projection)
United States	73.7	81.7	89.2
Sub-Saharan Africa	20.4	38.8	58.1
North Africa	39.4	51.4	64.1
East Asia	25.5	59.8	81.4
South Asia	21.3	34.5	53.8
Latin America and the Caribbean	61.0	79.9	87.8

Source: United Nations Population Division, *World Urbanization Prospects 2018.*

of growth in the region's largest cities has slowed, many have continued enormous growth in absolute terms. African cities, starting from a smaller base, expanded at an even faster pace. Between 1960 and 1983, Kinshasa (Congo) grew by nearly 600 percent and Abidjan (Côte d'Ivoire) by more than 800 percent. Today, a number of major cities in less developed countries are still doubling their populations in two decades or less.

As table 8.2 indicates, Latin America and the Caribbean is by far the most urbanized region in the developing world, having reached over 60 percent of the national population in 1975 and projected to be almost ninety percent by 2050. In 1975, urban population (25.5 percent) in sub-Saharan Africa (20.4 percent) and East Asia constituted a far lower portion of the national total. On the other hand, cities in those two regions are now growing far more rapidly than in the Americas and by 2025, they will have closed the gap with Latin America and the Caribbean considerably (especially East Asia).

Table 8.3 demonstrates the incredible growth that many of the developing world's largest cities will have experienced in one-half century (1975–2025). In 1975, Latin America, the developing world's most urbanized region, had two of the world's largest megacities—Mexico

Table 8.3 Populations of Selected Urban Areas, 1975–2025 (in millions)

Metropolitan Area	1975	2015	2025 (projection)
New York City–Newark (United States)	15.8	18.6	19.2
Mexico City (Mexico)	10.7	21.1	22.8
São Paulo (Brazil)	9.6	20.9	23.0
Cairo (Egypt)	6.4	18.8	23.1
Kinshasa (Congo)	1.5	11.6	17.8
Delhi (India)	4.4	25.9	34.7
Karachi (Pakistan)	4.0	14.3	18.1
Dhaka (Bangladesh)	2.2	17.6	24.7

Source: United Nations Population Division, *World Urbanization Prospects 2018.*

Table 8.4   Population Living in Urban Areas (in percentages)

Country	1975	2015	2050 (projected)
Mozambique	9.6	34.4	55.3
Egypt	43.3	42.8	55.6
China	17.4	55.5	80.0
India	21.3	32.8	52.8
Indonesia	4.5	53.3	72.8
Argentina	81.0	91.5	95.2
Brazil	60.8	85.8	92.4

Source: United Nations Population Division, *World Urbanization Prospects 2018.*

City (10.7 million) and São Paulo, Brazil (9.6 million). They have continued to grow and by 2025 will have more than doubled their populations in fifty years. On the other hand, two of the largest cities in South Asia—Delhi and Dhaka—trailed well behind their Latin American counterparts at the start of this era. But, by 2025, their populations will increase up to tenfold, putting both South Asian cities ahead of São Paulo and Mexico City.

Of course, within each region, the proportion of people residing in cities also varies considerably. As table 8.4 indicates, Indonesia (4.5 percent urban), Mozambique (9.6 percent), and China (17.4 percent) were far less urbanized in 1975 than Argentina (81 percent) or Brazil (60.8 percent). But, by 2050, fully 80 percent of Chinese citizens will live in cities, as will almost three-quarters of those in Indonesia and over half the population of Mozambique.

THE SOCIAL AND POLITICAL CONSEQUENCE
OF URBAN GROWTH

Next, we turn to two important aspects of urban politics. First, we look at the challenges that exploding urban populations present to political leaders and government planners. Specifically, we ask how poor countries can provide city dwellers with needed jobs, housing, sanitation, and other basic services, while also protecting them from crime. What is the government's role in those areas, and how do state policies interact with private-sector activities and self-help efforts? Second, we examine the political attitudes and behavior of the lower classes, who account for the majority of the urban population. To what extent do the inhabitants of urban shantytowns and slums have political orientations that are distinct from those of the rural poor and those of the urban middle and upper classes? Is rapid urbanization likely to contribute to political development, or does it carry the seeds of political instability?

The Search for Employment

It is worth remembering that just like today's less developed countries, Western nations experienced an urban explosion from the 1870s to the start of the First World War (1914). But rapid urbanization in Europe and North America occurred during an era of unprecedented industrialization and economic growth. As capitalism came of age, it needed the giant wave of migrant and immigrant laborers. By contrast, most contemporary developing countries are unable to provide sufficient employment to their rapidly expanding urban workforce.

To be sure, many people do find factory jobs, and some low-income workers achieve impressive upward mobility, but they are the exception. Most of the urban poor must engage in an ongoing struggle for economic survival. The severe recessions that gripped Africa and Latin America in the 1980s, parts of Asia in the late 1990s, and much of the world from 2008 to at least 2010, all exacerbated urban poverty, as industrial employment plummeted in scores of countries. Furthermore, at times, various countries in Latin America and Africa have suffered from high rates of inflation, making it difficult for many people, even those who were regularly employed, to support their families adequately.

Many of the urban poor who are unable to find work in the so-called formal segment of the urban economy (the government and modern, private-sector enterprises) turn to the **informal sector** for jobs. As noted in chapter 7, this sector is defined as the part of the economy that is "unregulated by the institutions of society [most notably the state], in a legal and social environment in which similar activities are regulated" and taxed.[14] Most of the workers in that sector are self-employed (an estimated 70 percent) in occupations ranging from garbage recyclers to shoeshine boys, street vendors, mechanics, electricians, plumbers, and drivers of unlicensed taxis. Others work in "underground" factories or other businesses that operate outside the law.

Of course, even cities such as New York, Los Angeles, and Milan in the industrialized world have informal sectors, including unlicensed street vendors, underground sweatshops, and other endeavors that are "off the books." In the less developed countries, however, this sector provides a substantial proportion of urban jobs. According to the World Bank, the informal sector may generate as much as 70 percent of urban employment and 30 percent of the less developed countries' GDP.

In the garbage dumps of Cairo and Mexico City, hordes of entrepreneurs sift through the refuse looking to recycle marketable materials. On the commercial boulevards of Manila (Philippines) and Nairobi (Kenya), an army of street vendors sells food, household appliances, and bootleg videos. In Lagos and Lahore (Pakistan), shoemakers and carpenters, working out of their homes, sell their wares to appreciative clients. All belong to the informal sector. While outside observers once assumed that people working in this sector were particularly impoverished, we now know that their earning power varies greatly and that in some countries they have average higher incomes than the typical factory worker does.

Over the years, government planners and social scientists have debated the informal sector's merits and faults. Critics point out that its workers are not protected by minimum-wage laws and may not have access to government health and welfare programs. Proponents respond that the sector not only employs vast numbers of people who would otherwise have no work, but also contributes a substantial proportion of the developing countries' consumer goods and services. Consequently, these analysts argue, governments should cease trying to regulate and license the informal sector and instead should allow it to flourish and expand.

Another source of employment is the public sector. The governments of less developed nations employ significant numbers of white-collar workers and bureaucrats. These jobs are a boon to the urban middle class since there is not enough work in the private sector. In addition, many governments own various economic enterprises (parastatals)—including petroleum fields and refineries, railroads, electric power plants, and steel mills—which provide relatively well-paid, blue-collar jobs in economies plagued by high unemployment.

Unfortunately, there are two major problems with some public-sector employment (earlier noted in chapter 4). First, in their efforts to gain popular support, the government or the ruling party has often padded bureaucratic and parastatal payrolls with unneeded employees. While this creates badly needed jobs, it adds to government budget deficits and makes these institutions highly inefficient. Second, public-sector employment is frequently treated as a political plum, with jobs going to activists in the ruling party and government supporters, rather than to the most qualified applicants. In many countries, government bureaucracies and parastatals hire unneeded white-collar workers as a form of political patronage. In fact, many employees never show up except to collect their paychecks. At one time, some 40 percent of Sierra Leone's government bureaucrats and state workers were "ghosts"—employees who were paid but never worked.

In recent decades, faced with spiraling government spending and large external debts, most less developed countries have been forced to reduce the size of their state sectors substantially. Although these cuts were usually necessary in order to cut huge government budget deficits and reduce inflation, they have imposed a heavy burden on white- and blue-collar workers who have been laid off and on young workers who faced more limited opportunities for future employment.

Only in communist countries such as China and Cuba has the state been a major employer of blue-collar workers. Those governments have commonly considered employment to be a fundamental workers' right and an important source of legitimacy for the system. Until recently, some communist governments created as many jobs as necessary to achieve full, or nearly full, employment, no matter how economically inefficient many of these jobs might be. Under China's "iron rice bowl" policy, factory workers were essentially guaranteed a job for life. But as the country has moved toward a capitalist economy, it has closed many inefficient plants and no longer guarantees workers permanent employment. In recent years, millions of workers have been laid off from state-owned enterprises. Similarly, Cuba has announced plans to shed up to 1 million government employees in the coming years.

Encouraged or pressured by the IMF, the World Bank, and private foreign banks, many heavily indebted African and Latin American countries have adopted macroeconomic policies, designed to reduce inflation rates. These measures seek to lower large budgetary and trade deficits by lowering government spending—including cuts in public-sector employment and the privatizing of many state enterprises (selling them to private investors). These policies—officially called structural adjustment and monetary stabilization programs, but widely known as austerity programs—are often successful in curtailing high-inflation rates (which sometimes had exceeded 100 percent annually). Curbing rampant inflation obviously helps consumers, especially the poor. But at the same time, stabilization entails major cutbacks in government and private-sector employment. For example, when the Mexican government privatized the previously state-owned steel industry, the new owners laid off half of the workforce.

The Struggle for Housing

Of all the challenges facing the urban poor, particularly the wave of new migrants, few are more pressing than finding adequate housing. With many cities doubling in size every ten to twenty-five years, private-sector housing cannot possibly expand fast enough to meet the need. Besides, most of the new homes and apartment houses constructed for private sale or rental are built for the middle and upper classes, since there is little profit to be made in building low-income housing. At the same time, although many governments have invested in public housing, their rents are commonly too high for low-income families to afford. So, lacking adequate options in both the private and state sectors, many of the urban poor live in squatter settlements and other forms of "self-help" (occupant-built) housing, called "spontaneous housing."* Others crowd into existing urban slums

---

* While squatter settlements (also called shantytowns) are poor neighborhoods, not everyone living in them is poor. A minority of shantytown residents are white-collar workers or well-paid blue-collar workers. Some of them achieved upward mobility since first settling there but have remained there because of attachments to friends and their community.

(decaying tenements). Building owners may add additional floors to their buildings to create more space, often in violation of poorly enforced local construction codes. The poorest city dwellers, lacking the resources to rent or build, are often homeless, residing in doorways, unused construction material, or the like. In the "City of the Dead"—a series of huge cemeteries on Cairo's outskirts—hundreds of thousands of the city's poor (largely migrants) live among the cemeteries' tombs.

In all, the total population of slum dwellers, those living in squatter settlements and homeless persons account for close to half the population of the developing world's cities. About 30 percent of the urban population in North Africa, Latin America, and the Caribbean live in slum (substandard) housing. This number rises to nearly 60 percent in South Asia and more than 70 percent in sub-Saharan Africa. Looking at individual nations, about 40 percent of the urban populations live in slums or squatter settlements in Brazil, Egypt, and Turkey. This figure rises to about 55 percent in India; 70–80 percent in Kenya, Pakistan, and Nigeria; and over 90 percent in Afghanistan.[15] Millions of the less developed countries' urban poor, including many of them who have built their own homes, have no direct access to clean water or sanitation facilities.

In recent decades, some countries have reduced their slum population by upgrading the quality of housing for many inhabitants and by providing drinking water and sanitation. Thus, from 1990 to 2010 four North Africa countries (Egypt, Morocco, Libya, and Tunisia) cut their slum dwelling population in half, from 20.8 million to 11.8 million. Throughout the less developed countries, housing upgrading enabled 227 million people to escape urban slums between 2000 and 2010. But, at the same time, some 282 million people were added to the slum population, meaning that the total number of slum dwellers actually increased by 55 million during that decade.[16]

Today, the availability of basic urban services in low-income neighborhoods varies considerably from region to region. For example, a survey of eight low-income neighborhoods in Latin America—located in Rio de Janeiro and Aracaju (Brazil) as well as Santiago and Temuco (Chile)—found that nearly all of the inhabitants had running water and electricity. On the other hand, a parallel study of eight poor African neighborhoods—in the cities of Abidjan and Man (Côte d'Ivoire) along with Nairobi and Kisumu (Kenya)—revealed that almost all the residents had to buy their drinking water. Similarly, very few homes in any of the eight African neighborhoods studied had electricity.[17] In light of these glaring needs, developing nations frequently have searched for appropriate state responses.

Public Housing and the Role of the State

Throughout the developing world, many governments have constructed **public housing** to alleviate housing shortages. In China, workers in state enterprises are commonly assigned apartments linked to their employment. Cuba's revolutionary government has built large apartment blocks, some of them housing 25,000–40,000 persons on the outskirts of its largest cities. During Venezuela's petroleum boom in the late 1970s and early 1980s, the government constructed as many as 34,000 urban housing units annually.[18] Hugo Chávez's populist government built many additional units during the oil boom years. In the 1960s and 1970s, various African governments established housing agencies with far fewer resources.

In time, however, it has become clear that public housing cannot provide sufficient shelter for the poor, and, in some cases, it actually worsens their plight. In the capital cities of India, Senegal, and Nigeria, for example, government housing projects have often been designed to eradicate "urban blight," that is, "unsightly," low-income slums built near the city center. To make the central city more aesthetically pleasing to upper- and middle-class residents, and foreign tourists, the government has sometimes removed those slums and replaced them with government buildings or government-built middle-class housing. Only a small portion of the poor families who had been evicted from their homes have subsequently secured a replacement in low-income public housing projects. Even those who received alternate housing were usually relocated on the edges of town, far removed from their workplace. Zimbabwe's government periodically ousted the same squatters from their settlements in different parts of the nation's capital, in effect "chasing them around town." Instead, the urban poor often turn to self-built housing, generally in sprawling shantytowns located in remote parts of the town. Many government planners, viewing these shacks from a middle-class perspective, believed that unless the squatters can afford "decent" urban housing with plumbing and multiple rooms for their families, they would be better off returning to the countryside.

In fact, many of the public housing projects do not serve the poor at all, housing lower-middle-class families instead. In order for a government to recoup its construction costs, it must sell or rent the new housing units at higher rates than the urban poor can afford. Consequently, the state faces two options: it can subsidize rents and mortgages to bring their cost down to a level within the reach of the poor or it can rent or sell the dwellings to those who have enough money to live there without state subsidies, namely the middle class.

Although many governments provide some subsidized housing to the poor, these programs have several drawbacks and by their nature must be limited. First, even when a government wants to subsidize substantial numbers of low-income units, it is too costly for most developing nations to sustain. For example, following the Cuban Revolution, the government committed itself to providing new homes for the urban lower class. To demonstrate its generosity and gain public support, it poured funds into a number of large housing projects, while recouping only a fraction of the costs out of the low rents that the new tenants paid. Projects such as Santiago's José Martí provided schools, day-care centers, theaters, clinics, and stores for its forty thousand inhabitants. However, by lavishing excessively "luxurious" housing on early recipients, the government soon ran out of funds for the many others needing shelter. Thus, the East Havana project, planned for 100,000 dwelling units, ultimately contained only 1,500.

But even though the state lacked the resources to meet the country's housing needs, it limited private ownership to families who owned their homes at the time of the revolution (1959). People could not build new private homes and those who already owned them were not allowed to sell them. To alleviate the country's severe housing shortage, the government has allowed the sale of existing private homes since 2011.

Elsewhere, another problem is that (subsidized) public housing is often allocated to supporters of the ruling party or the government rather than on the basis of need. Because political patronage plays such an important role, police officers, government bureaucrats, and teachers are often among the first served.[19] Consequently, residents in state housing are frequently from the middle class. They have enough political connections to secure access to public housing and can also afford to pay higher rents than low-income families can.

Most developing countries lack the resources to provide housing for a large segment of the urban poor. Consequently, many analysts believe that the state should not try to provide relatively costly, completed housing units to poor families, but instead should support cheaper alternatives that can serve far more people. With most less developed countries cutting back government spending since the 1980s, the case for cheaper, but more widely disbursed, housing solutions has become even stronger.

Spontaneous Housing

For years, many social scientists and urban planners have maintained that the most effective remedy for urban housing shortfalls is to allow or encourage **spontaneous** (self-built) **housing**—that is, the very shantytowns that have been considered urban blight. In cities throughout the developing world, the poor have built their own homes, sometimes with hired or volunteer assistance. While living in these dwellings, many proprietors, particularly in Africa, also rent part of their home to others. In some cases, the property owners are squatters, living on land that has been occupied illegally, often with the compliance of government authorities.

Spontaneous housing settlements range in size from a few isolated homes to communities of many thousands. For example, on the dried-up marshlands outside Mexico City, the municipality of Netzahualcóyotl began as an illegal squatter settlement in the 1940s. By 1970, it housed 600,000 people.[20] Organized protests eventually persuaded the national government to provide badly needed urban services and to grant the squatters legal titles to their homes. Elsewhere, up to 40 percent of Nairobi's population and one-fourth to one-third of the inhabitants of Jakarta, Karachi, and Lima live in squatter settlements. These homes, many analysts contend, often have been erroneously viewed by politicians and planners as a problem, when, in fact, they are a major part of the solution to urban housing needs. Rather than building public housing, they argue, governments can serve many more people by removing the legal and political obstacles to spontaneous housing settlements, giving squatters titles to their land and helping residents upgrade the dwellings that they have built.

Self-built homes have several important advantages over public housing. First, they actually serve the poor, whereas public housing generally does not. Second, they afford occupants the opportunity to upgrade their homes continuously. For example, in Lima's vast network of shantytowns, one can observe many wood and straw shacks whose owners are building brick walls around them, slowly constructing a better home as funds become available. Third, precisely because they are self-built, these homes better address the needs and desires of their owners than do units built by government planners. Finally, squatter settlements have the churches, bars, and neighborhood stores that help create a sense of community, which is too often lacking in large, impersonal public housing projects. Accepting these arguments, over the years, the governments of Peru, Brazil, and other nations have given millions of illegal squatters titles to their plots of land and provided public services such as sewage and drinking water.

Sites-and-Services Programs

Other analysts who favored a more active role for the state view this perspective as a convenient excuse for governments that do not wish to spend much on the poor. Championing self-help housing, these critics charged, merely perpetuated the status quo and allowed the state to direct its limited housing resources toward the middle class.

Ultimately, many developing world governments, the World Bank, and many foreign-aid donors have pursued a middle-ground policy that falls between providing expensive, fully built public housing units and a hands-off policy that leaves the government with little role to play. In countries as diverse as Colombia, India, Malawi, and Turkey, the state has sold or rented parcels of land to the poor that come with basic services such as running water, sewage, and electricity. Buyers then build their own homes on the sites as they do with spontaneous housing. In some cases, governments provide credit, technical assistance, or low-cost construction materials.

These **sites-and-services** programs have several obvious advantages. As with spontaneous housing, families lacking large savings are able to use their own semi-skilled labor to reduce the cost of acquiring housing and increase their assets by building some or all of it themselves—so-called sweat equity. However, unlike squatter settlements, such programs allow the government to steer self-built housing to locations that are safe and environmentally sound. By contrast, unregulated spontaneous shelters in Caracas illustrate the dangers of unzoned squatter settlements. There, more than half a million people live on precarious hillsides in shacks that are sometimes washed away by mudslides during the rainy season. In contrast to many sprawling squatter communities, inhabitants of sites-and-services settlements have electricity, sanitation, and other basic services from the outset. Furthermore, although occupants must purchase their sites, the lots are far more affordable than are fully built, state housing units.

The Problem of Urban Crime

Escalating crime is a major problem in Latin America (with the world's highest homicide rate) and in many African cities. On the other hand, Asia's murder rate is lower than Western Europe's. In fact, it is the lowest of any region in the world. In places such as San Salvador and Nairobi, large, well-armed youth gangs escalate the level of violence. In many developing countries, crime is more than a personal concern. It has become an important political issue, eliciting mass demonstrations and angry demands for better protection from robbery and violent crime. As in the United States and other industrialized nations, the origins of criminal activity often lie in poverty, discrimination, income inequality, inadequate schools, and broken families. Its victims, of course, come from all social classes, rich and poor alike. However, the urban poor make up a disproportionate share of both the perpetrators and the victims.

Although violent crime rates generally are associated with poverty, there are some important exceptions. For example, homicide and rape rates are significantly higher in the United States than in a number of developing countries such as Chile, Egypt, and Senegal. And, as we have noted, Asia—with severe poverty in a number of countries—has the lowest violent crime rate of any world region. One possible explanation for such anomalies is that income inequality may be a more important factor influencing the crime rate than is the absolute rate of poverty. A number of cross-national studies have found a positive correlation between inequality and violent crime.[21] Countries such as the United States, South Africa, and Brazil—all with high-income inequality—tend to have higher violent crime rates than other countries with comparable or lower per capita incomes, but greater equality. Conversely, although Asian countries such as Bangladesh, India, and Laos suffer from extensive and acute poverty, they also have low income inequality when compared to either affluent or developing countries. And all three have relatively low homicide rates.

Latin American and African cities (largely poor and unequal) suffer from high crime rates. For example, Honduras and South Africa, with some of the world's most extreme income inequality, have among the world's highest urban homicide and rape rates. Of course, the association between inequality and crime is not absolute. For example, while income is very unequally distributed in Chile, its cities have low levels of violent crime. Similarly, both Hong Kong and Singapore, though having moderately high-income concentration, are among the safest cities in the world. In some of these exceptional cases, other factors likely influence crime rate. These include cultural values, the strength of nuclear families, and the likelihood of being caught and punished by the criminal justice system. For the most part, however, a country's degree of income equality is a strong predictor of its crime rate.

Poor policing can contribute to the problem. As noted in chapter 4, police shakedowns and solicitation of protection money are common in many less developed countries. In some countries, police corruption is far more serious. In Mexico, many national and municipal policemen support major drug cartels and are involved in kidnappings, extortion, and murder. In early 2011, when mass graves containing at least 145 bodies were found not far from the Texas border, 16 local policemen were arrested for links to the brutal Zeta cartel and for involvement in those killings. In Argentina, one sociologist observed:

> Each division [of the Buenos Aires police department] dedicates itself to the area of crime that it is supposed to be fighting. The robbery division steals and robs, the narcotics division traffics drugs, auto theft controls the stealing of cars and the chop shops, and those in fraud and bunko, defraud and swindle.[22]

Not surprisingly, the Argentine public had the lowest level of trust in their police of any of the twenty-six countries surveyed in the Western Hemisphere.[23] In many other developing countries, rampant crime and, especially, extensive police corruption not only threaten the security of all city dwellers (regardless of economic status) but also undermine the government's legitimacy.

THE POLITICS OF THE URBAN POOR: CONFLICTING IMAGES

How do the urban poor react politically to their daily struggles for jobs, shelter, and personal safety? As with discussions of peasant politics, social scientists have presented sharply contrasting images of the politics of the urban poor. When political scientists and sociologists first noted the flood of migration and urban growth, many viewed the sprawling slums and squatter settlements as potential hotbeds of unrest or revolution. In a highly influential early work on the less developed countries, James Coleman warned that "there exist in most urban centers elements predisposed to anomic activity [that is, behavior caused by alienation, often lacking societal or moral constraints]."[24] Huntington maintained that the first generation of urban migrants was unlikely to challenge the existing order, but their children often would: "At some point, the slums [and shantytowns] of Rio and Lima are likely to be swept by social violence, as the children of the city demand the rewards of the city."[25] And economist Barbara Ward, taking note of shantytown poverty and the rise of radical urban movements, insisted that "unchecked, left to grow and fester, there is here enough explosive material to produce . . . bitter class conflict . . . erupting in guerrilla warfare, and threatening, ultimately, the security even of the comfortable West."[26]

As we will see, the urban poor have, indeed, contributed to several revolutions in less developed countries. Yet, the urban conflagrations that many analysts had once expected have been rare. For the most part, the poor have shunned radical political activity and violence. Even at the ballot box, they have been as likely to vote for right-wing or centrist political candidates as for radical ones. It now seems clear that initial expectations of a violent or radicalized urban lower class were based on erroneous premises. Many social scientists had assumed that urban migrants, coming to the cities with raised expectations and heightened political sensitivities, would surely turn militant when these expectations were not satisfied. Instead, although the slums of Cairo, Calcutta, and Caracas may appear horrendous to outside observers, most migrants find them preferable to their previous life in the countryside. For example, the urban poor are far more likely than their rural counterparts to have access to electricity, sewage, tap water, and nearby schools. In many countries, urban migration provides an escape from semifeudal social controls or ethnic civil war. Small wonder that early surveys of migrants to Ankara, Baghdad, Bogotá, Mexico City, Rio de Janeiro, and other cities have indicated that most respondents feel better off in their urban hovels than they had in their rural villages.[27] Periodic economic downturns have lowered urban living standards for a while and have undoubtedly embittered some of the poor. Yet, surveys over the years have shown that urbanites generally remain optimistic about the future, particularly their children's future.

When early expectations of urban radicalism and political violence generally failed to materialize, some scholars jumped to the opposite conclusion. For example, on the basis of his studies of low-income neighborhoods in Mexico and Puerto Rico, anthropologist Oscar Lewis concluded that most of the urban poor are prisoners of a "culture of poverty." By this he referred to an underclass that lacks class consciousness, economic and political organization, and long-term aspirations. While distrustful of government, they feel powerless and fatalistic about effecting change.

The culture of poverty, Lewis argued, is inherently apolitical and, hence, quite unlikely to generate radical activity or, for that matter, great pressure for any change.

Related scholarship describes the urban poor as marginal—outside the mainstream of their nation's political and economic life. This suggests a vicious circle in which the exclusion of the poor magnifies their political apathy, which, in turn, isolates them further. They demonstrate a "lack of active participation due to the fact that . . . marginal groups make no decisions; they do not contribute to the molding of society."[28] Like the victims of Lewis's culture of poverty, these "marginals" allegedly show little class consciousness or capacity for long-term collective action.

While it may be true that many poor city dwellers feel incapable of advancing their own lives or influencing the political system—often with good reason—they do not necessarily suffer from the apathy or helplessness that many scholars ascribed to them. Levels of fatalism or optimism vary from place to place and from time to time, depending on both the community's cultural values and its socioeconomic experiences. When poor slum dwellers in Côte d'Ivoire and Kenya—low-income African countries—were asked whether they believed that "when a person is born, the success he/she is going to have is already decided" (an obvious measure of fatalism), nearly 60 percent of them strongly agreed and an additional 11 percent agreed somewhat. In Brazil, a much more economically developed country with one of the world's most unequal income distributions, only about 15 percent strongly agreed, but some 30 percent agreed somewhat. Finally, in Chile, which since the start of the 1990s has experienced the most rapid economic growth in Latin America, with a sharp decline in urban poverty, a mere 4 percent of the respondents strongly agreed, while only 15 percent agreed somewhat.[29] In short, the level of fatalism or optimism among the urban poor varies considerably across nations and seems to correspond more to objective economic conditions than to culturally embedded values.

Just as initial predictions of radicalism and political violence among the urban lower class have turned out to be greatly exaggerated, so too have the reverse assertions that the poor are invariably apathetic and fatalistic. To be sure, low-income communities generally are not highly politicized. In his early study of the poor in Guatemala City, Bryan R. Roberts found that "they claim to avoid politics in their local work, and to them the term politician is synonymous with deceit and corruption."[30] Yet, these assessments often do not originate in the slum dwellers' innate apathy or fatalism. Rather, they come from their accurate perception that they have little chance of changing the political and economic order. On the other hand, when given the opportunity to organize and when there is a realistic chance of attaining some benefits from the political system, many low-income communities have seized the opportunity. The slums and shantytowns of

Caracas, Lima, and Rio, for example, have spawned numerous well-organized and politically effective community groups. Furthermore, their leaders often have a keen understanding of how to operate within the political system and manipulate it.

Increasingly, many social scientists question the earlier concepts of marginality and the culture of poverty. In the previously mentioned survey of poor neighborhoods in four African cities (in Côte d'Ivoire and Kenya) and four Latin American cities (in Brazil and Chile), political attitudes, levels of political interest, and political knowledge varied considerably. In all four countries, a majority of the people (ranging from 51 to 63 percent) surveyed responded that they were not interested in politics.[31]

Yet, despite their professed disinterest, many of these slum dwellers were well informed and communicative about politics. In Chile, Côte d'Ivoire, and Kenya, roughly half of them reported talking occasionally with other people "about the problems which [their] country has to face today." This proportion rose to almost two-thirds in Brazil. Moreover, although over half of them professed to have no interest in politics, about half of those surveyed in Chile and Côte d'Ivoire claimed that they regularly followed political news. When asked to name important government leaders, most were quite knowledgeable. In all four nations, at least two-thirds were able to name the president of their country (reaching 94 percent in Kenya and 96 percent in Chile). Moreover, about half the respondents in Chile and Kenya and two-thirds in Brazil and Côte d'Ivoire could name the mayor of their town. In short, these low-income city dwellers seemed to have a greater interest in politics than they were willing to admit. Perhaps the question on their level of political interest meant something different to them than it did to the people conducting the survey.

However, in all four countries the urban poor tended to take a rather dim view of their political system and their elected representatives. More than 80 percent of those surveyed in each of the four countries believed that "those we elect to parliament lose touch with people pretty quickly," with this number reaching 94 percent in Chile. When asked whether they believed that "public officials care what people like me think," a significant majority in all of the eight cities said "no." Surprisingly, Ivorians, living in a country that was not then democratic, were most positive about their public officials. On the other hand, Chileans, who live in the most democratic and politically responsive of the four nations, were least likely by far to believe that their government officials care about them and were also least likely to believe that their parliamentary representative keeps in touch with low-income constituents. Perhaps Chileans had harbored unrealistically high expectations of their new political leaders following the restoration of democracy in 1990 after a seventeen-year military dictatorship. Another important factor may be that Chilean parties, renowned for their strong linkages to the lower classes prior to the dictatorship, had become more elitist and distant during their years in exile.

Thus, there seems to be a wide variety of political attitudes among the urban poor. Moreover, their attitudes may vary over time in response to changes in national politics. Although the slums of Santiago (Chile) or Tehran (Iran) once boiled with unrest, the same neighborhoods were largely tranquil or even passive years later. Clearly, a more nuanced view of urban politics requires us to ask: Under what circumstances do the poor organize politically? What goals do they seek, and how do they pursue them? What factors determine whether their political organization is peaceful or violent, conservative or radical, reformist or revolutionary?

FORMS OF POLITICAL EXPRESSION AMONG THE URBAN POOR

Political scientists have long understood that the urban poor tend to be better informed and more politically active than their rural counterparts. Indeed, early scholarship on less developed countries used a nation's level of urbanization as an indirect indicator of its level of political participation. Lower-income city residents have higher levels of literacy than peasants do, greater exposure to the mass media, and more contact with political campaigns and rallies. This does not mean, however, that most of them are highly politicized. To the contrary, as we have noted, many of them are indifferent, apathetic, or fatalistic about political events (just as many Americans are). Nor does it mean that political activists in the community are necessarily radical or indignant about local living conditions or prone to violent protest. What it does mean is that the urban poor generally vote in higher numbers and follow politics more closely than the peasantry does. Furthermore, it appears that many low-income neighborhoods carefully calculate what benefits they can secure from the political system and then organize to secure them. Contrary to initial expectations that the disoriented and frustrated urban poor would riot and rebel, they have tended, instead, to be rather pragmatic and careful in their political behavior.

Individual Political Behavior

For most slum and shantytown dwellers, opportunities for individual political activity are rather restricted. In the many developing countries ruled by military or single-party dictatorships, voting is meaningless. And even in electoral democracies, where many candidates court the support of the urban poor, political officials tend to forget these voters until the next election.

An alternate, often more fruitful, type of individual political activity takes the form of **clientelism** (patron-client relationships). Members of the urban lower class often advance their interests by attaching themselves to a prominent patron within the government, an influential political party, or an organized political movement. Clientelism involves "the dispensing of public resources as favors by political power holders/seekers . . . in exchange for votes or other forms of popular support." While it does offer concrete advantages to the less powerful partner (i.e., the client), it is at its heart "a strategy of elite-controlled political participation fostering the status quo."[32] Potentially frustrated or radicalized individuals and groups are thereby co-opted into the political system with the lure of immediate, though limited, gains. As we have already seen in chapter 4, such clientelism is often associated with the corrupt diversion of state resources by political bosses as they seek to reward their supporters.

Of course, patron-client relations were also common tools of America's urban political bosses in the late nineteenth and early twentieth centuries. Big city political machines aided recently arrived immigrants by supplying jobs, access to local government authorities, and Christmas turkeys in exchange for their support at the polls. Today, in cities throughout the less developed countries, the poor use clientelistic relations to secure credit, government employment, and other economic goods. Dictators like Egypt's Hosni Mubarak (and his eventual successor, Abdel Fattah el-Sisi), and royal families like those in Saudi Arabia, Jordan, or Morocco maintained their regimes for years by dispensing patronage. Similarly, in democracies, such as India or Uruguay, political bosses garner votes and volunteers similarly.

For most of the urban poor, however, collective rather than individual activity appears to be the most productive form of political participation. Many low-income neighborhoods have organized rather effectively to extract government benefits. Often, one of their first goals is to secure land titles for their homes along with basic services such as sanitation, sewage, tap water, schools, and paved streets.

Collective Goals: Housing and Urban Services

On the outskirts of Lima, Peru, several million people live in squatter communities. For the most part, these settlements were started through organized invasions of unoccupied land—be it government property, church property, or land whose ownership had been in dispute:

> Some invasions involve relatively small groups of families who cooperate on an informal basis shortly before the occupation of the land. Others involve hundreds of families and are planned with great care. The leaders of these invasions often organize well before the invasion occurs and meet many times to recruit members, choose a site, and plan the occupation itself.[33]

Although these land seizures were illegal, one study found that nearly half of the earliest ones were carried out with either the explicit or tacit approval of local government officials. While the authorities did not want invasions to get out of hand, they understood that permitting a controlled number of them onto low-value land (much of it public) enabled the poor to build their own homes with little cost to the state. There were political benefits to be gained as well. By protecting the invaders from police eviction, a political leader or party could secure electoral support from that community. In many cases, squatters paid off local authorities prior to their invasions.

When a leftist military regime seized power in Peru in 1968, it was anxious to mobilize the urban poor but, at the same time, it also wanted to preempt independent political activity. The generals issued an urban reform law legalizing most of the existing squatter communities. They tried to mobilize, yet control, the poor through SINAMOS, a state-run political organization for the rural and urban masses. Henry Dietz's study of six poor neighborhoods in Lima reveals that community leaders in several locations were adept at switching their tactics from Peru's earlier competitive electoral politics to the new rules of enlightened authoritarianism.[34] Mobilized neighborhoods used an impressive array of tactics to secure assistance from the military regime. These included: working through SINAMOS, enlisting the aid of a sympathetic Catholic bishop whom the church had assigned to the shantytowns, gaining the support of foreign NGOs, publishing letters in major newspapers, pressuring local government bureaucrats, and directly petitioning the president.

Although Lima's squatter settlements have been unusually well organized, the urban poor in many other developing countries have also established useful ties between their neighborhoods and the state. For example, in her study of low-income neighborhoods in Mexico City, Susan Eckstein described how neighborhood leaders became active in the long-ruling political party at the time (the PRI), thereby establishing themselves as the links between the government and their communities. Because these community organizations were controlled from the top down and tended to be short-lived, Eckstein was skeptical about how much the poor really gained through this clientelistic system. Still, she conceded that, over the years, poor neighborhoods had successfully petitioned the government for such benefits as running water, electricity, local food markets, schools, and better public transportation. Following the PRI's defeat in the 2000 presidential election (after seventy-one years in power) and Mexico's transition to democracy, many low-income neighborhoods have been forced to establish new clientelistic relationships.

The politics of low-income neighborhoods throughout the less developed countries generally resemble the Peruvian and Mexican models in two important respects: the scope of their claims and their relationship to the national political system. Studies of politics in India, Pakistan, the Philippines, and other less developed countries demonstrate that the poor usually have limited and pragmatic demands. For example, when their demands focus on housing, as they often do, they may simply demand protection against eviction from their illegal settlements. Beyond this, they may ask for basic services (water, electricity, etc.) and titles to their plots so that they can build their own homes. Established neighborhoods often request a medical clinic, a market, or a preschool lunch program. None of these objectives presents a challenge to the established political system or a call for major redistribution of economic resources.

In fact, the very nature of their political organizations limits the demands of low-income communities since these groups tend to atrophy after a number of years. Consequently, as Alan Gilbert and Peter Ward charge, "The [government's] main aim [in supporting] community-action programs is less to improve conditions for the poor . . . than to legitimate the state . . . to help maintain existing power relations in society."[35] As an alternative to clientelism, critics favor a more independent, and perhaps more radical, form of mobilization that would raise the urban poor's political consciousness and lead to more sweeping redistributive policies benefiting far more people.

Other analysts, however, hold a more positive view of clientelism. While recognizing its shortcomings, they insist that the benefits that it brings are clearly better than nothing. Viewed in the broader context of society's tremendous inequalities, paved streets, clean drinking water, or a clinic may not seem like sufficient improvements to some outside observers. Nevertheless, the low-income neighborhoods that receive them appreciate their value. A radical regime might redistribute more to the poor, but this usually is not a viable option. Furthermore, the performance of radical regimes in helping the poor has been mixed. Marxist governments often redistribute significant resources to the urban poor soon after taking power. However, with the notable exception of China (after it transformed to an essentially capitalist economy) and Vietnam, they have usually had a poor record of generating economic growth.

The benefits of clientelism vary from country to country, depending on the nature of the political system and the health of the economy. In relatively open and democratic systems, the poor have broader opportunities to organize, demonstrate, petition, and vote. Consequently, their capacity to demand rewards from the state is normally greater than under authoritarian regimes. At the same time, the level of benefits clientelistic systems can allocate to low-income neighborhoods is also constrained by the state's economic resources. During their petroleum booms, the Mexican and Venezuelan governments could be more generous to the urban poor. Even in more difficult economic times, the Mexican government used revenues from the sale of state enterprises to finance public works projects in the urban slums. When Venezuela reaped the rewards of its petroleum wealth, then president Hugo Chávez financed extensive anti-poverty programs, which earned him strong support among the urban poor. (Lower oil prices, government overspending, and economic mismanagement have since caused widespread economic distress in the country.) On the other hand, the remaining dictatorships in sub-Saharan Africa, such as Zimbabwe, have neither the economic resources nor the political will to aid impoverished urban neighborhoods.

Whatever the merits or limits of clientelism, its scope and range refute certain earlier assumptions about the politics of the urban poor. On the one hand, their often delicate and complex patron-client negotiations demonstrate that numerous low-income neighborhood leaders are more politically skilled than many outside analysts had given them credit for. While many of the urban poor may feel alienated from the political system, others are capable of sophisticated political organization and tough bargaining with the state or political parties. On the other hand, the universality of clientelism indicates that the poor rarely engage in the radical politics, the violent upheavals, or the revolutionary activities that some political scientists had expected. During the recent global economic crisis and in regional economic meltdowns, various urban neighborhoods have erupted in violence. Nevertheless, the extent of rioting and social unrest has remained surprisingly limited. To be sure, unemployment and other economic difficulties helped motivate the slum dwellers of Tunis and Cairo to join in the mass protests that brought down the dictators of Tunisia and Egypt. But both these reformist uprisings succeeded in large part because their support extended well beyond the poor to the more influential middle class.

Radical Political Behavior

While most of the urban poor favor moderate and pragmatic forms of political expression, there have been important exceptions. In some countries, such as El Salvador since the mid-1990s, low-income neighborhoods have voted in substantial numbers for Marxist political candidates. And, in a few cases, residents of urban slums and shantytowns have been important players in revolutionary upheavals. In 1970, Salvador Allende, candidate of Chile's leftist Popular Unity (UP) coalition, became the developing world's first democratically elected Marxist president. Allende received considerable electoral support from the *campamentos* (squatter settlements) that ring the capital city of Santiago. In fact, a number of these neighborhoods were politically organized either by the UP or by the MIR (Revolutionary Left Movement), a more radical group than UP, which periodically engaged in armed action. The poor of Lima played a major role in electing a Marxist mayor, Alfonso Barrantes. These examples, as well as the Communist Party's electoral successes in several large Indian cities, indicate that the poor do support radical political parties under certain circumstances. However, they will favor those parties only if they have a realistic chance of winning at the local or national level so that they can be in a position to deliver tangible benefits to their supporters. Thus, even a slum dweller's decision to vote for a radical candidate is often based on very pragmatic calculations. Not long after supporting Barrantes for mayor, Lima's poor gave him few votes when he ran for the nation's presidency, believing that his Marxist policies might succeed in Lima but were not viable at the national level.

More often, the urban poor are attracted to charismatic populists (such as the late Venezuelan president Hugo Chávez) or to moderate leftists (such as former Brazilian president Luiz Inácio Lula da Silva). Squatters or slum dwellers are much less likely to embrace urban guerrillas or other revolutionary movements. Teodoro Petkoff, a former leader of the Venezuelan communists' urban guerrilla wing, noted that residents of Caracas's poor barrios, even those who belonged to leftist unions, rejected the guerrillas. Blue-collar workers often elected communist union representatives in those days, Petkoff observed, because they felt that those union militants would deliver more at the bargaining table. On the other hand, in national elections, the urban poor were more likely to vote for the two mainstream parties (Social Democrats and Christian Democrats) or for the country's former right-wing dictator, all of whom were more capable of quickly delivering rewards to their supporters than the guerrillas were.[36]

In the 1980s and 1990s, Peru's Sendero Luminoso (Shining Path) guerrillas had some success in the shantytowns of Lima. However, as often as not, they only earned that "support" through intimidation. For example, when a popular, women's political organizer in the large shantytown Villa El Salvador failed to cooperate with it, the guerrilla group assassinated her in front of her family and neighbors.

This is not to suggest that the urban poor never support revolutions. During the second half of the twentieth century, the cities played a central role in four of the developing world's revolutions—in Bolivia, Cuba, Iran, and Nicaragua. However, in most cases, other social classes took the lead: miners, unionized blue-collar workers, artisans, the lower middle class, and the national police in Bolivia; students and university graduates in Cuba; and theology students and petroleum workers in Iran. In contrast, Douglas Butterworth's study of the former inhabitants of a Havana slum, Las Yaguas, conducted almost twenty years after the revolutionary victory, found that most respondents were barely aware of Fidel Castro's existence during his rise to power.[37]

In the past years, some of the urban poor in Muslim countries have been attracted to a different type of revolutionary vision, Islamic fundamentalism. However, there is little evidence that poverty is their sole, or even primary reason for doing so—as noted in chapter 5, many leaders of radical jihadist groups have come from the middle and professional classes.

CONCLUSION: THE ROLE OF THE RURAL AND URBAN POOR IN DEMOCRATIC CHANGE

In future decades, the less developed countries will continue to experience a shift in population from its rural areas to its urban centers. While the rate of urbanization has slowed in parts of the developing world, absolute increases in urban populations (the increases in raw numbers) will be greater than ever in the coming decades. Thus, governments will have to heed urban needs, including those of the poor. Still, even with the best-intentioned public policies, developing economies will be hard-pressed to provide sufficient jobs, housing, sanitation, and social services. Various economic crises over the past few decades have made the task all the more difficult. Urban crime, pollution, and AIDS will add tremendously to the burdens on the political and economic systems. In countries such as South Africa and Guatemala, the fall of authoritarian regimes has led to a surge in crime. To the extent that rural-urban migration can be slowed by agrarian reform, rural development programs, and improved rural education and health care, it will give both urban planners and the urban poor more time and opportunity to deal with these problems.

As some developing countries try to consolidate new democracies, they will find the urban poor better equipped than their rural counterparts to become participatory citizens. But they are also more volatile and, should democratic governments disappoint them, they are more likely to turn to forms of antisystemic behavior. Both the rural and urban poor will need to refine and improve their strategies for securing state resources, while governments will have to become more responsive to both groups' needs. In many developing countries, however, urban crime and poverty are more likely than radical politics to threaten stability in the proximate future. Faced with rising crime rates and economic deprivation, the poor may become disillusioned with democracy. If the military and the middle class also fear rising crime and disorder, democracies may fall to repressive governments.

> **Practice and Review Online at**
> http://textbooks.rowman.com/handelman9e

KEY TERMS

agrarian reform
clientalism
concentrated land ownership
everyday forms of resistance
informal sector
land reform
landless (peasants)
moral economy
peasants
public housing
rural class system
sites-and-services programs
spontaneous housing
urbanization

DISCUSSION QUESTIONS

1. What kind of rural reform or development projects do you think would most benefit the rural poor? Why?
2. Discuss the political orientations of the urban poor. What does survey research tell us about the way that the urban poor look at their present circumstances and about their views on the prospects of improving their lot?
3. Discuss the growth of urban crime in the less developed countries, the major obstacles to reducing crime, and the possible political consequences of rising crime rates.
4. How might rapid urban growth contribute to the growth of democratic governments in the less developed countries? Under what circumstances might it undermine democracy?

NOTES

1. George Foster, "Introduction: What Is a Peasant?" in *Peasant Society*, eds. Jack Potter, George Foster, and May Diaz (Boston, MA: Little, Brown, 1967), 2–14.
2. Eric R. Wolf, *Peasants* (Upper Saddle River, NJ: Prentice Hall, 1966), 10.

3. Robert Redfield, *Peasant Society and Culture: An Anthropological Approach* (Chicago, IL: University of Chicago Press, 1965), 77.

4. Phyllis Arora, "Patterns of Political Response in Indian Peasant Society," *Western Political Quarterly* 20 (September 1967): 654.

5. James C. Scott, *Weapons of the Week: Everyday Forms of Peasant Resistance* (New Haven, CT: Yale University Press, 1986).

6. One of the most insightful books on the role of the peasantry in twentieth-century revolutions is Eric R. Wolf, *Peasant Wars of the Twentieth Century* (New York, NY: Harper & Row, 1969).

7. James C. Scott, *The Moral Economy of the Peasant: Rebellion and Subsistence in Southeast Asia* (New Haven, CT: Yale University Press, 1976).

8. Wolf, *Peasant Wars.*

9. Samuel P. Huntington, *Political Order in Changing Societies* (New Haven, CT: Yale University Press, 1968), 375.

10. Zander Navarro, "Expropriating Land in Brazil," in *Agricultural Land Redistribution: Toward Greater Consensus*, eds. Hans Binswanger-Mkhize, Camille Bourguignon, and Rogier van den Brink (Washington, DC: World Bank, 2010), 275.

11. T. S. Jane et al., "Smallholder Income and Land Distribution in Africa," *Food Policy* 28 (2003): 253–75.

12. Huntington, *Political Order*, 375.

13. "FAO's Contribution to Good Policies and Practices in Agrarian Reform and Rural Development: A Brief Overview," 3.

14. Manuel Castells and Alejandro Portes, "World Underneath: The Origins, Dynamics and Effects of the Informal Economy," in *The Informal Economy: Studies in Advanced and Developing Economies*, eds. Alejandro Portes, Manuel Castells, and Lauren A. Benton (Baltimore: Johns Hopkins University Press, 1989), 12.

15. UN-Habitat (United Nations Human Settlements Programme), Statistics.

16. UN Habitat, *State of the World's Cities 2010/2011.*

17. Silvia Schmitt, "Housing Conditions and Policies," in *Poverty and Democracy—Self-Help and Political Participation in Third World Cities*, eds. Dirk Berg-Schlosser and Norbert Kersting (London: Zed Books, 2003), 61.

18. Howard Handelman, "The Role of the State in Sheltering the Urban Poor," in *Spontaneous Shelter*, ed. Carl V. Patton (Philadelphia, PA: Temple University Press, 1988), 332–33.

19. Susan Eckstein, *The Poverty of Revolution: The State and the Urban Poor in Mexico*, 2nd ed. (Princeton, NJ: Princeton University Press, 1988), 41.

20. Alan Gilbert and Peter Ward, *Housing, the State, and the Poor* (New York, NY: Cambridge University Press, 1985), 86–87.

21. For example, *United Nations Office on Drugs and Crime, Global Study on Homicide*, 2015 (online).

22. *New York Times*, August 4, 2004.

23. "Trust in the National Police," based on a 2010 survey of 44,000 people by Americas Barometer, www.AmericasBarometer.org.

24. James Coleman, "Conclusion: The Political Systems of Developing Nations," in *The Politics of Developing Areas*, eds. Gabriel Almond and James Coleman (Princeton, NJ: Princeton University Press, 1960), 537.

25. Huntington, *Political Order*, 283.

26. Barbara Ward, "Creating Man's Future Goals for a World of Plenty," *Saturday Review* 9 (August 1964): 192.

27. Joan Nelson, *Migrants, Urban Poverty, and Instability in Developing Nations* (Cambridge, MA: AMS Press and the Harvard University Center for International Affairs, 1969).

28. Jorge Giusti, "Organizational Characteristics of the Latin American Urban Marginal Settler," *International Journal of Politics* 1, no. 1 (1971): 57.

29. Barbara Happe and Sylvia Schmit, "Political Culture," in *Poverty and Democracy*, eds. Dirk Berg-Schlosser and Norbert Kersting (London: Zed Books, 2003), 130.

30. Bryan R. Roberts, *Organizing Strangers: Poor Families in Guatemala City* (Austin, TX: University of Texas Press, 1973), 299.

31. Happe and Schmit, "Political Culture," 125. All of the survey results that follow come from that chapter (121–52) and from Norbert Kersting and Jaime Sperberg, "Political Participation," in *Poverty and Democracy*, 153–80.

32. Both quotes come from A. Bank, "Poverty, Politics and the Shaping of Urban Space: A Brazilian Example," *International Journal of Urban and Regional Research* 10, no. 4 (1986): 523.

33. David Collier, *Squatters and Oligarchs* (Baltimore, MD: Johns Hopkins University Press, 1976), 41, 44.

34. Henry Dietz, *Poverty and Problem Solving Under Military Rule* (Austin, TX: University of Texas Press, 1980).

35. Gilbert and Ward, *Housing, the State and the Poor*, 175.

36. Interviews by Howard Handelman with Petkoff in 1976 and 1978.

37. Douglas Butterworth, *The People of Buena Ventura* (Urbana, IL: University of Illinois Press, 1980), 19–20.

9

Revolutionary Change

Benghazi during the 2011 Libyan revolution. At that time, Tahrir ("Liberation") Square was filled with political speakers, street vendors selling revolutionary souvenirs, and displays commemorating martyrs lost in the fighting. While the revolution eventually succeeded in toppling dictator Muammar Qaddafi, Libya was unsuccessful at consolidating a transition to democracy—and instead collapsed into renewed civil war. *Source*: Rex Brynen.

THE OPENING DECADES OF THE TWENTIETH CENTURY ushered in the Mexican and Russian Revolutions. The closing decades witnessed the collapse of Soviet Communism and the transformation of the Chinese and Vietnamese revolutions.* Just when it looked as this "age of revolution" was over, a new type of revolutionary movement has erupted in part of the Muslim world—the rise of radical Islamism. No era in world history had encompassed more revolutionary upheaval.

Karl Marx, the most influential prophet of revolution, expected insurrections to take place in industrialized European nations where the organized working class would rise up against the oppressive capitalist system. Instead, communist revolutions have taken place almost exclusively in the developing world, fought primarily by the peasantry. Militant Islamist groups, on the other hand, have drawn support from a wide variety of social classes and groups (see chapter 5).

In the less developed countries, the appeal of revolutionary change has been its pledge of rapid and sweeping solutions to the problems of underdevelopment. Marxist revolutions promised to end colonial rule, terminate dependency, protect national sovereignty, reduce social and economic inequalities, accelerate economic development, mobilize the population, and transform the political culture. Islamist uprisings promise to drive out allegedly corrupt Western influence and values. Not surprisingly, many of the developing world's poor and oppressed along with numerous intellectuals and alienated members of the middle class have found revolutionary ideologies appealing.

Some revolutionary governments—in China, Cuba, and Mexico, for example—were able to deliver on a number of their promises. Under Mao Zedong's leadership, the Chinese Communist Party (CCP) redistributed land to the peasantry, industrialized the economy, and transformed the country into a world power. Fidel Castro's government implemented extensive land reform, an impressive adult literacy campaign, and significant public health programs. Mexico's revolutionary party reestablished national sovereignty over the country's most valuable natural resources (most notably, petroleum), initiated agrarian reform, and industrialized the nation.

Often, however, these gains have come at great cost, including considerable human suffering and loss of life during the revolutionary struggle and after its victory (Cambodia), political repression (China and Iran), and rampant corruption (Mexico, Laos). As a result of their revolution, the Chinese people now enjoy far better medical care, education, and general

---

*Leninist regimes remain in place in China and Vietnam (they still are officially communist), but their governments have largely abandoned communist economics and class-based politics. The Cuban government has also made more modest transformations of its economy.

living conditions than ever before. At the same time, however, perhaps 30 million people starved to death in the 1950s due to the mistaken experiments of Mao's Great Leap Forward.* Millions more suffered humiliation or imprisonment and perhaps four hundred thousand people died during the ultra-radical period called the Cultural Revolution (1966–76). Many other communist governments had their own gulags (networks of prisons or forced labor camps) for real and imagined political opponents. In Vietnam, the revolutionary government sent many suspected dissidents to "reeducation" camps, and in Cuba, a smaller, but still significant, number were imprisoned. Iran's Islamist revolution has produced military and some social gains, but has done so at the cost of internal repression and international isolation.

In the most unfortunate cases—Angola, Mozambique, and Cambodia—large portions of the population died as a result of the revolutionary conflicts and their aftermaths, with little or nothing positive to show for it.† In Cambodia, the fanatical Khmer Rouge government murdered or starved more than a million people, including much of the country's educated class, while failing to accomplish anything for its people. Over the years, even some of the more idealistic revolutionary regimes changed into corrupt bureaucracies, run by a new generation of opportunistic apparatchiks (party or government bureaucrats) who had never risked anything for the revolution's ideals. During its brief rule over areas of Syria and Iraq, Daesh argued it was constructing the foundations of a new "Islamic State"—but at the cost of horrendous tyranny and mass slaughters, especially of non-Muslims and Shi'ites.

After examining the meaning of the term "revolution" and classifying different types of twentieth- and twenty-first-century revolutions, this chapter will discuss the causes of revolutionary upheavals, their principal sources of leadership and support, and the policy objectives of their leaders once in power. Finally, it will discuss the decline of the revolutionary model at the end of the twentieth century and its possible resurrection in a new form in the twenty-first century.

DEFINING REVOLUTION

Scholars have argued endlessly about what constitutes a revolution and whether particular upheavals such as the American or Iranian Revolutions

---

* "The Great Leap Forward" (1958–61) was Chinese leader, Mao Zedong's, tragic attempt to convert the economy to full communism rapidly. Government policies in agriculture, including the abolition of private farming, resulted in mass starvation.

† In Angola and Mozambique, most of the killings were carried out by counterrevolutionary forces, supported by the then white minority regime in South Africa. For the hundreds of thousands of butchered innocent civilians, however, it mattered little which side killed them.

were, in fact, true social revolutions. Thus, Chalmers Johnson notes, "Half the battle will lie in answering the question, 'What is revolution?'"[1] In its broadest and least precise usage, the term is applied to any violent government overthrow. Peter Calvert offers the most open-ended definition when he maintains that revolution is "simply a form of governmental change through violence."[2] This kind of definition, however, seems too broad because it encompasses military coups and other upheavals that do little more than change the heads of government. Most scholars insist on a more rigorous definition, arguing that revolutions must bring fundamental political, economic, and social change. Samuel Huntington defined it in this way:

> A revolution is a rapid, fundamental, and violent domestic change in the dominant values and myths of society, in its political institutions, social structure, leadership and government activity and policies. Revolutions are thus to be distinguished from insurrections, revolts, coups and wars of independence.[3]

To be sure, it is frequently difficult to make the distinctions that Huntington proposes at the end of his definition. For example, some wars of independence against colonial powers (sometimes called "wars of national liberation"), such as in Algeria and Mozambique, brought about a political transformation and substantial social change. The Haitian Revolution (1794–1804) is a particularly striking example: a slave uprising that ended French colonial rule and brought about independence.

On the other hand, Theda Skocpol accepts Huntington's starting definition but narrows it by claiming that "social revolutions are accompanied and in part effectuated through [massive] class upheavals."[4] She adds,

> Social revolutions are set apart from other sorts of conflicts by the combination of two coincidences: the coincidence of societal structural change with class upheaval; and the coincidence of the political with social transformation.[5]

Skocpol concedes that according to her more restrictive, class-based definition, only "a handful of successful social revolutions have ever occurred." The most clear-cut cases are the three she has studied in great detail: France (1789–99), Russia (1917), and China (1911–49). Other less restrictive definitions of revolution apply to Mexico, Cuba, Algeria, Ethiopia, South Africa, Vietnam, Cambodia, Turkey, and Iran. What is common to all of those is that insurgency brought sweeping changes to the country's political, economic, and social systems.

Because revolutions involve a fundamental transfer of political and economic powers, rather than a mere change in political leaders (as is the case of most military coups), they are almost always violent. Not surprisingly, the government officials and social classes that have long held (and often abused) power now face bleak futures and invariably fight to stay on top. If the revolutionaries triumph, they remove old elites from power and install new ones. And, at least in some respects, they broaden political, economic, and social participation to include those further down the social and economic ladder. This does not imply that revolutionary governments are democratic. They rarely are. But they are sometimes more broadly participatory and egalitarian than the regimes that they have toppled.

This chapter classifies as a **revolution** any insurgency that brings about these kinds of comprehensive political and socioeconomic changes. These insurrections may be rooted in class struggles (China and Vietnam), as Skocpol insists, or, contrary to Huntington, they may be wars of national liberation (Algeria and Angola), or even ethnic conflict (South Sudan) and religious revivalism (Iran), as long as they overturn critical political and economic institutions and change the country's underlying power structure and social values. In fact, the borderline between nationalist and class-based revolutions is often difficult to discern. The Vietnamese Revolution most clearly combined anticolonial and class struggles. Moreover, even primarily class-based revolutions, such as China's, Mexico's, Cuba's, and Nicaragua's, had important nationalist, anti-imperialist components to them.

Revolutions may be Marxist (China, Russia, Vietnam, Cambodia, and Cuba) or not (Mexico, Bolivia, Tunisia, and Iran). Marxism was particularly appealing to many revolutionaries because it promised the ideological rigor, social and economic "justice," and new political myths that they sought. But the revolutionary's vision of social justice need not be communist. It may also come from nationalism, Islam, democracy, or other ideologies and religions.

Revolutionaries generally come to power either through urban uprisings featuring strikes, protest marches, and street riots (Russia, Bolivia, Egypt, and Iran), rural guerrilla warfare (China, Vietnam, and Cuba), or through a combination of both (Nicaragua and Libya). There have also been a few "elite revolutions" in which military officers or upper-level bureaucrats have overthrown governments and instituted far-reaching socioeconomic changes that far transcended the objectives of mere coups.[6] Primary examples include Mustafa Kemal Ataturk's military revolt in Turkey (1919), Gamal Abdel Nasser's officers' revolt in Egypt (1952), and Peru's "revolution from above" (1968)—all led by reformist military officers (see chapter 10).

The recent series of mass uprisings against authoritarian regimes in Tunisia, Egypt, Libya, Syria, Yemen, and Bahrain raises interesting challenges to these definitions of revolution. Do those mass uprisings against Arab dictators qualify as revolutions? Surely, the Tunisian transition to democracy meets this test. However, in the other countries involved in the **Arab Spring**, their revolutions were aborted before they had gotten off the ground.

UNDERLYING CAUSES OF REVOLUTION

Just as experts have disagreed about the definition of revolution, they have also differed over the causes of revolutionary insurrection. Some theories focus on broad historical trends, including changes in the world order that make revolution possible or likely. Other explanations center on weaknesses in the ancien régime (the old political and socioeconomic systems), examining factors that caused the prerevolutionary state to fall. And yet others concentrate on the revolutions' major players, particularly the peasantry, seeking the factors that cause them to revolt.

Inexorable Historical Forces

Karl Marx viewed revolution as an unstoppable historical force growing out of class inequalities that are rooted in the ownership of the means of production. Those who command the economic system, he argued, control the state as well. Over time, however, subordinate classes will become alienated from the political—economic order and will attain sufficient political skills and vision (class consciousness) to overthrow the political system. Thus, Marx maintained that in the seventeenth and eighteenth centuries, an ascendant **bourgeoisie** (capitalists or, more broadly, the middle class) had toppled the old order dominated by the aristocracy and landed oligarchy. Examples of such bourgeois revolutions included the British Civil War (Revolution) of 1640 and the French Revolution (1789). Both of those were part of a broader European transition from agrarian feudalism to industrial capitalism. Although Marx believed that this new capitalist order represented a more advanced and more productive historical stage, he also argued that it depended on the exploitation of the working class (**proletariat**). In time, he predicted, as the exploitation of the proletariat became more apparent and as workers developed sufficient class consciousness, they would overthrow capitalism and install revolutionary socialism.

More than any other revolutionary theorist, Marx influenced the course of history, as most of the leaders of the twentieth century's major revolutions—including V. I. Lenin, Mao Zedong, Ho Chi Minh, Che Guevara, and Fidel Castro—fervently believed in his ideology. His writings evoked the centrality of class struggle in most revolutionary movements. But as even sympathetic analysts have noted, "He was, first and foremost a nineteenth-century man" whose ideology was closely linked to the era in which he lived.[7] "Marx's theoretical approach," writes Irving Zeitlin, "enabled him to explain the past but failed him in his predictions."[8] Indeed, no country has ever had the succession of revolutions that he predicted, first capitalist, then socialist.* Instead, the primary locus of modern revolution

---

*In other words, no Marxist revolution took place in a country where capitalism was entrenched. And, by the end of the twentieth century, in a complete reversal of Marxist theory, communist regimes in the Soviet Union and Central Europe were changing to capitalism.

has been the developing world—not advanced capitalist nations—and the foremost protagonists, at least in the twentieth century, were peasants rather than industrial workers. In this century, leadership in the Arab Spring has come principally from students and young professionals (joined by tribal leaders in Libya and Yemen), although in Tunisia the trade union movement also played a key role.

Mao Zedong, the leader of the Chinese Revolution, accepted Marx's view of revolution as part of an unfolding historical process. Like other developing world Marxists, he viewed capitalist exploitation and its resulting class conflict as the root causes of communist upheavals. However, the CCP's military defeats in the 1920s convinced him that its orthodox commitment to proletarian revolution was not viable in a country in which the working class constituted only a small percentage of the population. Consequently, he reinterpreted Marxist theory to make it more applicable to China and other parts of the developing world. Mao established a model of peasant-based struggle and a military strategy designed to encircle and conquer China's cities following a period of protracted rural guerrilla conflict. The success of his strategy in the world's most populous country and its frequent use in other developing nations made Mao the most influential practitioner of revolutionary warfare in the twentieth century.

In Vietnam and Cuba, Ho Chi Minh and Che Guevara refined Mao's vision of "peoples' war" to make it more compatible with conditions in Southeast Asia and Latin America. While all of them demonstrated that communist revolutions could take place in countries that are not highly industrialized, those leaders still adhered to Marx's theory of history and his vision of class struggle.

Regime Decay

Even before the collapse of the Soviet bloc, it had become obvious that there was no inevitable march toward revolution and that, in fact, successful revolutions have been rather rare. Skocpol argues that neither the repression of the masses nor the skills of revolutionary leadership alone can bring success. These factors may be necessary, but they are not sufficient. Rather, true revolutions succeed only when international pressures such as war or economic weakness undermine the state. The modernization of Britain and other European powers, she contends, created severe military and economic pressures on competing countries within and outside Europe. Some of those states, such as royalist France, Czarist Russia, and imperial China, were unable to adjust to these challenges and hence fell victim to revolutionary forces.[9]

In Russia, excessive military entanglements, foreign indebtedness, and a disastrous involvement in the First World War undermined the Czarist state. Successive military defeats in two wars—first by the Japanese (1905) and then by the Germans (1917)—helped undermine the Czarist regime. Similarly, China's Manchu dynasty, having been fatally weakened by European and Japanese imperialism, was toppled by Nationalist forces in 1911, who, in turn, were overthrown by the communists nearly forty years later. Elsewhere, stronger regimes were able to withstand comparable challenges, but the Russian and Chinese states were too weak. Ultimately, disgruntled soldiers, workers, and peasants, led by "marginal elites" (university students and middle-class professionals alienated from the system), toppled the old orders.[10] Ironically, just as military competition undermined the Czarist government and set the stage for the Russian Revolution, some seventy years later, the Soviet—American arms race undercut the Soviet Union's financial health and contributed to the system's collapse.

Thus, Skocpol and others have argued that the most significant factor contributing to a successful revolutionary struggle is not the revolutionary leadership's strategy, tactics, or zeal, but rather the internal rot of the decaying old order. For example, Japan's invasion of China prior to the First World War undercut the legitimacy of the Kuomintang government. The Japanese occupation demonstrated that the Nationalist regime was too corrupt and incompetent to resist a foreign threat, while the communist People's Liberation Army (PLA) was far more effective. When the Chinese revolutionary war resumed after the Second World War, many of the areas in which the communists won major military victories were the same ones in which they had organized mass resistance against the Japanese.

In fact, military defeats have frequently delegitimized the existing political order, setting the stage for subsequent revolutions. Thus, the destruction of the Ottoman Empire in the First World War and the Japanese capture of British, French, and Dutch colonies in Asia during the Second World War (including Myanmar, Vietnam, and Indonesia) all undermined the imperial or colonial governments' legitimacy and led, respectively, to Ataturk's military revolt in Turkey, the communist revolution in Vietnam, and various independence movements in South and Southeast Asia. Similarly, Egypt's defeat by Israel (1948–49) helped precipitate Nasser's overthrow of the Egyptian monarchy (1952).

War has the additional effect of disrupting peasant life, forcing many to seek the new social structure and physical protection offered by the revolutionary forces. For example, in accounts of life in rural China during its civil war and the Japanese invasion, "one is struck by the number of peasants . . . who had their routines upset through the [war-related] death of their kin before they joined revolutionary organizations."[11]

Of course, there are other factors besides military defeats that may undermine governments. In Cuba and Nicaragua, prolonged dictatorships became obscenely corrupt. Fulgencio Batista rose from the rank of army sergeant in 1933 to become Cuba's dominant political actor over the next two decades. During that period, corruption infested all ranks of government. Batista's links to the American mafia helped turn Havana into a playground for affluent foreign tourists seeking gambling and prostitution. In Nicaragua, members of the ruling Somoza Dynasty commandeered a huge share of the economy for decades. The National Guard—virtually the Somozas' personal army—enriched themselves as well. When an earthquake leveled the nation's capital (Managua) in 1972, aid meant for reconstruction was diverted into the dictator's pockets.

A further element undermining the legitimacy of both the Cuban and the Nicaraguan dictatorships was their subservience to the United States. Because the US military had occupied both countries for years early in the twentieth century, this was a particularly sensitive issue. The occupying American Marines had installed Anastasio Somoza Sr., the dynasty's founder, as the first commander of the country's hated National Guard, a position that he subsequently used to seize the presidency. In both Cuba and Nicaragua, the combination of rampant corruption and injuries to nationalist self-respect united people across class lines against the government—from peasants to students to business owners.

Revolutionary opportunities may also arise when the economy deteriorates, standards of living decline, and the government is unable to meet long-standing economic responsibilities to its people. For example, runaway inflation undermined support for China's Kuomintang government. Declining living standards helped spark the Kenyan rebellion against British colonialism. Thus, maintains Charles Tilly, one cause of revolution is "the sudden failure of government to meet specific obligations which members of the subject population regarded as well established and crucial to their welfare."[12]

While Skocpol, Tilly, and others emphasize the decay of state authority at the national level, revolutions can also arise from the breakdown of authority at the local level. We observed earlier (chapter 8) that a web of patron—client relationships linking peasants to their landlords and other local power brokers helps maintain stability in the countryside. Peasants will tolerate considerable injustice if their landlords and the village political bosses compensate by providing them with needed benefits, such as secure access to land, credit, and protection from harassment by the police. However, if the expansion of market forces makes rural patrons unwilling or unable to continue providing benefits that peasants had come to expect, their authority will likely break down. At this point, the state may try to replace the traditional patrons by providing social services such as credit, technical assistance, schools, and clinics. If, however, government authorities fail to satisfy the peasants' needs as well, the rural poor may turn to revolutionary groups as their new patrons and protectors.

Challenges from Below

While revolutionary movements generally succeed only against discredited or weakened governments, they must also mount a well-organized and politically coherent challenge from below. Without this, the old regime, weak though it may be, will either cling to power or collapse into disorder or anarchy.

Tilly contends that three things must happen before a revolutionary movement can succeed: first, the revolutionaries must establish themselves as an "alternative sovereignty"; that is, the rebel leadership must convince its would-be supporters that it can function as a viable alternate government. Second, a sizable portion of the population must support that revolutionary option. Finally, the established government must be incapable of suppressing the revolutionary opposition.[13] There are a number of well-known cases in which revolutionaries successfully established alternative sovereignties. During the Chinese Revolution, the PLA (the Communist Party's military arm) controlled "liberated zones" in which the communists distributed land to the peasants, organized military and political support, and demonstrated their ability to govern. The same was true of South Vietnam's National Liberation Front (Viet Cong).

But, even after understanding these broad preconditions for successful revolutionary activity, we still must ask what causes a revolution to break out in a particular country, at a particular time and not in others. Huntington argued that the probability of a successful insurrection is determined by the balance of power between the capabilities of government political institutions, on the one hand, and the level of anti-government political and social mobilization, on the other. Most revolutions, he notes, do not take place in either highly traditional or modern societies. Rather, they are most likely to erupt in modernizing countries—those in transition from traditional culture to modernity. As greater urbanization, increased education and literacy, and expanded mass-media communication stimulate widespread political mobilization, civil society (the network of organized groups independent of government control) increases its demands on the political system. Unless the governing order can establish institutions capable of accommodating some of these demands in a timely manner, the system will become overloaded and hence more unstable.

James Davies shifts our attention from the broad historical—social forces that make revolution possible to the question of why particular individuals choose to join a revolt or a revolution. He asserts that, contrary to what we might expect, people rarely rebel when they are experiencing prolonged or permanent suffering. "Far from making people revolutionaries, enduring poverty makes for concern with one's solitary self or solitary family, at best, resignation or mute despair at worst."[14] To uncover the source of political upheavals, Davies combines economic and psychological explanations. Unlike

Marx, Skocpol, or Tilly, his analysis lumps together mass revolutions with local uprisings and military "revolutions from above." Drawing upon historical data ranging from the Dorr Rebellion (an 1842 uprising in Rhode Island) to the Egyptian military revolution of 1952, he concludes that each upheaval took place after a period of sustained economic growth that was followed by a sharp downturn. A diagram of that growth and subsequent downturn produces what Davies calls the **J-curve**.* As a country's economy grows for a period of time, he suggests, people's expectations rise correspondingly (parallel to the long side of the "J"). However, these expectations continue to rise even after the economy experiences a downturn. What emerges is "an intolerable gap between what people want and what they get."[15] Davies argues that this economic J-curve also explains the American and French Revolutions, the American Civil War, the rise of German Nazism, student unrest in the United States during the 1960s, and the African American civil rights movement.

Using only twentieth-century data from seventeen less developed countries, Raymond Tanter and Manus Midlarsky confirmed Davies's thesis in Asia and the Middle East (long before the recent uprisings) but not in Latin America. Interestingly, their Asian and Middle Eastern cases also indicated that the higher the rate of economic growth prior to a downturn and the sharper the slide immediately preceding the outbreak of unrest, the longer and more violent the upheaval will be.[16]

Davies's theory is one of the most influential psychologically based explanations of revolutionary behavior. There is, however, an important limitation to his findings. He based his conclusions exclusively on data from countries that have experienced revolts or revolutions. This raises the question of whether there are countries that experienced a J-curve of growth and decline in their economies, yet did not have social upheavals. In fact, Davies admits that there are. For example, he notes the absence of mass unrest in the United States during the Great Depression, a devastating economic downturn. The same holds true for many Latin American countries that enjoyed strong economic growth in the 1960s and 1970s followed by a precipitous decline in the 1980s. Argentina had a comparable cycle from 1990 to 1998. Thus, as Davies concedes, his theory identifies common but not sufficient conditions for unrest. Although a J-curve often leads to revolution, it does not necessarily do so.

Ted Gurr has also developed a psychological model examining the gap between expectations and reality. Like Davies, he examines various types of civil violence, not just revolution. Gurr argues that "the necessary precondition for violent civil conflict is relative deprivation defined as [the]

---

* More precisely, the economic pattern he described can be drawn as the letter "J" tipped over, with the long side representing the period of economic growth and the rounded part depicting the downturn.

actors' perception of the discrepancy between their value expectations [i.e., what people believe they deserve] and value capabilities . . . conditions that determine people's perceived chances of getting . . . what they . . . expect to attain."[17] In other words, **relative deprivation** is the gap between what people want or expect from life and what they actually get.

Unlike Davies's theory, however, Gurr's notion of relative deprivation is not solely economic. Thus, he posits that there is also a high probability of civil unrest if many people are deprived of an important, noneconomic benefit that they have come to expect, or if they have suffered a blow to their status and their preferred social order. In Iran, for example, many of the reforms introduced by the Shah violated the "preferred social order" of the nation's Shi'ite population. This, as we have seen, helped set the stage for the Islamist Revolution.

Finally, Gurr maintains that the type of civil violence that a country experiences will depend on which segments of society are experiencing relative deprivation. If the poor alone feel frustrated, there may be political "turmoil" (spontaneous, disorganized violence) but not a revolution. Only if important elements of the middle class and the elite—more educated and politically experienced individuals who can provide political leadership—also suffer relative deprivation can there be revolutionary upheaval. This was certainly true in the recent upheavals in the Arab World, especially in Egypt, where young professionals and students often took the lead.

Explaining the "Arab Spring"

The "Arab Spring" revolts of 2011 provide some of the most important cases of revolutionary turmoil in recent years. The spark came in Tunisia, and specifically with a confrontation on December 17, 2010, between a female police officer and a 26-year-old street vendor, Mohamed Bouazizi. Angered at his treatment by authorities, Bouazizi set himself alight in protest, an act which quickly sparked anti-government riots in the small provincial town of Sidi Bouzid where he lived.

Many of the initial protesters were unemployed and underemployed youth, and the area itself suffered from a stagnant local economy. Improved education and modern mass media exposure had contributed to hope among the young for a better society and greater political freedom. On the other hand, the labor force provided few suitable jobs, and Tunisia had known only authoritarian rule since independence.* The protesters

---

*One contributing factor to economic discontent was the so-called youth bulge which occurs when developing countries undergo **demographic transition**. Death rates decline (due better health care and higher income), while birth rates fall more slowly (in part, for cultural reasons). This leads to a temporary period of higher population growth, and—for a period—a larger group of young people entering the labor market. Eventually, as in most industrialized countries, the population again stabilizes with lower birth and death rates.

demanded improved economic opportunities, and end to corruption, and political reform. Interestingly, Tunisia had enjoyed better than average economic growth in the preceding years, and the degree of corruption was lower than in most countries in the Middle East and Africa. However, as Gurr suggested, perception matters, and what was important was the apparent gap between the protesters' condition and what they felt the Tunisian government ought to be able to achieve.

Subsequently, the protests spread to the capital, Tunis. While social media and other developments in information and communication technology played a role in this, Merouan Mekouar has persuasively argued that even great impetus was provided when trade unions, and middle class and professional groups, joined the uprising—thus signaling that it was a society-wide revolt and not simply local rioting by angry young men.[18] Of equal importance, the Tunisian military refused orders to use major force against the protesters (exactly the sort of failure of state power that Skocpol points to). On January 14, 2011, President Zine El Abidine Ben Ali had little choice but to flee the country.

Tunisia held national elections later that year and has today made an apparently successful transition to democracy—albeit one that still grapples with serious economic challenges and corruption. The successful overthrow of a dictator in one part of the Arab World also emboldened protesters in other countries, with Arabic television coverage (notably by the Qatari-owned station al-Jazeera) and digital media helping to spread the word. In Egypt, the dictatorship of President Hosni Mubarak was overthrown in February 2011, after a similar popular uprising. Other dictators were toppled in Libya (Muammar Qaddafi) and Yemen (Ali Abdullah Saleh).

However, the Arab Spring also highlighted how difficult revolutions are to undertake, and the difficulties of subsequent transition to a more democratic political regime. In Bahrain, the ruling monarchy successfully suppressed peaceful protests with the aid of its conservative Gulf allies. In Syria, bloody repression of protesters by the regime of President Bashar al-Asad soon escalated to brutal, extended civil war. Today, the regime is winning that war (with the help of its Iranian and Russian allies), but at a horrific cost. As we have seen in chapter 5, the civil war also helped spur Islamist radicalization among the Syrian opposition and contributed to the emergence of Daesh. In Egypt, successful democratic elections brought the (Islamist) Muslim Brotherhood to power—only for the newly elected president, Mohamed Morsi, to be toppled in a military coup (an aspect we will return to in chapter 10). The military-backed regime of President Abdel Fateh el-Sisi has now returned Egypt to authoritarian rule. Thousands of Islamists have been imprisoned and tortured. Not surprisingly, some have been alienated and angered by the failed democratic experience and have joined more radical Islamist groups. In Libya and Yemen, transitional processes also failed, resulting in collapse into more violent civil conflict.

Causes of Revolution: A Summary

None of these theories of revolution offers a single "correct" explanation. For one thing, they often focus on different aspects of the question. For example, while Gurr and Davies ask why individuals join revolts or revolutionary movements, Skocpol focuses on the international economic and military factors that have weakened the state prior to successful revolutionary insurrections.

Clearly, revolutions are never inevitable and, in fact, successful revolutions are rare. While the causes of unrest may lie in relative deprivation or the regime's loss of legitimacy, the ultimate success or failure of revolutionary movements also depends on the relative military and political capabilities of the contending forces. Only by comparing the political-military strength of those who rebel with the state's capacity to defend itself can we understand why some revolutionary movements succeed, while others fail.

As we have seen, revolutions often occur after a country has been defeated or badly weakened in war (Russia, China, and Turkey) or after its government has been ousted temporarily (as several colonial powers were in the Second World War). They may also take place when a government is particularly corrupt (Cuba and Egypt) or subservient to foreign powers (Cuba, Mexico, and Iran). In all of these cases, the incumbent regime lost its legitimacy. Thus, Russia's Czarist regime and China's Kuomintang government both fell when they proved incapable of defending their people's sovereignty against foreign armies. Similarly, Cuban president Fulgencio Batista lost his authority when he turned Havana into "the brothel of the Caribbean" in league with the American mafia. And, the Shah of Iran lost his legitimacy after his modernization program offended Iran's Muslim clerics. British, French, and Dutch colonial rule in Asia was secure as long as the indigenous populations believed that Europeans were too powerful to topple and perhaps better equipped to govern. When the Japanese ousted the colonial governments of Indonesia, Malaysia, Myanmar and Vietnam, they demonstrated that Asian armed forces could defeat the European powers. Once the Europeans lost their aura of invincibility, they were unable to reestablish sustained colonial rule after the Second World War.

Finally, the very authoritarianism of many governments often ultimately undermines them. Cuba's Batista, the Shah of Iran, and Nicaragua's Anastasio Somoza Jr. illustrate this point. Because their governments had never been legitimized through free and honest elections, they could not convincingly claim to represent the people. Ignoring this problem during the Cold War, the United States supported authoritarian governments in countries such as El Salvador, Chile, Zaire (Congo), South Korea, Iran, and Pakistan. Responding to criticisms by human rights groups, Washington argued that, whatever their faults, these repressive governments were the last remaining firewalls against communist subversion and the rise of totalitarianism. In truth, however, a democratic government offers the best inoculation against revolution. Indeed, no consolidated democracy has ever been toppled by a revolution.*

LEVELS OF POPULAR SUPPORT

Che Guevara, the leading military strategist of the Cuban Revolution, once observed that those who undertake revolutions either win or die. Though perhaps overstating his point, Guevara's remark highlights the tremendous risk revolutionary fighters take, be they poor peasants or radicalized university students. Rebels almost always face superior firepower and a range of formidable state institutions (including the police and the military). Not surprisingly, most of the time the insurgents lose. One study counted twenty-eight guerrilla movements in Latin America from 1956 to 1990. Of this total, only two succeeded (Cuba's July 26 movement and Nicaragua's Sandinistas). Asia and Africa are also littered with the corpses of failed revolutionaries. Even victorious revolutions, such as Vietnam's and China's, leave behind vast numbers of fallen rebel fighters and supporters. Those who survive often return home to devastated villages and suffering families. Not surprisingly, then, peasants, workers, students, and professionals do not take lightly the decision to join a revolutionary force.

What portion of the population must support a revolution if it is to succeed? What types of people are most likely to join the movement? The answer to the first question is uncertain. There is no fixed or knowable percentage of the population that must support an insurrection in order for it to triumph. Following the Second World War, a majority of Ukrainians are believed to have supported a separatist movement fighting to end Russian control, yet this uprising was crushed by the powerful Soviet army. On the other hand, insurgencies elsewhere have succeeded with the active support of less than 20 percent of the civilian population.

Any evaluation of popular sentiment during a revolutionary upheaval needs to identify at least five different groups. First, there are those who strongly support the incumbent government and believe that their own fates are linked to the regime's survival. Government officials, military officers, landowners, and businesspeople with close links to the prerevolutionary state normally fall in this category. It may also include ethnic groups tied to the regime (such as the Hmong people of Laos), people ideologically

---

*The only case of a communist regime replacing a democratic government is in postwar Czechoslovakia. But the new government took power through a Russian-supported coup, not through revolution.

committed to the political system and an assortment of others with a stake in preserving the status quo.

A second group in society also supports the government, but more conditionally. For example, during the 1960s, most Venezuelans supported the government's battle against Marxist guerrillas. Even though many of them shared the guerrillas' objections to the country's severe inequality and poverty, they were repulsed by the rebels' use of violence and their refusal to work within the country's new democratic framework. Because the government's public support was broad but thin (i.e., many Venezuelans were conditional supporters), it could easily have lost its advantage had it used the repressive antiguerrilla tactics so widely employed elsewhere in Latin America. By showing moderation, the government held its ground.

A third, often critical, segment of the population supports neither the revolutionaries nor the government. Its members are generally alienated and probably dislike both sides. In the 1980s and 1990s, many Peruvian Indian villages were victimized by the Sendero Luminoso (Shining Path) guerrillas, an extremely fanatical and brutal revolutionary movement. At the same time, these peasants were also often brutalized by the Peruvian army, which flagrantly violated their human rights. Not surprisingly, most peasants feared and hated both sides. Caught in the middle, for their own preservation they avoided taking sides, though some did join government-supported defense militias.

A fourth group—drawn primarily from the peasantry, workers, the urban poor, and alienated members of the middle class who sympathize with the revolutionary cause—occasionally lends support to the insurgents but does not actually join them. For example, sympathetic peasants in China, Cuba, and Vietnam offered intelligence information, food, and shelter to rebel guerrillas. In countries such as China and El Salvador, where the guerrillas controlled "liberated zones" for long periods of time, these support networks were very extensive. In other countries where the revolution was fought primarily through urban street protests rather than guerrilla war (Iran) and in revolutions with important urban and rural components (Mexico, Nicaragua), revolutionaries also depended on the sympathy and occasional support of the urban poor, workers, and parts of the middle class.

Finally, there is a relatively small portion of the population that fully involves itself in the revolutionary struggle. In Cuba and Mexico, for example, committed students, teachers, and professionals assumed leadership positions. In those countries, as well as in China, Vietnam, and El Salvador, many peasants became the revolution's foot soldiers. Given the enormous risks involved for the participants and their families, it is not surprising that only a small portion of the people took up arms. Some peasants joined out of desperation, because the armed forces had destroyed their farms or villages or because they feared being drafted into an army that they despised. Others were attracted to the revolutionaries' promises of a more just social order.

One can only guess the proportion of a country's population in each of these five groups at a particular point in time. Public opinion surveys in countries experiencing revolutionary upheavals are unlikely to elicit honest responses. But we do know that if they are to succeed, revolutionary movements must attract a core of firmly committed activists willing to risk their lives for the cause, as well as a larger circle of sympathizers. How large their numbers must be depends on the extent of government decay and loss of legitimacy. It also depends on how well-armed and committed government troops are, how effectively those troops fight, and how much foreign support they have. Thus, for example, Fidel Castro's small rural force of only a few hundred troops (supported by a comparable number of urban guerrillas) defeated Batista's much larger but dispirited army. On the other hand, El Salvador's FMLN (the Farabundo Martí National Liberation Front)—a far larger and better-equipped guerrilla army than Castro's—could not unseat a government that was bolstered by extensive American economic and military aid. Yet even the United States' commitment of massive military assistance could not save the South Vietnamese government from the Viet Cong (communist) guerrillas and their North Vietnamese allies.

The people in the second category (mild government supporters) and the third (neutrals) are equally important targets for any revolutionary movement. In developing countries that have substantial urban populations, governments can maintain power in the face of considerable peasant unrest and rural guerrilla activity as long as they control the cities and retain the support of the urban middle class, particularly civil servants, businesspeople, and professionals. These middle-class groups are not normally radical, but they can become disenchanted with particularly corrupt, repressive, or ineffectual regimes. In Iran, the tide turned in favor of the revolutionary mullahs when Tehran's bazaar shopkeepers lost confidence in the Shah's government. In Tunisia, as we have seen, the uprising against the Ben Ali dictatorship reached a turning point when trade unions and middle class professionals joined the ranks of the protesters.

In short, if a revolutionary movement is to gain power, there must be widespread alienation from the government, a disaffection that reaches beyond the ranks of the poor and the oppressed to the heart of the middle class and the business community. It is neither likely nor necessary for a large portion of those groups to actively support the insurrection. For the revolution to succeed, it is only essential that some of them, including a highly committed core, do so, while many others simply cease supporting the government.

PEASANTS AS REVOLUTIONARIES

Let us now turn our attention to the ranks of committed revolutionary supporters, particularly the last group, revolutionary activists. Most revolutions in less developed countries have been fought primarily by peasants. The Chinese Red Army and the Viet Cong, for example, consisted overwhelmingly of the rural poor. Indeed, almost all African and Asian revolutionary movements have been overwhelmingly rural in character (the recent urban uprisings in the Arab World being obvious exceptions). And even in Latin America's revolutions, where the urban populations often played key roles, peasants were also very important actors. Consequently, it is important to ask, "What factors induce some peasants to risk joining a revolution, and what types of peasants join?"

Why Peasants Rebel

In our analysis of rural society (chapter 8), we noted that traditional peasant culture tends to be rather conservative. Because early economic modernization frequently affects them negatively, they have good reason to cling to tradition. But the intrusion of market forces into their communities sometimes so unsettles their world that it radicalizes them as they struggle to protect what they have. For one thing, increasing numbers of subsistence farmers (peasants producing primarily for their family's consumption) in a modernizing economy are induced or pressured to enter the commercial market for the first time. Once involved in commercial agriculture, however, they must deal with fluctuations in the price of their crops, including volatile shifts that they are ill-equipped to handle.

At the same time, rural landlords, whose precapitalist exploitation of local peasants had been constrained by their neofeudal obligations, now viewed their tenants merely as factors of production in the new market economy. In Latin America, many landlords, who had previously funded their peons' fiestas or lent them money when they were in special need, concluded that such expenditures were no longer financially prudent in the more competitive market environment. Other landlords entering the commercial market decided to mechanize production and evict tenant farmers from their lands. For all of these reasons, rural society's transition from neofeudal to capitalist production precipitated many of the twentieth-century revolutions.[19] James Scott notes that the pain peasants suffered during that transformation was not merely economic or physical but also psychological.

To be sure, the precapitalist rural order had its share of grave injustices, but these inequities were somewhat mitigated by a web of reciprocal obligations between landlords and peasants and among peasants. It is the collapse of this "moral economy," Scott argues, that drives many peasants to revolution.[20] Similarly, as noted in chapter 8, Eric Wolf insists that in countries as disparate as Cuba, Mexico, Algeria, Vietnam, and China, most peasant participants in revolutionary movements were not trying to create a new socialist order. Rather, they were seeking to restore the security of their old way of life.

Which Peasants Rebel

Even in a single country or region, peasants are not a homogeneous mass. Some of them own comparatively large plots of land and employ other peasants to work on their farms with them. Others are landless or own extremely small plots. And still others work as wage laborers on large estates or rent parcels of land from the landlord, paying their rent in cash, labor, or sharecropping.* Each group has distinct political and economic needs.

The peasants most threatened by the economic change in the country-side are the ones most likely to join local revolts or broader revolutionary movements. Analyzing data collected from seventy developing nations over a twenty-year period, Jeffrey M. Paige found that the peasant groups most liable to join insurgencies were wage laborers and sharecroppers who worked for landlords.[21] Not only are these peasants particularly vulnerable to changing economic conditions, but their landlords are also less likely to grant them financial concessions because they depend exclusively on their farmland for their incomes. Research on Latin American guerrilla movements reveals that squatters (poor farmers who illegally occupy land) and other peasants who face eviction from the land that they cultivate are also more prone to rebel.[22]

But even peasants with more secure access to the land may feel threatened by declining crop prices. For example, in Peru's Ayacucho province, the birthplace of the Shining Path guerrilla movement, peasants suffered from declining terms of trade for two decades; that is, the cost of the goods they consumed had been rising faster than the price of the crops that they sold. Caught in an ongoing financial squeeze, they felt increasingly insecure and hence became more receptive to the Shining Path's appeals.[23]

Peasants who are more prone to support revolutions, then, have one element in common—they are threatened by the prospect of losing their land and/or their livelihood. Conversely, the most conservative peasants are those with secure titles to their landholdings and relatively stable prices for their crops. It is for this reason that many analysts maintain that the best protection against rural revolution is an agrarian reform program that

---

*Sharecroppers are tenant farmers who pay their rent by giving the landlord a portion of their crop.

distributes land and offers the recipients secure titles and support services (see chapter 8).

Peasant insurrections are also more likely to arise in areas that have traditions of rebellion. For example, the revolutionary forces in China, Vietnam, Cuba, Mexico, and Nicaragua all received their greatest support in regions that had long records of peasant resistance, what one author calls a "rebellious culture."[24] Fidel Castro's home province of Oriente, known as "the cradle of the Cuban Revolution," had a history of unrest dating back to nineteenth-century slave revolts against their owners and against Spanish colonial rule. China's Hunan Province (Mao Zedong's home) also had a rebellious tradition. Similarly, some revolutionary movements take root in areas with a long record of lawlessness and hostility toward the legal authorities. For example, Mexican revolutionary leader Pancho Villa operated in a region known for cattle rustling and other forms of social banditry. Villa himself was a bandit-turned-revolutionary. And Castro's guerrillas based themselves in the Sierra Maestra Mountains, a region with a history of smuggling, marijuana production, and banditry.

Daesh is perhaps the only revolutionary movement in which not only the leadership but also a large portion of the rank-and-file rebels come from educated, middle-class backgrounds, particularly among the unusually high proportion of foreign fighters in its ranks.* However, the temporary success of the movement in Syria and Iraq was also made possible by passive acceptance among segments of the local Sunni population, who felt little affinity to the (brutal) Syrian regime or (Shiite-dominated) Iraqi government in Baghdad. Daesh's behavior ultimately alienated this passive constituency too, however—helping to accelerate its military defeat.

REVOLUTIONARY LEADERSHIP

Although peasants furnish the foot soldiers for revolutions, they rarely hold the highest leadership posts. They may stage spontaneous uprisings or even more extensive revolts on their own, but they usually lack the organizational and political skills needed to lead a national revolution. Consequently, the top revolutionary leaders and many at the middle level are typically people with more education and greater political experience. To be sure, there are exceptions. Mexico's Emiliano Zapata was a horse trainer from a peasant family who only became literate as an adult. Pancho Villa was also of humble origins. More recently, peasants held important leadership posts in the Colombian Revolutionary Armed Forces of Colombia (FARC) guerrillas. Ultimately, however, their political inexperience

---

*Perhaps 30 percent of Daesh forces are foreign volunteers, many of them university educated.

and lack of external contacts proved costly. Thus, Villa and Zapata jointly conquered Mexico City, the nation's capital, but then left it because neither man felt ready to run the country.

More typically, then, the top revolutionary leadership comes from middle-class or even upper-class origins. Trained as a librarian, China's Mao Zedong was the son of a grain merchant. In Vietnam, Ho Chi Minh, the son of a rural schoolteacher, practiced a number of professions, including photography, while living in Paris, where he became an activist in the French Communist Party. Fidel Castro received a law degree at the University of Havana, where he was a leader in student politics. His father, a Spanish immigrant, had started life in Cuba as a worker, but eventually became a well-to-do landowner. Castro's comrade, Che Guevara, was a doctor whose parents, though not rich, were of aristocratic origin. Similarly, most of the nine comandantes who directed the Sandinista Revolution in Nicaragua came from solid middle- or upper-class families and were well educated. For example, President Daniel Ortega and his brother, Defense Minister Humberto Ortega, were the sons of an accountant-businessman. Luis Carrión, the son of a millionaire, had attended an American prep school. Only one comandante, Henry Ruiz, came from a poor urban family, and none were of peasant origin.[25] Finally, a Vietnamese Communist Party study of nearly two thousand party activists (conducted after the Second World War, at the start of their long revolutionary struggle) revealed that 74 percent of them were either intellectuals or were from bourgeois (middle-class or capitalist) families, while only 7 percent were the children of workers, and 19 percent came from peasant families.[26] These are remarkable statistics for a party trying to speak for the country's peasantry and working class.

Not surprisingly, a larger number of lower-ranking revolutionary leaders are of peasant or working-class backgrounds. Compared to Latin America, more of the rural poor have held leadership positions in Asia's revolutionary governments (including China, Vietnam, and Cambodia), in countries where peasants accounted for most of the national population. During their two-decade revolutionary struggle and after taking power, the CCP and its Red Army offered peasant activists unprecedented opportunities for upward mobility. From its early days, the party gave peasants and children of peasants—heretofore at the bottom of the social ladder—preference for admission to its ranks. And as recently as 1985, decades after it took power, one-third of all CCP members were peasants (some 25 percent of whom were illiterate).* Similarly, many of the lower- and middle-level

---

*Although the percentages of peasants and illiterates in the party were still well below their corresponding shares of the general population, they were higher than in most less developed countries. Since the late 1980s, however, the educational level and professional training of mid-level party leaders have risen, meaning that they are more skilled but somewhat less representative of the population.

guerrilla leaders in El Salvador and Peru were of peasant origin, although they often were upwardly mobile children of peasants, who themselves had become teachers, health workers, and the like.

The educational and social gaps separating aspiring revolutionary leaders from the peasant rank and file can be considerable problems unless those leaders have a firm understanding of the local culture. Although Mao Zedong was an urban professional, his rural upbringing had given him an understanding of village life. Fidel Castro was no peasant, but his childhood on his father's farm had familiarized him with the region's rural poor.

On the other hand, the rural poor often spurn aspiring guerrilla organizers who come to them with little understanding of their problems. Hence, they usually reject the overtures of radical university students from other regions of the country, other countries, or other ethnic backgrounds. Given their history of exploitation, peasants tend to be understandably wary of outsiders. The wider the language, cultural, or racial gaps between would-be revolutionary leaders and the local villagers, and the greater the peasants' prior suspicion of outsiders, the harder it is for aspiring organizers to break through that wall of distrust. In Cuba, where racial and ethnic divisions were relatively less important, the peasants of the Sierra Maestra Mountains accepted Che Guevara, an urban middle-class Argentinean. When he later ventured to Bolivia to spread the revolution, he was ill-prepared for the Indian peasants' deep mistrust of white outsiders such as himself. There, an antiguerrilla unit of the Bolivian armed forces captured and killed him, aided by local villagers who saw no reason to risk their safety for an outside agitator. Similarly, Hector Béjar, a failed Peruvian guerrilla leader, later wrote candidly in his memoirs about how he—a coastal, white journalist and poet—was unable to gain the trust of the highland Indians whom he had hoped to lead.[27]

REVOLUTIONARIES IN POWER

While many comparative studies have examined the causes of revolution, there is less cross-national research on the policies revolutionary regimes implement once in office. Perhaps guerrilla fighters in the hills have inspired more interest and romanticism (or fear) than have revolutionary bureaucrats in the corridors of power. The record suggests that revolutions in developing nations commonly have accomplished more than their detractors admit but less than their supporters claim.

A major goal of many revolutionary governments (especially Marxist ones) has been to achieve greater socioeconomic equality. This quest usually begins with the struggle for power itself, when revolutionary leaders use egalitarian appeals to garner support from downtrodden peasants and workers. Recognizing the critical importance of this support, Mao Zedong wrote that the peasantry is to the guerrilla army what water is to a fish.

To win their loyalty, the Red Army treated peasants whom they encountered with greater respect than other Chinese military forces or governments had. Similarly, in Cuba, "the army's brutal treatment of the peasants" contrasted with "Castro's policy of paying for the food purchased from the peasants . . . and putting his [mostly urban] men to work in the . . . fields."[28]

Once in power, revolutionary governments have generally continued to emphasize economic and social equality. In addition to redistributing land and other economic resources, they may also introduce other egalitarian cultural reforms. Efforts at economic and social egalitarianism have been more limited in non-Marxist revolutions. Still, insurgencies such as Bolivia's and Mexico's have improved the social status of the rural poor, including that of the indigenous peoples.

As we have seen, revolutions open up new channels of upward social mobility for peasants and workers who previously had few such opportunities. To be sure, people of middle-class origins hold most of the government and party leadership positions. And ethnic minorities are also underrepresented at that level. For example, Cuba's Black and Mulatto populations and China's (non-Han) ethnic minorities have been severely underrepresented in their Communist Party politburos and government cabinets. But many revolutionary activists from humble backgrounds do hold political offices that they could never have attained under the old order. Consequently, revolutionary parties and associated mass organizations often give peasants and workers a greater sense of participation in the political system.

Finally, revolutions usually reduce economic inequality, though the degree of change varies from country to country. Agrarian reform programs in China, Vietnam, Bolivia, Cuba, Mexico, and Nicaragua redistributed land from the rural oligarchy to the peasantry. Many Marxist regimes have offered guaranteed employment, subsidized food and housing, state-sponsored medical care, and other measures that particularly benefit the poor. In countries such as Cuba, government wage policies have reduced prior income inequalities. On the other hand, however, in more moderate revolutions, such as Mexico's, the prerevolutionary concentration of income has continued or even worsened.

To be sure, inequalities persist even in radical revolutionary societies. For example, while many of them have reduced disparities between rural and urban living standards, significant gaps persist. Since China has applied free-market reforms to its economy, income inequality—which had declined substantially in the 1980s—has increased sharply. In fact, currently economic inequality (as measured by the Gini index) is greater in China than in the United States, India, Mexico, or any country in Europe. On the other hand, other communist countries in Asia—such as Vietnam and Laos—as well as many former communist nations—Mongolia, Eastern European countries, and many of the former republics of the Soviet Union—have relatively low-income inequality.

At the same time, a new form of inequality invariably emerges in revolutionary societies as newly entrenched party and government officials begin to appropriate special perquisites for themselves and their families. Many years ago, Milovan Djilas, a disillusioned former leader of Yugoslavia's communist government, complained about the rise of a "new class" in revolutionary regimes, a new elite of party officials who enjoy special privileges and a better standard of living.[29] Today in China, the foremost Communist Party leaders are well known for their lavish lifestyles, while the children of party cadre are despised for their arrogance and corruption. While the effect of this "new class" is not sufficient to substantially affect their nations' Gini indexes, it often demoralizes the public. Widespread government corruption (even technically legal corruption) is disheartening in any setting, but even more so in a population that fought a revolution in the name of equality.*

Another major revolutionary objective has been mass political mobilization. As Huntington notes, "A full-scale revolution involves the rapid and violent destruction of existing political institutions, the mobilization of new groups into politics, and the creation of new political institutions."[30] Thus, in China, Vietnam, Cuba, and Nicaragua, the revolutionary governments created incentives and pressures that induced a large portion of the population to join revolutionary support groups. At one time, close to 90 percent of Cuban adults belonged to their neighborhood Committees for the Defense of the Revolution. In the 1980s, substantial portions of the Nicaraguan population joined Sandinista Defense Committees.

At its best, mass political mobilization has increased the government's capacity to build the economy by mobilizing volunteer labor and spreading labor discipline. At times, revolutionary support groups have also helped combat sexism, racism, and crime. At their worst, however, these groups have been used as vigilantes against alleged counterrevolutionaries and as agents of thought control. At Cuban CDR meetings, government spokespersons familiarize the members with current government political positions, while citizens are allegedly imbued with greater revolutionary consciousness and are encouraged to volunteer for projects such as planting neighborhood gardens or conducting mass inoculations. But in Mao Zedong's China, mass mobilization often involved brutal political campaigns that called upon citizens to root out and punish alleged enemies of the revolution. Hundreds of thousands, perhaps more, were persecuted,

---

*The British essayist George Orwell (himself an active radical) foresaw this danger in his famed novel *Animal Farm* (1945). It notes that "all animals [who had carried out a successful revolution against the humans] are equal, but some animals are more equal."

jailed, or killed during the government's Anti-Rightist Campaign (1957) and its Cultural Revolution (1966–76).

Mass mobilization can be used either to activate citizens who support the revolution's goals or to isolate and persecute those who do not. Most revolutionary regimes are led by a dominant party, such as the CCP or the Mexican PRI (Institutionalized Party of the Revolution), which stands at the center of the mobilization process. Opposition parties are either prohibited or are only tolerated in a weakened condition. Among Marxist governments, only Nicaragua's Sandinistas allowed themselves to be voted out of office in 1990. Elsewhere, a number of non-Marxist revolutionary parties have lost favor over time. They may resort to fraud when faced with the prospect of losing control (as in Mexico until 2000), cancel elections that the opposition is expected to win (Algeria), or hand over the reins of power and become just another competing party (Bolivia and, most recently, Mexico).

In short, while revolutionary regimes often have broad popular support, as we have already noted, they are not democratic. Because they view themselves as the only legitimate voice of the people and the sole custodians of the general good, most radical regimes tend to regard opposition groups as enemies of the people who should be denied political space. The Sandinistas, a rare exception, allowed opposition parties and interest groups to function, though they were occasionally harassed. Although the major opposition newspaper, *La Prensa*, was periodically censored or briefly shut down, it continued to vigorously, and sometimes outrageously, attack the government right up to the time its publisher, Violeta Chamorro, was elected the nation's president. For the most part, however, even communist governments that have opened up their economies to free-market reforms (China and Vietnam) have maintained a repressive political structure that tightly limits opposition voices.

While members of the first generation of revolutionary leaders tend to be true believers in their movement's ideology, the next generation is frequently more corrupted by power. In China and Vietnam—where rapid economic growth and the expansion of the private sector have opened up new opportunities for corruption—bribing the right state official is often a necessity for doing business. Cubans, who generally had believed that their revolutionary leaders were more honest than their extremely corrupt predecessors, were shocked by the "Ochoa affair" (1989), which revealed that high-ranking military and security officers were involved in drug trafficking. Since the 1990s, more mundane government corruption has increased as a result of the frequent scarcities of consumer goods.[31] And, after the Sandinistas left office in 1990, disillusioned Nicaraguans learned that top party officials had kept for themselves some of the luxurious mansions that had been confiscated from the

Somoza regime.* It is not that these revolutionary regimes are necessarily more corrupt than other governments in developing nations; often they are less so. It is just that their supporters, some of whom may have made considerable sacrifices for the revolutionary cause, had expected more.

CONCLUSION: REVOLUTIONARY CHANGE AND DEMOCRACY

Revolutionary change was an important force in many less developed countries throughout the twentieth century. Its impact was probably greatest in Asia, where the Chinese Revolution transformed the lives of one-fifth of humanity and where revolutionary struggles in Vietnam, Laos, and Cambodia involved France and then the United States in major wars. Elsewhere in Asia, there were failed communist insurgencies in the Philippines and Malaysia and, most recently, a partially successful one in Nepal. Most of Africa's revolutions were wars of national liberation from European colonialism (Algeria, Angola, and Kenya, among others) or secessionist wars (including Biafra, Eritrea, and South Sudan). In some African nations, military rulers imposed revolutions from above—most notably in Ethiopia—usually with unfortunate results. Latin America experienced two Marxist revolutions (Cuba and Nicaragua), two non-Marxist insurrections (Bolivia and Mexico), and a number of unsuccessful revolutionary movements (including Colombia, El Salvador, Guatemala, and Peru). Both the revolutions and the failed insurgencies had spillover effects on neighboring countries. For example, the Cuban Revolution prompted a number of Latin American governments to initiate agrarian reform programs designed to avert "another Cuba." But it also intensified government repression in El Salvador and elsewhere.

However, in the past two decades, the appeal of classical revolutions, discussed earlier (those that fit the models of revolutionary theorists and analysts), particularly Marxist revolutions, seemed to have waned considerably. Indeed, today's world is a veritable graveyard of failed insurrections. The Soviet Union, once the fountainhead of Communism, collapsed. Communism is equally discredited throughout Eastern and Central Europe, where it held sway until recently. In Nicaragua, an American-backed counterrevolutionary war and the Sandinista regime's own errors undid many of the revolution's early social and economic gains and led to their defeat in the 1990 presidential election. Cuba's impressive achievements in education and health care were partially eroded in the 1990s after the collapse of the Soviet Union, previously a major source of economic assistance. Elsewhere in developing nations, other revolutionary governments performed far more poorly. Countries such as Angola, Cambodia, Ethiopia, and Mozambique

---

*Yet, in spite of that, in 2006, Sandinista leader Daniel Ortega was once again elected president. He was reelected in 2011 and 2016.

Supporters of the ruling Sandinista National Liberation Front (FSLN) celebrate the thirty-ninth anniversary of the Nicaraguan Revolution in July 2018. President Daniel Ortega and the FSLN also faced a series of major protests against government policy through the spring and summer of 2018—many of which were suppressed by force by police and progovernment paramilitaries. *Source*: Carlos Herrera/Picture-Alliance/dpa/AP Images.

suffered enormous losses of life and economic devastation, having achieved little or nothing in return.

Judging the accomplishment and failures of revolutionary change in countries such as China, Cuba, and Vietnam is not easy because evaluations are invariably influenced by the analysts' ideological orientations. Furthermore, even the most objective social scientist finds it difficult to isolate the effects of revolutionary policy from a host of other overlapping factors. For example, critics of the Chinese Revolution argue that the socioeconomic gains attained under Mao were achieved in spite of his radical policies, not because of them. They further insist that the country's rapid economic growth since the 1980s demonstrates the advantages of free-market reforms. On the other hand, other analysts maintain that China could never have achieved its market-based economic boom without the revolution's earlier advances in education.

In the same way, the Cuban Revolution's detractors contend that the country's progress in health care and education could have been achieved under a democratic system, noting that Costa Rica (one of the strongest democracies in the region) has made comparable gains in social welfare. Furthermore, they maintain that Cuba's strong record in those areas was possible only because of massive Soviet aid over a period of thirty years. Nevertheless, more sympathetic observers note that Cuba achieved its impressive educational and health gains in spite of an American trade embargo.*

Neither side can definitively prove its position because there are so many independent variables that make it difficult or impossible to establish causal relationships. In any event, while there may yet be future revolutions in the developing world, it is likely that the era of leftist revolutions is drawing to an end. The demise of Soviet and Central European Communism exposed more clearly the deficiencies of Marxist-Leninist regimes. So too have China's and Vietnam's introduction of free-market (capitalist) components into their economic systems.

With Communism seemingly discredited, even among some of its once-fervent followers, it is unlikely to find many adherents willing to risk their lives fighting for its ideals. Marxist ideology, once chic among intellectuals and political activists, has become far less fashionable. At the end of the 1980s, facing defeat by its mujahideen opponents, Afghanistan's then-ruling People's Democratic Party (a communist party beholden to Moscow at the time) renounced its Marxist ideology in a failed effort to maintain power. One of its leaders dismissed the party's long-standing communist position by claiming that it had adopted that ideology at "a time when Marxism-Leninism was quite in fashion in underdeveloped countries." In Angola, where the governing party made a similar ideological conversion, the president explained that continuing to support the Marxist-Leninist model "would be rowing against the tide [of capitalist democracy]."[32] Similar transformations have occurred within Nicaragua's Sandinista party and El Salvador's FMLN, both former revolutionary movements that subsequently transformed themselves into democratic socialist political parties. In his successful 2006 campaign to regain the presidency, Sandinista leader Daniel Ortega insisted that Jesus Christ, not Marx, was his first inspiration when he led the country's revolution nearly thirty years earlier. Modifying his earlier leftist views, he declared that "in this new context, to which we had to adjust, the market economy plays its role."

How many revolutionary upheavals will take place in the coming years is hard to predict, and the answer may be partly an issue of semantics (i.e., how we choose to define a revolution). However, now that colonialism has essentially come to an end in Africa and Asia, there are few possibilities for wars of national liberation. The collapse of the Soviet bloc, the abandonment of Marxist economics in China and Vietnam, and Cuba's economic problems after it lost Soviet aid have all substantially diminished the appeal of revolutionary Marxism. But, the Arab Spring indicates that other types of revolutions will very likely erupt in some less developed countries.

---

*Prior to the revolution, the United States was Cuba's dominant trading partner.

> **Practice and Review Online at**
> http://textbooks.rowman.com/handelman9e

KEY TERMS

Arab Spring
bourgeoisie
demographic transition
J-curve
proletariat
relative deprivation
revolution

DISCUSSION QUESTIONS

1. What conditions or developments have convinced people in less developed countries to join revolutionary movements?
2. What is the likelihood of further revolutions in the twenty-first century? What kinds of revolutions are most likely to occur?
3. What sorts of challenges and political dynamics are faced by countries after a successful revolution?

NOTES

1. Chalmers Johnson, *Revolution and the Social System* (Stanford, CA: Hoover Institution, 1964).

2. Peter Calvert, "Revolution: The Politics of Violence," *Political Studies* 15, no. 1 (1967): 2; and *Revolution and Counter Revolution* (Minneapolis, MN: University of Minnesota Press, 1990).

3. Samuel P. Huntington, *Political Order in Changing Societies* (New Haven, CT: Yale University Press, 1968), 264.

4. Theda Skocpol, "France, Russia, China: A Structural Analysis of Social Revolutions," *Comparative Studies in Society and History* 18, no. 2 (1976): 176.

5. Theda Skocpol, *States and Social Revolutions: A Comparative Analysis of France, Russia and China* (Cambridge, MA: Cambridge University Press, 1979), 4.

6. Ellen Kay Trimberger, "A Theory of Elite Revolutions," *Studies in Comparative International Development* 7, no. 3 (1972): 191–207.

7. A. S. Cohan, *Theories of Revolution* (London: Thomas Nelson and Sons, 1975), 72.

8. Irving Zeitlin, *Marxism: A Re-examination* (Princeton, NJ: Princeton University Press, 1967), 142.

9. Skocpol, *States and Social Revolutions*.

10. Skocpol, "France, Russia, China."

11. Joel Migdal, *Peasants, Politics and Revolution* (Princeton, NJ: Princeton University Press, 1974), 252.

12. Charles Tilly, *From Mobilization to Revolution* (New York, NY: Addison-Wesley, 1978), 204–5.

13. Charles Tilly, "Does Modernization Breed Revolution?" *Comparative Politics* 5, no. 3 (April 1974): 425–47.

14. James C. Davies, "Toward a Theory of Revolution," *American Sociological Review* 27, no. 1 (February 1962): 7.

15. Ibid. For other theories on the causes of revolution, see James Davies, ed., *When Men Revolt and Why* (New York, NY: Free Press, 1971).

16. Raymond Tanter and Manus Midlarsky, "A Theory of Revolution," *Journal of Conflict Resolution* 11, no. 3 (1967): 264–80.

17. Ted Robert Gurr, "Psychological Factors in Civil Violence," *World Politics* 20, no. 2 (1967–68): 252–53; see also Ted Robert Gurr, *Why Men Rebel* (Princeton, NJ: Princeton University Press, 1970).

18. Merouan Mekouar, *Protest and Mass Mobilization: Authoritarian Collapse and Political Change in North Africa* (New York, NY: Routledge, 2016).

19. Eric R. Wolf, *Peasant Wars of the Twentieth Century* (New York, NY: Harper & Row, 1969).

20. James C. Scott, *The Moral Economy of the Peasant: Rebellion and Subsistence in Southeast Asia* (New Haven, CT: Yale University Press, 1976).

21. Jeffrey Paige, *Agrarian Revolution: Social Movements and Export Agriculture in the Underdeveloped World* (New York, NY: Free Press, 1975), chaps. 1–2.

22. Timothy P. Wickham-Crowley, *Guerrillas and Revolution in Latin America* (Princeton, NJ: Princeton University Press, 1992), chap. 6.

23. Cynthia McClintock, "Sendero Luminoso: Peru's Maoist Guerrillas," *Problems of Communism* 32, no. 5 (September–October 1983): 19–34.

24. Wickham-Crowley, *Guerrillas and Revolution*, 246–50; Wolf, *Peasant Wars*.

25. Dennis Gilbert, *Sandinistas: The Party and the Revolution* (New York, NY: B. Blackwell, 1988).

26. Thomas H. Green, *Comparative Revolutionary Movements* (Upper Saddle River, NJ: Prentice Hall, 1974), 18.

27. Hector Béjar, *Peru 1965: Notes on a Guerrilla Experience* (New York, NY: Monthly Review Press, 1970).

28. Sebastian Balfour, *Fidel Castro* (New York, NY: Longman, 1990), 49.

29. Milovan Djilas, *The New Class* (New York, NY: Praeger, 1957).

30. Huntington, *Political Order*, 266.

31. Sergio Díaz-Briquets and Jorge Pérez López, *Corruption in Cuba: Castro and Beyond* (Austin, TX: University of Texas Press, 2006).

32. Both quotations come from Forrest Colburn, *The Vogue of Revolution in Poor Countries* (Princeton, NJ: Princeton University Press, 1994), 89.

10

Soldiers and Politics

The Egyptian Army patrols the streets of Cairo shortly after overthrowing the democratically elected government of President Mohamed Morsi in July 2013. The following year, military rule was institutionalized through the stage-managed "election" of former field marshal Abdel Fattah el-Sisi. Such military regimes have become less common in the developing world in recent years. *Source*: ZUMA Press, Inc./Alamy Stock Photo.

FOR MANY YEARS, THE POLITICAL SYSTEMS of many developing countries were distinguished by a high degree of military interference, either through direct rule or as a dominant interest group. Unlike their counterparts in industrialized democracies, soldiers in the less developed countries often reject any dividing line between military and political activity. A pronouncement by the Indonesian armed forces prior to their assumption of power in the 1960s illustrates this perspective well:

> The army, which was born in the cauldron of the Revolution, has never been a dead instrument of the government, concerned exclusively with security matters. The army, as a fighter for freedom, cannot remain neutral toward the course of state policy, the quality of government, and the safety of the state.[1]

To be sure, there are countries such as India, Malaysia, Kenya, and Costa Rica where the armed forces have not ventured deeply into politics for decades. But, until the 1980s, such restraint was the exception rather than the rule. Indeed, until recently, the military's political involvement in most of the less developed countries was so pervasive that it was almost a defining characteristic of political underdevelopment.

One early study of military intervention revealed that the 59 developing nations scrutinized had had a total of 274 attempted **military coups*** between 1946 and 1970.[2] At the start of the 1980s, most countries in South America—most notably Argentina, Brazil, Chile, and Peru—were governed by the armed forces. During that decade, the armed forces also dominated politics in much of Africa, including Algeria, Ghana, Nigeria, and Sudan. From 1958 to 1984, there were more than sixty-two successful and sixty failed coup attempts in sub-Saharan Africa alone, affecting more than 80 percent of the nations in that region.[3] During an average year in the 1980s, military rulers governed 65 percent of Africa's population. Noting the scarcity of democratic elections in the region for most of that period, one observer argued that "coups had become the functional equivalent of elections, virtually the sole manner of ousting incumbent political leaders."[4] In all, sub-Saharan Africa had 80 coups and 108 failed coup attempts from 1956 to 2001, affecting 41 of the region's 48 countries. Three countries (including Nigeria, the continent's most populous nation) had six successful coups each.[5]

Military intervention was less prevalent in Asia, where India, Sri Lanka, and Malaysia, among others, were able to maintain elected civilian governments. Elsewhere in Asia, authoritarian civilian governments in Singapore,

---

*A military coup is a sudden and illegal removal of the incumbent government and the seizure of political power by the armed forces or a faction of the military, using violence or the threat of violence. Usually, the coup makers install themselves in power, but sometimes they install a new civilian government or call new elections.

Vietnam, and China also kept the armed forces in check. Still, military takeovers in some countries have continued into the twenty-first century.

Although several Middle Eastern countries have been controlled directly by the armed forces or by military strongmen, indirect military dominance has been more common. Former Egyptian president Hosni Mubarak (1981–2011) and Syria's longtime strongman Hafez al-Assad (1970–2000) entered politics as military men and then assumed civilian roles. Similarly, current Egyptian dictator Abdel Fattah el-Sisi hung up his military uniform to run for president in dubious elections in 2014. Elsewhere in the region, monarchs in Morocco, Jordan, Saudi Arabia, Kuwait, and the smaller Gulf States have successfully controlled their armed forces.

Change has been most dramatic in Latin America, where democratically elected governments have become the norm. In a remarkable turnabout, successful military coups have virtually ended in the region (excepting Ecuador, Haiti, and Honduras) since the end of the Cold War. In Asia, military regimes have ended in countries such as Indonesia, Bangladesh, and South Korea. But, since 2000, military rulers have returned to power in Thailand after previously having stepped down in favor of civilian governments. Finally, the military government in Myanmar (in power since 1962) has largely turned the reins of government to Aung San Sui Kyi and her National League for Democracy (NLD) party, which won a landslide victory in the 2015 parliamentary election. However, in most of these countries—especially Myanmar—the armed forces continue to hold veto power and exercises considerable power behind the scenes. Pakistan is a similar case. It experienced its last military coup in 1999, and it has had regular elections since 2002. However, the military and intelligence service remain a very powerful actor in national (and local) politics.

In Africa, where military governments predominated into the 1990s, important transitions to civilian government have occurred in such nations as Nigeria and Ghana, leaving few military governments in power (though periodic coups and attempted coups continue). Since 2001, the rate of new military coups in sub-Saharan Africa has declined to less than one per year. Still, while fewer African countries remain under formal military rule today, several armed forces leaders have resigned their positions and subsequently become presidents through rigged elections. Moreover, there have been a number of coup attempts (multiple times in some nations), which have destabilized their political systems. When soldiers in Mali overthrew the elected government in 2012, for example, it so weakened the state that both Islamist and ethnic Toureg rebels made major military advances—leading to intervention first by French and African forces, and later by United Nations peacekeepers, to stabilize the situation. New presidential elections were held in 2018, but the political situation remained highly uncertain.

While the number of military governments throughout the developing world has declined substantially, the armed forces continue to wield considerable political influence over many civilian regimes. Often they are able to veto decisions by elected civilian officials regarding national security and foreign policy. In some countries, military leaders protect their own budgets, determine who serves as defense minister, or control military promotions. For example, while elected civilian presidents have governed Guatemala since 1985, they still hesitate to pursue policies that threaten the army's interests. In some countries, such as Algeria, Nigeria, and Pakistan, the armed forces remain a commanding force in politics.

On the other hand, in a number of other nations once dominated by the military (such as Argentina and Brazil), the generals now accept civilian control. Turkey's 2016 coup attempt failed, for example, because most military personnel—even if they disliked President Recep Tayyip Erdoğan or his policies—no longer believed that governments should be changed in such a manner.

In order to examine military participation in developing world politics and the changing nature of civil-military relations, this chapter explores a series of interrelated questions: What accounts for so much military involvement in politics? How do the structures of military regimes differ from one country to another? What do the armed forces hope to accomplish when they seize power? How successfully have military governments achieved their political and economic goals? Is military rule generally beneficial or detrimental to economic and political development? What factors have induced military governments to step down in recent decades? What political roles do the armed forces continue to play after the establishment or reestablishment of civilian rule? How can civilian governments best control the military?

THE CAUSES OF MILITARY INTERVENTIONS

Political scientists have offered three alternative perspectives for explaining the frequency and nature of military intervention in developing countries. The first focuses on the internal characteristics of the armed forces themselves. The second stresses the broader political environment in which the military operates, most notably the weakness of civilian regimes. The third looks at the specific measures that governments might take to protect themselves from their own soldiers, a process sometimes called "coup-proofing."

The Nature of the Armed Forces
In early research on the less developed nations, many analysts maintained that the armed forces enjoyed greater organizational cohesion and clarity of purpose than civilian political institutions did, hence their penchant for

intervention. As one leading analyst concluded, "The ability of officers to intervene in domestic politics and produce stable leadership is [directly] related to internal [military] social cohesion."[6] In their efforts to better understand the military's inner workings, scholars examined the class origins, educational levels, ideological orientations, and internal organization of the officer corps. These factors all seemed to affect the probability of military involvement in politics and to influence the officers' goals.

Obviously, the officers' education and training greatly influence their political values. A country wishing to keep the military out of politics must impart professional values to its officers. Ideally, as military training and tactics become more sophisticated, officers develop specialized and complex military skills, while distancing themselves from politics. However, such a division of function will develop only if military training focuses on external threats such as wars with other nations. Should the focus of military education shift toward internal warfare—controlling guerrilla unrest or other civil insurrections—professionalization will not suffice to keep the military out of politics.

Building on this theme, Alfred Stepan distinguished between "old" and "new" military professionalism. The former, typical of developed countries such as the United States, emphasizes skills relevant to "external security." As military officers train to repel foreign enemies, we can expect them to remove themselves from domestic politics. In many developing nations, however, military training (the new professionalism) has primarily prepared officers for internal warfare against class-based or ethnically based insurgencies.

In his study of civilian relations with the military, Michael Desch found that the level of civilian control over the armed forces correlates with the level of external threat that the country faces from a foreign adversary and the extent of any domestic threat from internal upheaval. He argues that civilian control over the military is likely to be strongest when the country faces a high external threat and a low internal threat. Conversely, civilian control is generally weakest when the country faces a low external threat and a high internal threat, precisely the situation that has prevailed in many Latin American and African nations in the recent past.

Political Institutions and Civil Society

Though research into the internal structure and dynamics of the armed forces is very useful, it fails to tell the entire story. In other words, we cannot ascertain the probability of military intervention in politics and the objectives of this intervention merely by evaluating internal military factors such as the armed forces' cohesion, size, professionalism, and ideological orientation. For example, there is surprisingly little correlation between the military's size and firepower, on the one hand, and its propensity to topple civilian governments, on the other. Indeed, Africa, home to some of the world's smallest militaries, has had one of the highest incidences of military rule. In Togo, an army of only 250 men and a small number of retirees from the former French colonial force carried out West Africa's first military coup. In Benin, one president was overthrown by only sixty paratroopers. Indeed, small and poorly armed military units executed a number of other takeovers in the region. In the closing years of the twentieth century, of nearly forty-five African countries, thirty-five had armed forces of fewer than thirty thousand, and twenty-three of these had fewer than ten thousand men. In contrast, China, India, Israel, Sweden, and the United States—with far larger militaries—have never suffered a coup.

Ultimately, then, the military's propensity to intervene in politics is less a function of its own capabilities than a consequence of the weaknesses of civilian political institutions. As Samuel Huntington insisted, "The most important causes of military intervention in politics are not military, but political and reflect, not the social and organizational characteristics of the military establishment, but the political and institutional structure of society."[7] Hence, the second group of explanatory theories focuses its attention on the nature of civil society.

If a civilian government enjoys substantial support from political and economic elites, influential political parties, and the general public, and if it provides political stability and a healthy economy, it is relatively immune from military coups. Conversely, "In times of uncertainty and the breakdown of [civilian political] institutions, soldiers come into their own; when there is no other effective organization of society, even a small, weak army may take command over a large, unorganized mass."[8] Samuel Finer maintained that the quality of a nation's political culture helps determine whether or not its civilian government can resist military intervention. Countries are relatively safe from coups if their citizens (including political and military elites) believe that only civilian political leaders and institutions are legitimate and that elections are the only legitimate means of changing governments. Civilian government is also more secure if a country has a strong civil society, that is, a network of independent groups such as labor unions and business organizations.[9] But, in many developing nations, civilian governments have low legitimacy and few members of civil society are willing to defend them. Consequently, disgruntled military leaders have more opportunities to overthrow them, while civilians and other troops are less likely to risk their lives defending them.

From an institutional perspective, civilian regimes are strongest when broadly based political parties support them. Where party systems are deeply entrenched in the fabric of society and elicit widespread support, the likelihood of military intervention is greatly diminished. In fact, a country's susceptibility to coups is more strongly influenced by the degree to which its party system penetrates and organizes society than by how democratic it is. Thus, once-authoritarian governments in Mexico and Taiwan (dominated by a single party) controlled the military effectively for years, just as the autocratic Chinese Communist Party does now. But when placed under great stress, not even a strong party system can fully immunize a political system from military interference. For example, strong party systems, which had kept Uruguay and Chile free of military coups for decades, collapsed under the strains of intense class conflict in the 1970s.

Civilian governments are most vulnerable during periods of economic decline or high inflation. They are also at risk when they are perceived as corrupt and when they are unable to maintain political stability. All these circumstances undermine their legitimacy and often increase popular expectations (or hopes) that military rule could improve the situation. In nations such as Nigeria, Thailand, and Pakistan, soon after taking power, military leaders declared their intention to root out widespread corruption. In such cases, military intervention has often drawn broad support initially from civil society. Following severe economic and political crises in Argentina, Brazil, Chile, and Uruguay, the new military dictatorships committed themselves to crush leftist movements, restore social order, and reinvigorate the economy.

As modernization theory would lead us to believe, countries that are more socioeconomically developed are less likely to suffer military takeovers.

> Countries with per-capita GNPs of $1,000 or more [in 1995 dollars] do not
> have successful coups; countries with per-capita GNPs of $3,000 or more do
> not have coup attempts. The area between $1,000 and $3,000 per-capita GNP
> is where unsuccessful coups occur, while successful coups . . . were [most com-
> mon] in countries with per-capita GNPs under $500.[10]

While there have been a few exceptions to that claim, it has remained largely true.*

In summary, a nation's ability to limit military intervention reflects, in large part, the strength of its political institutions, the values of its political culture, and its level of economic development. Yet, these factors alone do not account for all the variations in civil-military relations. Elite values and behavior also play an important role. For example, India and Costa Rica, with political and socioeconomic circumstances comparable to those of their neighbors, have experienced little or no military intervention in politics. The explanation may lie in the values of their political and economic elites: elected officials, government bureaucrats, political party leaders, business leaders, and labor leaders, as well as military officers themselves.

---

*These GNP levels are expressed in constant dollars to eliminate the effects of inflation.

India illustrates this point well. Located near several countries with long histories of military intervention (Pakistan, Bangladesh, Myanmar, and Thailand), it has been governed exclusively by civilians since independence. There is little to suggest that the Indian public, still heavily rural and one-third illiterate, is much more opposed to military rule than others in the region.* Nor, until the 1990s, was its economy much more advanced than theirs. It appears, however, that political and economic elites in India have long endorsed civilian control more strongly than have their counterparts in neighboring countries.

Elite values, however, may change more quickly than entire political cultures do. In a process of "political learning," a nation's civilian leaders may understand from previous experience how better to avert military coups.

Coup-Proofing

Regimes may also introduce **coup-proofing** strategies designed to reduce the risk of being overthrown by their own military. Appointments and promotions may be carefully managed to ensure that senior officers support the political system, be it a democracy, hybrid regime, or authoritarian dictatorship. Countries like China and Vietnam place political commissars in military units to monitor and report on the loyalty of personnel to the Communist Party. Some countries recruit key military units from especially loyal segments of the population. In Jordan, for example, combat units and officers tend to be of "East Bank" rather than Palestinian origin, while in Syria, elite units and senior officers are disproportionately drawn from the Alawi (Shi'ite) community and other religious minorities. Special military units may be organized to counterbalance the regular military and to provide protection to members of the regime and key centers of government power, such as the National Guard in Saudi Arabia, the Revolutionary Guards and Basij militia in Iran, or the presidential guard units of many African leaders. Military salaries and other benefits may be increased to secure the loyalty of the troops. A number of Arab countries did this in response to the Arab Spring protests of 2011, for example.

In very rare cases, such as Costa Rica, the military may be reduced in size, or dissolved entirely to reduce the risk of future coups. In Latin America, investigation and prosecution of abuses by former military regimes have been a useful tool in delegitimizing past military intervention, and instilling democratic values across the armed forces. High-profile purges may be used in extreme cases to rid the military of disloyal officers and deter future coup plotting. In Turkey, for example, more than one hundred

---

*According to World Values Survey data, 38 percent of Indians believe that military rule could be "good" or "very good," compared to 35 percent of Thais, 51 percent of Filipinos, 59 percent of Pakistanis—and a rather alarming 17 percent of Americans.

generals were detained following the 2016 coup, as were thousands of military and police personnel.* More subtly, officers with dubious loyalties can be assigned to unimportant posts. Such measures need to be undertaken carefully, however—lest they provoke a military coup.

PROGRESSIVE SOLDIERS AND MILITARY CONSERVATIVES

Having examined the factors that either promote or inhibit military intervention, we will now consider the political behavior and policies of military regimes after they have established control. Given the disorder and conflict that characterize so many developing world nations, we must ask whether military rule produces greater political stability and socioeconomic development, at least in the short run. Also, once in office, are the generals and colonels likely to be a force for progressive change or defenders of the status quo?

Many of the early modernization theorists felt strongly that the armed forces could contribute to development. Marion Levy was impressed by the military's alleged rationality, disciplined organization, and commitment to modern values. Taking their critics to task, he maintained that the armed forces might be "the most efficient type of organization for combining maximum rates of modernization with maximum levels of stability and control."[11] Lucian Pye also saw the military as one of the best-organized national institutions in otherwise "disorganized transitional societies."[12] For Manfred Halpern, the Middle Eastern military was "the vanguard of nationalism and social change."[13]

Positive evaluations such as these predominated in the early modernization literature. Frequently, they were based on an idealized vision of the professional soldier: trained in modern organizational skills, nationalistic, and above narrow tribal, class, and regional interests. At times, these writings reflected the authors' strong preference for order and stability, coupled with the assumption that the military could bring order out of political and economic chaos. Occasionally, they drew on a few military success stories— such as the modernization and secularization undertaken by Ataturk (Mustafa Kemal) in Turkey after 1919—and projected them onto a larger screen.

Over the years, very different kinds of officers (and sometimes enlisted men) have seized power, promising to modernize their countries through industrialization, greater labor discipline, expanded education, agrarian reform, or other fundamental reforms. In countries such as Upper Volta,

---

* Well over one hundred thousand judges, teachers, and other public-sector employees in Turkey have been suspended, dismissed, or detained since the 2016 coup attempt. This goes well beyond coup-proofing and represents part of a broader recent shift to ever greater authoritarianism under President Erdoğan.

Libya, and Peru, leftist militaries have promoted one or more of the following causes: economic redistribution, greater state intervention in the economy, mass mobilization, agrarian reform, or a struggle against imperialism.

On the other hand, conservative generals in Brazil, Chile, Indonesia, and South Korea repressed mass political participation, while encouraging investment by domestic firms and multinational corporations. In the 1960s and 1970s, conservative military juntas across Latin America imprisoned, tortured, and executed leftists, trade unionist, and others.

Why have some military governments championed the poor, while others have supported wealthy corporate and landowning interests? To find the answer, we must examine the class origins of the officers' corps, their nation's level of socioeconomic development, and the class alliances that had developed in their political system. Research in a range of less developed countries has shown that officers tend to come from middle-class backgrounds, particularly in Asia and Latin America. Typically, their fathers were military officers, shopkeepers, merchants, midsized landowners, teachers, or civil servants. Not surprisingly, then, military regimes have commonly identified with the goals and aspirations of their country's civilian middle class.

But what are those goals, and what political ideologies and development policies have emerged from them? In the least developed countries, officers have often viewed economic elites, including large landowners and foreign corporations, as the source of their country's backwardness. Members of the middle class frequently resent those same elites for obstructing their own rise to political and economic prominence. In such a setting, both the armed forces and the civilian middle class may perceive the relatively unmobilized lower class as a potential ally in the battle against the oligarchy. For example, soon after taking power, Peruvian general Juan Velasco blamed the traditional landowning class and Peru's economic dependency for the nation's underdevelopment. In the following years, the military's ambitious land redistribution, shantytown reform, expropriations of property belonging to MNCs, expansion of the state economic sector, and mass mobilization greatly altered the country's political and economic landscape. Elsewhere, "General Omar Torrijos of Panama railed against oligarchic control and encouraged the lower class to participate in politics."[14] Muammar Qaddafi's government in Libya and a number of Marxist military governments in Africa used similar revolutionary rhetoric, but were quick to enrich themselves, their friends, and their relatives.

In the more modern and industrialized developing nations, however, where workers and the poor are more mobilized, the military confronts a different political landscape. Urbanization, the spread of secondary and university education, and economic development all have enlarged and strengthened the middle class, enabling it to wrest a share of political power from the economic elites. At the same time, industrialization has increased the size of the working class and enhanced the trade union movement. Urbanization also creates a growing and sometimes organized shantytown population. And the commercialization of agriculture often triggers unrest in the countryside. Not surprisingly, the middle class (having achieved a share of political influence) and its military partners see the more galvanized and politicized lower classes as a threat rather than a useful ally.

If left-wing political parties and trade unions have gained considerable mass support and if there has been growing political unrest, the military and the middle class are more likely to ally themselves with the economic elite and to repress mass mobilization. In Chile, the election of Salvador Allende's Marxist government and the accompanying mobilization of workers, peasants, and urban poor polarized the country along class lines. In nearby Uruguay, the Left's electoral appeal was not as strong, but labor-industrial conflict was intense, and the Tupamaros, a potent urban guerrilla group, were engaged in a campaign of political kidnappings and insurgency. In both countries, the perceived threat of guerrilla groups, mass mobilization, and an ascendant Left (including strong leftist political parties) prompted the military to topple long-standing democracies.

Conservative military officers' concerns are not limited to leftist mass movements. They generally oppose any mobilization of lower-class groups that threaten the nation's stability. For example, in recent times, the Algerian and Egyptian armed forces have stood in the way of mass mobilization by Islamist groups.

In short, then, the more underdeveloped a country is and the weaker its middle class, the greater the likelihood that the country will have a left-of-center military.* However, notes Eric Nordlinger, "The soldiers who have power in countries with an established middle class . . . act as more or less ardent defenders of the status quo."[15] Similarly, Huntington observes,

> In the world of the oligarchy, the soldier is a radical; in the middle class world, he is a participant and arbitrator; as mass society looms on the horizon he becomes the guardian of the existing order. . . . The more advanced a society becomes, the more conservative and reactionary becomes the role of the military.[16]

Huntington went on to identify three major types of coups: reformist **breakthrough coups**, where military officers from relatively humble backgrounds seek to break the power of established oligarchs and elites; **guardian coups**,

---

* But the armed forces in the least developed nations are not always reform oriented. In Africa and other impoverished areas, the military often has seized power out of self-interest or for narrow ethnic goals. Similarly, while the military has sometimes been progressive in the less developed nations of South America, Africa, and the Middle East, it has generally been reactionary in Central America and the Caribbean, where it has been co-opted by the upper class.

where the military is acting to protect its own immediate interests, or those of the regime to which it is attached; and conservative **veto coups**, in which the generals are acting to protect the established social order and slow social change by taking action against a radical challenge from below.

THE TYPES AND GOALS OF MILITARY REGIMES

Having observed the range of ideological orientations among military governments, we now examine the structures and goals of those regimes.

Personalistic Regimes

In the least developed countries—those with low levels of military professionalization, limited mass political participation, extensive political corruption, and little semblance of representative government—military officers frequently seize power for their own personal enrichment and aggrandizement, usually with little or no interest in economic or political reform. Their governments tend to be personalistic; that is, a single charismatic officer with a strong personal following leads them. In order to bolster his support, however, the leader allows part of the government plunder to pass on to the military and civilian cliques surrounding him. "Legitimacy is secured through patronage, clientelistic alliances, [and] systemic intimidation."[17]

In Latin America, personalistic dictatorships were most common in the less developed political and economic systems of Central America and the Caribbean. One of the most prominent examples was the Somoza Dynasty in Nicaragua. As leader of the country's National Guard (its only military force), Anastasio Somoza Sr. overthrew the government in 1937, primarily seeking his own enrichment. Governing a small and impoverished nation, he amassed a fortune of several hundred million dollars using state resources to purchase construction firms, urban real estate, electrical power plants, air and shipping lines, cement factories, and much of the nation's best farmland. Following Somoza's assassination in 1956, his political and financial empire passed to his two sons, who ruled the country in succession until the 1979 Sandinista Revolution. Other personalistic regimes in the Americas included the Batista government in Cuba (eventually toppled by Fidel Castro's revolutionary army) and Alfredo Stroessner's long dictatorship in Paraguay (1954–89). Batista had links to the American mafia's gambling and prostitution operations in Havana. Stroessner and his associates enriched themselves by collaborating with international smugglers and drug dealers.*

---

*To be sure, a few personalistic dictators, such as Argentina's Juan Perón and Venezuela's Hugo Chávez, introduced broad social and economic reform programs. But even benevolent personalistic military regimes are usually corrupt and concentrate excessive power in the hands of one person.

Personalistic military regimes have been especially common in sub-Saharan Africa, sometimes led by upwardly mobile junior officers or even enlisted men such as Ghana's Flight Sergeant Jerry Rawlings and Liberia's Sergeant-Major Samuel Doe. While some were well intentioned, most have done little to develop their countries. The most infamous personalistic dictators in the continent have been Uganda's Idi Amin Dada, the Central African Republic's Jean-Bédel Bokassa, and Congo's Mobutu Sese Seko. Ironically, in light of his regime's subsequent enormous brutality, Amin initially justified his coup by citing the human rights violations of ousted president Milton Obote. Enamored of power as much as wealth, Amin played upon and exacerbated Uganda's ethnic divisions during his brutal eight-year reign (1971–79). He not only expelled the country's sizable Asian population (mostly Indian) but also murdered an estimated three hundred thousand to five hundred thousand people, most notably members of the previously influential Langi and Acholi tribes. Seeing enemies at every turn, he even executed one of his wives. In an attempt to maintain absolute control over the armed forces, he purged or executed a large portion of the officers' corps, eventually creating an army composed largely of foreign troops (principally Sudanese and Zairian).

Equally megalomaniacal, the Central African Republic's Jean-Bedel Bokassa unleashed a reign of death and terror on his country following his takeover in a 1966 coup. Plundering the treasury of one of the world's more impoverished nations, he concluded that the presidency was not a sufficiently exalted position, so he lavished millions of dollars on his own coronation as the country's new emperor. In time, Amin and Bokassa so outraged the world community that they were ousted through external intervention. Amin fell to a Tanzanian invasion, while a French-supported coup toppled Bokassa.

Because most personalistic dictators lack a meaningful ideology or program to legitimize their regime, they typically must share some of the spoils with their military and civilian supporters in order to maintain themselves in office. For example, President Mobutu, Africa's most enduring military dictator (1965–97), made himself a multibillionaire while opening up the floodgates of corruption to benefit his military and civil service. In this manner, he kept himself in office for decades while bankrupting the national government and destroying a once-dynamic economy. By the late 1990s, however, as the Zairian economy collapsed, his regime unraveled, falling rapidly to a Rwandan-backed rebel force whose new government, unfortunately, turned out to be almost as corrupt and just as repressive. In the 1990s, warlords (regionally based, military/political bosses who plunder the region they control) in Sierra Leone and Liberia overthrew the government with few goals other than looting the country.

Institutional Military Regimes

As developing countries' political and economic systems modernize, corresponding changes take place in military institutions and attitudes. Frequently, officers attend advanced military academies at home or abroad. Sometimes, they enroll in specialized seminars with civilian leaders, establishing links with politicians, businesspeople, and academics. These programs more intensely expose military officers to their country's political and economic challenges.

If these "new soldiers" seize power, they are likely to govern collectively rather than vest authority in the hands of a single leader. To be sure, many **institutional military regimes** have been dominated by a single figure, such as Indonesia's Suharto and Chile's Augusto Pinochet. Like purely personalistic dictators, some of these men are motivated by ambition, fear, and greed. Even in such cases, a substantial number of officers hold influential government positions (not just the paramount leader), and there is a degree of institutional decision making. In Indonesia, for example, active and retired military officers at one time held nearly half the positions in the national bureaucracy and some two-thirds of the provincial governorships. Furthermore, the goals of these institutional regimes are broader than any single leader's ambitions.

Institutionalized military governments have generally been headed by councils or juntas such as Niger's Supreme Military Council and Burma's Revolutionary Council. Comparable groups have governed Algeria, Argentina, Brazil, Ethiopia, Thailand, Uruguay, and a number of other countries. These are relatively small governing committees made up of officers from the various branches of the armed forces.* Typically, one active or retired officer serves as president and wields the most influence. Often, however, his term of office is limited. For example, in Argentina and Brazil, the military juntas limited the president to a single term. In contrast, Chile's General Augusto Pinochet was all powerful and was not constrained by term limits. In some countries, including South Korea, Brazil, and Indonesia, the armed forces tried to legitimize its rule by creating a ruling political party that ran candidates in tightly controlled elections. Frequently, presidents and other leading government officials retire from active military duty before taking office. And in Egypt and Syria, military and civilian elites joined together to form a ruling party.

Institutional military regimes can be as repressive and brutal as personalistic dictatorships—sometimes even more so. Their day-to-day governing

---

*In some cases such councils have been mere façades, with one officer really in power. Thus, it is not always easy to distinguish between personalistic and institutional military regimes. Ultimately, the determining factor is where real power resides rather than what the formal structures are.

style, however, is generally more bureaucratic and sophisticated—commonly drawing on the talents of highly trained civilian technocrats. Moreover, unlike self-aggrandizing personalistic leaders, they are more likely to support the aspirations of the middle class, more prone to espouse a coherent political ideology, and more likely to champion nationalistic goals. Most institutional military governments pursue four broad objectives, or at least claim to do so.

First, they usually justify their seizure of power by denouncing the alleged corruption of the government that they have ousted. Thus, when Bangladesh's Lieutenant General Hussain Muhammad Ershad led a 1982 army coup, he charged that the outgoing administration had "failed totally because of [its] petty selfishness . . . and unbounded corruption."[18] Incoming military leaders in Uruguay, Pakistan, Thailand, and much of Africa have made similar proclamations. All of them promised to clean up the mess.

A second goal—one not normally publicly articulated or acknowledged—is the advancement of the military's own corporate interests. As Ruth First observed, while African coup leaders may claim to have acted for the good of the nation or for other noble political purposes, "when the army acts, it generally acts for army reasons."[19] When officers are unhappy with their salaries, the size of the defense budget, or the quantity and quality of their weapons, they often take action. They also react negatively to civilian "interference" in military affairs, such as the president deviating from normal promotion practices for officers.

Ever since the 1960s—a decade featuring coups in Togo, Ghana, Mali, Congo-Brazzaville, and Algeria—a number of African armies have taken power to protect themselves from competing military units (such as presidential guards), to increase their troop strength, to raise their salaries, or to augment their budgets. In South Asia, repeated coups in Bangladesh have been motivated by resentment over civilian interference in military promotions and by desires for greater military spending.

A third common goal is to maintain or restore order and stability. Institutional coups have often occurred during periods of civil unrest, guerrilla insurgencies, or civil war. For example, the army first involved itself deeply in South Korean politics when student demonstrations and labor protests challenged the civilian administrations of Syngman Rhee and Chang Myon. Thailand's many coups have usually followed strikes and street demonstrations in Bangkok.

Military officers are particularly troubled by radical challenges to the political and economic systems and by threats to the safety and integrity of the armed forces. During the early 1960s, Indonesia's civilian president, Sukarno, moved his regime leftward and became increasingly dependent on the country's large communist party, much to the discomfort of his conservative military commanders. Their fears intensified in 1965, when a small group of leftist officers assassinated Lieutenant General Ahmad Yani and five other officers, claiming that these men had been plotting a coup against Sukarno. The country's top military command responded with a massive attack against the communist party, eventually killing some half million alleged party supporters. At the same time, many Indonesian civilians used the chaos as an opportunity to loot and kill members of the country's prosperous Chinese minority. In time, army chief General Suharto ousted Sukarno and established a military dictatorship that lasted more than thirty years.*

Similarly, in Argentina, Brazil, Chile, and Uruguay, the generals' fear of leftist unions, guerrillas, and radical political parties prompted extended military dictatorships. In 1992, the Algerian armed forces halted the second round of parliamentary elections that seemed certain to result in victory for the Islamic Salvation Front, a party of militant Islamic fundamentalists.

A final goal of many institutionalized military regimes has been to revive and stimulate the economy. As we have noted, coups frequently follow periods of rampant inflation, labor conflict, or economic stagnation. A study of thirty-eight sub-Saharan African governments over a two-decade period revealed that military takeovers were most likely to occur after an economic downturn. Asian and Latin American coups have frequently followed this pattern as well.

Developing world militaries are frequently committed to industrialization. For one thing, industrial growth can provide them with arms and supplies that previously needed to be imported. In the least developed countries, such production may be limited to uniforms or rifles. On the other hand, in countries such as Brazil, Indonesia, and South Korea, highly advanced arms industries now produce planes, tanks, and other sophisticated weaponry for both domestic consumption and export. Even when it has no direct military payoff, industrialization contributes to national pride and international prestige. Small wonder, then, that many Latin American and Asian countries have seen a political alliance between industrialists and the armed forces.

Having reviewed the goals of institutionalized military governments in general, we now focus on two distinct regime types that have received considerable attention in recent years: the bureaucratic-authoritarian regime and the revolutionary military government. While each type has represented only a minority of military governments, they have had a significant impact both within and outside their borders.

---

*Like many Indonesians, both Suharto and Sukarno had only one name and did not use a family name.

Bureaucratic-Authoritarian Regimes

Beginning with the Brazilian coup d'état of 1964, through the 1973 coups in Uruguay and Chile, to the Argentine military takeovers of 1966 and 1976, four of the most socioeconomically developed countries in South America succumbed to military rule. Chile and Uruguay had also been the strongest democracies in the region, free of military domination for decades. Thus, their coups contradicted the widely held assumption that both socioeconomic development and a strong political party system limit military intervention.

Once in power, these regimes lasted longer than typical military governments in the region, from twelve years (in Uruguay) to twenty-one (in Brazil). They suspended political party activity, crushed labor unions and other grassroots organizations, prohibited strikes, and jailed and tortured many suspected political dissidents. In Argentina and Chile, thousands of people were murdered or "disappeared" (covertly taken away, never to be seen again).

Argentine political scientist Guillermo O'Donnell referred to these military governments as **bureaucratic-authoritarian** (BA) **regimes**. Compared to previous military dictatorships, they had a more extensive bureaucratic structure that included like-minded civilian technocrats; they penetrated more deeply into civil society; established close links to multinational corporations; and were particularly repressive. O'Donnell focused on the closely related economic and political factors that explained the rise of these BA regimes in Latin America's most developed nations. First, he noted, economic growth in these countries had begun to stagnate by the 1960s. Many analysts argued that further growth would require investment in capital-goods industries and new technologies, which only MNCs had the resources to provide. But international corporations (as well as domestic companies) had been reluctant to invest because of the rising labor strife, civil unrest, and leftist electoral strength, all caused by the countries' economic stagnation, high-inflation, and declining living standards.

Growing radicalism among the poor and portions of the middle class and the resulting political polarization of society deeply alarmed the armed forces. In Argentina, Chile, and Uruguay, urban guerrillas added to the perceived threat. The goals of the new BA regimes, then, were to crush leftist political parties, unions, and guerrilla movements; limit workers' wages; create a "stable environment for investment"; and work closely with MNCs and domestic corporations to control inflation and reinvigorate the economy. Beyond repressing the Left, the generals wanted to depoliticize society and terminate most forms of political participation for an extended period. In addition, they wanted to extend the role of the private sector and roll back state economic activity, including welfare programs, minimum-wage guarantees, and public ownership of economic resources. While the analysis of BA regimes focused on Latin America, this type of military government later developed in South Korea and other East Asian countries.

Revolutionary Military Regimes

In a number of developing nations, the military has pursued goals diametrically different from those of the conservative BA regimes. Rather than excluding most of the population from the political system, they instead extended political and economic participation to formerly excluded groups. At the same time, however, their authoritarian political structure tightly controlled mass participation. In Africa, a number of Marxist, military governments proclaimed policies of cultural nationalism, anti-imperialism, peasant and working-class political mobilization, expansion of the state's economic role, and redistribution of economic resources to the poor.

Revolutionary coups have often been led by radicalized officers from the middle ranks (captains, majors, colonels), rather than generals. In a speech outlining the goals of Upper Volta's military government, Captain Thomas Sankara articulated the Marxist rhetoric typical of such regimes:

> The triumph of the Revolution [i.e., the military takeover] . . . is the crowning moment of the struggle of the Volta People against its internal enemies. It is a victory against international imperialism and its internal allies. . . . These enemies of the people . . . are: the bourgeoisie of Volta [and] . . . reactionary forces whose strength derives from the traditional feudal structures of our society. . . . The People in our revolution comprises: The working class . . . the petty bourgeoisie . . . the peasantry . . . [and] the lumpenproletariat [the poorest urban inhabitants].[20]

Military governments in Ethiopia, Sudan, Somalia, Congo-Brazzaville, Benin, and Madagascar made similarly radical declarations. Like most African military regimes, however, these governments have been led by men without significant political skills or advanced education. Consequently, their Marxist ideals were "self-taught, ideologically immature and crude, and riddled with inconsistencies."[21] For some of them, Marxism simply expressed their strong nationalism and distaste for the European nations that had colonized the continent. For others, revolutionary rhetoric came almost as an afterthought, a means of justifying their earlier seizure of power and authoritarian control. Thus, the government of Colonel Mengistu in Ethiopia, perhaps Africa's most prominent radical military government, did not embrace Marxism-Leninism until it had been in office for three years.

In other world regions, leftist (though not Marxist) military regimes have governed countries as disparate as Libya, Panama, and Peru. Peru's military came to power seeking to curtail the influence of the rural oligarchy and incorporate the peasantry, working class, and urban poor into the political system. Finally, military governments in Panama and Ecuador introduced comparable, though far more modest, reform programs.

THE ACCOMPLISHMENTS AND FAILURES OF MILITARY REGIMES

How successfully have military governments achieved their goals and how well have they served their countries? Little needs to be said about personalistic military dictatorships. With a few notable exceptions, they are rarely seriously interested in benefiting their countries. Even those with broader goals have had blatantly self-serving objectives. Thus, it would be very hard to argue seriously that dictators such as Batista (Cuba), Somoza (Nicaragua), Stroessner (Paraguay), Amin (Uganda), and Bokassa (Central African Republic) contributed to the long-term political or economic growth of their respective countries. Consequently, the analysis in our next section focuses exclusively on the record of institutional military governments, which often have serious intentions, be it for left-wing or right-wing reform.

Combating Corruption

Let us first look at one of the most commonly professed objectives of institutional regimes—eliminating government corruption. Because government malfeasance is so pervasive, denouncing corruption is a convenient means of legitimizing the armed forces' unconstitutional seizure of power. Yet, most soldiers in office prove every bit as corrupt as their predecessors, or more so. To be sure, a few military governments have been quite honest, but they are the exceptions. As one leading scholar has observed,

> Every Nigerian and Ghanaian coup . . . has had as its prime goal the elimination of deeply ingrained corruption from society. Yet, not one military administration has made truly consistent efforts in that direction . . . or for that matter remained immune to it itself. . . . [Elsewhere in Africa] in two . . . military regimes—Guinea and Burkina Faso—nepotism and accumulation of wealth commenced the very day the officers' hierarchy took office.[22]

Ironically, the continent's continual military intervention has tended to increase corruption in the civilian governments that they oust. "The fear that [civilian] power may not last encourages the incoming politicians to grab what is grabbable."[23] In Asian nations such as Thailand and Indonesia, the military's record has been equally disappointing. In those few military governments that avoid gross corruption, the more modest lure of contraband automobiles and tax-supported vacation homes often proves irresistible. In short, even those military governments that seized power with noble intentions are generally soon corrupted.

Defending Military Interests

When it comes to pursuing their second major objective—advancing their own corporate interests—not surprisingly, military governments have been more successful, at least in the short term. More often than not, military rulers enhance the nation's defense budget. Unfortunately, however, these outlays draw government resources away from badly needed programs such as health care and education.

Typically, military governments increase spending on armaments, military salaries, military housing, and officers' clubs. In much of Asia, officers have benefited from preferential treatment in the distribution of governmental contracts. After leading a coup in Libya in 1969, Muammar Qaddafi ensured his officers' loyalty by doubling their salaries. Even in the face of a mass insurgency and the defection of many regular army troops in 2011, the military's elite units (those best armed and trained) remained loyal right to the end. In their first five years in office, Uruguay's generals raised the military and security share of the national budget from 26 percent to more than 40 percent. A parallel "bias in favor of army, police and civil service salaries and benefits can be observed in practically every military regime in Africa."[24]

Throughout the developing world, even when soldiers do not actually govern, the mere specter of intervention has often led civilian governments to bestow salary hikes and expensive weapon systems on the armed forces. For example, it would be very imprudent for elected leaders in the Philippines or Thailand to slash their country's defense budget. Even Malaysia and Singapore, with no history of coups d'état, pay their officers generously to keep them out of politics.

But, while military rule may enlarge military budgets, it usually damages the armed forces in the long run by reducing their institutional cohesion. The longer the armed forces stay in power, the more generals, colonels, and admirals begin to squabble over resource allocation and other policy issues. New economic and political challenges inevitably arise, which drive a wedge between the officers in command. Furthermore, even military governments that took power with considerable popular support usually lose their legitimacy as they confront difficult economic and social problems. As a consequence, in some regions, most notably sub-Saharan Africa, internal coups (one military faction ousting another) have produced a series of unstable military governments. Nearly half of Africa's twentieth-century coups and failed coup attempts sought to topple incumbent military regimes.[25] Hence, for the most part in recent decades, militaries have returned to the barracks to avoid further internal divisions, restoring the government to civilian hands.

Establishing Stability

Military officers almost always react negatively to popular unrest and political instability. For one thing, disorder violates their hierarchical view of society. Furthermore, it frequently threatens the interests of their middle-class and industrialist allies. Often, mass protests or other types of unrest pose an imminent danger to the armed forces themselves. The generals and colonels of Latin America, for example, have been keenly aware that Marxist revolutions in Cuba and Nicaragua destroyed their country's old military establishment. In Cuba, a number of Batista's officers faced the firing squad, while in Nicaragua, many National Guardsmen were imprisoned or had to flee the country. In Chile and Brazil, leftist political leaders threatened the officers' hierarchical control of the armed forces. Similarly, the generals in Algeria felt endangered by the growing strength of Islamic fundamentalists. Even "revolutionary soldiers" in Ethiopia, Libya, and Peru preferred to dictate change from the top, with tight government controls over mass mobilization.

In many respects, military governments are particularly well suited for controlling civil unrest. They can use force with impunity to combat guerrilla insurrections, disperse street demonstrations, and ban strikes. In some cases, their extensive intelligence agencies enabled them to penetrate deeply into society to control dissent. The Argentine, Brazilian, Chilean, and Uruguayan armies used mass arrests, torture, and death squads to crush potent urban guerrilla movements. In Indonesia, the military destroyed one of the world's largest communist parties and later decimated various separatist movements.

But the generals restored order in these countries at a tremendous cost in human suffering. Some twenty to thirty thousand people died in the Argentine army's "dirty war" against the Left, while many more were imprisoned and tortured. Students and other young people were the primary victims, many of them incorrectly identified as part of the leftist opposition. In Chile, thousands of intellectuals and professionals fled the country, devastating one of the developing world's most advanced university systems and artistic communities. Some three thousand Chileans died; many others were the victims of torture. During Indonesia's "year of living dangerously," perhaps 500,000 communists and ethnic Chinese were massacred, while some 150,000 other people died subsequently (largely from starvation) in the army's struggle against East Timorian separatists. Another twelve thousand died in the separatist rebellion in Aceh. Of course, many military regimes are not repressive. However, it is precisely those that seize power to restore order in highly polarized societies that normally are the most brutal.

Moreover, in the long term, the military has not been particularly successful in providing political stability. To be sure, in several Asian and Latin

American countries, state repression, coupled with technocratic develop-ment policies, either co-opted or decimated opposition groups. In South Korea, sharply improved living standards and a gradual political transition paved the way to a stable elected government. And in Argentina, Brazil, Chile, and Uruguay, the BA regimes' brutality against radical movements convinced political leaders on both sides of the ideological spectrum (but especially the Left) to moderate their positions so as not to provoke further military intervention. Ironically, all of these countries now have democrati-cally elected leftist governments, not what the BA regimes hoped to achieve.

But these "successes" are the exception. Despite their brute strength, the armed forces' hold on power has generally been relatively brief. Eric Nordlinger's pioneering study of military governments found that, on aver-age, they dissolved in five to seven years.[26] Karen Remmer's later work on twelve South American military governments between 1960 and 1990 showed four to be quite durable (twelve to thirty-five years); the remaining eight, however, averaged less than seven years.[27] Moreover, military rule, no matter what its accomplishments are, ultimately impedes the maturation of political parties and other civilian institutions necessary for long-term stability.

In Africa, more often than not, coups have only led to further coups, hampering political development as they turned politics into a fight for survival. The brutal regime of Sergeant Samuel Doe exposed Liberia to a devastating civil war and to a far more sinister ruler, Charles Taylor, who fomented unspeakably brutal internal warfare at home and in nearby Sierra Leone. Military rule in Ethiopia and the Sudan only worsened ethnically based civil wars. Elsewhere, extended suppression of dissident groups will likely lead to greater upheavals after those regimes eventually fall, as it did in Libya.

Improving the Economy

Earlier we noted that coups often are provoked by economic recessions or severe inflation. Consequently, many newly installed military governments promise to impose fiscal discipline and revitalize the economy. In South Korea, Indonesia, Brazil, and Chile, for example, conservative military governments curtailed union activity in order to suppress wage demands. By reducing strike activity and weakening unions, the generals expected to lower inflation and attract foreign investment.

Proponents of military dictatorships assert that they can more easily make economic decisions consistent with the national interest because they need not pander to special interest groups. Critics counter that soldiers lack the expertise to manage an economy. Even when well intentioned, they tend to allocate excessive funds to defense and to wasteful, chauvin-istic projects. Examining the economic performance of specific military governments provides evidence to support both sides of the debate. South Korea demonstrated that a military government can oversee a very successful economic development program. Following General Park Chung-hee's seizure of power in 1961, the armed forces governed the country for more than twenty-five years. During this period, the Republic of Korea changed from an underdeveloped nation into one of the world's most dynamic industrial economies. Moreover, the country enjoyed sustained economic growth while still maintaining very equitable income distribution. Indeed, economists frequently cite South Korea as a model of well-executed economic modernization.

Elsewhere in Asia, Indonesia's military also presided over rapid economic growth from the mid-1960s to late 1990s. During the 1970s and early 1980s, the Suharto dictatorship plowed back a portion of the country's extensive petroleum revenues into labor-intensive export industries. At the same time, rural development programs and mass education improved income distribution and, coupled with economic growth, substantially reduced the number of Indonesians living in poverty. Nearby Thailand, governed by the military for much of the last seventy years, has also enjoyed an economic boom, though it was somewhat flawed by corruption and "crony capitalism" (plentiful government loans and contracts awarded to politically well-connected businesspeople).

Two of Latin America's major bureaucratic-authoritarian regimes—Brazil and, especially, Chile—also had relatively successful economic records. After several false starts, Chile's pro-business, export-oriented policies ushered in a period of strong economic expansion with low inflation. These achievements, however, followed a period of severe economic hardship, which forced the poor to bear a disproportionate share of the sacrifice. As with other bureaucratic-authoritarian regimes, income distribution deteriorated. After the restoration of democracy in 1990, the civilian governments of Patricio Aylwin and Eduardo Frei maintained high-growth rates, while using targeted programs to reduce poverty. During that decade, that combination of high-growth and remedial programs for those left behind halved the number of Chileans living in poverty.

Brazil's bureaucratic-authoritarian regime achieved dramatic economic growth during the late 1960s and 1970s, turning the country into an important industrial power. The benefits of this growth, however, were very poorly distributed, leaving many of the poor worse off than before. Moreover, Brazil's "economic miracle" was built on excessive foreign borrowing that turned the country into the less developed countries' largest external debtor. In recent years, civilian president Luiz Inácio Lula da Silva's administration (2003–10) was able to accelerate economic growth, while sharply reducing the percentage of the population living in poverty.

Many other Latin American military governments performed poorly in the economic sphere. They spent far too much on defense, borrowed excessively, were corrupt, and frequently failed to understand development economics. In Africa, the armed forces' economic record, with few exceptions, has ranged from poor to disastrous. And, the Myanmar military government wrecked the national economy.

Moving beyond examinations of individual cases such as these, some analysts have engaged in more systematic statistical comparison of regime types. Examining data on economic indicators such as growth rates and inflation, they have compared the economic performance of military and civilian governments in specific regions or throughout the less developed countries. Unfortunately, these comparisons face a number of methodological problems. For one thing, the economies of individual less developed countries are greatly influenced by world economic conditions, particularly the level of demand from highly industrialized countries for their major exports. Moreover, a military regime's economic policies may either negatively or positively influence the performance of civilian government that replaces it. Thus, for example, some military governments have stimulated short-term economic growth by borrowing excessively from foreign banks or institutions. But in doing so, they bequeathed high inflation and a debt crisis to their civilian successors. Few analytical comparisons have been able to control for all such factors. In general, though, cross-national statistical research has uncovered little difference between the economic growth rates of democratic and military governments, though in some regions (including sub-Saharan Africa), civilian governments have outperformed military regimes.

MILITARY WITHDRAWAL FROM POLITICS

Once the armed forces have become entrenched in the political system, dislodging them is usually no easy task. Domestic protests (Indonesia) or external intervention (Uganda) sometimes induce the military to withdraw from power. More often, however, the armed forces voluntarily relinquish power for one or more of the following reasons: having accomplished their major objectives, they see no value in retaining power; deteriorating economic conditions make continued rule unappealing; extended rule has undermined internal military cohesion; or the regime has become so unpopular that staying in office would reduce the military's legitimacy as an institution.

Many military governments come into office as "caretakers" whose goal is to restore stability or solve a particular problem quickly and then return control to civilians. In Ecuador, for example, the armed forces frequently ousted elected leaders whom they considered too demagogic, too

populist, or too incompetent. After ruling relatively briefly, they then voluntarily stepped down.

Because the perpetrators of institutional coups usually take power with
expectations of augmenting military budgets and accelerating economic
growth, their interest in governing, not surprisingly, wanes if the economy
turns sour (as it does for at least some period of time in many less developed
countries). In countries such as Peru, Uruguay, and Thailand, economic
downturns have convinced military governments to step down. These
declines may also aggravate internal divisions within the armed forces.

In sub-Saharan Africa, military rule may also aggravate ethnic tensions within the armed forces, particularly when officers from one tribe or
religion dominate top government positions. For example, in Nigeria, the
military's entry into the political arena unleashed four internal coups in a
ten-year span, with ethnic divisions playing an important role. Two heads
of government and a number of other senior officers were killed in the
military's internal struggles. Elsewhere, other military governments, fearing
similar deteriorations in military cohesiveness, have preferred to step down,
leaving the nation's problems to civilian governments. In some countries,
soldiers from one tribe or ethnic group may dominate the armed forces.
For example, in Togo as of 2005, the Kabyé tribe made up only 15 percent of the country's population but constituted 70 percent of all soldiers
and 90 percent of the officer corps. Ultimate power has been in the hands
of a Kabyé military dictator who ruled the country for thirty-eight years
(1967–2005) and his son who has reigned since 2005.

Just as military coups are most likely to take place when civilian governments lack legitimacy, the army is most likely to return to the barracks
when its own legitimacy declines. This happens most dramatically when
the country has been defeated in war. For example, following its humiliating defeat by the British in the Falklands (or Malvinas) war, the Argentine
military regime was forced to step down. And Pakistan's military had to
transfer power to its leading civilian critic after it lost East Pakistan (now
Bangladesh) in a war with India.

In recent years, influential nations and international organizations in
both developed countries and less developed countries have taken a stronger stance against military takeovers. Thus, countries such as Madagascar
and Ecuador, which have had coups during that period, found themselves
isolated in the African Union (AU) or the Organization of American
States (OAS) until they restored civilian government. Moreover, in 2009,
the OAS unanimously ousted Honduras from that organization shortly
after that country's armed forces removed an elected president, who was
replaced with a more conservative civilian official. The coup was universally condemned by governments of all political stripes, whereas such a
coup would have gone virtually unnoticed in decades past. Later in that

year, both the European Union and the Economic Community of West African States imposed an arms embargo on Guinea when its military government's soldiers fired on opposition protesters, killing some 150 of them.

During the Cold War (1945–91), the United States had worked closely with a number of military governments, occasionally even encouraging military coups against elected leftist governments (in Brazil and Chile, for example). Since the 1990s, however, it has opposed most military takeovers, while members of the world community generally have toughened their position against military governments.

But these international pressures are usually ineffective unless the military has also lost its legitimacy at home. In Uruguay, economic decay and public revulsion against the regime's political repression so weakened the military government that it unexpectedly lost a national referendum that it had been confident it could tightly control. Eventually, popular discontent induced the generals to negotiate a return to civilian government. Similarly, in 1992, in Thailand, massive student-led prodemocracy demonstrations convinced the armed forces to withdraw. And in 2008, mass protests led by Pakistan's lawyers' association brought down the Pervez Musharraf dictatorship.

While some combination of these factors has accounted for the departure of most military regimes, it has not guaranteed that the armed forces would stay out of power. Indeed, until the 1980s, the soldiers were likely to return to power. Talukder Maniruzzaman examined seventy-one instances of military withdrawal from office from 1946 to 1984. He only considered cases in which military rulers were replaced by civilian government. In 65 percent of these cases examined, the armed forces were back in power within five years.[28] In 2006, the Thai military returned to power for several years and returned again in 2014. And the Pakistani military has been in and out of power a number of times.

This historical record notwithstanding, since the 1990s, those military governments that have stepped down have been more likely to stay out of office. In most of the developing world, there has been a dramatic decline in military rule. This trend has been weaker in Africa, where military governments or quasimilitary governments remain in such nations as Equatorial Guinea, Sudan, Algeria, Uganda, and Rwanda.* For example, as of 2018, the Latin American nations of Argentina, Ecuador, Brazil, Guatemala, and El Salvador, all with long histories of armed forces intervention, had enjoyed anywhere from three to four decades without military government. In South Korea, decades of military dominance ended in 1993. Even in sub-Saharan Africa, military regimes in several countries, including Nigeria,

---

*Quasimilitary governments are nominally headed by civilians but depend on the backing of the military, which is the final authority.

Soldiers outside the Presidential Palace in Mali. Rebellious troops toppled the government in 2012 and retained considerable influence despite the subsequent formation of a "unity government." Often, even when soldiers do not rule directly, the military may be a powerful behind-the-scenes actor in many developing countries. *Source*: dpa Picture-Alliance/Alamy Stock Photo.

Benin, and Congo (Brazzaville), have given way to elected civilian governments in recent times.

In some cases, years of misrule undermined the military's institutional legitimacy. The brutality and incompetence of Argentine military dictatorship (1976–83) so discredited it that succeeding civilian governments were able to reduce the armed forces to one-third their previous size. Elsewhere, as in Mozambique, El Salvador, and Nicaragua, peace treaties ending long civil wars also mandated sharp reductions in the size of the military.

From the military's point of view, there are dangers in "returning to the barracks," especially if their rule has been brutal or oppressive. Senior officers might face criminal charges for human rights abuses. Post-military elections might see their political opponents brought to power. For that reason, many transitions have involved **political pacts** between the outgoing regime and civilian political leaders. These agreements might guarantee amnesties for former military rulers, or structure transitional political arrangements in such a way as to favor the military's political allies. In Latin America, such agreements made it easier for military juntas to give up power. In some cases, once democracy was well established and the risk of military coup had receded, the protections afforded to military leaders were rescinded by the courts or legislatures on the grounds they were illegitimate and obtained under duress. Former Chilean dictator Augusto Pinochet, for example, was eventually arrested in 2004, and faced hundreds of criminal charges at the time of his death (due to ill health) two years later.

Ultimately, if the armed forces are to relinquish political power and not return, they will need to find new responsibilities to justify their role in society and their share of the national budget. This is particularly true in countries that face no serious foreign threats. In Latin America and much of Africa, for example, wars between nation-states, as opposed to civil conflicts, have been quite rare. In assigning the military new roles, however, civilian governments must be careful not to involve it in tasks that may draw it back into politics—a danger some analysts see in the Latin American military's growing involvement in the "war on drugs." Furthermore, to maintain their restored political power and their control over the armed forces, civilian governments will have to establish more effective civil-military relationships.

THE MILITARY AS A DECIDING FACTOR IN THE ARAB SPRING

In the recent wave of reformist uprisings across North Africa and the Middle East, the outside world has correctly focused its attention on the factors that led to the uprising and the character of the people who bravely put their lives on the line for a more open political system. But if we examine these rebellions closely, we find that the most important factor determining the success or failure of each uprising is probably the willingness or reluctance of the armed forces to defend the authoritarian regime.

In both Tunisia and Egypt, the armed forces were widely respected institutions. Early in both protest movements, the military made a decision not to use force against the demonstrators despite the fact that Presidents Ben Ali and Mubarak had been high-ranking military officers before taking office. While it is impossible to know whether the two dictators would have been able to hold onto power had the armed forces defended them, at the very least overthrowing those regimes would have taken an enormous toll in human lives. However, the Egyptian case also shows the limits of a democratic transition facilitated by the military. Although the mass uprising coupled with military restraint led to the first democratically elected president in that country's history, the armed forces—long the most powerful force in Egyptian political life—remained as powerful as they had always been. When the elected president, Mohamed Morsi, alienated the military, it overthrew him and reinstalled a military dictatorship more repressive than ever.

More so than many Arab nations, Syria is a country highly divided between various religious and ethnic groups: Sunnis, Alawites, Kurds,

Christians, and others. The Alawite minority is a sect that split from Shi'ite Islam centuries ago and suffered persecution over the years at the hands of the Sunni majority. Long one of the poorest and least powerful ethnic groups in the country, the Alawites were marginalized from Syrian society. Hence, unlike the Sunnis, they established a somewhat close relationship with the French colonial government that took power after the First World War. The French, in turn, encouraged them to enter the colonial army, where they became entrenched in the officers' corps. In 1970, after independence, backed by his fellow Alawite officers, General Hafez al-Asad led a coup that put him in power until his death in 2000, when he was succeeded by his son, Bashar. While ethnically mixed, Syria's armed forces and security units are dominated by Alawite officers. Because the fall of the Asad regime would almost certainly strip them of their power and very likely subject them to discrimination, there is little chance that the country's elite troops will abandon the regime.

In Libya and Yemen, the military split, with many elite units remaining loyal to the old regime, but many ordinary soldiers supporting protesters. In (Shi'ite-majority) Bahrain, the security forces had largely been recruited from Sunnis, many of them hired from outside the country. They had few qualms about suppressing protests.

NEW ROLES FOR THE ARMED FORCES

Many of the proposed "new roles" for the military are not really entirely new. They include combating drug trafficking (in parts of Latin America, the Caribbean, and Asia), antiterrorist activity, and emergency relief efforts following natural disasters. Unfortunately, in the past, some of these activities have brought as many new problems as solutions. In Mexico, Colombia, the Caribbean, and Central America, antidrug efforts have frequently corrupted the armed forces, as some officers have changed from enforcers to well-paid protectors of the drug cartels.

In Mexico, for example, there have even been gunfights between military antidrug units and soldiers who were paid by the drug cartels to protect them. Furthermore, in countries such as Colombia and Sri Lanka, the armed forces have often used their mandates to combat terrorism and internal subversion as carte blanche for violating human rights and crushing peaceful and legitimate political opposition groups.

Another popular military activity is civic action—using troops in projects that are beneficial to the civilian population, such as building roads, medical clinics, sanitation projects, and schools. During the Cold War, US military missions in the less developed countries, particularly in Central America, encouraged and financed civic action designed to win local support for the government. Many governments have continued similar projects in countries such as Senegal, Thailand, and the Philippines. These activities have been far too limited to make a significant dent in national poverty. Indeed, there is no reason to believe that military institutions are particularly skilled at development initiatives, compared to aid workers, civilian public employees, or the private sector.

Finally, another role for militaries in the less developed countries has emerged in recent times. Developing countries having increasingly taken on the primary burden of providing military personnel for international peace-keeping missions (discussed in chapter 6), whether under the auspices of the United Nations, or regional organizations such as the African Union and ECOWAS (Economic Community of West African States). The vast majority of United Nations peacekeepers today come from developing countries such as Ethiopia, Bangladesh, India, Rwanda, Pakistan, Nepal, and Ghana. Indeed, in 2018, Ethiopia alone contributed more troops to UN peacekeeping missions (over eight thousand) than did all of the industrialized democracies combined, suffering some 120 deaths during such deployments.

Improving Civil-Military Relationships

Although there are now far fewer military regimes, in many less developed countries, particularly those with prior histories of military dominance, the armed forces continue to interfere frequently in politics. Consequently, civilian governments need to shore up their positions by modernizing and improving civil-military relationships. They must create or strengthen political institutions, attitudes, and behavior that reinforce civilian control.

One important area is the education of military officers. They are normally trained at military academies, often after graduating from military high schools. In the larger and more advanced less developed countries, many senior officers continue their education through much of their careers, with the most promising ones attending advanced academies for specialized training. All of these schools are decisive in socializing military officers into the values of both the armed forces and the political system. If those officers are to stay out of national politics, their training must stress the importance of civilian control over the armed forces.

Second, the nation's constitution and legal system must bestow upon the chief executive (president or prime minister) final control over the armed forces. Unfortunately, in some countries, the constitution requires the civilian president to secure the approval of the military high command before appointing the defense minister or promoting the most senior generals and admirals. Other nations require the defense minister to be a military officer. To establish civilian control, governments need to eliminate such restrictions. Indeed, it is best if civilians serve as defense ministers.

Third, the country's political institutions must give the civilian president and defense minister clear and direct control over the armed forces.

In the United States, for example, the president is legally the commander in chief and officers who criticize his policies publicly may be relieved of duty. In addition, it is important that the country's parliament or congress determines the defense budget and has some level of oversight (through committee hearings and the like) over the armed forces.

Fourth, an important, but rarely discussed, requirement for civilian dominance is that civilian officials control military intelligence activities. Primarily, these intelligence activities involve clandestine gathering of information at home and possibly abroad regarding national security. But often they also include covert operations. In countries such as Chile under General Pinochet and Pakistan today, military intelligence units have operated as an independent force in defense, foreign, and even domestic policy. For example, Pakistan's powerful Directorate for Inter-Service Intelligence has assisted the Afghan Taliban (and probably al-Qaida) in the hopes of having an Afghan ally against India. It is also believed to maintain links to the Pakistani Taliban and to Muslim terrorist groups operating in India.

Finally, government leaders need to walk a fine line in their relationships with the armed forces. While insisting on civilian control, they also need to fund the military sufficiently to protect national security, and they must take seriously the opinions of military commanders in matters related to national defense. To do otherwise would be to invite a coup attempt.

CONCLUSION: DEMOCRACY AND THE MILITARY

By definition, the spread of democracy has reduced the number of military governments. This does not mean that the specter of military takeovers has disappeared. But, since the 1990s, attempted military coups have been largely limited to sub-Saharan Africa and, to a lesser extent, Asia.

Even in democratically elected governments, the armed forces often exercise considerable political influence in certain policy areas. Furthermore, in a number of countries, the military has remained outside civilian control. For example, in Chile, where General Pinochet's outgoing dictatorship was able to dictate the terms of the 1989 transition to democracy, the new constitution afforded the armed forces considerable influence. The military was granted amnesty for most of its human rights violations, including the murder of some two thousand to three thousand civilians. The elected president lacked authority to remove the military's chief of staff, and the armed forces appointed several members of the senate. General Pinochet himself, as a former president, served initially as senator for life. It took more than ten years until the Chilean Congress was able to end those special powers.

In order to consolidate democracy, less developed countries must do more than merely restore elected governments. A stable and secure democracy requires a professionalized military that is committed to staying out of politics. Officers must largely limit their professional role to defending their country from potential threats and must recognize that their involvement in national politics will only divide the armed forces and diminish their professional capacity. But just as the generals and colonels must keep out of national politics, civilian political leaders must respect the military's domain and not attempt to politicize the armed forces. All too often, aspiring political leaders or political parties who are unable to gain office through legitimate channels have approached the military for support. In Egypt, for example, many opposition parties who had done poorly in democratic elections in 2011–12 supported the 2013 military coup as a way of removing the democratic winners, the Muslim Brotherhood, from power.

Even the most successful military governments inhibit political development. They do so because their very rationale for taking office is "the politics of antipolitics." With their hierarchical perspective and their distaste for disorder, military commanders believe in a managed society. Most reject the give-and-take of political competition and the compromises inherent in politics. Consequently, they

> fail to see the functional aspects of the great game of politics: They severely restrict the free flow of the political process and force would-be politicians into a long period of hibernation. . . . The opportunity for gaining political skills by a people once under a military regime is continually postponed by every new military regime.[29]

Practice and Review Online at
http://textbooks.rowman.com/handelman9e

KEY TERMS

breakthrough coups

bureaucratic-authoritarian regimes

coup-proofing

guardian coups

institutional military regimes

military coups

military withdrawal (from politics)

political pacts

revolutionary military regimes

veto coups

DISCUSSION QUESTIONS

1. What factors contributed to the frequency of military intervention in politics in the postcolonial developing world? Why might the frequency of military coups have declined in more recent years?

2. Imagine you have been appointed as an advisor to the government of a newly established—and fragile—democracy. What methods might the new government take to reduce the risk of a military coup? What are the strengths and weaknesses of these various approaches?

3. How successful have military regimes been at delivering political order and economic development? Why/why not?

4. What important role did the military play in determining the outcome of the "Arab Spring" uprisings in the Arab World? Discuss how that role varied from country to country.

NOTES

1. Harold Crouch, *The Army and Politics in Indonesia* (Ithaca, NY: Cornell University Press, 1978), 345.

2. William Thompson, "Explanations of the Military Coup," PhD dissertation, University of Washington, Seattle, 1972, 11. Quoted in Amos Perlmutter, *The Military and Politics in Modern Times* (New Haven, CT: Yale University Press, 1977), 115.

3. Claude E. Welch, "Military Disengagements from Politics: Incentives and Obstacles in Political Change," in *Military Power and Politics in Black Africa*, ed. Simon Baynham (New York, NY: St. Martin's Press, 1986), 89–90.

4. Samuel Decalo, *Coups and Army Rule in Africa* (New Haven, CT: Yale University Press, 1990), 2.

5. Patrick J. McGowan, "African Military Coups D'état, 1956–2001: Frequency, Trends and Distribution," *Journal of Modern African Studies* 41, no. 3 (September 2003): 339.

6. Morris Janowitz, *Military Institutions and Coercion in the Developing Nations: Expanded Edition of the Military in the Political Development of New Nations* (Chicago, IL: University of Chicago Press, 1977), 105.

7. Samuel P. Huntington, *Political Order in Changing Societies* (New Haven, CT: Yale University Press, 1968), 194.

8. Robert Wesson, "Preface," in *New Military Politics in Latin America*, ed. Robert Wesson (New York: Praeger, 1982), v.

9. Samuel E. Finer, *The Man on Horseback: The Role of the Military in Politics*, 2nd ed. (London: Penguin Books, 1976), 78–82.

10. Samuel P. Huntington, "Reforming Civil-Military Relations," in *Civil–Military Relations and Democracy*, eds. Larry Diamond and Marc Plattner (Baltimore, MD: Johns Hopkins University Press, 1996), 9. Italics added.

11. Marion J. Levy Jr., *Modernization and the Structure of Societies* (Princeton, NJ: Princeton University Press, 1966), vol. 2, 603.

12. Lucian W. Pye, "Armies in the Process of Political Modernization," in *The Role of the Military in Underdeveloped Countries*, ed. John Johnson (Princeton, NJ: Princeton University Press, 1962), 69–89.

13. Manfred Halpern, *The Politics of Social Change in the Middle East and North Africa* (Princeton, NJ: Princeton University Press, 1963), 75, 253.

14. Karen L. Remmer, *Military Rule in Latin America* (Boston, MA: Unwin Hyman, 1989), 3.

15. Eric A. Nordlinger, *Soldiers in Politics: Military Coups and Governments* (Englewood Cliffs, NJ: Prentice Hall, 1977), 173; also Huntington, *Political Order*, chap. 4.

16. Huntington, *Political Order*, 221.

17. Decalo, *Coups and Army Rule in Africa*, 133.

18. Jeffrey Lunstead, "The Armed Forces in Bangladesh Society," in *The Armed Forces in Contemporary Asian Society*, ed. Edward Olsen et al. (Boulder, CO: Westview Press, 1986), 316.

19. Ruth First, *Power in Africa* (New York, NY: Pantheon Books, 1970), 20.

20. "The Political Orientation Speech Delivered by Captain Thomas Sankara in Ouagadougou, Upper Volta, on October 2, 1983," in *Military Marxist Regimes in Africa*, eds. John Markakis and Michael Waller (London: Frank Cass, 1986), 145–53 (selected portions).

21. Samuel Decalo, "The Morphology of Radical Military Rule in Africa," in *Military Marxist Regimes in Africa*, ed. John Markakis and Michael Waller (New York: Routledge, 1986), 123.

22. Samuel Decalo, "Military Rule in Africa: Etiology and Morphology," in *Military Power and Politics in Black Africa*, ed. Simon Baynham (London: Croom Helm, 1986), 56, 58.

23. J. Bayo Adekanye, "The Post-Military State in Africa," in *The Political Dilemma of Military Regimes*, eds. Christopher Clapham and George Philip (London: Croom Helm, 1985), 87.

24. Decalo, *Coups and Army Rule in Africa*, 20.

25. McGowan, "African Military Coups D'état, 1956–2001," 347.

26. Nordlinger, *Soldiers in Politics*, 139.

27. Remmer, *Military Rule*, 40.

28. Talukder Maniruzzaman, *Military Withdrawal from Politics: A Comparative Study* (Cambridge, MA: Ballinger Publishing, 1987), 21, 24–25.

29. Brian Loveman and Thomas M. Davies Jr., eds., *The Politics of Antipolitics: The Military in Latin America*, 2nd ed. (Lincoln: University of Nebraska Press, 1989), 6.

Glossary

African Union (AU) An organization representing fifty-five African states and seeking to promote cooperation between them. It was founded in 2002 to succeed the Organization of African Unity.

agrarian reform Distribution of farmland to needy peasants along with government-support programs such as roads, technical assistance, and lines of credit needed to make beneficiaries economically viable.

ancien régime The old political order. The term is often used to describe a decaying regime threatened or ousted by a revolutionary movement.

anti-corruption initiatives Reforms (such as increased transparency and criminal investigation of corruption allegations) intended to reduce the level of corruption in politics and the economy.

apparatchiks A privileged class of state and party bureaucrats, especially in communist countries.

Arab Spring The term used to describe the rise of anti-government protests in the Arab world, starting with Tunisia and Egypt in early 2011 and soon spreading to other Arab countries, including Libya, Syria, Yemen, and Bahrain. Of these, only Tunisia achieved a democratic transition.

Arab World Countries in North Africa and the Middle East that are predominantly Arabic-speaking. All of these are also predominantly Muslim.

Asian tigers The so-called four Asian tigers are South Korea, Taiwan, Singapore, and Hong Kong—the first Asian nations, after Japan, to develop rapidly growing, export-oriented economies.

associated-dependent development A type of Third World industrialization based on an alliance of the local, political, economic, and military elites with multinational corporations and Western governments.

autarky An economic strategy that severely limits trade and foreign investment and emphasizes self-reliance.

authoritarian government (regime, system) A political system that limits or prohibits opposition groups and otherwise restricts political activity and expression.

bicameral legislature A legislature comprised of an upper and lower house (such as the US Senate and House of Representatives).

bourgeoisie Business or capitalist class.

breakthrough coup A military coup, generally by lower- and middle-ranking officers from relatively humble social backgrounds, that seeks to break the power of established elites and promote social change.

bureaucratic-authoritarian (BA) regimes Military dictatorships, found most often in Latin America's more developed countries that were based on an alliance between the military, government bureaucrats, local business elites, and multinational corporations.

candidate quota An electoral system that requires that certain candidates be women (or from certain ethnic or religious groups).

capital-intensive Industrial or agricultural production that relies more heavily on machinery and technology than on human labor.

caste system A rigid social hierarchy in which each person is born with a status that he or she retains regardless of his or her education or achievement.

chaebol A family/clan-based business empire, especially in South Korea.

Christian or Ecclesial Base Communities (CEBs) Small Catholic neighborhood groups in Latin America that discuss religious questions and community problems. Commonly located in poor neighborhoods, many CEBs were politicized or radicalized in the 1960s and 1970s.

civil society The array of voluntary organizations—including churches, unions, business groups, farmers' organizations, and women's groups—whose members often influence the political system but are free of government control.

class consciousness A measure of how much a social class (workers, peasants, or the middle class) views itself as having common goals that are distinct from, and often opposed to, the interests of other classes.

class structure The socioeconomic structure of society, based on wealth, influence, and economic power.

clientelism Supporting a patron in exchange for rewards. See **patron-client relations**.

climate change The current warming of the Earth's climate. There is a broad scientific consensus that this is largely caused by human activity, specifically the release of CO_2 and other "greenhouse gases."

collectivization (collective farm) The act of merging individual farms into a collective (joint) unit. Collectivization may be undertaken voluntarily (as in the Israeli Kibbutz) or may be forced by the state against the will of the affected peasant smallholders. Forced collectivization led to considerable bloodshed in countries such as the Soviet Union.

colonialism The conquest and subjugation of another country, for the purposes of extracting economic advantage or enhancing strategic power. The era of European colonialism in the sixteenth through twentieth centuries had profound effects on the developing world.

colored(s) A South African term coined during the period of white rule (Apartheid) to describe people of mixed racial background.

command economy An economy in which most of the means of production are owned and managed by the state and in which prices and production decisions are determined by state planners.

comparative advantage A country's capacity to engage in a particular economic activity efficiently and cheaply relative to other nations.

concentrated land holdings A situation where the vast majority of land is held by a small number of large landowners, and most of the rural population are smallholding or landless peasants.

conflict trap The linkage between conflict and underdevelopment, whereby civil war inhibits political and economic development, and underdevelopment increases the likelihood of future conflict.

consociationalism A system of ethnic power-sharing, in which groups have an agreed share of political power, relative autonomy and a veto over major decisions that affect them.

constant dollars Inflation-adjusted data—for example, "2000 constant dollars" would mean that all figures are expressed in terms of currency values in the year 2000.

core nations The richer, highly industrialized nations of the world.

corruption The illegal misuse of public office for private gain, through bribery, extortion, vote buying, and similar actions.

coup d'état A seizure of political power by the military; a **military coup**.

coup-proofing Efforts undertaken by a regime to reduce the risk of a military coup.

critical mass The observation that women need to comprise around 30 percent of political leaders before women's issues are seriously addressed by government.

crony capitalism A corrupt form of capitalism in which powerful, well-connected business leaders use their government ties to accumulate wealth.

cultural pluralism A diversity of ethnic groups.

culture of poverty A sense of powerlessness and fatalism allegedly found commonly among the urban poor.

democratic consolidation The process through which democratic norms (democratic "rules of the game") become accepted by all powerful groups in society, including labor unions, business, rural landlords, the church, and the military.

democratic recession The possible decline of democracy and democratization in recent years, including the growth of **hybrid regimes**.

democratic transition The process of moving from an authoritarian regime to a democratic one.

demographic transition Temporary rapid population growth that occurs when death rates have declined (due to social and economic development), but (culturally rooted) birth rates have not yet fallen accordingly.

demonstration effects The process whereby events in one country encourage or discourage others to take similar action in other countries.

dependency theory A theory that attributes underdevelopment in the developing world ("periphery") to these countries' economic and political dependence on the advanced industrial nations ("the core").

developmental corruption Bribe paying by businesses to secure government contracts or avoid regulations.

developmental state A government system that intervenes actively in the capitalist economy in order to guide or promote the state's economic development goals.

economies of scale Economic efficiencies achieved through large-scale operations.

electoral democracy A country that has free and fair elections, but may not honor its citizens' rights in some areas, such as freedom of expression.

endemic corruption Routine, generally low-level corruption in everyday life—for example, bribing a police officer to avoid a ticket.

ethnicity (ethnic group) A group that feels it has common culture, traditions, beliefs, values, and history that unite it and distinguish it from other cultures.

everyday forms of resistance Largely passive resistance to state authority through non-cooperation, tax evasion, and minor acts of sabotage.

export-oriented industrialization (EOI) An industrialization model heavily tied to exporting manufactured goods. This strategy has been the linchpin of East Asia's economic boom.

federalism A system of governance in which territorial subunits have a degree of autonomy from the national government in defined areas. May be used to address regional or ethnic tensions.

foreign direct investment Economic investment in a country by foreign firms and multinational corporations.

fundamentalism A desire to address the perceived corruption and moral crisis of modern society by returning to the real or imagined roots of religious belief.

gender The socially constructed roles that are assigned to men and women by society and culture.

gender equality Conditions under which men and women have similar rights and opportunities, and where there are no major disparities in economic, social, and political circumstances.

gender gap A systematic difference in social status or achievement between men and women (e.g., a difference in income levels).

gender inequality index (GII) The GII is a composite index comparing men and women on three dimensions—empowerment, labor force participation, and health.

gender parity index (GPI) An index comparing the female literacy rate to the male rate.

gender-related development index (GDI) A composite score that compares female life expectancy, education, and income with those of men.

gender quota Requirement that a certain number of candidates or legislative seats be assigned to women.

genocide Efforts to destroy an ethnic or other group, in whole or part, through violence.

globalization The growth of international trade, finance, communications, migration, and interdependence.

gross domestic product (GDP) A measure of a nation's total production. Similar to the **gross national product** (GNP), but it excludes certain financial transfers that are included in GNP.

growth with equity Economic growth that also reduces economic inequality within countries.

gini index A measure of economic inequality in a society, whereby 0.00 indicates no inequality, and 1.00 maximal inequality.

globalization The tendency of today's national economies to become increasingly intertwined and interdependent, usually coupled with increased interdependence of cultures.

Great Leap Forward China's effort (1958–62) to rapidly industrialize and increase agricultural production by forcing the peasantry into large communes (a type of collective farm) and by having the country's huge urban and rural workforce put forth tremendous effort. That experiment had disastrous effects on the economy and led to the starvation and death of millions of Chinese.

greenhouse gases Carbon gases produced by burning fossil fuels that threaten to warm the world's climate dangerously by limiting the dispersion of heat from the atmosphere.

gross national product (GNP) A measure of a country's total production. GNP per capita is often used as a measure of average income in an individual country.

guardian coup A coup in which the military (or a portion of it) acts to protect its institutional and other interests.

guerilla warfare Hit-and-run attacks by insurgent forces during a civil war or revolution.

human development index (HDI) A composite measure of educational level, life expectancy, and per capita GDP.

hurting stalemate An ethnic or other conflict in which no side can "win," and continued conflict comes at a cost. Such situations are more likely to produce a negotiated peace agreement.

honor killings Murders of women who have allegedly "dishonored" their families by engaging in sexual activity or some related "lesser offense" (sometimes as innocent as being seen in public with an unacceptable man). Honor killings are commonly committed by close male relatives of the victim.

hybrid regime A country with formal elections, but also aspects of authoritarian rule that limit effective popular participation in, and influence over, politics. The terms "**illiberal democracy**" and "**semi-democracy**" are also used.

illiberal democracy A political system with regular elections, but limits of free association and expression. The terms "**semi-democracy**" and "**hybrid regime**" are also used.

import-substitution industrialization (ISI) A policy of industrial development based on manufacturing goods domestically that were previously imported. Usually involves tariff and other trade barriers to raise the price of imports that compete with local industries.

informal sector The part of the economy that is unregulated by the government while similar activities are regulated and taxed. Also defined as "all unregistered (unincorporated) enterprises below a certain size."

infrastructure The underlying structures (including transportation, communication, and agricultural irrigation) that are needed for effective production.

institutionalism An approach to comparative politics which emphasizes the role that institutions and historical legacies play in constraining or enabling political choices.

institutional military regime A government in which many of the armed forces' commanding officers take part. That is, the armed forces as an institution take command of government, rather than a charismatic officer with a personal following.

International Monetary Fund (IMF) A United Nations-affiliated international organization that assists countries in dealing with budget deficits, trade deficits, and monetary policy through technical advice and loans.

Islamist Social and political movements that advance a political ideology rooted in a particular view of Islam.

jihad Righteous struggle. While the term is often understood in the West to refer solely to religiously motivated violence, it can be used to describe the defense of Muslim communities against external threat or the struggle against sin.

j-curve A graph depicting the political instability that can result when a prolonged period of economic growth is followed by economic stagnation or recession, resulting in unmet expectations.

laissez-faire A policy of minimal state intervention in the economy.

landless peasants Rural peasants with no land, forced to work as renters, sharecroppers, or agricultural laborers.

land reform The process of redistributing land from large landowners to smallholding and landless peasants.

latifundia Large agricultural estates owned by wealthy landowners (or multinational corporations).

legitimacy A population's acceptance of the government's or its leaders' right to rule.

LDCs This term can be used to refer to either *less* developed countries (meaning the developing world in general), or the *least* developed countries (meaning the very poorest developing countries).

LGBT+ Lesbian, gay, bisexual, transgender, and other sexual minorities.

liberal democracy A democracy that not only has free and fair elections, but also respects civil liberties and upholds basic freedoms.

liberalization (of the economic system) Reducing the degree of state intervention in the economy (referring to the eighteenth-century classical liberalism of Adam Smith).

liberalization (of the political system) A process whereby an authoritarian government begins to reduce repression and loosen restraints on freedom, often in response to organized protest.

liberated zones Areas (most notably in the countryside) controlled by the revolutionary army during an insurgency.

liberation theology A reformist interpretation of Catholic doctrine that stresses the emancipation of the poor. It was born and spread in Latin America from the 1960s to the 1990s and still has many adherents today.

lingua franca A widely understood language used for interaction between groups in a multilingual society.

majoritarian democracy A type of democracy in which the party or group that wins elections makes decisions without affording constitutional or other institutional protections to minority groups, who are not given any special representation.

market socialism A hybrid of Marxist economics and free enterprise that has been adopted by countries such as China.

mass mobilization The process whereby large segments of the population are activated politically. Governments or revolutionary movements may choose to mobilize the population.

military coup The seizure of political power by military personnel.

military withdrawal (from politics) The transfer of political power from a military regime to civilian control. The military may still exercise considerable behind-the-scenes power, however.

Millennium Development Goals (MDGs) A series of eight major development goals agreed in 2000 by 191 members of the United Nations intended to reduce global poverty by the year 2015. These were later supplanted by the **Sustainable Development Goals.**

modernization theory An approach to comparative politics that argues that all countries experience a broad and interconnected process of economic, social, political, and cultural modernization. Later revisionist approaches argued that, in the short and medium term, modernization might provoke great political instability in some countries. Modernization theory has been increasingly criticized since the 1970s for treating Western experience and values as the model for all countries.

moral economy The web of economic and moral obligations that binds a social unit together. Often used in reference to peasant-landlord relations in the countryside.

multinational corporations (MNCs) Corporations with holdings and operations in a number of countries. Primarily based in the developed world, many of them exercise considerable economic power in the developing world.

nation A population with its own language, cultural traditions, historical aspirations, and, sometimes, its own geographical home.

nationalization The transfer of private firms to state ownership.

neocolonialism Economic or cultural dominance of one sovereign state over another.

neoliberalism Economic policies, now widely in favor, based on an adaptation of Adam Smith's "classical liberalism." These reforms reduce the role of the state in the economy, enhance the role of the private sector, and allow free-market forces to operate without government interference. Specific reforms have included balancing the budget, letting the market (not government regulations) determine the value of the national currency, removing barriers to free trade, and privatizing state enterprises.

neopatrimonialism A system of **patron-client relations** fueled by state resources (e.g., government hiring of political supporters as a reward for their loyalty).

nongovernmental organization (NGO) An organization at the local, national, or international level that is privately funded and has no connection with the government. Most NGOs stress grassroots organization. Commonly, they support goals such as democratization, human rights, women's rights, environmental protection, housing, health care, and education.

newly industrialized country (NIC) Countries in East Asia and Latin America (such as Taiwan and Mexico) that have developed a substantial industrial base in recent decades.

new social movements Grassroots reformist movements that are free of traditional political party ties or class-based ideologies.

official development assistance Foreign aid (whether in the form of grants, concessional loans, or technical assistance) intended to promote economic and social development in developing countries. Relative to the size of their economies, European (especially Scandinavian) countries tend to be the most generous aid donors.

oil curse The potential adverse effects of oil (and other natural resources) on political and economic development through corruption, neopatrimonial politics, and distortion of the local economy.

parastatals Semiautonomous, state-run business enterprises, such as government-owned power plants, petroleum firms, and food-processing plants.

Paris Agreement An international agreement negotiated in 2015 by 196 states calling for reduction in greenhouse gas emissions so as to slow global warming.

patriarchy A pattern of male domination of politics and the economy.

patronage Support by a patron for a client, in exchange for loyalty. See **patron-client relations** and **neopatrimonialism**.

patron-client relations Relations between more powerful figures (patrons) and less powerful ones (clients), involving a series of reciprocal obligations that benefit both sides but are more advantageous to the patron. Also referred to as **clientelism**.

peacekeeping operation A military mission undertaken by the United Nations or others to end violence and support a peace agreement in a conflict-affected country.

peasant A person in a traditional rural society, who earns his or her living from agriculture either as the owner or renter of a small plot of land, who often produces (wholly or in part) for their own family's consumption. Peasants, by definition, have a culture and lifestyle that is distinct from urban society, and are dependent for their survival on relationships with more powerful outsiders, such as landlords (who own larger farms), merchants, and moneylenders.

per capita income Total national income (whether measured by GNP or GDP) divided by the size of the population. While this provides a general measure of economic development, it says nothing about how (un)equally income might be distributed within a country.

periphery Third World countries, commonly seen by dependency theorists as occupying a lesser rank in the international economy.

personalistic military regime A form of military dictatorship in which a single officer dominates. Often that regime's legitimacy is based on his charisma or his web of contacts with powerful groups.

planned corruption Tolerance of corruption by political leaders as part of a **neopatrominial** strategy of regime maintenance.

pluralism (pluralist democracy) A form of government that allows a wide variety of groups and viewpoints to flourish and to engage in political activity independent of government control.

political culture The set of political beliefs and values that underlie a society's political system.

political economy The interrelated dynamics of economics, politics, and government policy.

populism Political movements, parties, or leaders claiming to speak for the needs of "ordinary" people and critical of elite politics. Some populist leaders in the developing world (and elsewhere) may tend to demagoguery by fanning fears, scapegoating minorities, and appealing to societal prejudices.

private sector The sector of the economy that is owned by individuals or private companies.

private sphere Family caregiving and other domestic functions (contrasted with the **public sphere**).

privatization The process of transferring to the private-sector portions of the economy formerly owned by the state.

procedural democracy Standards of democracy based on political procedures (such as free elections) rather than outcomes (such as social justice).

progressive church The reformist and radical wings of the Catholic Church (primarily in Latin America).

proletariat Marxist term for the working class (blue-collar workers).

proportional representation (PR) A method of electing legislatures in which voters select from party lists in multimember districts; seats are then allocated in proportion to the percentage of votes each party receives.

public housing Housing projects built, owned, and operated by the state, often intended for low-income households.

public sphere Participation in politics and the formal economy. Contrast with **private sphere**.

purchasing power parity An adjustment made to national income (GNP or GDP) statistics to allow for differences in local purchasing power.

race Identity based on similar physical appearance and supposed shared ancestry.

reconciliation approach A contemporary perspective in modernization theory that holds that it is possible for developing countries to simultaneously attain some development goals that were previously considered contradictory, at least in the short run (such as early economic growth and equitable income distribution).

relative deprivation The gap between an individual's or group's expectations and desires and their actual achievement.

remittances Income sent by workers in one country to support family members in another.

rentier state A state which receives substantial income from outside sources (through oil sales, typically) and is able to use patronage and repression to maintain authoritarian rule. See also the **oil curse.**

reserved seats Seats in a government body, such as the national parliament, that are specifically set aside for women or other underrepresented groups.

responsibility to protect The idea that the international community has a shared responsibility to stop mass atrocities and other large-scale human rights abuses.

revivalism An attempt to revive traditional religious practices and, sometimes, to revive the role of religion in politics. See also **fundamentalism.**

revolution A successful insurgency that results in comprehensive political and socioeconomic change.

revolutionary military regimes Regimes established through a **military coup** that seek to impose major political and economic changes; successful revolutions undertaken through a military coup.

rural class system The system of agrarian social relations, usually characterized by a small class of large landowners, a group of middle peasants, and a large number of small-holding and landless peasants.

Salafists Fundamentalists who favor a return to the religious and social structures of the Muslim faith as practiced in the time of the Prophet Muhammed.

secession When a region of a country seeks to exit from current political arrangements and form its own independent state.

secularization The separation of religion and the state and, more generally, the removal of religion from politics.

semi-democracy A democracy where the power of the electorate is limited by intimidation and other constraints. The terms "**illiberal democracy**" and "**hybrid regime**" are also used.

shantytown A community of poor homes or shacks built by the inhabitants. Unlike slums, they are commonly in outlying urban areas rather than the central city.

Shi'ite (Muslim) A (minority) branch of Islam, predominant in Iran, Iraq, and Bahrain. Shi'ism differs from **Sunni** Islam over the nature of religious authority as well as aspects of religious practice.

sites-and-services programs Housing initiatives in which the state sells or gives each inhabitant legal title to a plot with basic services such as electricity and water, leaving the recipient to build their own home.

smallholders Peasants owning small plots of land.

single-member districts (SMDs) An electoral system in which the country is divided into a relatively large number of districts with comparable populations, with only one representative (member) elected to the legislature in each district. SMD is largely confined to English-speaking countries such as Britain, Canada, and the United States. Other democracies are more likely to use proportional representation.

South (global) A term sometimes used to refer to the developing world.

spontaneous housing Urban housing built independently by the occupants without government permission, often in urban slums.

squatter settlements Communities built by the poor who illegally or semi-legally occupy unused land.

state-led industrialization Government policies intended to spur industrialization, usually through investment in key sectors. In Latin America, in particular, this also often involved trade protection for domestic industries (**import-substitution industrialization**).

structural adjustment program (SAP) A series of economic reforms designed to address budget deficits and promote business-friendly reform. These may involve government austerity measures, deregulation, and privatization of **parastatals**, and are often supported by the **International Monetary Fund**.

substantive democracy A democracy system that is not merely procedural (electoral democracy), but also effectively represents public opinion and produces equitable public policy.

Sunni (Muslim) The majority branch of Islam. Sunnis differ with Shi'ite Muslims over the nature of religious authority as well as aspects of religious practice.

sustainable development Economic development that does not place undue burdens on resources or the environment and is thus sustainable for future generations.

Sustainable Development Goals (SDGs) A series of seventeen United Nations development goals, to be achieved by the year 2030. These call for poverty reduction, improved social conditions, reduced inequality, and greater attention to the environment.

technocrat A government bureaucrat or adviser with technical expertise, who often has advanced training in fields such as engineering, economics, and the sciences.

theocracy (theocratic state) a country, state, or city that is subject to the rule of God as interpreted and enforced by religious leaders.

Third Wave The widespread transition from authoritarian to democratic government that has taken place in the Third World and Eastern Europe since the mid-1970s (some say it ended around the year 2000, though some democratic transitions continue).

Third World A term sometimes used to refer to the developing world.

traditional culture (values, society) A culture or society that adheres to long-standing values and customs that have not been extensively transformed by modernization.

tribe Subnational groups who share a collective identity and language and believe themselves to hold a common lineage.

unicameral legislature A legislature with only a single house (in contrast to a **bicameral legislature**).

United Nations Development Programme (UNDP) A UN organization dedicated to supporting social and economic development. UNDP published much of the data used in this text.

urbanization The process of urban growth, including the migration of rural populations to towns and cities.

veto coup A conservative military coup, generally by well-connected senior officers, that seeks to slow social change and protect the established social order.

wars of national liberation Wars of independence fought against colonial powers.

World Bank A United Nations-affiliated international organization that supports economic and social development in the developing world through loans, grants, and technical advice.

World Trade Organization (WTO) An intergovernmental organization of over 160 states that establishes trading rules in an effort to promote freer and fairer global trade.

zipper quotas A type of quota system for electoral lists of candidates for parliament or other government bodies, in which the list must alternate between male and female candidates (or vice-versa).

Index